# ESSENTIAL
# HUMAN RIGHTS
# CASES

## SECOND EDITION

# ESSENTIAL
# HUMAN RIGHTS
# CASES

## SECOND EDITION

Susan Nash, Barrister, Gray's Inn

Mark Furse

JORDANS
2002

Published by
Jordan Publishing Limited
21 St Thomas Street,
Bristol BS1 6JS

**British Library Cataloguing-in-Publication Data**
A catalogue record for this book is available from the British Library.


ISBN 0 85308 800 4

Typeset by Mendip Communications Ltd, Frome, Somerset
Printed and bound in Great Britain by Bell & Bain Ltd, Glasgow

# Preface

When the first edition of this book was published, the Human Rights Act 1998 had not yet entered into force in the UK, and human rights law could still be viewed as a 'foreign' subject. That of course has now changed, and in this edition of the book we have been faced with an avalanche of case-law to consider for inclusion. We have included additional Convention cases where these have been brought to our attention as meriting inclusion in the first edition, or in response to our own considerations of the earlier material, or to new cases. Our response to the current plethora of domestic cases has been to include only those which appear to us to be of the utmost significance or interest, and our watchword in the preparation of this second edition has been the first word of the title: 'essential'.

There have been a number of developments that have affected human rights case-law since the first edition. Institutional changes within the Convention architecture have altered the procedures by which case-law emerges from Strasbourg and these are dealt with in the first chapter. The accession to the Council of Europe of new States, with differing traditions, has been reflected in the work of the Court, and of course, in the UK, domestic courts have grappled with human rights issues across a wide range of areas.

In addition to the inclusion of new material, we have made some substantial reorganisation of existing material. The incidents of duplication of treatment of cases has been reduced, although we will continue to refer to cases in more than one entry where this is appropriate to the treatment of the subject matter. Material referred to in that part of the first edition dealing with discrimination has been absorbed into the substantive chapters of the book to which the discrimination relates. Nothing has been lost in this process, and we hope that the end result makes the book easier to use.

It is clear that as the role played by human rights law in the UK expands, an increasing number of cases will be come to be regarded as 'essential', and we would be pleased to hear from any reader of this book who would like to recommend material for inclusion.

In the preparation of this edition we are both jointly responsible for all the content, and any errors are ours alone. However, Susan Nash has been primarily responsible for the first chapter and areas of the book relating to criminal law, and immigration and deportation issues, while Mark Furse has been primarily responsible for the commercial areas. Other areas have been shared out more or less equally.

In the preparation of this edition the publication team at Jordans have done an excellent job in dealing with a great number of changes, and we are grateful to them for their patience and professionalism. While we have prepared this edition ourselves, and have made changes to material included in the first edition where it has been retained, we remain grateful to those who made contributions to the first edition. Contributions by Merris Amos, Leroy Bunbury, Amanda Hopkins, Charles King and Claire de Than that were present in the first edition continue to appear in this edition.

The cut off date for the inclusion of cases in this edition was 1 June 2002.

SUSAN NASH, MARK FURSE
*October 2002*

# Contents

# Table of Cases

References are to *page* numbers. References in bold type are to where cases are considered.

# Table of Statutes

**References are to *section* numbers**

# Table of Statutory Instruments

**References are to *section* numbers**

# Table of Conventions and EC Materials

**References are to *section* numbers**

# Table of National Materials

**References are to *section* numbers**

# Table of Abbreviations

| | |
|---|---|
| the Convention | Convention for the Protection of Human Rights and Fundamental Freedoms 1950 (European Convention on Human Rights) |
| the Court | European Court of Human Rights |
| AID | artificial insemination by donor |
| CFI | Court of First Instance |
| DLP | Discretionary Lifer Panel |
| DPP | Director of Public Prosecutions |
| DTI | Department of Trade and Industry |
| EC | European Community |
| ECJ | European Court of Justice |
| ECSC | European Coal and Steel Community |
| EU | European Union |
| FEA | Fair Employment Agency for Northern Ireland |
| FRG | Federal Republic of Germany |
| GDR | German Democratic Republic |
| HIV | human immunodeficiency virus |
| HRA 1998 | Human Rights Act 1998 |
| IAP | Independent Appeal Panel |
| ILEA | Inner London Education Authority |
| IRA | Irish Republican Army |
| ISKCON | International Society for Krishna Consciousness |
| LEA | Local Education Authority |
| OACI | Occupational Association for the Chemical Industry |
| PACE | Police and Criminal Evidence Act 1984 |
| PTT | (Swiss) Post, Telegraph and Telephone Services |
| RPC | Restrictive Practices Court |
| RUC | Royal Ulster Constabulary |
| SPUC | Society for the Protection of Unborn Children Ireland Ltd |
| TRNC | Turkish Republic of Northern Cyprus |
| UNHCR | United Nations High Commission for Refugees |

# Part 1
# INTRODUCTION

# Chapter 1

# THE EUROPEAN CONVENTION ON HUMAN RIGHTS AND THE UNITED KINGDOM

## 1.1  INTRODUCTION

The long-awaited implementation of the Human Rights Act 1998 (HRA 1998), which imposes new duties on public authorities to act compatibly with the Convention for the Protection of Human Rights and Fundamental Freedoms 1950 (the Convention), has brought about a change in legal culture. Despite preserving the principle of Parliamentary sovereignty, the HRA 1998 provides that, insofar as it is possible to do so, primary legislation must be read and given effect in a way that is compatible with Convention rights (HRA 1998, s 3(1)). However, if legislation fails to conform to the standards of the Convention, courts may not disapply rogue provisions but are required to issue a declaration of incompatibility (HRA 1998, s 4(1)). The power to make a declaration of incompatibility is reserved for the superior courts. Ministers responsible for the passage of new legislation through Parliament have a duty to make a statement with regard to its compatibility with Convention rights (HRA 1998, s 19). Public authorities, including courts and tribunals, are obliged to act in a way which is compatible with Convention rights (HRA 1998, s 6(1)), unless provisions in primary legislation require them to act differently (HRA 1998, s 6(2)), and must take into account judgments of the European Court of Human Rights (the Court). Thus, in order to interpret the provisions of the HRA 1998 appropriately, domestic courts are obliged not only to adopt a broad, purposive approach to legislation but also to embrace Convention jurisprudence. Statutory provisions must be 'read down' in order to render them compatible with Convention rights, and cases dealt with in a manner which corresponds with the approach of the Court. As a consequence, courts throughout the UK can now apply and develop Convention principles instead of awaiting decisions from Strasbourg. Whereas fears that the HRA 1998 would bring chaos to the legal system appear to be unfounded, the task of interpreting its provisions and applying Convention rights in British courts is currently producing a considerable body of interesting case-law. In order to advise clients effectively, practitioners are required to know the extent of the substantive rights and freedoms guaranteed under the Convention and to have a sound understanding of Convention jurisprudence. For a more detailed account of the HRA 1998 and the substantive rights and freedoms guaranteed by the Convention, see R Clayton and H Tomlinson *The Law of Human Rights* (Oxford University Press, 2000); B Emmerson and A Ashworth *Human Rights and Criminal Justice* (Sweet & Maxwell, 2001); M Janis, R Kay and A Bradley *European Human Rights Law* (Oxford University Press, 2000); D Feldman *Civil Liberties and Human Rights in England and Wales* (Oxford University Press, 2002).

## 1.2   THE COUNCIL OF EUROPE AND THE EUROPEAN CONVENTION ON HUMAN RIGHTS

The Council of Europe, the first pan-European political institution, was formed in the aftermath of the Second World War. Its aim was to achieve a greater degree of unity and understanding within Europe in order to reduce the chance of further conflict. One of the first tasks of the Council was to draft a European human rights charter to reflect the standards laid down in the United Nations Universal Declaration of Human Rights. In November 1949 the Committee of Ministers, the decision-making body of the Council of Europe which is composed of the foreign ministers of the Member States or their representatives, appointed a Committee of Experts to prepare a draft text. On 7 August 1950 the Committee of Ministers approved a text which, although less extensive than originally planned, provides an effective regional enforcement mechanism for the protection of fundamental rights. The European Convention on Human Rights is a treaty, binding in international law, which sets out minimum international standards for the protection of human rights and provides effective enforcement procedures to ensure Contracting States comply with their obligations. The Convention established the first international complaints procedure and the first international court dealing exclusively with human rights. The European Court of Human Rights was established in 1959. Although constructed as an international treaty, the Convention differs from other treaties in several respects: it places an obligation on contracting parties to ensure that everyone within their jurisdiction receives protection irrespective of nationality; it provides for the right of individual petition before the Court and the acceptance of the Court's compulsory jurisdiction. In the event of an alleged violation of a Convention right, an individual, a group of individuals or a non-governmental organisation claiming to be a victim, may lodge a complaint with the Court. A Contracting State may also bring a complaint against another State. These procedures do not replace the protection of human rights at national level; indeed, before there is recourse to proceedings under the Convention all remedies at the domestic level must have been exhausted.

Although the UK was one of the first States to sign and ratify the Convention, which entered into force on 3 September 1953, it refused to recognise the right of individual petition and the jurisdiction of the Court until 1966. Since the Convention entered into force, 11 Protocols have been adopted which extend the list of rights protected and address the organisation and procedure of the Convention organs. The ratification of the Eleventh Protocol, which came into operation in November 1998, resulted in a radical restructuring of the Convention's enforcement machinery. The position relating to the Twelfth Protocol is discussed below. While all States within the European Union belong to the Council of Europe, the drafting of the Convention and the enforcement of the rights and freedoms it guarantees remain the responsibility of the Member States of the Council of Europe. In the last decade the membership of this body has increased significantly. On 31 May 2002 there were 43 Member States of the Council of Europe. An update of the state of signatures and ratification of the Convention and its Protocols can be found at the Council of Europe's website at www.echr.co.int.

## 1.3   RIGHTS AND FREEDOMS GUARANTEED UNDER THE CONVENTION AND ITS PROTOCOLS

Contracting parties undertake 'to secure to everyone within their jurisdiction the rights and freedoms defined in Section I of this Convention' (Art 1). The Convention recognises that human rights are possessed by all human beings and are not dependent upon a person's nationality. Article 1 has the effect of imposing positive and negative obligations upon contracting parties. Thus, Contracting States are obliged to take positive steps to ensure that the rights and freedoms are secured and to undertake to refrain from hindering the effective exercise of these rights. This may require States to introduce legislation to alter domestic law and practice insofar as it is incompatible with obligations under the Convention.

The Convention protects a range of mainly civil and political rights, including:

the right to life (Art 2);
liberty and security of the person (Art 5);
the right to a fair trial in civil and criminal matters (Art 6);
respect for private and family life, home and correspondence (Art 8);
the right to freedom of thought, conscience and religion (Art 9) and freedom of expression (Art 10);
freedom of association and peaceful assembly (Art 11);
the right to marry and found a family (Art 12).

Further rights are guaranteed by the inclusion of a number of prohibitions, including:

a prohibition on torture and inhuman or degrading treatment or punishment (Art 3);
the requirement that persons should be free from slavery and forced or compulsory labour (Art 4); and
the prohibition on the enactment of retroactive criminal laws (Art 7).

Currently, there are four Protocols relating to substantive rights. These may be regarded as additional Articles to the original Convention and are binding on those States which have ratified them.

The First Protocol guarantees:
the right to peaceful enjoyment of one's possessions (Art 1);
the right to education (Art 2); and
the right to free elections by secret ballot (Art 3).

The Fourth Protocol:
provides that a State allows freedom of movement to everyone lawfully within the territory (Art 2);
prohibits the deprivation of liberty due to an inability to fulfil a contractual obligation (Art 1);
prohibits the expulsion of nationals (Art 3); and
prohibits the collective expulsion of aliens (Art 4).

The Sixth Protocol provides that the death penalty be abolished and that no one shall be condemned to death or executed, thereby amending Art 2 of the original Convention which expressly permits the death penalty.

In addition to providing procedural guarantees in the event of the expulsion of aliens lawfully resident in the territory of the State (Art 1), the Seventh Protocol provides that everyone convicted of a criminal offence shall have:

the right to have their sentence reviewed by a higher tribunal (Art 2);

the right to compensation in the event of a miscarriage of justice (Art 3);

the right, following an acquittal or conviction, not to be tried for the same offence (Art 4); and

equality of rights and responsibilities between spouses (Art 5).

In November 2000 the Council of Europe opened the Twelfth Protocol for signature in order to extend the protection from discrimination provided in Art 14, which only offers individuals protection from discrimination in relation to the rights and freedoms guaranteed by the Convention. The Twelfth Protocol, which is not linked to other Convention rights, will not take effect until it has been signed and ratified by at least 10 Member States.

The UK has signed and ratified the First and Sixth Protocols and has signed but not ratified the Fourth.

## 1.4   RESERVATION, DEROGATION AND RESTRICTION

The Convention provides that States may, prior to ratification, lodge a reservation in respect of a particular provision 'to the extent that any law then in force in its territory is not in conformity with the provision' (Art 57). Thus, a State is prohibited from lodging a reservation in relation to a law passed *after* it has ratified the Convention. There are a number of provisions allowing contracting parties to modify or limit the exercise of the rights guaranteed. In the event of a war or other public emergency threatening the life of the nation, for example, a State may take appropriate measures to derogate from its obligations under the Convention 'to the extent strictly required by the exigencies of the situation' (Art 15(1)). Derogation is only permitted in certain well-defined circumstances and in accordance with specific procedures. The Secretary-General of the Council of Europe must be informed of the measures taken and kept abreast of any developments (Art 15(3)). Although the State has a wide margin of appreciation in determining whether derogation is necessary, the Court has responsibility for ensuring that States act reasonably and has the jurisdiction to assess the proportionality of the measures taken.

Some rights and obligations cannot be restricted or suspended (Art 15(2)). Under no circumstances can a State derogate from its obligation to prohibit torture and inhuman or degrading treatment or punishment (Art 3) and slavery (Art 4(1)). Derogation in respect of the right to life (Art 2) is permitted only 'in respect of deaths resulting from lawful acts of war'. Although there can be no derogation from an obligation to abolish the death penalty (Sixth Protocol), there is a substantive provision which allows States to make provision for the death penalty 'in respect of acts committed in time of war or imminent threat of war' (Sixth Protocol, Art 2). The prohibition against the enactment of criminal laws that are retroactive and retrospective criminal penalties (Art 7) does not apply to war crimes and crimes against humanity which would be considered 'criminal according to the general principles of law recognised by civilised nations'. Some Articles contain restrictive clauses which limit the exercise of a specific right in order to achieve a balance between the rights of the individual and the interests of a democratic society (Arts 8, 9, 10, 11 and Art 2 of the Fourth Protocol). A restriction may not be used for any purpose other than the one for which it is authorised (Art 18). The restrictive clauses are considered in more detail in the section on substantive rights.

## 1.5 THE DOCTRINE OF THE MARGIN OF APPRECIATION AND THE PRINCIPLE OF PROPORTIONALITY

The Court when determining whether a Contracting State has taken sufficient measures to discharge its positive obligations under the Convention applies the 'margin of appreciation' test. By conceding a margin of appreciation, the Court accepts that national authorities are generally in a better position to judge whether local conditions necessitate limiting, derogating or restricting the rights and freedoms guaranteed by the Convention. Accordingly, States have a degree of discretion when deciding whether their actions are reconcilable with their obligations. The margin of appreciation will vary according to the nature of the activities restricted and the aims pursued. Although national authorities can make an initial assessment, the final evaluation as to whether any interference with a Convention right is necessary rests with the Court, which on occasion has construed the margin of appreciation narrowly. (See eg *Smith and Grady v United Kingdom* (2000) 29 EHRR 493.) Lord Hope in *R v DPP, ex parte Kebilene* [1999] 4 All ER 801, considered that by conceding a margin of appreciation, the Court acknowledged that the manner in which the Convention is applied by national authorities is subject to local needs and conditions. However, States are required to justify any derogation from an obligation and bear the burden of establishing that any action is reasonable and proportional.

The principle of proportionality requires that a fair balance is maintained between the rights of the individual and the requirements of the community at large. This principle has frequently been invoked in cases involving the restriction of a right guaranteed by the Convention. In *Goodwin v United Kingdom* (1996) 22 EHRR 123, for example, a journalist complained that an order requiring him to disclose his notes and reveal his source amounted to an unnecessary interference with his freedom of expression guaranteed by Art 10. The Court considered that any restriction on this right could be justified only if there was 'a reasonable relationship of proportionality between the legitimate aim pursued by the disclosure order and the means deployed to achieve that aim'.

## 1.6 THE ENFORCEMENT MACHINERY

The Convention provides an effective regional enforcement mechanism for the protection of fundamental rights. Its success has been due, in part, to the acceptance of both the right of individual petition and the jurisdiction of the Court. Under the original system, the Commission, the Court and the Committee of Ministers shared the task of ensuring Contracting States complied with their obligations. The primary role of the Commission was to conduct the initial examination into complaints alleging violations of the Convention and to determine admissibility. A petition was declared inadmissible if it was anonymous, manifestly ill-founded or the applicant had failed to exhaust available domestic remedies. Admissible claims were then examined in order to establish the facts and the Commission attempted to reach a friendly settlement. This could involve the offer of compensation, an undertaking to amend rules and regulations and the preparation of amending legislation. When a friendly settlement proved impossible, the Commission drew up a report containing a statement of the facts and an opinion as to whether there had been a violation of the Convention. The report was sent to the Committee of Ministers. Within 3 months of the drafting of the report, the Commission and any Contracting State could refer the case to the Court.

Under the original machinery, individuals complaining of a violation of their rights under the Convention did not have the right to refer a case to the Court. If the case was not referred to the Court, the Committee of Ministers determined the outcome of the case. Decisions of the Committee of Ministers are final and Member States undertake to regard them as binding. Despite assistance by a permanent secretariat, the expanding workload and the complexity of the issues raised by the cases resulted in proceedings becoming increasingly protracted. It could take up to 5 years from the lodging of a petition to the delivery of the Court's judgment. Recognising the need to improve efficiency, Member States agreed to the restructuring and streamlining of the enforcement machinery. The principal element of reform was the elimination of the time-consuming examination of cases by two separate bodies. On 1 November 1998, the Eleventh Protocol entered into force, replacing the Commission and the Court with a new, single permanent European Court of Human Rights. This radical development has shortened the length of proceedings and strengthened the judicial character of the system by making recognition of the Court's jurisdiction mandatory and abolishing the Committee of Ministers' adjudicative role. The new Court delivered its first judgment in January 1999.

Judges are elected by the Parliamentary Assembly of the Council of Europe and sit for a term of 6 years. Although the Court is composed of judges equal to that of the Contracting States, judges sit in their individual capacity and do not represent the interests of any State. The Plenary Court elects its President, two Vice-Presidents and two Presidents for each section. Under the Rules of Court, the Court is divided into four sections which are geographically and gender balanced and take account of the different legal systems of the Contracting States. Each section has a President, a Committee of three judges and Chambers of seven judges. A Grand Chamber of 17 judges, which includes the President, Vice-Presidents and section Presidents, will hear cases which raise a serious question affecting the interpretation of the Convention and its Protocols.

The Committee is an important feature of the restructured system and is responsible for the filtering process which was carried out by the Commission. It may unanimously declare inadmissible or strike out an individual application and its decision is final (Art 28). Where no decision is made, a Chamber shall decide upon the admissibility and merits of an individual application and can also decide upon the admissibility of inter-State applications (Art 29). The Chamber may relinquish jurisdiction in favour of the Grand Chamber in cases which raise a serious question affecting the interpretation of the Convention or its Protocols, or where the decision may be inconsistent with a previous decision of the Court, unless one of the parties objects

(Art 30). In exceptional cases, parties may request a referral to the Grand Chamber providing the request is made within a period of 3 months of the delivery of the judgment of the Chamber (Art 43). Although the new Court is not strictly bound by existing case-law, it will consider the existing jurisprudence of the Court to be relevant and persuasive.

## (1)  INDIVIDUAL PETITION, ADMISSIBILITY CRITERIA AND THIRD-PARTY INTERVENTION

The right of individual petition has proved to be an effective means of protecting human rights and was considered to be the most progressive provision of the Convention. However, prior to the introduction of the Eleventh Protocol, the Commission was unable to consider petitions from individuals unless the contracting party against which the complaint had been made declared that it recognised the competence of the Commission to receive such petitions. The right of individual complaint and recognition of the Court's jurisdiction are now mandatory. The Court can receive applications from any person, non-governmental organisation or group of individuals claiming to be the victim of a violation and Contracting States undertake not to 'hinder in any way the effective exercise of this right' (Art 34). Contracting States may also lodge applications against other States directly with the Court (Art 33). On many occasions, the Court has emphasised that applicants should be able to communicate with the Convention organs without being subjected to any form of pressure from the authorities to withdraw or modify their complaints (see *Akkoc v Turkey* (2002) 34 EHRR 51). Undue pressure may stem not only from direct acts of intimidation but also from indirect actions designed to discourage applicants. In *McShane v United Kingdom* (2002) 35 EHRR 23, for example, the Court considered that using sanctions against a solicitor in respect of the alleged disclosure of information for use in proceedings before the Court could have 'a chilling effect on the exercise of the right of individual petition by the applicants and their representatives' (para 151). The applicant's solicitor in domestic inquest proceedings allegedly disclosed witness statements supplied by the Royal Ulster Constabulary (RUC) to the Committee for Administration for Justice, who represented the applicant before the Court. The applicant complained that a formal complaint lodged by the RUC with the Law Society of Northern Ireland alleging that the applicant's solicitor was responsible either directly or indirectly for breaching an undertaking of confidentiality was contrary to Art 34. Although the Law Society considered that there was insufficient evidence to show a prima facie case of unprofessional conduct against the solicitor, the Court considered that the threat of disciplinary proceedings could amount to a restriction on the free and unhindered access to the Convention organs.

Each application is assigned to a section. The President of each section appoints a rapporteur who is responsible for deciding whether applications should be dealt with by a Committee or a Chamber. A Committee may decide unanimously to strike out an application or declare it inadmissible. State applications and applications either sent directly to the Chamber by the rapporteur or not declared inadmissible by a Committee are examined by a Chamber which has jurisdiction to determine both admissibility and merit. Chamber decisions on admissibility, which are taken by majority vote, must give reasons and be made public. In dealing with matters of admissibility, the Court applies similar criteria to those used by the Commission under the old procedures (Art 35). In cases before a Chamber or Grand Chamber of the Court, an applicant will be able to take part in the hearings and the President of the Court can extend an invitation to take part to any person considered to be concerned with the application (Art 36). Once proceedings have commenced, the Court can continue its examination of the application if 'respect for human rights as defined by the Convention and the protocols thereto so requires' (Art 37). However, the Court is given the power to strike out applications if the applicant does not intend to pursue the application or the matter has been resolved or if it considers that an examination of the matter is no longer justified. The Court has the power to restore applications which have been struck out. The applicant's State is entitled to intervene as of right.

## (2) FRIENDLY SETTLEMENTS, JUDGMENTS, ADVISORY OPINIONS AND JUST SATISFACTION

The Commission was originally charged with the task of conducting an investigation to ascertain the facts and place itself at the disposal of the parties with a view to securing a friendly settlement. The Court was only permitted to consider a case after the Commission had acknowledged the failure of efforts to achieve a friendly settlement. Under the restructured enforcement machinery, the Court is required to 'place itself at the disposal of the parties concerned with a view to securing a friendly settlement of the matter' (Art 38). Friendly settlement negotiations are confidential. If successful, the Court is required to 'strike the case out of its list by means of a decision which shall be confined to a brief statement of the facts and of the solution reached' (Art 39). Thus, in agreeing to settle the matter, a contracting party is able to avoid any significantly adverse publicity. Usually, hearings before the Court will be in public and documents deposited with the Registrar will be made accessible to the public (Art 40). However, in exceptional circumstances, the President of the Court can decide not to make documents available and the public can be excluded from the proceedings.

In the event of a finding that there has been a violation of the Convention or its Protocols, the Court shall afford just satisfaction to the injured party (Art 41). If national law fails to make satisfactory reparation for a violation, the Court has the power to award compensation. Although a finding of a violation will frequently be sufficient to amount to just satisfaction, the Court can award substantial sums of money to successful applicants. Just satisfaction is generally divided into three categories: pecuniary loss; non-pecuniary loss; and costs and expenses. Pecuniary loss will be awarded if it can be established that there is a causal link between the violation and loss. Where an applicant has suffered pain and suffering as a result of a violation which caused mental or physical harm, the Court can award a sum for non-pecuniary loss. The amount to be awarded is determined by the Court on the basis of what is considered an equitable sum in the circumstances. An award can also be made to cover necessary legal costs and expenses incurred by applicants to prevent a violation of their rights or to obtain redress in national courts. This figure is likely to be reduced if the applicant was in receipt of legal aid (now public funding).

The Court is required to give reasons for judgments and for its decisions on the issue of admissibility. The decision is reached by a majority vote; however, any judge who does not concur with the decision is entitled to deliver a dissenting opinion (Art 45).

Although the procedures do not give the Court jurisdiction to issue directions on the measures to be taken to address a violation, contracting parties undertake to abide by the final decision of the Court in any case to which they are parties (Art 46). The judgments of a Chamber can become final when the parties declare that they will not request that the case be referred to the Grand Chamber; or if after a period of 3 months following the judgment, no request has been received; or when the panel of the Grand Chamber rejects the request to refer the case to the Grand Chamber (Art 44). There is no appeal from a judgment delivered by the Grand Chamber. Responsibility for supervising the execution of the judgment remains with the Committee of Ministers (Art 46), although the Court may give advisory opinions on legal questions concerning the interpretation of the Convention and its Protocols if the Committee of Ministers (Art 47) submits a request. If a member of the Court does not agree with the advisory opinion, any judge will be entitled to deliver a separate, dissenting opinion (Art 49).

## 1.7  SUBSTANTIVE RIGHTS AND FREEDOMS

The rights and freedoms guaranteed under the Convention are set out in Section I and in the First, Fourth, Sixth and Seventh Protocols of the Convention. Whilst the Convention recognises that some rights are absolute, requiring States to give an inviolable guarantee, the exercise of other rights can be subject to some restriction and qualification.

## (1)  RIGHT TO LIFE: ARTICLE 2 AND THE SIXTH PROTOCOL

The protection of human life is acknowledged as being the 'supreme value in the international hierarchy of human rights' (*Streletz, Kessler and Krenz v Germany* (2001) 33 EHRR 31, para 87). Article 2 imposes an obligation on Contracting States not only to refrain from the intentional and unlawful taking of life but also to take positive measures to safeguard the lives of those within their jurisdiction (*LCB v United Kingdom* (1999) 27 EHRR 212, para 36). The State incurs a duty to ensure the effective enforcement of criminal law provisions which deter the commission of offences against the person, and in appropriate circumstances the authorities may need to take operational measures to protect an individual from the criminal acts of others (*Edwards v United Kingdom* (2002) 35 EHRR 19). However, this obligation should not impose an impossible or disproportionate obligation on the authorities (*Kilic v Turkey* (2001) 33 EHRR 58, para 62). The Court considers that before States incur a positive obligation to take protective measures, it must be established that the authorities knew or ought to have known that there was a real and immediate risk to life (*Osman v United Kingdom* (2000) 29 EHRR 245, paras 115–116). The obligation to protect life requires by implication that there should be an effective official investigation when individuals are killed as a result of the use of force. The purpose of the inquiry is to secure the effective implementation of the domestic laws which protect the right to life, and, in cases involving State authorities, to ensure accountability for deaths occurring under their responsibility. Although the form of investigation may vary according to the circumstances, the initiative to launch an inquiry rests with the authorities and should not be left to the next of kin. For an investigation to be effective, the persons conducting the inquiry must be independent from those implicated in the events, which requires not only a lack of institutional connection but also practical independence. Any deficiency in the investigation which undermines its ability to establish the cause of death or the person responsible will risk falling foul of this standard (*Hugh Jordan v United Kingdom* (2002) 34 EHRR 20).

Given the importance of the protection afforded by Art 2, the Court subjects any deprivation of life to careful scrutiny. The obligation to protect life is particularly onerous in the case of persons in custody, who are considered to be in a particularly vulnerable position (*Keenan v United Kingdom* (2001) 33 EHRR 38). When a person in good health dies in police custody, the burden of providing a satisfactory account for their treatment during detention rests with the authorities. Strong presumptions of fact will arise in respect of the cause of death (*Salman v Turkey* (2002) 34 EHRR 17). The use of lethal force in self defence, lawful arrest or to prevent an escape from lawful custody or to quell a riot or insurrection is not contrary to Art 2 provided the force used was no more than absolutely necessary. In assessing whether the use of force is strictly proportionate, regard must be had to the nature of the aim pursued, the dangers to life and limb inherent in the situation and the degree of risk that the force employed might result in loss of life. It is necessary to scrutinise carefully the deliberate use of force by State agents to determine whether the authorities minimised the need for force (*McCann v United Kingdom* (1996) 21 EHRR 97). Although the death penalty is not contrary to Art 2, ratification of the Sixth Protocol requires Contracting States to abolish this form of punishment.

## (2)   FREEDOM FROM TORTURE, INHUMAN OR DEGRADING TREATMENT OR PUNISHMENT: ARTICLE 3

States have an obligation to take measures to ensure that individuals within their jurisdiction are not subjected to torture or inhuman or degrading treatment or punishment, including such ill-treatment administered by private individuals. In *Soering v United Kingdom* (1989) 11 EHRR 439, the Court considered that the absolute prohibition on particular forms of treatment or punishment 'enshrines one of the fundamental values of the democratic societies making up the Council of Europe'. Thus, there may be no derogation from this obligation. In determining whether a State has violated this provision, the Court has tended to adopt a strict interpretation of the notions of torture and inhuman and degrading treatment. In *Ireland v United Kingdom* (1978) 2 EHRR 25, the Court, drawing a distinction between different categories of prohibited State practices, found that interrogation techniques used to obtain information from Republican detainees in Northern Ireland did not amount to torture. 'Torture' required 'deliberate inhuman treatment causing very serious and cruel suffering', whereas inhuman treatment or punishment involved the 'infliction of intense physical and mental suffering' which reached a minimum level of severity, and degrading treatment required 'ill-treatment designed to arouse in victims feelings of fear, anguish and inferiority capable of humiliating and debasing them and possibly breaking their physical or moral resistance'.

The Court notes that, in addition to the severity of the treatment, torture involves a purposive element (*Salman v Turkey* (2002) 34 EHRR 17). This is recognised in the UN Convention against Torture and Other Cruel, Inhuman and Degrading

Treatment and Punishment, which defines torture in terms of the intentional infliction of severe pain or suffering with the aim, inter alia, of obtaining information, inflicting punishment or intimidating.

Under Art 3, the Court has been asked to consider cases involving corporal punishment, the treatment of persons held in detention, conditions in prison and mental hospitals, deportation and extradition, and the application and operation of asylum and immigration procedures. In *Tyrer v United Kingdom* (1978) 2 EHRR 1, the Court held that corporal punishment cannot be justified if the punishment is considered to be inhuman or degrading. In assessing whether the punishment is sufficiently humiliating to cross the minimum threshold, regard will be had to all the circumstances of the case including the 'nature and context of the punishment itself and the manner and method of its execution'. The personal characteristics of the victim can have a bearing on the case: thus factors including age, gender and state of health of the applicant have been considered relevant. The Court is reluctant to sanction the physical chastisement of children and considers that children and other vulnerable individuals are entitled to effective protection from the State against breaches of their personal integrity. In *A v United Kingdom (Human Rights: Punishment of Child)* [1998] 2 FLR 959, the applicant, who was 9 years old, received punishment at the hand of his stepfather that reached the level of severity prohibited by Art 3. The stepfather was charged with assault but successfully raised the defence of reasonable chastisement in the national court. The Court found that the State was in violation of its obligation under the Convention on the ground that national law failed to provide the applicant with adequate protection from a violation of Art 3.

In *McFeely v United Kingdom* (1984) 38 D&R 11, IRA prisoners complained that detention in cells which they had smeared with food and excrement constituted an inhuman and degrading system of treatment. The Commission noted that, whilst the Convention required prison authorities to have due regard to the welfare of prisoners, the self-imposed deterioration in living conditions can relieve the respondent government from responsibility. Nevertheless, the State had an obligation to exercise its custodial authority to safeguard the health and well-being of all prisoners and needed to keep the situation under review. In addition, the Commission found that there was nothing inherently degrading or objectionable about the requirement to wear prison uniform or to be subjected to intimate body searches. However, the authorities have an obligation to ensure that prison conditions meet the needs of prisoners with special needs (*Price v United Kingdom* 11 BHRC 401). A prisoner on remand in HM Prison Barlinnie in Glasgow has successfully argued before a national court that prison conditions were sufficiently inadequate to be contrary to Art 3. His complaint related to overcrowding, inadequate light, ventilation and exercise, and lavatory arrangements which involved the process known as 'slopping out', which required prisoners to empty vessels used for urine and faeces (*Napier v The Scottish Ministers* [2002] UKHRR 308).

Although States have the right to control the entry, residence and expulsion of aliens, immigration, extradition and deportation may give rise to issues under Art 3. In *Soering v United Kingdom* (1989) 11 EHRR 439, the Court considered that to return the applicant to the USA on charges of capital murder would infringe his rights under the Convention. Although the Convention does not prohibit the death penalty, subjecting the applicant to the death-row phenomenon would be contrary to Art 3. It is now well established in Convention case-law that where there are substantial grounds for believing that the person would face a real risk of being subjected to torture or ill-treatment in the receiving State, Art 3 implies an obligation not to expel the person to that country (*Ahmed v Austria* (1996) 24 EHRR 278; *Hilal v United Kingdom* (2001) 33 EHRR 2). Similarly, although the right to political asylum is not contained in either the Convention or its Protocols, it may give rise to an issue under Art 3 (*Vilvarajah v United Kingdom* (1991) 14 EHRR 248). The Court has emphasised that, having regard to the absolute nature of Art 3, a rigorous scrutiny must necessarily be conducted of an individual's claim that his or her deportation to a third country will expose that individual to treatment prohibited by Art 3 (*Amuur v France* (1996) 22 EHRR 533; *Jabari v Turkey* (2000) 9 BHRC 1, para 39). Notwithstanding that the use of immigration controls is not in itself a violation of the Convention, immigration controls based on gender or racial discrimination will amount to degrading treatment which is contrary to Art 3 (*Abdulaziz, Cabales and Balkandali v United Kingdom* (1985) 7 EHRR 471; *East African Asians v United Kingdom* (1973) 3 EHRR 76).

## (3)   PROHIBITION OF SLAVERY AND FORCED LABOUR: ARTICLE 4

The Convention draws a distinction between slavery and servitude and forced or compulsory labour. The Court and Commission have been asked to consider very few claims involving slavery and servitude, which are considered to be the most extreme form of control over another individual. In *Van Droogenbroeck v Belgium* (1982) EHRR 443, the Commission considered that servitude necessarily involved an obligation on the part of the 'serf' to live on another's property and the 'impossibility of changing his condition'. An absolute prohibition is placed on slavery and servitude but forced or compulsory labour is subject to the exceptions set out in Art 4(3). In *W, X, Y and Z v United Kingdom* (1968) 11 YB 562, the Commission rejected a claim by four young men who claimed that a refusal to discharge them from the navy resulted in 'oppressive compulsory service tantamount to the status of servitude'. The Commission considered that the men had not been held in servitude and that military service was not forced labour because it was specifically excluded by Art 4(3).

The Commission and the Court have rejected claims arising from an obligation on members of a profession to provide services free of charge. In *Van Der Mussele v Belgium* (1983) 6 EHRR 163, a lawyer claimed that the requirement to provide pro bono services to indigent defendants was forced labour and amounted to a violation of Art 4. In rejecting this claim, the Court noted that the work performed was within the scope of normal legal duties and could be considered as forming part of his 'normal civic obligation'. The majority of complaints under Art 4 have been brought by convicted prisoners and concern compulsory work done in prison whilst serving a sentence.

## (4)   RIGHT TO LIBERTY AND SECURITY: ARTICLE 5

The primary purpose of this provision is to protect individuals against arbitrary arrest and detention. The Court has emphasised that the right to liberty and security of the person is a fundamental right in a democratic society and any interference with this right by the authorities must be compatible with the rule of law (*Brogan and Others v United Kingdom* (1988) 11 EHRR 117 and *De Wilde, Ooms and Versyp v Belgium* (1971) 1 EHRR 373). Accordingly, no one may be deprived of his or her liberty save in a limited number of circumstances which must be in accordance with a procedure prescribed by law (*Winterwerp v The Netherlands* (1979–80) 2 EHRR 387). Not all restrictions on movement will amount to a deprivation of liberty for the purposes of the Convention. The distinction is one of degree or intensity rather than one of nature or substance and will depend upon the circumstances of each case (*Guzzardi v Italy* (1980) 3 EHRR 333 and *Conka v Belgium* (2002) 34 EHRR 54). Where the lawfulness of detention is in issue, the Convention refers in the first instance to national law and presupposes conformity with domestic law (*Weeks v United Kingdom* (1987) 10 EHRR 293). Thus the Convention requires that arrest and detention have a legal basis in domestic law. However, since failure to comply with domestic law can result in a breach of Art 5, the Court will examine whether national law is formulated with sufficient precision for the purposes of the Convention (*Steel v United Kingdom* (1999) 28 EHRR 603 and *Hashman and Harrup v United Kingdom* (2000) 30 EHRR 241). The circumstances in which a person may be deprived of his or her liberty are set out in Art 5(1)(a)–(f).

Article 5(1)(a) provides for detention after conviction by a competent court. The word 'after' has been interpreted as meaning more than 'subsequent to a conviction' and detention must be as a consequence of a conviction. The Court has interpreted the requirements of the Convention for this provision as meaning that there must be a causal connection between conviction and detention (*Van Droogenbroeck v Belgium* (1982) 4 EHRR 443). The continued detention of a person serving a discretionary life sentence on the grounds of mental instability and dangerousness to the public from risk of further violence was not incompatible with Art 5 (*Weeks v United Kingdom* (1987) 10 EHRR 293). However, if the decision to revoke the licence of a person serving a mandatory life sentence were based on objectives inconsistent with the objectives of the original sentencing court, continued detention would no longer be justified in terms of Art 5(1)(a) (*Stafford v United Kingdom* (2002) 152 NLJ 880). Article 5(1)(b) provides for detention or arrest for non-compliance with a court order. Under this provision, detention has been allowed for non-payment of the community charge, non-payment of a fine and to allow security checks to be carried out (*Benham v United Kingdom* (1996) 22 EHRR 293).

Article 5(1)(c) requires that arrest or detention must be based on reasonable suspicion that an offence has been committed. Thus, in the absence of adequate facts or information supporting the basis for reasonable suspicion, detention will be unjustified. The purpose of detention under this provision is to confirm or dispel the suspicion that formed the basis for the arrest and the fact that a person is eventually released without charge does not necessarily mean that his or her detention was in breach of Art 5 (*Brogan and Others v United Kingdom* (1988) 11 EHRR 117). The Court's task is to determine whether the objective standard of reasonable suspicion has been met. Although lawful detention must be based on reasonable suspicion, after a lapse of time reasonable suspicion will no longer be a sufficient reason for continued detention (*Szeloch v Poland* Application No 33079/96). Provided an arrest is for the purpose of initiating a criminal prosecution and not merely for preventative detention, facts which raise a suspicion need not be of the same level as those necessary to justify a conviction or even the bringing of a charge (*Murray v United Kingdom* (1995) 19 EHRR 193).

Although accepting that suspected terrorists could be detained on the basis of confidential information, which was not disclosed to either the suspect or the court on the ground of public interest, the Court observed that it was necessary for the respondent government to furnish sufficient information to establish that an arrest was based on reasonable suspicion and considered that 'the exigencies of dealing with terrorist crime cannot justify stretching the notion of reasonableness to the point where the safeguard secured by Article 5(1)(c) is impaired' (*Fox, Campbell and Hartley v United Kingdom* (1990) 13 EHRR 157 and *O'Hara v United Kingdom* (2002) 34 EHRR 32, para 35). Article 5(1)(c) imposes an obligation to bring the person under arrest or detention before a competent judicial authority. This requirement applies whether the person is arrested to prevent the commission of an offence or to prevent him absconding (*Lawless v Ireland* (1979–80) 1 EHRR 15).

Article 5(1)(d) allows children to be detained for the purpose of educational supervision or in order to bring them before a competent legal authority (*Bouamar v Belgium* (1988) 11 EHRR 1), and Art 5(1)(e) permits persons to be detained for purposes relating to social control (*Riera Blume and Others v Spain* (2000) 30 EHRR 632). Many cases under this latter provision have concerned the detention of psychiatric patients (*Winterwerp v The Netherlands* (1979–80) 2 EHRR 387). Provided domestic law provides adequate legal safeguards against arbitrary decisions, arrest and detention pending deportation or expulsion is permitted under Art 5(1)(f) (*Chahal v United Kingdom* (1996) 23 EHRR 413). The Court in *Bozano v France* (1987) 9 EHRR 297 expressed grave doubts as to whether the applicant's detention was lawful and found that the authorities had deprived the applicant of his liberty to effect a disguised extradition and to circumvent an order of the court.

Article 5(2) provides that, following an arrest, a person has the right to be informed promptly, in a language he understands, of the reasons for his arrest and any charge brought against him. This provides an elementary safeguard for persons under arrest in that it allows them to know why they are being detained (*Fox, Campbell and Hartley v United Kingdom* (1990) 13 EHRR 157). Although the authorities must provide sufficient information for the person to know the essential legal and factual grounds for his arrest, the information given under this provision need not be as detailed as that prescribed in Art 6(3). In order to reduce the risk of arbitrariness in pre-trial detention, Art 5(3) requires that, on arrest, a person should be brought promptly before a judicial body which has the power to order his release pending trial. Whether continued detention is reasonable will be assessed by reference to the facts of each case (*Wemhoff v Federal Republic of Germany* (1979–80) 1 EHRR 55). The tribunal which has the power to order release must be sufficiently independent of the parties (*Jordan (Stephen) v United Kingdom* (2001) 31 EHRR 6). Although States are allowed a margin of appreciation, the Court has expressed concern that an excessively liberal interpretation of the word 'promptly' would seriously weaken this procedural guarantee which is to protect the individual from arbitrary detention (*Brogan and Others v United Kingdom* (1988) 11 EHRR 117). The Court has considered that a period of detention in excess of 4 days is not compatible with the requirement of prompt judicial control (*O'Hara v United Kingdom* (2002) 34 EHRR 32). The reasons for denying bail pending trial will be subject to careful scrutiny by the Court (*Toth v Austria* (1992) 14 EHRR 551). Although the Convention permits conditions to be attached to bail, the Court considers that measures which effectively fetter judicial decisions in relation to bail will be contrary to Art 5(3) (*Caballero v United Kingdom* (2000) 30 EHRR 643 and *SBC v United Kingdom* (2002) 34 EHRR 21).

Article 5(4) provides persons under arrest or detention with a substantive right to challenge the lawfulness of detention, which may be reviewed if circumstances change. The Court considers that the dramatic impact of deprivation of liberty on fundamental rights requires that proceedings conducted under Art 5(4) should in principle meet as far as possible the basic requirements of a fair trial (*Schops v Germany* Application No 25116/94). A request for release from detention must be decided 'speedily'. Undue delay in hearing a request under this provision will not be justified on the grounds of complexity of national judicial systems (*MB v Switzerland* Application No 28256/95). This provision requires that national courts not only reach a decision promptly but also, where an automatic review of detention exists, make decisions at regular intervals. Although it is not the Court's function to determine the maximum period of time between reviews, the Court and the Commission have accepted periods of less than one year between reviews and rejected periods of more than one year (*Hirst v United Kingdom* [2001] Crim LR 919). In *Oldham v United Kingdom* (2001) 31 EHRR 34, the Court acknowledged the need for a flexible system of review which takes account of the personal circumstances of the prisoner but noted that in this case the applicant had no power to seek a review within 2 years, which was excessive and contrary to Art 5(4). The body reviewing the lawfulness of continued detention should have the power to order release or must have a procedure which meets with the necessary judicial safeguards (*Thynne, Wilson and Gunnell v United Kingdom* (1990) 13 EHRR 666). Convention case-law establishes that prisoners detained during Her Majesty's pleasure are entitled, after the expiry of the tariff period, to have the lawfulness of their detention reviewed by a judicial body (*Hussain v United Kingdom* (1996) 22 EHRR 1; *T v United Kingdom* (2000) 30 EHRR 121). If the power to direct the prisoner's release remains the prerogative of the Home Secretary, this requirement will not be met (*Curley v United Kingdom* (2000) 31 EHRR 14). The Court is satisfied that the tariff period of a life sentence represents the punishment element of the offence and continued detention after this period should be based on matters associated with the objectives of the original sentence. Accordingly, the body determining the continued detention of a prisoner serving a life sentence must satisfy the procedural requirements of Art 5(4) (*Stafford v United Kingdom* (2002) 152 NLJ 880). Although the arrest and detention of persons suspected of involvement in terrorist activities present the authorities with special problems, decisions of national authorities are still subject to effective control by the Court (*Chahal v United Kingdom* (1996) 23 EHRR 413). However, the rights protected by this provision are not absolute and States are permitted to issue a notice of derogation in time of an emergency (Art 15(1)). In the event of a violation of Art 5, there is an enforceable right to compensation under Art 5(5).

## (5) FAIR TRIAL: ARTICLE 6 AND ARTICLES 2–4 OF THE SEVENTH PROTOCOL

Article 6 provides that in the determination of their civil rights and obligations or of any criminal charge against them, everyone shall be entitled to a fair and public hearing, within a reasonable time, by an independent and impartial tribunal. The terms 'civil rights and obligations' and the nature of a 'criminal charge' are autonomous concepts, which have not been construed solely by reference to national law (*Ashingdane v United Kingdom* (1985) 7 EHRR 528; *Air Canada v United Kingdom* (1995) 20 EHRR 150; *Adolf v Austria* (1982) 4 EHRR 313; *Schmautzer v Austria* (1995) 21 EHRR 511; *Campbell and Fell v United Kingdom* (1984) 7 EHRR 165). This provision applies to all proceedings whose outcome has a direct bearing upon the determination of a private right or obligation and has been used in cases involving the law of tort, family law and commercial law (*Fayed v United Kingdom* (1994) 18 EHRR 393). In determining whether the offence in question is classified as criminal, the Court takes account of three main criteria: the legal classification of the offence in national law; the nature of the offence; and the nature and degree of severity of the penalty (*Funke v France* (1993) 16 EHRR 297). Similarly, the term 'charged with a criminal offence' has been held to have an autonomous meaning requiring the Court to examine the realities of the situation and determine whether the applicant was 'substantially affected' by the steps taken against him (*Quinn v Ireland* (2000) 29 EHRR CD 234). Everyone charged with a criminal offence is provided with certain minimum rights in the preparation and presentation of his or her defence. In order to understand the nature of the allegations, the accused has the right to be given sufficient information, in a language he understands (*Steel v United Kingdom* (1999) 28 EHRR 603; *Mattoccia v Italy* [2001] EHRLR 89). Charge sheets have been found to contain sufficient information to satisfy this requirement.

Procedural guarantees laid down in Art 6 are meaningless in the absence of the right of effective access to a court (*Golder v United Kingdom* (1975) 1 EHRR 524). However, this right is not absolute and can be subject to legitimate restrictions (eg statutory limitation periods and national security considerations), provided any restriction on access serves a legitimate aim and complies with the principle of proportionality (*Stubbings and Others v United Kingdom* (1996) 23 EHRR 213; *Luisa Diamantina Romero de Ibanez and Roberto Guillermo Rojas v United Kingdom* Application No 58692/00; *Osman v United Kingdom* (2000) 29 EHRR 245; *Devenney v United Kingdom* (2002) 35 EHRR 24; and *Devlin v United Kingdom* (2002) 34 EHRR 43). The hearing should be in public and take place within a reasonable time, but the press and public can be excluded from the trial in the interest of morals, public order, national security or if publicity would prejudice the interests of justice (see *Ferrantelli and Santangelo v Italy* (1997) 23 EHRR 288; *Kuopila v Finland* (2001) 33 EHRR 25). Thus it is permissible for witnesses to give evidence in camera (see *Kostovski v The Netherlands* (1989) 12 EHRR 434; *Visser v The Netherlands* [2002] 13 HRCD 65). Delays that could jeopardise the effectiveness and credibility of the trial process or leave the accused in a state of uncertainty about his fate for a lengthy period will violate Art 6 (*Dede and Others v Turkey* Application No 32981/96). However, the Convention does not set a time-limit on proceedings and each case is assessed on its facts.

In determining whether a tribunal is sufficiently independent, the Court considers the manner of appointment of its members and the duration of their term of office, the existence of guarantees against outside pressures and the question whether the body presents an appearance of independence (*Piersack v Belgium* (1982) 5 EHRR 169; *Sander v United Kingdom* (2001) 31 EHRR 44; *Ahmed and Others v United Kingdom* (2000) 29 EHRR 1; *McGonnell v United Kingdom* (2000) 30 EHRR 289; and *Morris v United Kingdom* (2002) 34 EHRR 52). However, administrative authorities may play a role in adjudication without infringing the Convention, provided the person concerned has an opportunity to challenge any decision made against him before a tribunal that offered the guarantees of Art 6 (*W v United Kingdom* (1988) 10 EHRR 29; *Kingsley v United Kingdom* (2001) 33 EHRR 13). Many cases considered by the Court have concerned the impartiality of the investigating magistrate in civil law systems (*Lauko v Slovakia* [1998] HRCD 838). While the primary purpose of Art 6 is to focus on the trial proceedings, there is nothing to prevent it from applying to pre-trial proceedings (*Imbrioscia v Switzerland* (1994) 17 EHRR 441). In addition to a general right to a fair trial, this provision incorporates a number of specific rights, all of which are linked to the notion of a fair hearing. These specific rights, which are manifestations of the general right to a fair hearing, include the right to be presumed innocent until proven guilty, which places the burden of proof on the prosecution (*Salabiaku v France* (1988) 13 EHRR 379; *Phillips v United Kingdom* 11 BHRC 280; *Saunders v United Kingdom* (1996) 23 EHRR 313; *Telfner v Austria* (2002) 34 EHRR 7); the right to be informed promptly of the nature of the charge (*Kamanski v Austria* (1989) 13 EHRR 36); the right to defend oneself and to have adequate time and facilities to organise one's defence in an appropriate way (*Murray v United Kingdom* (1996) 22 EHRR 29), and without restrictions in order to put forward all the relevant arguments before the court (*Chichilian and Ekindjian v France* (1989) 13 EHRR 553); the right to effective legal assistance, which may involve the accused conducting his own defence (*McVicar v United Kingdom* (2002) 35 EHRR 22), obtaining the services of a lawyer of his choosing and in some circumstances receiving free legal representation (*Pakelli v Federal Republic of Germany* (1983) 6 EHRR 1; *Averill v United Kingdom* (2002) 31 EHRR 36; *McGee v United Kingdom* Application No 28135/95; *Brennan v United Kingdom* (2002) 34 EHRR 18).

The accused also has the right to obtain the attendance and examination of defence witnesses and the opportunity to cross-examine prosecution witnesses and, in principle, all evidence must be produced in the presence of the accused (*Unterpertinger v Austria* (1986) 13 EHRR 175; *Saidi v France* (1994) 17 EHRR 251). The Convention does not exclude the possibility that witnesses living abroad whose presence at trial cannot be enforced by the trial court can be examined in their country of residence. Although the Court has been reluctant to sanction the use of anonymous witnesses, it has accepted that in some circumstances evidence can be given by an unidentified witness, provided the accused has ample opportunity to challenge the evidence (*Doorson v The Netherlands* (1996) 22 EHRR 330). Similarly, the Court has found that the use of written statements at trial is not in itself inconsistent with the right to a fair trial, provided the rights of the defence are respected (*Kostovski v The Netherlands* (1989) 12 EHRR 434; *Visser v The Netherlands* [2002] HRCD 65). While Art 6 does not guarantee the right of appeal, many judicial systems do provide for an appeals process which is required to comply with these provisions. In assessing the matter of procedural fairness, the Court insists on examining national proceedings in their entirety, including any appeals process (*Khan v United Kingdom* (2001) 31 EHRR 45; *CG v United Kingdom* (2002) 34 EHRR 31).

Fair trial rights are considered to be so fundamental to the principle of the rule of law that Art 6 has been interpreted fairly widely and the Court has applied the general right to a fair hearing, even though it is not possible to point to a violation of a specific right (*Barbera, Messegue and Jabardo v Spain* (1988) 11 EHRR 360). Although not expressly mentioned in Art 6, the Court considers that the privilege against self-incrimination, the right to remain silent and the principle of equality of arms are internationally recognised standards which are implicit in the right to a fair trial (*Funke v France* (1993) 16 EHRR 297; *Saunders v United Kingdom* (1996) 23 EHRR 313; *Dombo Beheer BV v The Netherlands* (1993) 18 EHRR 213; *Fitt v United Kingdom* (2000) 30 EHRR 481). However, the Court has noted, in the context of jury trial, that the right to silence is not an absolute right and the drawing of inferences from silence cannot by itself be considered incompatible with the requirements of Art 6 (*Murray v United Kingdom* (1996) 22 EHRR 29; *Condron v United Kingdom* (2001) 31 EHRR 1). Notwithstanding the need to combat serious crime, the Court has held that the requirement of a fair hearing cannot be sacrificed for the sake of expediency, thus the public interest cannot justify the use of evidence obtained in a manner which offends against fundamental principles of fairness (*Teixeira de Castro v Portugal* (1998) 28 EHRR 101; *Saunders v United Kingdom* (1996) 23 EHRR 313). However, as a general rule, when the issue relates to the rules of evidence, the Court has taken the view that it should not usurp the role of the national court in assessing the evidence (*Schenk v Switzerland* (1988) 13 EHRR 242). Its function was to scrutinise the decision-making process in its entirety to ensure that, as far as possible, it complied with the requirements of Art 6 (*Khan v United Kingdom* (2001) 31 EHRR 45; *PG and JH v United Kingdom* [2001] HRCD 707).

Any restriction on defence rights must be limited to measures that are strictly necessary and national authorities are required to ensure that the limitation is sufficiently counterbalanced by safeguards (*Rowe and Davis v United Kingdom* (2000) 30 EHRR 1). While the right of a suspect to have access to a lawyer when in police custody has been inferred from Art 6, and a refusal to allow a suspect access to legal advice without good cause has consistently incurred the Court's disapproval, consultations between a solicitor and the accused can be subject to restriction (*Campbell and Fell v United Kingdom* (1984) 2 EHRR 165). Whether any restriction on the right of access to a solicitor does in fact result in the accused being deprived of a fair trial should be considered in the light of the whole proceedings. On the ground that the Convention is intended to guarantee rights that are practical and effective, the Court attaches considerable importance to the right to consult a solicitor in private (*Averill v United Kingdom* (2002) 31 EHRR 36; *McGee v United Kingdom* Application No 28135/95). If solicitors were unable to receive instructions in confidence, there was a risk that legal advice would lose much of its effectiveness (*Brennan v United Kingdom* (2002) 34 EHRR 18). The Convention does not guarantee the right to trial by jury and does not explicitly require the interests of witnesses to be taken into consideration (*Doorson v The Netherlands* (1996) 23 EHRR 330, para 70). Furthermore, whilst the Court considers that, in principle, prosecuting authorities should disclose all material evidence, there is no absolute right to disclosure of all prosecution evidence (see *Edwards v United Kingdom* (1992) 15 EHRR 417; *Rowe and Davis v United Kingdom* (2000) 30 EHRR 1). Although legal presumptions are not in principle contrary to the Convention, Art 6(2) requires that the court does not start with the preconceived idea that the accused committed the offence (*Telfner v Austria* (2002) 34 EHRR 7). The Convention does not provide for an automatic exclusionary rule in relation to irregularly obtained evidence (see *Schenk v Switzerland* (1988) 13 EHRR 242).

Although Art 6 does not guarantee the right of appeal, many judicial systems do provide for an appeals process whereupon the procedural guarantees set out in this provision will generally apply. The right to appeal in criminal cases is provided by Art 2 of the Seventh Protocol, which gives everyone convicted of a criminal offence the right to have his conviction or sentence reviewed by a higher tribunal. In *Edwards v United Kingdom* (1992) 15 EHRR 417, the Court was prepared to accept that the appeals process could rectify earlier procedural violations. Article 3 of the Seventh Protocol provides the right to compensation if it is established conclusively that there has been a miscarriage of justice. Article 4 of the Seventh Protocol provides that no one may be tried or punished twice for the same offence unless there is fresh evidence or there was a fundamental defect in the initial proceedings. Thus, a second conviction arising from the same set of facts as an earlier conviction will be contrary to the Convention (see *Fischer (Franz) v Austria* [2001] HRCD 341).

## (6) FREEDOM FROM RETROACTIVE CRIMINAL LAW: ARTICLE 7

A conviction based on acts or omissions which did not constitute a criminal offence under national or international law at the time they were committed will be contrary to Art 7(1) of the Convention. The prohibition on the retrospective application of criminal law is based on the principle of legal certainty, which requires that an offence must be clearly defined in law (*Kokkinakis v Greece* (1993) 17 EHRR 397). However, this provision does not prohibit the progressive development of the criminal law through judicial law-making, providing it is consistent with the essence of the offence and could reasonably be foreseen (*SW v United Kingdom; CR v United Kingdom* (1996) 21 EHRR 363). Similarly, a heavier penalty cannot be imposed than was applicable at the time the offence was committed. The Court considers that the concept of 'penalty' has an autonomous meaning and was satisfied that a confiscation order imposed following conviction for a criminal offence was a penalty within the meaning of Art 7 (*Welch v United Kingdom* (1995) 20 EHRR 247). Confiscation proceedings are considered to be part of the sentencing process and do not invoke the procedural protections provided by Art 6(2) (*Phillips v United Kingdom* 11 BHRC 280). Retrospective application of national criminal law is acceptable in respect of acts which were acknowledged as crimes under international law. Thus, notwithstanding that it was not recognised as a crime in national law at the time, a conviction for torture will not be contrary to Art 7.

## (7) RIGHT TO RESPECT FOR PRIVATE AND FAMILY LIFE: ARTICLE 8

Article 8(1) provides that everyone has the right to respect for private and family life, his home and his correspondence. The object of this provision is to offer the individual protection against unnecessary interference by public authorities (*Kroon v The Netherlands* (1994) 19 EHRR 263). States have an obligation not only to refrain from interfering with these rights but also to adopt positive measures to ensure they are protected (*Johnston v Ireland* (1986) 9 EHRR 203; *Ignaccolo-Zenide v Romania* (2001) 31 EHRR 7). The Court and the Commission have interpreted the notion of respect for private life to include the right to establish relationships with other persons for personal development and fulfilment (*Niemietz v Germany* (1992) 16 EHRR 97; *Dudgeon v United Kingdom* (1981) 4 EHRR 149). It has been held to cover the right to physical and moral integrity, the right to develop sexual relationships and the right to establish a personal identity (*X and Y v Netherlands* (1985) 8 EHRR 235; *Sheffield and Horsham v United Kingdom* (1998) 27 EHRR 163; *Costello-Roberts v United Kingdom* (1993) 19 EHRR 112; *Gaskin v United Kingdom* (1989) 12 EHRR 36). The notion of family life has been interpreted widely and covers de facto as well as marriage-based relationships and relationships between grandparents and grandchildren, uncles and nephews, and children and foster-parents (*Sahin v Germany; Sommerfield v Germany; Hoffmann v Germany* [2002] 1 FLR 119; *X, Y and Z v United Kingdom* (1997) 24 EHRR 143; *Bronda v Italy* [1998] HRCD 641; *Boyle v United Kingdom* (1994) 19 EHRR 179). Although Art 8 guarantees both parents and children a right of mutual contact, the authorities can justifiably restrict access if necessary to protect the health and rights and freedoms of the child (*Andersson v Sweden* (1992) 14 EHRR 615; *W v United Kingdom* (1988) 10 EHRR 29; *Glaser v United Kingdom* (2001) 33 EHRR 1; *Z and Others v United Kingdom* (2002) 34 EHRR 3). In assessing whether there are sufficiently close links to bring the relationship within the scope of the concept of family life, the Court takes account of many factors including cohabitation, marriage and frequency of contact (*Kroon v The Netherlands* (1994) 19 EHRR 263; *Berrehab v The Netherlands* (1988) 11 EHRR 322). The existence of close family ties will not prevent the deportation or extradition of a family member if it is justified under Art 8(2) (*Moustaquim v Belgium* (1991) 13 EHRR 802). Although States enjoy a margin of appreciation in matters related to the entry and expulsion of non-nationals, a fair balance must be struck between the competing interests of the individual and the community (*Gül v Switzerland* (1996) 22 EHRR 93).

Article 8 also provides the right to live in one's home without unnecessary interference by the authorities (*Buckley v United Kingdom* (1996) 23 EHRR 101; *Chapman (Sally) and Others v United Kingdom* (2001) 33 EHRR 18). States have an obligation to take reasonable and appropriate measures to ensure compliance with this provision, which also applies to business premises (*Hatton v United Kingdom* (2002) 34 EHRR 1; *Niemietz v Germany* (1992) 16 EHRR 97). The right to respect for correspondence gives a right to communicate freely with other people and covers written forms of communication and telephone conversations (*Silver v United Kingdom* (1983) 5 EHRR 347; *Huvig v France* (1990) 12 EHRR 528; *A v France* (1993) 17 EHRR 462; *Petra v Romania* (2001) 33 EHRR 5; *Foxley v United Kingdom* (2001) 31 EHRR 25). The entry into and search of premises and vehicles by police officers will be contrary to Art 8 unless the requirements set out in Art 8(2) are satisfied (*Funke v France* (1993) 16 EHRR 297; *McLeod v United Kingdom* [1998] 2 FLR 1048). Any interference with a right guaranteed by this provision must comply with national law, which should be formulated with sufficient clarity to give citizens an adequate indication as to the circumstances in which and the conditions on which authorities are empowered to interfere with their rights (*Malone v United Kingdom* (1984) 7 EHRR 14). The relevant law and practice must afford adequate and effective safeguards against abuse by the authorities (*Miailhe v France* (1993) 16 EHRR 332; *Cremieux v France* (1993) 16 EHRR 357; *Lambert v France* [1998] HRCD 806). To be considered necessary, the interference must correspond to a pressing social need and be proportionate to the legitimate aim pursued (*Funke v France* (1993) 16 EHRR 297). Intrusive surveillance may be Convention compliant provided the methods used do not undermine democracy and are accompanied by safeguards which provide adequate protection against misuse (*Klass and Others v Federal Republic of Germany* (1978) 2 EHRR 214;

*Khan v United Kingdom* (2001) 31 EHRR 45; *PG and JH v United Kingdom* [2001] HRCD 707). Although States enjoy a margin of appreciation, the final evaluation as to whether any restrictions placed on Art 8 rights are compatible with the Convention rests with the Court (*Laskey, Jaggard and Brown v United Kingdom* (1997) 24 EHRR 39; *ADT v United Kingdom* (2001) 31 EHRR 33; *Smith and Grady v United Kingdom* (2001) 31 EHRR 24).

## (8) FREEDOM OF THOUGHT, CONSCIENCE AND RELIGION: ARTICLE 9

Article 9 provides the right to freedom of thought, conscience and religion. While religious freedom is a matter of individual conscience, this provision includes the right to worship with others either in public or private and to teach and practise a religion or belief. However, those who choose to exercise the freedom to practise their religion must tolerate the denial by others of their religious beliefs and accept the dissemination of other doctrines which may be hostile to their faith (*Kokkinakis v Greece* (1993) 17 EHRR 397). Strong links between church and State will not violate this provision provided membership is on a voluntary basis (*Darby v Sweden* (1991) 13 EHRR 774). It includes the freedom to hold or not to hold a religious belief and to practise or not to practise a religion (*Buscarini v San Marino* (2000) 30 EHRR 208). This provision embraces the freedom to hold non-religious beliefs and philosophies including pacifism. However, the freedom to practise does not cover every act associated with a religion or belief (*Arrowsmith v United Kingdom* (1978) 19 D&R 5). The Court has drawn a distinction between freedom of thought and the dissemination of ideas which may be subject to justified restrictions (*Handyside v United Kingdom* (1976) 1 EHRR 737). States incur an obligation to ensure that the holders of a belief or philosophy can enjoy the rights guaranteed under Art 9. In extreme cases this obligation may result in States controlling the manner in which religious doctrines are opposed or denied (*Otto-Preminger Institute v Austria* (1994) 19 EHRR 34). Although the Convention provides the right to worship with others, practical difficulties may limit the exercise of this aspect of Art 9 (*Ahmad v United Kingdom* (1982) 4 EHRR 126). In democratic societies States do not need to take measures to ensure that religious communities remain under a unified leadership (*Serif v Greece* (2001) 31 EHRR 20). The freedom to manifest one's religion or belief may be subject to limitations as are prescribed by law and are necessary in a democratic society in the interests of public safety for the protection of public order, health or morals, and for the protection of the rights and freedom of others. Although States enjoy a wide margin of appreciation in this area, legislation permitting significant interference with the exercise of religious freedoms by political, administrative and ecclesiastical authorities will be contrary to the Convention (*Manoussakis v Greece* (1996) 23 EHRR 387). The freedom of thought enshrined in Art 9 is important to believers and has been acknowledged as 'a precious asset for atheists, agnostics, sceptics and the unconcerned' (*Kokkinakis v Greece* (1993) 17 EHRR 397).

## (9) FREEDOM OF EXPRESSION: ARTICLE 10

Article 10 protects the right to freedom of expression, and provides the opportunity to take part in the exchange of cultural, political and social information and ideas and to receive and impart information without unjustified interference by public authorities. The rights provided by Art 10 apply to everyone including natural and legal personalities. The Court has taken the view that this right forms one of the essential foundations of a democratic society and is one of the basic conditions for its progress and individual self-fulfilment. Accordingly, the Court has been prepared to give it an expansive definition (*Handyside v United Kingdom* (1976) 1 EHRR 737). The circumstances whereby States may limit this right, which are set out in Art 10(2), have been narrowly interpreted and the necessity for any restriction must be convincingly established (*Observer and Guardian v United Kingdom* (1992) 14 EHRR 153). Although Art 10 rights have particular relevance to press freedom and the media, they also apply to artistic expression, some forms of entertainment and commercial matters (*Sunday Times v United Kingdom* (1979–80) 2 EHRR 245; *Goodwin v United Kingdom* (1996) 22 EHRR 123; *Muller and Others v Switzerland* (1988) 13 EHRR 212; *Markt Intern Verlag GmbH and Beermann v Federal Republic of Germany* (1989) 12 EHRR 161). Artists who promote their work incur duties and responsibilities in accordance with Art 10(2) (*Muller and Others v Switzerland* (1988) 13 EHRR 212). The freedom of expression applies not only to ideas and information which are regarded as generally acceptable and inoffensive but also to those which may offend, shock or disturb (*Handyside v United Kingdom* (1976) 1 EHRR 737). Thus, although causing gratuitous offence may be legitimately restricted, the publication of extreme and offensive views will not necessarily be prohibited (*Otto-Preminger Institute v Austria* (1994) 19 EHRR 34; *Jersild v Denmark* (1994) 19 EHRR 1). In some circumstances, States may legitimately restrict the publication of confidential material (*Vereniging Weekblad Bluf! v The Netherlands* (1995) 20 EHRR 189; *Observer and Guardian v United Kingdom* (1992) 14 EHRR 153). Although this provision imposes a positive obligation on the State to protect an individual's right to freedom of expression, and prohibits the authorities from preventing a person from receiving information from those who are willing to give it, it does not impose an obligation on public authorities to provide information (*VGT Verein Gegen Tierfabriken v Switzerland* (2002) 34 EHRR 4; *Open Door Counselling Ltd and Dublin Well Woman Centre v Ireland* (1992) 15 EHRR 244; *Gaskin v United Kingdom* (1989) 12 EHRR 36). However, it does not give the right of access to information held on a police file (*Leander v Sweden* (1987) 9 EHRR 433).

Any legislation placing restrictions on Art 10 rights must be adequate, accessible and precise (*Sunday Times v United Kingdom* (1979–80) 2 EHRR 245). Although States have a margin of appreciation in assessing whether a restriction is necessary, this is not unlimited and goes hand in hand with the supervisory function of the Court (*Handyside v United Kingdom* (1976) 1 EHRR 737). Article 10 guarantees not only the freedom of the press and the media to inform the public but also the right of the public to be properly informed and to receive information and ideas (*Sunday Times v United Kingdom* (1979) 2 EHRR 245). Thus when the government seeks to restrict the freedom of the press and the media, the Court has generally adopted a very strict test of necessity (*Observer and Guardian v United Kingdom* (1992) 14 EHRR 153). The Court considers that journalists play a vital role as public watchdogs in imparting information of serious public concern and on occasion has held that defamation proceedings amount to a disproportionate interference with the freedom of expression (*Lingens v Austria* (1986) 8 EHRR 103; *Oberschlick v Austria (No 2)* (1998) 25 EHRR 357). However, the Court allows a wider margin of appreciation in matters affecting the imposition of limits on artistic expression and accepts that national authorities are generally better placed to assess the need for restrictions. Thus the seizure of a satirical film restricting freedom of expression may be justified to protect the religious sensitivities of others (*Otto-Preminger Institute v Austria* (1994) 19 EHRR 34).

Although the right of recruitment to the civil service was expressly excluded from the Convention, the Court is increasingly called upon to consider the legitimacy of imposing restrictions on the activities of civil servants (*Wille v Liechtenstein* (2000) 30 EHRR 558). Once in post, a civil servant has the right to complain if his or her rights under the Convention are breached (*Vogt v Germany* (1996) 21 EHRR 205). A restriction on the political activities of certain categories of senior personnel has been justified as a valid response to the legitimate aim of maintaining the political impartiality of local government officers (*Ahmed and Others v United Kingdom* (2000) 29 EHRR 1). Notwithstanding the wide margin of appreciation given to States in this area, restrictions found to be disproportionate will be contrary to the Convention (*Vogt v Germany* (1996) 21 EHRR 205). Article 10 allows States to regulate the manner in which broadcasting is authorised. While there is no longer a justification for restricting licences to a single broadcasting monopoly, it is not disproportionate to limit the granting of terrestrial broadcasting licences (*Autronic AG v Switzerland* (1990) 12 EHRR 485; *Tele 1 Privatfernsehgesellschaft mbH v Austria* (2002) 34 EHRR 5).

## (10) FREEDOM OF ASSEMBLY AND ASSOCIATION: ARTICLE 11

Article 11 provides the right to freedom of association and freedom of peaceful assembly. It imposes a positive obligation on the State to ensure that the right to peaceful demonstration and assembly can be exercised (*Plattform 'Ärzte für das Leben' v Austria* (1988) 13 EHRR 204). It gives the right to join trade unions, to attend public and private meetings and to take part in peaceful demonstrations. However, compulsory membership of a trade union or an association would strike at the very substance of the freedom it is designed to guarantee and would be contrary to the Convention (*Young, James and Webster v United Kingdom* (1981) 4 EHRR 38; *Sigurdur A Sigurjonsson v Iceland* (1993) 16 EHRR 462; *Chassagnou v France* (2000) 29 EHRR 615). The imposition of disciplinary sanctions for taking part in a public demonstration may interfere with the right to peaceful assembly (*Ezelin v France* (1991) 14 EHRR 362). This provision can be invoked by associations as well as named individuals (*Grande Oriente D'Italia Di Palazzo Giustiniani v Italy* (2002) 34 EHRR 22). Restrictions can be imposed by the authorities provided they are prescribed by law and are necessary in a democratic society in the interests of national security or public safety, for the prevention of disorder or crime, for the protection of health or morals or for the protection of the rights or freedoms of others. Any restriction imposed must be proportionate to the aim pursued (*Young, James and Webster v United Kingdom* (1981) 4 EHRR 38). The balancing of individual interests which may be in conflict is a difficult task and States have a broad margin of appreciation since national authorities are in a better position to determine whether or not there is a pressing social need (*Chassagnou v France* (2000) 29 EHRR 615). Restrictions may be imposed on the rights of members of the armed forces, the police or others employed in State administration (*Council of Civil Service Unions v United Kingdom* (1987) 50 D&R 228; *Ahmed and Others v United Kingdom* (2000) 29 EHRR 1; *Rekvenyi v Hungary* (2000) 30 EHRR 519).

## (11)   RIGHT TO MARRY: ARTICLE 12

Article 12 provides that men and women have the right to marry and found a family. This right refers to the traditional marriage between persons of the opposite biological sex which is 'a matter encompassed within the power of the state to regulate by national law' (*Rees v United Kingdom* (1986) 9 EHRR 56). Accordingly, States are given a wide margin of appreciation in these matters. The Court has been unwilling to find a violation where a State has refused to permit the marriage of transsexuals or persons of the same gender (*Sheffield and Horsham v United Kingdom* (1998) 27 EHRR 163). The Convention does not guarantee the right to divorce (*Johnston v Ireland* (1986) 9 EHRR 203). However, where national legislation permits divorce, the State cannot impose unreasonable restrictions on remarriage (*F v Switzerland* (1987) 10 EHRR 411).

## (12)   RIGHT TO AN EFFECTIVE REMEDY: ARTICLE 13

States are obliged under Art 13 to provide 'an effective remedy before a national authority' for an alleged breach of the Convention. The Court has accepted that Art 13 only requires a remedy to be 'as effective as can be' in circumstances where national security issues require the non-disclosure of sensitive material (*Leander v Sweden* (1987) 9 EHRR 433). However, the notion of an effective remedy under Art 13 requires independent scrutiny of the claim without regard to any perceived threat to national security if there is real risk of treatment in breach of Art 3 (*Chahal v United Kingdom* (1996) 23 EHRR 413). While the national authority may not necessarily be a judicial authority, if it is not, its powers and procedural guarantees will be relevant in determining whether the remedy before it is effective (*Klass and Others v Federal Republic of Germany* (1978) 2 EHRR 214). Thus an effective remedy may involve a hearing before an administrative or a judicial body provided the national authority has the power to deal with the substance of the relevant Convention complaint and grant appropriate relief. Judicial review proceedings have been found to provide an effective degree of control over the decisions of administrative decisions in extradition proceedings and asylum cases (*Soering v United Kingdom* (1989) 11 EHRR 439; *Vilvarajah v United Kingdom* (1991) 14 EHRR 248). However, the Court will look at the circumstances of each case and on occasion judicial review may not provide the necessary guarantees to meet the requirements of Art 13 (*Smith and Grady v United Kingdom* (2000) 29 EHRR 493). States have a margin of appreciation in conforming to their obligation under this provision, but bear the burden of proving the existence of an effective national remedy.

## (13)   FREEDOM FROM DISCRIMINATION: ARTICLE 14

While Art 14 does not provide for a general prohibition on discrimination, it complements the other substantive provisions of the Convention and States have an obligation to ensure that all individuals enjoy Convention rights without discrimination (*Belgian Linguistic Case (No 2)* (1968) 1 EHRR 252; *Rasmussen v Denmark* (1985) 7 EHRR 371). This provision only offers safeguards against discrimination to persons who are in similar situations (*Johnston v Ireland* (1986) 9 EHRR 203). The State is required to justify any differential treatment with respect to the exercise of a substantive right on reasonable and objective grounds (*Inze v Austria* (1987) 10 EHRR 394).

## (14)   RIGHT TO PEACEFUL ENJOYMENT OF PROPERTY: ARTICLE 1 OF FIRST PROTOCOL

Article 1 of the First Protocol guarantees the right to peaceful enjoyment of property, although, as is the case with other rights, there is a margin of appreciation on the State in its application of the provision. The concept of 'property' has an autonomous meaning in Convention law, and is not therefore subject to national formal classification. The Article provides that the right to peaceful enjoyment can only be curtailed by legal measures, and that this must be in the public interest, and that any interference must strike a fair balance between this legitimate public interest and the rights of the individual. The most extreme example of the State's interference with this right relates to expropriation, which is not in itself prohibited. As with other interferences, expropriation must be the proportionate response to a legitimate public policy concern. In such cases the Convention requires that appropriate compensation be paid, and that this be paid in a timely fashion (see eg *Former King of Greece v Greece* (2001) 33 EHRR 21). At a less extreme level the Court has held on a number of occasions that there are obligations on the State to protect property rights from interference by others. Thus, for example, the Court has held that a State will be in breach where it does not provide, contrary to its own legislation, appropriate mechanisms by which a landlord may repossess its property when a court order allowing the repossession has been made (*GL v Italy* (2002) 34 EHRR 41).

## 1.8   THE HUMAN RIGHTS ACT 1998

The Human Rights Act 1998 (HRA 1998) received Royal Assent on 9 November 1998 and came into effect on 2 October 2000. The HRA 1998 is the result of almost 30 years of lobbying by politicians, judges, academics, lawyers and various human rights organisations to incorporate the Convention into domestic law. The first substantial breakthrough was made in March 1993, when incorporation was adopted as Labour Party policy and quickly became an important issue distinguishing the Party from the existing Conservative government. Following the meetings of the Joint Consultative Committee on Constitutional Reform between Liberal Democrat and Labour representatives in Summer 1996, the Labour Party released its consultation paper, *Bringing Rights Home* in December 1996. In this paper, it outlined its proposals to 'bring rights home to British people' to 'cut costs, save time and give power back to British courts'.

Following Labour's victory in the 1997 General Election, the Human Rights Bill was announced in the Queen's Speech as part of the new Government's first wave of legislation devoted to constitutional reform. In the White Paper, *Rights Brought Home*, released in October 1997, the Government stated that it is no longer sufficient to rely on the common law for the protection of rights and freedoms and that to enforce Convention rights 'takes too long and costs too much'. The aim of the Human Rights Bill, introduced in the House of Lords, was to enable UK people to argue for their rights in UK courts without 'inordinate delay and cost', and to bring the rights more fully into the jurisprudence of UK courts. It is hoped that the HRA 1998 will 'make more directly accessible the rights which the British people already enjoy under the Convention ... to bring those rights home'.

The HRA 1998 gives 'further effect' to the 'Convention rights'. These are defined as the rights and freedoms set out in Arts 2 to 12 and Art 14 of the Convention, Arts 1 to 3 of the First Protocol, and Arts 1 and 2 of the Sixth Protocol (Abolition of the Death Penalty). All of these rights and freedoms must be read in conjunction with Arts 16 to 18 of the Convention.

The Convention rights must also be read subject to existing UK derogations and reservations to the Convention and Protocols. Currently, the UK maintains a derogation from Art 5(3) of the Convention (right to be brought promptly before a judge following arrest or detention) to permit the continued use of certain powers in the Prevention of Terrorism Acts. The UK has also made a reservation to the second sentence of Art 2 of the First Protocol (right of parents to ensure education and teaching in conformity with their own religious and philosophical convictions). This part of Art 2 is accepted 'only so far as it is compatible with the provision of efficient instruction and training, and the avoidance of unreasonable public expenditure'.

Article 13 of the Convention (the right to an effective remedy) is not included as one of the Articles to be given further effect by the HRA 1998. This was the subject of much debate in Parliament, but the Government maintained that its inclusion was unnecessary as s 8 of the HRA 1998 (remedies) already provides for effective remedies before UK courts. However, it was conceded by the Lord Chancellor in the debates that courts may have regard to Art 13 when considering the provisions of s 8. Therefore, it can be argued that a remedy for breach of the HRA 1998 must not only be 'just and appropriate' but should also be effective.

## (1)  OBLIGATIONS IMPOSED BY THE ACT

Pursuant to s 6 of the HRA 1998, it is unlawful for a public authority to act in a way which is incompatible with a Convention right. Although 'public authority' is not defined in the HRA 1998, it is made clear in s 6(3) that the term includes courts and tribunals and any person 'certain of whose functions are functions of a public nature'. According to the White Paper, this includes, but is not limited to, central government (including government ministers), local government, the police, immigration officers, prisons and companies responsible for areas of activity 'previously within the public sector'. Placing courts and tribunals under a duty to act compatibly with Convention rights effectively means that these rights must be considered and applied wherever relevant.

Section 7 of the HRA 1998 provides that victims of the unlawful acts of public authorities, as defined in s 6, may bring proceedings against the authority or rely on Convention rights in any legal proceedings. Thus victims can rely on Convention points in any legal proceedings involving a public authority, which includes referring to Convention points as part of a defence to criminal or civil proceedings, or when acting as a plaintiff in civil proceedings, or in seeking judicial review, or on appeal.

It is also possible to bring proceedings against a public authority on Convention grounds alone. As such, proceedings will be by way of an application for judicial review, and the applicant must satisfy the test for standing to seek judicial review by demonstrating a 'sufficient interest' in the subject matter of the action. However, the sufficient interest test has been slightly altered by the HRA 1998. Section 7(3) provides that an applicant will be taken to have a sufficient interest in relation to the unlawful act, 'only if he is, or would be, a victim of that act'. This change to the sufficient interest test prevents public interest groups from bringing Convention test cases, as generally they will be unable to show that they are a victim of the unlawful act.

Section 7(5) provides that proceedings must be brought before the end of one year, beginning with the date on which the act complained of took place, or such longer period as the court considers equitable. This is subject to any rule imposing a stricter time-limit. Therefore, if proceedings are to be by way of judicial review, an application must still be made within 3 months from the date on which the act complained of took place.

## (2)  REMEDIES

In relation to the acts of a public authority found to be incompatible with a Convention right, courts and tribunals are empowered by s 8 of the HRA 1998 to grant 'such relief or remedy, or make such order, within its powers as it considers just and appropriate'. Possible remedies include injunctions, declarations, orders of mandamus and damages but it is with the latter that s 8 is primarily concerned. Displaying caution in making such a remedy available for the acts of public authorities, the government has attempted to impose a number of limits on its use.

Only a court which has power to award damages or to order the payment of compensation in civil proceedings may award damages, and criminal courts therefore cannot award damages. No award of damages is to be made unless, taking account of all the circumstances of the case, it is necessary to afford just satisfaction. In determining whether to award damages, or the amount of an award, the court must take into account the principles applied by the Court in relation to the award of compensation under Art 41 of the Convention.

Whenever a court or tribunal is determining a question concerning a Convention right, it must, according to s 2 of the HRA 1998, 'take into account' relevant judgments, decisions, declarations or advisory opinions of the Court; opinions and decisions of the Commission; and decisions of the Committee of Ministers. This wealth of Convention case-law is proving invaluable to UK judges grappling with the interpretation of particular Convention rights but they are required to take it into account, and not to follow it. Binding UK judges too strictly to Strasbourg-made law would have defeated one of the primary objectives of the Act as set out in the White Paper: to allow UK judges 'to make a distinctively British contribution to the development of the jurisprudence of human rights in Europe'.

## (3)  FREEDOM OF EXPRESSION AND FREEDOM OF RELIGION

As a result of concerns raised by various media interest and religious organisations during the passage of the Bill through Parliament, some Convention rights have received special treatment in the HRA 1998.

Section 12 deals with concerns about the right to privacy (Art 8) and applies if a court is considering whether to grant any relief which, if granted, might affect the exercise of the Convention right to freedom of expression (Art 10). Safeguards include a provision that no relief is to be granted so as to restrain publication before trial 'unless the court is satisfied that the applicant is likely to establish that publication should not be allowed'. Courts are also reminded 'to have particular regard to the importance of the Convention right to freedom of expression'.

In the Parliamentary debates on the Bill, it was argued by various Peers and MPs that if religious organisations are classified as public authorities, Art 14 (prohibition of discrimination in the enjoyment of rights and freedoms) may deny their right to freedom of thought, conscience and religion (Art 9). Examples raised of areas which may be affected included taking into account religious opinions and practices in appointing teachers to religious schools and refusals to carry out certain marriages on religious grounds.

Section 13 of the HRA 1998 was inserted to address these fears. It provides that if a court's determination of any question arising under the HRA 1998 might affect the exercise by a religious organisation of the Convention right to freedom of thought, conscience and religion, 'it must have particular regard to the importance of that right'.

## (4)   CONVENTION RIGHTS AND ACTS OF PARLIAMENT

The relationship between Convention rights and Acts of Parliament was one of the most contentious issues in the debate leading up to the release of the White Paper and the Bill. There were two main options: the European Communities Act (or Canadian) model and what became known as the New Zealand model. The primary difference between the models is the power of judges to strike down Acts of Parliament inconsistent with Convention rights. According to the EC model, as is the case with Community law, judges should be able to strike down Acts of Parliament incompatible with Convention rights. Under the New Zealand model, judges would not have this power.

Due to the importance which the government attaches to parliamentary sovereignty, the model adopted in the HRA 1998 can be described as basically a New Zealand model with added extras. Section 3 of the Act imposes an obligation on courts and tribunals 'so far as it is possible to do so' to read and give effect to primary and subordinate legislation, whenever enacted, in a way which is compatible with the Convention rights. It was hoped that this would give judges the flexibility to avoid clashes between Acts of Parliament and Convention rights as, according to the White Paper, s 3 'goes far beyond the present rule which enables the courts to take the Convention into account in resolving any ambiguity'.

However, in some cases it has been impossible to interpret primary legislation in this way. Where there is a clear incompatibility between primary legislation, whenever enacted, and a Convention right, pursuant to s 4 of the HRA 1998, the court may make a 'declaration of incompatibility'. A declaration may also be made where there is a clear incompatibility between subordinate legislation and a Convention right, and the primary legislation concerned prevents removal of the incompatibility.

Only the higher courts such as the House of Lords, Court of Appeal and High Court can make such declarations and a declaration does not affect the validity, continuing operation, or enforcement of the provision in respect of which it is given. In keeping with the overriding respect for parliamentary sovereignty, it is only Parliament which can amend the offending primary legislation although the Act does make provision for a 'fast-track' amendment procedure.

Section 10 grants a Minister the power to make, by order, such amendments to primary legislation 'as he considers necessary to remove the incompatibility'. An order may not be made unless a draft of the order has been approved by a resolution of each House of Parliament made after the expiration of 60 days from when the order was laid. However, in cases of urgency it is possible to make the order without a draft being so approved but the special procedure set out in Sch 2 to the HRA 1998 must be followed, and the order will cease to have effect if not approved by each House within 120 days from the date when it was made.

The HRA 1998 also attaches importance to improving compliance with Convention rights. Section 19 of the HRA 1998 provides that a Minister in charge of a Bill must, before Second Reading, make a statement in writing that, in his view, the provisions of the Bill are compatible with the Convention rights. If this is not possible, a statement must be made to the effect that the Minister is unable to make a statement of compatibility but nevertheless wishes the House to proceed with the Bill.

## 1.9 THE EUROPEAN CONVENTION ON HUMAN RIGHTS AND THE EUROPEAN UNION

The legal landscape in Western Europe is now a particularly complicated one, and the 15 Member States of the European Union (EU) (Belgium, The Netherlands, Luxembourg, France, Germany, Italy, the UK, Ireland, Denmark, Greece, Spain, Portugal, Austria, Finland and Sweden) must ensure the correct application and compliance with their domestic law, EC law, and the law of the Convention. National courts, in which certain aspects of EC law are justiciable, face particular problems if they encounter a seeming incompatibility between the demands of the Community, on the one hand, and of the Convention, on the other. The relationship between the EU and the Convention architecture is a complex one, and leading cases are summarised in Part 6 of this book. Strictly, there is no legal link between the two systems, which exist independently of each other, and have different membership. However, all Member States of the EU are members of the Council of Europe, and it is considered to be essential that any States wishing to accede to the EU are similarly committed to the Convention and the norms set out therein. Article 49 of the Treaty of European Union provides that it is a requirement that States applying to join comply with the obligations of Art 6(1) EU. These include respect for human rights.

The Strasbourg authorities will not generally recognise a right to challenge Community law on the basis of the latter's compatibility with the Convention. However, as has been recently demonstrated, certain rights guaranteed under the Convention may be invoked even in the context of measures which are closely, or inextricably related to the Community (see eg *Matthews v United Kingdom* (1999) 28 EHRR 361). Many of the provisions of 'Community' law have in fact been enacted into national laws. This is the case, for example, with EC Directives which are 'binding as to the result to be achieved, upon each Member State' (Art 249 EC). National legislation, irrespective of whether it is introduced in order to comply with a Community requirement, is reviewable under the Convention. So too are national measures taken in the context of EC obligations which nevertheless have an impact on an applicant within the domestic legal order. In *M & Co v Federal Republic of Germany* (1990) 64 D&R 138, the Commission considered a case in which a fine imposed under Art 81 EC was being recovered under procedures provided for in German law. The Commission reaffirmed that it was not competent to examine proceedings before, or decisions of, the EC organs. On the other hand, it held that:

> '... this does not mean, however, that by granting executory power to a judgment of the [ECJ] the competent German authorities acted quasi as Community organs and are to that extent beyond the scope of control exercised by the Convention organs.'

The EU itself lacks, according to the European Court of Justice (ECJ), the competence to accede to the Convention in its own right (see *Opinion 2/94* [1996] ECR I-1759). On several occasions, however, the EU Member States have affirmed, within the structure of the Union, their commitment to the principles enshrined in the Convention, and the ECJ has, to a considerable extent, but arguably not completely, assimilated Convention principles and practice into the jurisprudence of the EU.

Broadly, the position is that the application of EC law, whether by the EC Commission, the Council of Ministers or the ECJ and Court of First Instance (CFI), or whether in the Member States in response to EU obligations, should proceed in a manner which is compatible with that of the Convention. Prior to the incorporation of the Convention into UK law, this meant, for example, that, in a situation based in EU law, affected parties could rely more directly on Convention law, albeit as applied by the ECJ, than they could in an analogous national case. If this were the full picture, the position would be relatively straightforward and would need no further clarification. Unfortunately, this is not the case, and the application of Convention law in the context of EC law does not proceed as straightforwardly as does its application in the context of national law. In particular, there is the possibility, albeit an unlikely one, that a court in the UK might find itself facing differing obligations under the law of the EC and the law of the Convention. For example, it has been confirmed by the Court that citizens of Gibraltar have been deprived of a fundamental right to vote in elections to the European Parliament. However, the rules governing those elections and the rights to vote in them are a matter of EC law, and no such right has been given. Such conflicts are, it is to be hoped, likely to be rare, and their resolution can be achieved only at the political level. More important, however, is the way in which Convention law is to be applied to situations falling under the umbrella of EC law. The approach has been developed tentatively by the ECJ, and continues to be somewhat controversial.

The founding treaties of the EU, most important of which is the Treaty of Rome (or EC Treaty), are silent on the issue of 'rights' or general principles of law. In 2000 the Member States enacted the Charter of Fundamental Rights of the European Union at Nice. The Treaty of Nice leaves the precise legal status of the Charter open for consideration at a future Inter-Governmental Conference. The Charter makes many references to the rights set out in the Convention, and reproduces some of these rights in its articles, although not necessarily with identical wording.

In an early decision taken in the context of the European Coal and Steel Community (ECSC), the ECJ dismissed the arguments of the applicant that were based on breaches of fundamental rights (Case 1/58 *Stork v High Authority* [1959] ECR 17). The role of the ECJ, under Art 220, is to 'ensure that in the application of this Treaty the law is observed'. The ECJ has, in subsequent cases, given this provision a wide interpretation so that it extends not to 'the law' of the Treaty in particular, but 'the law' in general. This has been held to constitute both the legal traditions common to the Member States, in particular their constitutions, as well as Treaties in which the Member States have participated. It is significant to the development of these principles and the approach taken by the ECJ that early cases arose in such a way that the Court was faced with challenges to its authority and to the supremacy of Community law, in particular by the German Constitutional Court. The concern expressed in the Member States was that national protections went further than those accorded to applicants under Community law, and that constitutional provisions guaranteeing the observance of fundamental rights could not be pushed aside by competing Community obligations. The response of the ECJ has been to recognise such rights, and to assert that it is engaged in a partnership with national courts under which it too will protect those rights. At the same time it has asserted its sole jurisdiction, given to it under Art 230 EC, to rule on the validity of Community law and the actions of the institutions. Thus, where there is an alleged conflict between a fundamental right, whatever the derivation of that right is, and Community law, the Court has held that it alone is in a position to resolve the matter, as it is best placed to balance the demands of the two competing provisions. The ECJ has thus skilfully dealt with issues of supremacy, while assuring the Member States' courts that the protections valued by the latter would be recognised at the centre.

The result of this approach, however, is that there have arisen situations in which the ECJ's approach to matters raised by parties on the basis of the Convention appears to sit uneasily with the resolution of similar questions by the Convention authorities themselves. It is for this reason that a selection of relevant cases are dealt with in Part 6.

# Chapter 2

# GENERAL PRINCIPLES OF THE CONVENTION AND GUARANTEES

## 2.1 MARGIN OF APPRECIATION

### (1) DOMESTIC AUTHORITIES IN BEST POSITION TO JUDGE

**Rees v United Kingdom**

**(1986) 9 EHRR 56**

*Facts:* The applicant had undergone a sex change operation and wanted to amend his birth certificate. He campaigned unsuccessfully to persuade MPs to introduce legislation to allow gender reassignment to be acknowledged by the issue of a new certificate. He claimed the production of his birth certificate caused humiliation and embarrassment.

*Commission:* The Commission unanimously expressed the opinion that Art 8 had been violated. The Commission agreed with the applicant that the change in his sexual identity should be given full recognition by the Contracting State. It was not within the State's margin of appreciation to decide whether the change should be fully recognised, although there was room for discretion as to how it was recognised and against which countervailing public interests it was balanced.

*Court:* The Court disagreed with the Commission. The Court found that States have a wide margin of appreciation in this area. Whilst recognising that several States had given transsexuals the option of changing their personal status to fit their newly gained identity, this option has been subject to conditions of varying strictness. In other States, the option does not exist. It was therefore not inherent within Art 8 that transsexuals should be given full legal recognition.

## Tyrer v United Kingdom

**(1978) 2 EHRR 1**

*Facts:* The applicant, when aged 15, had been found guilty in a juvenile court of unlawful assault. In 1972, the court sentenced him to three strokes of the birch. Before receiving the punishment, the applicant was made to wait for a considerable time in the police station for the doctor to arrive. He was then made to take down his trousers and underpants and bend over a table. Two policemen held him down whilst a third administered the punishment. The applicant claimed a violation of Art 3 of the Convention. The government, seeking to rely on Art 63(3) of the Convention, argued that public opinion within the Isle of Man, where the punishment took place, supported the practice of birching, therefore making it a 'local requirement'.

*Commission:*   The Commission expressed the opinion that judicial corporal punishment was degrading and therefore constituted a breach of Art 3.

*Court:*   The Court agreed with the Commission's finding of a violation of Art 3 due to it being degrading. The fact that the majority of the island's population did not believe it to be degrading was not conclusive. The Court went on to consider the government's arguments in relation to Art 63(3). The fact that there existed a consensus within the population of the Isle of Man as to the appropriateness and effect of judicial punishment was not enough to bring it within the scope of Art 63(3). For this, there would have to be positive and conclusive proof of a requirement and the Court could not consider beliefs and local opinion on their own as constituting such proof.

## Ireland v United Kingdom
## (1978) 2 EHRR 25

*Facts:*   The applicant complained that the emergency provisions employed by the UK to deal with the problem of terrorism in Northern Ireland infringed, inter alia, Art 5, and was not saved by a derogation under Art 15.

*Court:*   The Court found that, in situations where States have to determine whether the life of the nation was threatened by a public emergency and how far the State should go in attempting to overcome it, the State should be given a wide margin of appreciation, although this was not unlimited. The Court reserved the right to rule upon whether the State had gone beyond that which was necessary. However, this merely meant that it had to take into account the conditions and circumstances prevailing when the measures were taken. It was not for the Court to substitute the British government's assessment, in this case, of the situation or its policy to combat the situation.

## Handyside v United Kingdom
## (1976) 1 EHRR 737

*Facts:*   The applicant was the owner of a publishing firm which published a book entitled *The Little Red Schoolbook*. He was charged and convicted under the Obscene Publications Acts 1959 and 1964. The book had also been published elsewhere in Europe and circulated in the UK. The applicant claimed, inter alia, violation of Art 10 of the Convention, freedom of expression.

*Commission:*   The majority of the Commission was of the opinion that the State's interference with the applicant's freedom of expression was 'necessary in a democratic society', 'for the protection of morals' and therefore was not a violation of Art 10. The majority of the Commission was also of the opinion that the Court's task was only to ensure that the English courts acted reasonably, in good faith and within the limits of the margin of appreciation left to the Contracting States by Art 10(2). However, the minority saw the Court's task as being to examine the *Schoolbook* directly in the light of the Convention and of nothing but the Convention.

*Court:*   The protection offered by the Convention is subsidiary to national systems safeguarding human rights. It leaves to each Contracting State the task of securing the rights and freedoms it enshrines. In particular, there is no uniform European conception of morals, therefore, '[by] reason of [the Contracting States'] direct and continuous contact with the vital forces of their countries, State authorities are in principle in a better position than the international judges to give an opinion'. The Court held that the domestic margin of appreciation goes hand in hand with European supervision. In this case, the Court held on the same grounds as the Commission that there was no violation of Art 10.

## Stubbings and Others v United Kingdom
## (1996) 23 EHRR 213

*Facts:*   The applicants were victims of child abuse and suffered severe psychological disturbances as a result in their childhood. The applicants were held to be time-barred by virtue of the Limitation Act 1980 from bringing any action against the alleged perpetrators of the abuse. They complained to the Commission that they were denied access to a court in respect of their claims for compensation for psychological injury caused by childhood sexual abuse in violation of Art 6(1). They alleged discrimination based on the fact that victims of unintentional injury were treated more favourably by the legislation.

*Commission:*   The Commission acknowledged that the right of access to a court is not absolute and may be regulated by States which have a certain margin of appreciation, provided that the limitation does not restrict or reduce the access left to the individual in such a way or to such an extent that the very essence of the right is impaired. It also held that a limitation will not be compatible with the Convention if it does not pursue a legitimate aim and if there is not a reasonable relationship of proportionality between the means employed and the aim sought to be achieved. The Commission found that the application of the 6-year time-limit to the applicants' claims was not objectively or reasonably justified and it disclosed discriminatory treatment in the regulation of their access to a court for the determination of their civil rights. Accordingly, there had been a violation of Art 6.

*Court:*   The Court reiterated that the right of access to a court is not absolute. It may be subject to limitations and these are permitted by implication since the right of access, by its very nature, calls for regulation by the State. Although the Contracting States enjoy a certain margin of appreciation, the final decision as to the observance of the Convention's requirements rests with the Court. The Court applied the same criteria as the Commission, ie the essence of the right must not be impaired and the relationship between the means employed and the aim sought must be proportionate. The Court found that the UK had complied with these requirements and that it was not for the Court to substitute its own view for that of the State authorities as to what would be the most appropriate policy in this regard. Consequently, there was no violation of Art 6(1).

## LACK/PRESENCE OF CONSENSUS

## X, Y and Z v United Kingdom
## (1997) 24 EHRR 143

*Facts:* The applicant, X, was a female-to-male transsexual and had lived with the second applicant, Y, a woman, since 1979. The third applicant was Z, a child born to Y through artificial insemination by donor (AID) in 1992. In February 1992, X inquired about being registered as the father of Z. He was told by the Registrar-General that only a biological man could be regarded as the father for the purposes of registration. The applicants claimed that the failure in English law to give legal recognition to the de facto father–child relationship constituted a violation of Art 8.

*Commission:* In considering whether respect for the applicants' family life imposed a positive obligation on the UK to change its legal system as it applied to transsexuals, the Commission was of the opinion that regard must be had to the fact that there is a clear trend in Contracting States towards legal acknowledgement of gender reassignment.

*Court:* The Court held that a wide margin of appreciation should be given to the Government as there was little common ground amongst the Contracting States regarding the standard of parental rights given to transsexuals. Further, this lack of consensus extended to the legal system which surrounds the social relationship between a child conceived by AID and the person who performs the role of the father. Where lack of consensus existed, the Court should not adopt or impose any single viewpoint.

## Cossey v United Kingdom
## (1990) 13 EHRR 622

*Facts:* Miss Cossey was a male-to-female transsexual. In 1983, Miss Cossey wished to marry Mr L. The Registrar-General informed the applicant that such a marriage would be void as a matter of English law because she was still classified as a male. He also informed her that she could not be granted a birth certificate showing her to be female as such a certificate records details at the date of birth. The applicant went through a so-called marriage ceremony with another man, Mr X. The applicant claimed that the respondent State's refusal to permit changes to birth certificates resulted in a violation of the Convention.

*Commission:* The Commission noted that although there existed in the UK 'no uniform, general decision as to the civil status of post-operative transsexuals', other Contracting States had begun to implement policies which allowed for the alteration of birth certificates.

*Court:* The Court was not persuaded by the above argument as this would have been tantamount to saying that the UK should adopt a system which was in principle the same as other Contracting States for determining and recording civil status. It drew attention to the fact that the reports surrounding the Resolution adopted by the European Parliament on 12 September 1989, and Recommendation 1117 (1989), which sought to harmonise laws and practices in this area, still showed degrees of diversity. Accordingly, having regard to the existence of little common ground between the Contracting States in this matter, there was still an area in which they enjoy a wide margin of appreciation.

## B v France

## (1992) 16 EHRR 1

*Facts:*   The applicant was a male-to-female transsexual who claimed that medical intervention had merely revealed her true sexual identity rather than changed it. She claimed, inter alia, that her rights guaranteed under Art 8 had been violated by the French authorities' refusal to recognise her true sexual identity, and in particular the refusal to allow her a change of civil status on the official register. This resulted in the disclosure of intimate personal information to third parties and caused difficulties in her professional life.

*Commission:*   The Commission held that there had been a violation of Art 8. The Commission distinguished the present case from previous English transsexual cases, where no violation had been found, by the differences between the French and English systems. The fact that there existed no consensus between Contracting States meant that the same criteria could not be applied in the present case as was applied in *Rees v United Kingdom* (1986) 9 EHRR 56 and *Cossey v United Kingdom* (above). The Commission would need to consider the merits of the case, particularly as regards the exercise of France's margin of appreciation.

*Court:*   The Court acknowledged that there were noticeable differences between France and England as regards their law and practice on, inter alia, a change of civil status. It distinguished the present case from previous English cases and was of the opinion that France had not struck a fair balance between the general interest and the interest of the individual and that, accordingly, there had been a violation of Art 8.

## (2)   MARGIN OF APPRECIATION AS DEFINING THE SCOPE OF RIGHTS

## Marckx v Belgium

## (1979) 2 EHRR 330

*Facts:*   The applicants were a mother and infant daughter who claimed that the illegitimacy laws in Belgium infringed, inter alia, Arts 8 and 14. The aspects of the Belgian Civil Code at issue were the requirement that maternal affiliation could be established only by a formal act of recognition (Arts 334 and 341a), the existence of limitations on the mother's capacity to give or bequeath property, and the child's capacity to take or inherit property.

*Commission:*   The Commission found a violation of Art 8 with respect to the illegitimate child and to the mother.

*Court:*   The Court found that, notwithstanding the margin of appreciation allowed to national authorities, domestic law must render possible, from the moment of birth, the child's integration within the family. In this case, national law which drew a distinction between legitimate and illegitimate children was discriminatory and in violation of Art 14 of the Convention.

## Abdulaziz, Cabales and Balkandali v United Kingdom
## (1985) 7 EHRR 471

*Facts:*   The applicants were immigrants, lawfully and permanently settled in the UK. Their husbands were refused permission to remain, in accordance with the immigration rules then in place. Stricter controls applied to men wishing to join their partners than to women, or nationals of Member States of the EU. The applicants claimed, inter alia, breaches of Arts 8 and 14.

*Commission:*   The Commission unanimously held that there had been a violation of Art 14 and Art 8, on the ground of sexual discrimination. No violation was found as regards racial discrimination.

*Court:*   The Court agreed unanimously with the Commission to the extent that there had been a violation of Arts 14 and 8 on the grounds of sex but no other violations were found. In discussing the scope of possible positive obligations arising under Art 8 in relation to 'respect' for family life, the Court found that, due to the diversity of practices amongst the Contracting States, the requirements will vary from case to case. Therefore, this was an area in which Contracting States enjoyed a wide margin of appreciation in determining the steps to be taken to ensure compliance with the Convention. Further, the Court held that although Contracting States enjoy a certain margin of appreciation in assessing whether and to what extent differences in otherwise similar situations justify a difference in treatment in law, it is for the Court to give the final ruling.

## Airey v Ireland
## (1979) 2 EHRR 305

*Facts:*   The applicant had attempted to obtain a judicial separation from her husband due to his alleged physical and mental cruelty to her and their children. She was unable to find a solicitor willing to act for her due to her inability to meet the financial costs for which legal aid was not available. The applicant claimed, inter alia, a breach of Art 6, due to the fact that her right of access to a court was effectively denied, and a breach of Art 8 due to the State's failure to provide an accessible legal procedure for the determination of rights and obligations created by Irish family law.

*Commission:*   The Commission held unanimously that the failure of the State to ensure the applicant's effective access to court to enable her to obtain a judicial separation amounted to a breach of Art 6(1). In this particular case, where facts were difficult to prove and the subject matter emotive, right of access to a court was not satisfied by the applicant being able to represent herself.

*Court:*   The Court accepted the government's argument that the Commission's opinion would result in an obligation on the State to provide free legal aid in all cases concerning the determination of a 'civil right'. It is for the State to determine effective right of access to the courts. Legal aid is only one scheme; another could be to simplify the procedure. It is not for the Court to dictate the measures.

## Smith and Grady v United Kingdom
## (2000) 29 EHRR 493

*Facts:* The applicants complained that intrusive investigations into their private life, which resulted in their administrative discharge from the Royal Navy on the ground of homosexuality, was in violation of the right to private life which is guaranteed by Art 8. Furthermore, their treatment was degrading and in violation of Art 3. The Ministry of Defence submitted that the policy of excluding homosexuals from the armed forces was designed to ensure operational effectiveness. It was accepted by both parties that the interference with the applicants' private life was in accordance with domestic law and Community law. The Court accepted that the investigations undertaken to establish whether the person concerned was a homosexual to whom the policy applied did pursue the legitimate aim of 'the interests of national security'. Therefore, the issue for the Court to decide was whether the level of interference was 'necessary in a democratic society'.

*Court:* Noting that the hallmarks of a democratic society were pluralism, tolerance and broadmindedness, the Court acknowledged that in assessing whether any interference was necessary, Contracting States have a margin of appreciation which varies according to the nature of the activities restricted and the aims pursued. Although national authorities can make an initial assessment, the final evaluation as to whether the interference is necessary rests with the Court. In this case, the Court required the government to provide 'particularly convincing and weighty reasons' (para 94) to justify an investigation which interfered with intimate aspects of the applicants' private life. Construing the margin of appreciation narrowly, the Court noted that only a minority of European States continued to operate a blanket ban on homosexuals in the armed forces, and could not accept that the interference with the applicants' private life was necessary. Accordingly, there was a violation of Art 8. However, although the Court accepted that the government's policy and the investigation were humiliating and distressing for the applicants, it did not consider that the applicants' treatment reached the level of severity which would amount to a violation of Art 3.

## *UNITED KINGDOM CASES*

## R v DPP, ex parte Kebilene
## House of Lords, [1999] 4 All ER 801

*Facts:* The respondents were charged under s 16A of the Prevention of Terrorism (Temporary Provisions) Act 1989 which, they argued, reversed the legal burden of proof and was therefore in conflict with the presumption of innocence and in breach of Art 6(2) of the Convention.

*Held:* It was arguable that this provision did not reverse the legal burden, but merely placed an evidential burden on the defendant. Statutory provisions which partially reverse the burden of proof are not necessarily inconsistent with the Convention. In each case the question will be whether the court considers a presumption to be within reasonable limits. With respect to the discretionary area of judgement given to a national court, Lord Hope of Craighead remarked that:

> 'The European Court has acknowledged that, by reason of their direct and continuous contact with the vital forces of their countries, the national authorities are in principle better placed to evaluate local needs and conditions than an international court: *Buckley v UK* (1996) 23 EHRR 101 at 129 (paras 74–75). Although this means that, as the European Court explained in *Handyside v UK* (1976) 1 EHRR 737 at 753 (para 48), "the machinery of protection established by the Convention is subsidiary to the national systems safeguarding human rights", it goes hand in hand with European supervision. The extent of this supervision will vary according to such factors as the nature of the Convention right in issue, the importance of the right for the individual and the nature of the activities involved in the case.

> The doctrine is an integral part of the supervisory jurisdiction which is exercised over state conduct by the international court. By conceding a margin of appreciation to each national system, the Court has recognised that the Convention, as a living system, does not need to be applied uniformly by all states but may vary in its application according to local needs and conditions. This technique is not available to the national courts when they are considering Convention issues within their own countries. But in the hands of the national courts also the Convention should be seen as an expression of fundamental principles rather than a set of mere rules. The questions which the courts will have to decide in the application of these principles will involve questions of balance between competing interests and issues of proportionality' (at p 844).

## R v Stratford Justices, ex parte Imbert
## Divisional Court, [1999] 2 Cr App R 276

*Facts:*   The applicant applied for judicial review of a decision of the Stratford Justices who refused an order that proceedings be stayed as being an abuse of process. He claimed that there was a conflict between Art 6, which, he submitted, required the prosecution to disclose all the relevant material in its possession to the defence in advance of trial, and the absence of any requirement of advance disclosure in summary trials in the Magistrates' Courts (Advance Information) Rules 1985, SI 1985/601.

*Held:*   Lord Buxton considered that the jurisprudence of the Strasbourg Court did not lay down 'any rules with regard to, and certainly has not made mandatory, pre-trial disclosure of the order contended for in the present application' (at p 286). He observed that the Court interprets Convention rights as subject to the doctrine of the margin of appreciation, thereby recognising that:

> 'the detailed content of at least some Convention obligations is more appropriately determined in the light of national conditions. In the hands of the Strasbourg Court, however, that approach is necessarily translated into a view of the meaning and reach of the detailed provisions of the Convention that is flexible or, according to the observer's point of view, relativist. . . . The English judge cannot therefore himself apply or have recourse to the doctrine of the margin of appreciation as implemented by the Strasbourg Court. He must, however, recognise the impact of that doctrine upon the Strasbourg Court's analysis of the meaning and implications of the broad terms of the Convention provisions: which is

the obvious source of guidance as to those provisions, and a source that in any event the English court will be obliged, once section 2(1)(a) of the 1998 Act has come into force, to take into account' (at pp 286–287).

Although the Court has not expressly referred to this doctrine in respect to rights conferred by Art 6, it has used 'very similar expressions of policy' (at p 287) when called on to consider rules of criminal procedure and evidence. In dismissing the application, Lord Buxton observed that the Court 'strongly warns that criminal proceedings must be assessed as a whole, and stands against the contention advanced in our case that failure to give disclosure at a particular stage of those proceedings must necessarily render them unfair' (at p 289).

## Brown v Stott

## High Court of Justiciary, 2000 SLT 379
## Privy Council, [2001] 2 WLR 817

*Facts:* In response to police questioning, the respondent had admitted driving and was subsequently prosecuted for driving after consuming excess alcohol. It was submitted for the respondent that leading evidence at trial of her admission made under s 172 of the Road Traffic Act 1988 violated her right to a fair trial.

*High Court of Justiciary:* In finding for the respondent, the court was strongly influenced by the decision of the European Court in *Saunders v United Kingdom* (1996) 23 EHRR 313. The Lord Justice General noted that, to be effective, the right to silence and the privilege against self-incrimination at trial implied the recognition of similar rights at the stage when the suspect was being questioned during the criminal investigation. To assess whether a person had incriminated himself or herself, it was necessary to consider the use made of evidence obtained under compulsion. In this case, the respondent's replies to questions were self-incriminating because they contributed to the proof that she had driven a car on the occasion in question, which provided an essential link in the chain of testimony against her. There was nothing exceptional in s 172 of the 1988 Act to justify a breach of the privilege against self-incrimination.

*Held:* The Privy Council considered that the High Court had interpreted the decision in *Saunders* as laying down a more absolute standard than was intended by the European Court. While acknowledging that the overall fairness of the criminal trial must not be compromised, the Privy Council considered that treating the privilege against self-incrimination as an absolute right could not be reconciled with Convention case-law. Observing that Strasbourg jurisprudence established the need to strike a balance between the general interests of the community and the personal rights of the individual, the Privy Council considered that the Convention provided for a graduation of rights which depend upon the seriousness of the criminal charge or the circumstances of the case. The Court noted that while a national court does not apply the doctrine of the margin of appreciation, it could give weight to the decisions of Parliament and a democratically elected government 'within the discretionary area of judgment accorded to those bodies'. Overturning the decision of the High Court of Justiciary, the Privy Council was unanimous in its opinion that the Procurator Fiscal could adduce the respondent's answers to police questions without infringing her privilege against self-incrimination. Referring to the high incidence of death and injury on the roads, and noting the public interest in the enforcement of road traffic legislation, Lord Bingham considered that s 172 constituted a proportionate response to the problem of maintaining road safety. Given the need to attain a balance between conflicting interests, he was not persuaded that the use at trial of the respondent's answers to questions obtained as a consequence of this provision compromised her right to a fair trial. Accordingly, in this case a limited qualification of the rights contained within Art 6 was acceptable.

## 2.2   LIMITATIONS ON INTERFERENCE WITH CONVENTION RIGHTS BY THE STATE

### (1)   STRICT LIMITATIONS

### Fox, Campbell and Hartley v United Kingdom

### (1990) 13 EHRR 157

*Facts:*   The applicants were arrested under s 11(1) of the Northern Ireland (Emergency Provisions) Act 1978 on suspicion of being terrorists, for which they could be held for a period of up to 72 hours. They were questioned over a period of 44 hours, 44 hours and 5 minutes, and 30 hours and 15 minutes respectively, although no charges were brought against them. They were not brought before a judge or given any opportunity to apply for release on bail. The applicants claimed, inter alia, that their arrest and detention was not justified under Art 5(1) of the Convention.

*Commission:*   The Commission concluded, inter alia, that there had been a violation of Art 5.

*Court:*   The Court, in finding a violation of Art 5(1), stressed that the suspicion, as defined in that paragraph, must be 'reasonable'. What may be regarded as 'reasonable' will depend upon all the circumstances and the Court recognised that terrorist crime falls into a special category. However, the interpretation of 'reasonableness' is restricted to maintaining the essence of the right. The failure of the government to provide further information concerning their suspicions did not satisfy the objective element of 'reasonable', and therefore the minimum standard set by Art 5(1)(c) for judging the reasonableness of a suspicion for the arrest of an individual had not been met.

### Campbell and Cosans v United Kingdom

### (1982) 4 EHRR 293

*Facts:*   The applicants each had children of compulsory school age attending State schools in Scotland where corporal punishment was used as a disciplinary measure. Both parents refused to accept the right of the school to administer such punishment and claimed, inter alia, that it violated Art 2 of the First Protocol of the Convention.

*Commission:*   The Commission held that disciplinary procedures form part of what is meant by 'education' and therefore fell within the relevant Protocol. The parents' and pupils' opposition to corporal punishment amounted to 'philosophical convictions' which governments are obliged to respect in the administration of education. By failing to allow for the objections against corporal punishment, the government had violated Art 2 of the First Protocol.

*Court:*  The Court, agreeing with the Commission, held that the duty to respect parental convictions in this sphere cannot be overridden by the alleged necessity of striking a balance between the conflicting views involved. The government's policy to move gradually towards the abolition of corporal punishment was not in itself enough to comply with this obligation. The right to education guaranteed by the first sentence of Art 2 of the First Protocol by its very nature calls for regulation by the State, but the Court held that this regulation must never injure the substance of the right nor conflict with other rights enshrined in the Convention or its Protocols. Accordingly, there was a violation of the Convention.

## Guzzardi v Italy

## (1980) 3 EHRR 333

*Facts:*  The applicant had been placed under special supervision on the island of Asinara in accordance with legislation which allowed compulsory residence orders to be made in respect of dangerous persons. Asinara was 50 sq km in area, but the residence order was restricted to 2.5 sq km.

*Commission:*  The Commission held unanimously that Art 5(1) requirements had not been observed.

*Court:*  The Court agreed with the Commission, although on a narrow margin of 10 votes to 8. The government's initial arguments concerned the situation that it faced in Italy as regards public order due to terrorism and the Mafia. The Court acknowledged this, but said that its attention must be confined, so far as possible, to the applicant's specific case. For the applicant's 'right to liberty' to be restricted, the justifications must fall within the exhaustive exceptions listed in Art 5(1)(a)–(f) and not on any general contextual arguments. The Court considered each potentially relevant exception, even those not raised by the government, and held that the deprivation of liberty was not justified in the applicant's case.

## Lawless v Ireland (No 3)

## (1961) 1 EHRR 15

*Facts:*  The applicant was a member of the IRA. He alleged that the Convention had been violated by virtue of his detention for 5 months without trial in a military detention camp under the Offences Against the State Act 1939.

*Commission:*  The Irish government argued that the detention without trial did not constitute a violation of Art 5 of the Convention. Its argument was based on the construction it placed on sub-para (c) of Art 5(1). The sub-paragraphs refer to an exhaustive list of cases in which it is lawful to deprive someone of their liberty. The government argued that the applicant's detention fell within the boundaries of sub-para (c) because it consists of two categories: those who have been detained or arrested 'on reasonable suspicion of having committed an offence' and those who have been detained or arrested 'when it is reasonably considered necessary to prevent him committing an offence'. It maintained that it was clear from the wording of the clause that the obligation to bring the person before a competent judicial authority as contained within Art 5(3) applies only to the former category. The Commission disagreed. The obligation referred to all of Art 5(1)(c) and therefore the detention fell outside its boundaries. However, the Commission also held that the Irish government was entitled to derogate from its Convention obligations by virtue of the existence of a public emergency as defined by Art 15.

*Court:*  Agreeing with the Commission, the Court held that the clause permits deprivation of liberty only when such deprivation is effected for the purpose of bringing the person arrested or detained before a competent judicial authority. In addition, the Court stressed that the measures governments can take when derogating are strictly limited to what is required by the exigencies of the situation and also that they do not conflict with other obligations under international law. The Court was satisfied that these strict limitations were met.

## (2)  IMPLIED LIMITATIONS

### Johnston v Ireland

### (1986) 9 EHRR 203

*Facts:*  The case involved three applicants. The first applicant was Mr Johnston who had separated from his wife and now lived with the second applicant, Ms Williams-Johnston and the third applicant, their child, as a family. The first and second applicants were unable to marry due to divorce being illegal under the Irish Constitution. They were particularly concerned about the legal status of cohabiting couples and illegitimate children. They alleged violation, inter alia, of Art 8 of the Convention.

*Commission:*  The Commission found that the Convention did not guarantee the right to divorce and subsequently to remarry. However, the legal status of illegitimate children in Ireland did amount to a violation of Art 8.

*Court:*  The Court acknowledged that States have a wide margin of appreciation in this area. Although it was for the State to choose how legal safeguards are imposed to protect rights guaranteed under the Convention, this discretion was not unlimited. The margin of appreciation was also subject to the implied limitations of striking a fair balance between the demands of the general interest of the community and the interests of the individual; and the implied rights of the individuals.

In finding that there had been no violation of Art 8 as regards the first and second applicants, the Court, while recognising the evolutionary nature of attitudes towards 'respect' for family life, stressed that the Convention must be read as a whole. Therefore, having found that the scope of Art 12 did not include the right to divorce, the Court held that it would be inconsistent to derive such a right from Art 8, a provision of more general purpose and scope.

## (3) PROPORTIONALITY AND THE BALANCE BETWEEN THE INTERESTS OF THE INDIVIDUAL AND OF THE COMMUNITY

### Rees v United Kingdom

### (1986) 9 EHRR 56

*Facts:* See **2.1**(1).

*Court:* Whilst finding there was no violation of Art 8, the Court recognised that it was part of the States' margin of appreciation to decide which countervailing public interests should be balanced against the individual's interests. The applicant had requested the adjustment in the form of an annotation to the present birth register. Under the UK's legal system, this would constitute falsification of the facts. The Court accepted that the demands of the public interest weighed strongly against any such alteration. Further, altering the birth certificate would not constitute an effective safeguard for ensuring the integrity of the applicant's private life as it would reveal his change of sexual identity. For such information to be kept secret, this would require a fundamental change to the UK's legal system. Having regard to the wide margin of appreciation to be afforded the State in this area and to the relevance of protecting the interests of others in striking the requisite balance, the positive obligations arising from Art 8 cannot be held to extend that far.

### X, Y and Z v United Kingdom

### (1997) 24 EHRR 143

*Facts:* See **2.1**(1).

*Commission:* In considering whether an effective respect for the applicants' family life imposed a positive obligation on the UK to change its legal system in respect of transsexuals, the Commission was of the opinion that regard must be had to the fair balance that has to be struck between the general interest of the community and the interests of the individual. The applicants' interests centred around those of the child, Z, who may be prejudiced as regards rights of inheritance and the stigma of being an illegitimate child, threatening the child's sense of security within the family. In the Commission's view, the government had not put forward any countervailing public concern which outweighed the applicants' interests. Therefore, the absence of an appropriate legal regime reflecting the applicants' family ties disclosed a breach of Art 8.

*Court:* The Court accepted the government's rather than Commission's and applicants' arguments that there were prevailing Community interests which outweighed those of the applicants. The Court stressed that in maintaining a coherent system of family law (a community interest) the best interests of the child should be at the forefront. First, considering the community interest, the Court noted that the proposed change in the legal system did not make it clear that it would be to the advantage of Z, or children conceived by AID in general. Indeed, the Court accepted the government's argument that any change in the law may have undesirable or unforeseen ramifications for children in Z's position. Against this, the Court balanced the applicants' interests. In respect of Z's interest regarding inheritance rights, this could be protected by X making a will. In respect of Z's security within the family unit due to the lack of a named father on the birth certificate, this was no different to many other families and was negligible as the certificate is not in common use for administrative or identification purposes within the UK. Further, the alleged stigma attached to such illegitimacy was not established. There was also nothing preventing X from acting as Z's father in the social sense. The Court therefore held that there was no obligation on the government to recognise as the father of a child a person who is not the biological father, and consequently no violation of Art 8.

## Artico v Italy

## (1980) 3 EHRR 1

*Facts:*  The applicant had been imprisoned for offences of fraud. He appealed and was appointed a legal aid lawyer. However, the lawyer nominated refused to act for the applicant. Unable to secure a different legal aid lawyer, the applicant was not represented at his appeal. The applicant complained to the Commission that the failure to provide him with legal assistance was in breach of Art 6(3)(c).

*Commission:*  The Commission held unanimously that there had been a violation of Art 6(3)(c) by virtue of the absence of legal assistance.

*Court:*  The Court stressed that the Convention is intended to guarantee rights that are practical and effective, not theoretical and illusory. Mere nomination of a lawyer does not ensure effective assistance as many situations may result in the nominated lawyer failing to carry out his duties. If the authorities are notified of the situation, they must either replace the lawyer or compel him to carry out his duties. The applicant did not receive effective assistance. Therefore, a violation of Art 6(3)(c) was found.

## *THE PROTECTION OF A DEMOCRATIC SOCIETY*

## Castells v Spain

## (1992) 14 EHRR 445

*Facts:*  The applicant was a lawyer and senator belonging to a political group supporting independence for the Basque region. In 1979, a weekly magazine published an article entitled 'Outrageous Impunity' which was signed by the applicant. The prosecuting authorities instituted criminal proceedings against the applicant for insulting the government. The applicant brought proceedings before the Commission alleging, inter alia, violation of Art 10, freedom of expression, particularly in relation to not being allowed to establish the truth of the statements contained in the article.

*Commission:*  The Commission found a violation of Art 10.

*Court:*  The Court stressed that freedom of expression constitutes one of the essential foundations of a democratic society and one of the basic conditions for its progress. It is particularly important for an elected representative of the people. Therefore, interference with the freedom of expression of an opposition Member of Parliament, like the applicant, calls for the closest scrutiny on the part of the Court. The Court also held that the press has a primary role in a State governed by the rule of law and it is morally obliged to impart information and ideas on political questions and on other matters of public interest. Freedom of the press enables everyone to participate in the free political debate which is at the very core of the concept of a democratic society. However, the Court also held that this freedom is not absolute in nature. A Contracting State may make it subject to certain restrictions or penalties, but it is for the Court to give the final ruling on the compatibility of such measures with the freedom of expression. As regards the government, the limits of permissible criticism are wider than in relation to a private citizen or politician. This does not mean that a State cannot adopt measures intended to protect against defamatory accusations devoid of foundation or formulated in bad faith in the interests of public order. However, these measures must fulfil the requirements of Art 10(2). In this case, the Court held that the interference suffered by the applicant was not necessary in a democratic society.

## Malone v United Kingdom
## (1984) 7 EHRR 14

*Facts:*   Following his acquittal for dishonestly handling stolen goods, the applicant brought a civil action seeking to establish that the interception of his telephone by the police during the criminal investigation had been unlawful. Although the government consistently denied that the applicant's phone had been tapped, it conceded that, as a suspected handler of stolen goods, he belonged to a class of persons liable to have their calls intercepted. At the time, the relevant national law and procedure required that the police obtain a warrant issued by the Home Secretary prior to intercepting telephone calls. The applicant complained that the interception of his telephone and his correspondence was in violation of Art 8.

*Commission:*   The Commission found that there had been a breach of the applicant's rights under Art 8 by virtue of the intercepted telephone conversation to which the applicant had been a party. Further, the existence in England and Wales of laws and practices which permitted and established a system for effecting secret surveillance of communications amounted in itself to an interference with the applicant's rights under Art 8.

*Court:*   The Court agreed with the Commission's above findings whilst stressing that this case did not refer to communications in general, but only interceptions effected by the police. The principal issue was whether the interference was justified under the terms of Art 8(2), in particular whether it was 'in accordance with the law' and 'necessary in a democratic society'. The Court held that 'in accordance with the law' should be interpreted in light of the same general principles as stated in *Sunday Times v United Kingdom* (1979–80) 2 EHRR 245. Therefore, the principle covers unwritten law and the interference must have some basis in domestic law. This also relates to the quality of law and requires the domestic law to be compatible with the rule of law as expressly mentioned in the preamble to the Convention. The law must be sufficiently clear in its terms to give citizens an adequate indication as to the circumstances in which, and the conditions on which, public authorities are empowered to resort to such measures. The law must also indicate the scope of any discretion conferred on the competent authorities and the manner of its exercise with sufficient clarity, having regard to the legitimate aim of the measure in question, to give the individual adequate protection against arbitrary interference. In this case, the Court held that the law of England and Wales did not indicate with reasonable clarity the scope and manner of exercise of the relevant discretion conferred on the public authorities. Consequently, the minimum degree of legal protection to which citizens are entitled under the rule of law in a democratic society was lacking.

# McCann v United Kingdom
## (1996) 21 EHRR 97

*Facts:*   The authorities were aware that the IRA was planning a terrorist attack on Gibraltar. The exact date of their knowledge was not ascertained, although it was before 4 March 1988 and probably from at least the beginning of the year. The attack was believed to be arranged for 8 March by way of a car bomb. Military forces had arrived on the island before 4 March with the purpose of assisting the Gibraltar police in arresting the IRA suspects if requested. The request was made on 6 March after the suspects had been identified as being in the vicinity of the expected attack area where they had parked a car believed to contain a bomb. McCann and Farrell, two of the IRA suspects, were shot and killed by two soldiers who, on their own evidence, opened fire after they believed the suspects had attempted to detonate the bomb. Eye-witness accounts were at variance with the soldiers' evidence. The third suspect, Savage, was also shot by two soldiers who claimed they opened fire to prevent the suspect from detonating the bomb. After opening fire, the soldiers acknowledged that their intention was to shoot to kill as they had been trained. Again, eye-witness accounts were at variance with the soldiers' evidence. The suspects' bodies and car were searched; no weapons or devices were found. However, a car connected to the suspect, Farrell, was later found and searched. It contained an explosive. The applicants claimed that either the decision to shoot to kill the suspects had been made by the UK government prior to the incident and the soldiers were ordered to carry out the shootings, or that the operation was planned and implemented in such a way that the killing of the suspects by the soldiers was the inevitable result. In any event, in light of the circumstances, the use of lethal force by the soldiers was not necessary or, if it was necessary, the force used was excessive and therefore not justified. The applicants, therefore, claimed a violation of Art 2.

*Commission:*   One of the applicants' claims was that Art 2 should be interpreted as including a procedural element, namely the provision of an effective procedure after the event for establishing the facts. The Commission found that, although a general legal prohibition of arbitrary killing by State authorities was rendered futile if, in practice, there was no mechanism for reviewing the action by the State, Art 2 cannot be interpreted as including a requirement of access to the Court in the determination of any resulting civil rights disputes or an effective remedy before the courts where there is a complaint of deprivation of life. Instead these matters would fall to be considered under Arts 6 and 13 of the Convention which were not invoked by the applicants in the present case. However, the Commission held that the obligation imposed on the State that everyone's right to life shall be 'protected by law' may include a procedural aspect.

This includes the minimum requirement of a mechanism whereby the circumstances of a deprivation of life by the agents of a State may receive public and independent scrutiny. The Commission held in this case that the inquest conducted after the shootings provided sufficient procedural safeguards for the purposes of Art 2(1) of the Convention.

In relation to the alleged 'shoot to kill' policy, the Commission highlighted the fact that such a policy would constitute a violation of the rights guaranteed under the Convention. A terrorist who is suspected of having committed or of intending to commit an act of violence continues to enjoy the protection of the right to life and the right to a fair trial (Arts 2 and 6 respectively). In this case, however, the Commission found no evidence to support the applicants' claims of a premeditated design to kill the suspects. The Commission therefore held, 11 votes to 6, that there had been no violation of Art 2.

*Court:* The Court immediately drew attention to the fact that the Convention, as an instrument for the protection of individual human beings, requires that its provisions be interpreted and applied so as to make its safeguards practical and effective. It was noted that, in connection with the force which can be used, the use of the phrase 'absolutely necessary' in Art 2(2) requires that a stricter and more compelling test of necessity must be employed from that normally applicable when determining whether State action is 'necessary in a democratic society' under para 2 of Arts 8–11. In particular, the force used must be strictly proportionate to the achievement of the aims set out in sub-paras 2(a), (b) and (c) of Art 2. The Court, in applying this to the facts of the case, ultimately held that there had been a violation of Art 2, although by a very narrow margin of 10 votes to 9.

## PROPORTIONALITY: GOALS ACHIEVED BY OTHER MEANS?

# Chahal v United Kingdom
# (1996) 23 EHRR 413

*Facts:* The applicant had been detained in custody for deportation purposes since 1990 after the Home Secretary decided that he was a threat to national security and had been denied asylum. The applicant relied upon, inter alia, Art 3 of the Convention, complaining that his deportation to India would expose him to a real risk of torture or inhuman or degrading treatment and that his detention pending deportation had been too long. He was joined by his wife and children as applicants, who claimed that his deportation would breach their right to respect for family life under Art 8.

*Commission:* The applicant claimed that Art 3 of the Convention provides absolute protection against being sent to a country where such a real risk exists. Further, this absolute protection is not subject to a qualification of proportionality. However, if there is a proportionality issue, the applicant maintained that he had not violated English rules or regulations by denying the government's allegations of terrorist activity. Such allegations could have been dealt with by the criminal process, not a deportation order. In response, the government argued that Art 3 was never intended to cover such cases as this. Contracting Parties have a right and duty to weigh the risk of torture against the harm caused to national security by the continued presence of an alien on its territory.

However, the government claimed that this balancing exercise is non-justiciable. It cannot be the role of the national courts or the Convention organs to make any searching judicial scrutiny of national security matters. The Commission was of the opinion that the guarantees of Art 3 are of an absolute character, permitting no exception, and did not accept the government's submission that the risk of ill-treatment was to be weighed against the threat to national security. Once the risk to the individual has been established, it is not the case that the individual's background, or the threat posed by him to national security of the deporting State, can be weighed in the balance so as to reduce the level of protection afforded by the Convention.

In addition, the Commission noted that the interference with the applicant's right to respect for private and family life was in accordance with the law and pursued the legitimate aim of protecting the interests of national security. Therefore, it would only have to be decided whether the deportation of the applicant would be proportionate to that aim and 'necessary in a democratic society' within the meaning of Art 8(2). The Commission considered the interference to be a serious one. The deportation of the applicant would almost certainly lead to the break up of the family. The Commission took into consideration the fact that the applicant had not been convicted of any serious crime. Indeed, the allegations against him had remained untested. The Commission therefore held that deportation was not proportionate to the legitimate aim pursued, and would not therefore be necessary within the meaning of Art 8(2) of the Convention.

*Court:* The Court agreed with the Commission's opinion that the prohibition against ill-treatment as guaranteed by Art 3 is absolute. Therefore, whenever substantial grounds have been shown for believing that an individual would face a real risk of being subjected to treatment contrary to Art 3 if removed to another State, the responsibility of the Contracting State to safeguard the person against such treatment is engaged in the event of expulsion. The activities of the person, however undesirable or dangerous, cannot be a material consideration.

## FAIR TRIAL: JUDICIAL SAFEGUARDS

## McCann v United Kingdom
## (1996) 21 EHRR 97

*Facts and Commission:* See **2.2**(3), at p 50.

*Court:* The Court considered it unnecessary to decide whether a right of access to the Court to bring civil proceedings in connection with deprivation of life can be inferred from Art 2(1) since it held that it was an issue which would be more appropriately considered under Arts 6 and 13. However, it agreed with the Commission that a general legal prohibition of arbitrary killing by the agents of the State would be ineffective if there existed no procedure for reviewing the lawfulness of the use of lethal force by State authorities. The obligation to protect the right to life, read in conjunction with the State's general duty under Art 1 to 'secure to everyone within their jurisdiction the rights and freedoms defined in [the] Convention' requires, by implication, that there should be some form of effective official investigation. The Court agreed with the Commission's finding that the inquest fulfilled such an investigation and it rejected as unsubstantiated the applicants' claims that the killings were premeditated. However, because the force used was not 'absolutely necessary' within the meaning of Art 2(2), the Court held by 10 votes to 9 that there had been a violation of Art 2.

## Klass and Others v Federal Republic of Germany
## (1978) 2 EHRR 214

*Facts:* The applicants claimed that legislation which permitted State authorities to open and inspect mail and listen to telephone conversations in the interests of the security and order of the State, infringed, inter alia, Arts 6 (right to a fair hearing) and 8 (right to respect for correspondence). They accepted the State's right to have recourse to such measures, but challenged the legislation on the grounds that it contained no absolute requirement to notify the person after surveillance had ceased.

*Commission:* The Commission held that the legislation did not infringe the Convention. As regards Art 6, the Commission agreed with the government and held that the Article did not apply to the facts. As regards Art 8, although the Commission found that the surveillance did constitute interference with the Convention right, this interference fell within the scope of the exceptions laid out in Art 8(2).

*Court:* The Court considered the merits of Art 6 without deciding whether it actually applied to this situation. The Court found that the decision could come within the ambit of Art 6 only after the discontinuance of surveillance. While it is secret, the lack of judicial control does not infringe Art 6 so long as the secrecy is justified by the exceptions contained within the said provision. As regards Art 8, the Court referred specifically to the Preamble of the Convention which expresses the fundamental principle of the rule of law in a democratic society. The Court found that the rule of law implies that interference by the executive authorities with an individual's rights should be subject to an effective control which should normally be assured by the judiciary. It considered that in a field where abuse is potentially so easy and could have harmful consequences for democratic society, it is in principle desirable to entrust supervisory control to a judge. However, the Court held that in this particular case, due to the legislation's inbuilt safeguards, the exclusion of judicial control did not exceed the limits of what may be deemed necessary in a democratic society.

## (4) AUTONOMOUS CONCEPTS – INTERPRETATION OF PARTICULAR TERMS
### Abdulaziz, Cabales and Balkandali v United Kingdom
### (1985) 7 EHRR 471

*Facts:* See 2.1(2).

*Commission:* The government argued that the right guaranteed under Art 8 referred solely to existing family life, which the applicants had not established. It also claimed that the applicants were, in effect, claiming a right to choose their country of residence which is not within the scope of Art 8. The Commission did not examine the applications under Art 8 and therefore this aspect of the Convention was not discussed. However, it was considered that such arguments did not lie outside the scope of Art 8.

*Court:*   The Court agreed with the government to the extent that Art 8 'presupposes the existence of a family', but held this does not mean that all intended family life falls entirely outside the ambit. The term 'family' must at any rate include the relationship that arises from a lawful and genuine marriage.

## Engel v The Netherlands (No 1)
## (1976) 1 EHRR 647

*Facts:*   The five applicants were conscript soldiers serving in different non-commissioned ranks in The Netherlands armed forces. On separate occasions, various penalties had been passed on them by their commanding officers for offences against military discipline. In particular, Mr Dona and Mr Schul were involved in the publication and distribution of certain prohibited writings, Mr Engel left his residence without authorisation, Mr Van der Wiel was 4 hours late for duty and Mr De Wit had driven his vehicle in an irresponsible manner. The applicants appealed to the complaints officer and the Supreme Military Court, which upheld the punishments in all cases, although it reduced the level imposed in two cases. The applicants claimed that the penalties imposed constituted deprivation of liberty, contrary to Art 5, and that the proceedings before the military authorities were not in conformity with Art 6 of the Convention.

*Commission:*   The alleged violation under Art 6 raised serious interpretation problems. The question was asked 'Does Art 6 cease to be applicable just because the competent organs of a Contracting State classify as disciplinary an act or omission and the proceedings it takes against the author, or does it, on the contrary, apply in certain cases notwithstanding this classification?'. The applicants, the government and the Commission termed this as relating to the 'autonomy' of the concept of a criminal charge as contained within Art 6.

*Court:*   The Court held that the 'autonomy' of the concept of 'criminal' operates one way only. States are free to designate as a criminal offence an act or omission not constituting the normal exercise of one of the rights the Convention protects. However, the ability of States to designate as disciplinary offences those which would normally constitute criminal offences is much stricter. If this were not the case, States would be able to escape their obligations under the Convention as Arts 6 and 7 refer to guaranteeing rights in connection with 'criminal offences' not 'disciplinary' matters. The Court, therefore, held that it was within its jurisdiction to satisfy itself that the 'disciplinary does not encroach upon the criminal'. The Court then went on to define what it considered to be criminal offences with reference to certain factors – how it is classified by the State, the nature of the offence and the severity of the punishment.

## (5)   AUTONOMOUS CONCEPTS – INTERPRET CONVENTION AS A WHOLE

### Abdulaziz, Cabales and Balkandali v United Kingdom

### (1985) 7 EHRR 471

*Facts:*   See **2.1(2)**.

*Commission:*   In response to the government's submission that the Convention did not apply to immigration control as the Fourth Protocol only was relevant and the UK had not ratified it, the Commission confirmed its previous case-law in holding that the right of a foreigner to enter or remain in a country was not, as such, guaranteed by the Convention, but immigration controls had to be exercised consistently with the Convention obligations. Therefore, the exclusion of a person from a State where members of his family were living might raise an issue under Art 8.

*Court:*   The Court was also unable to accept the government's submission. It said that not only the Convention, but also its Protocols, must be read as a whole. Therefore, a matter dealt with mainly by one of its provisions may also, in some of its aspects, be subject to other provisions thereof. Applying this to the present case, the Court held that, although some aspects of the right to enter a country are governed by the Fourth Protocol as regards States bound by that instrument, it is not to be excluded that measures taken in the field of immigration may affect the right to respect for family life under Art 8.

## 2.3   THE CONVENTION AS A LIVING INSTRUMENT

### (1)   INTERPRETATION IN THE LIGHT OF PRESENT-DAY CONDITIONS

### Tyrer v United Kingdom

### (1978) 2 EHRR 1

*Facts:*   See **2.1(1)**.

*Court:*   The Court agreed with the Commission that it was only the provision 'degrading' which it needed to consider as regards Art 3. In defining 'degrading', the Court stressed that the Convention is a living instrument which must be interpreted in the light of present-day conditions. In the present case, the Court was influenced by the developments and commonly accepted standards in the penal policy of the Member States of the Council of Europe in this area. Further, the provisions of Manx legislation concerning judicial corporal punishment had been under review for a number of years. The Court went on to hold that the applicant had been subjected to a punishment in which the element of humiliation attained the level inherent in the notion of 'degrading punishment', thereby finding a violation of Art 3.

# Johnston v Ireland
## (1986) 9 EHRR 203

*Facts:*   See 2.2(2).

*Court:*   In holding that the Convention's scope did not extend to including divorce, the Court acknowledged the applicants' claims that the Convention should be interpreted in the light of present-day conditions. In particular, there had been social developments which had occurred since the Convention was drafted, notably an alleged substantial increase in marriage breakdown. However, the Convention, as a living instrument, was outweighed by the fact that the right to divorce was not intended to be included and, moreover, it was deliberately omitted. Further, while also acknowledging that the meaning of the right to 'respect' for family life has evolved, this was outweighed by the fact that the Convention must be interpreted as a whole. In doing so, the right to 'respect' for family life did not include that of the right to divorce.

# Rees v United Kingdom
## (1986) 9 EHRR 56

*Facts:*   See 2.1(1).

*Court:*   Whilst according the UK a wide margin of appreciation in the area of the legal status of transsexuals, the Court concluded its judgment as regards no violation of Art 8 with the reminder that the Convention should be interpreted in the light of current circumstances. Therefore, the need for appropriate legal measures should be kept under review, having regard particularly to scientific and societal developments.

# Marckx v Belgium
## (1979) 2 EHRR 330

*Facts:*   See 2.1(2).

*Court:*   In finding a violation, the Court stressed that the Convention must be interpreted in the light of present-day conditions. It acknowledged the government's argument that, at the time the Convention was drafted, it was regarded as permissible and normal in many European countries to draw a distinction between the 'illegitimate' and 'legitimate' family. In the present case, however, the Court was 'struck' by the fact that there had been an evolution in thinking and there now existed a 'clear measure of common ground' amongst the Contracting States to treat each family with legal equality. The Belgian law was therefore considered discriminatory.

# Dudgeon v United Kingdom
## (1981) 4 EHRR 149

*Facts:*   The applicant was part of a campaign aimed at bringing the law relating to homosexuality in Northern Ireland into line with that in force in England and Wales. In January 1976, he was questioned by police officers about his sexuality. The police file was sent to the Director of Public Prosecutions with a view to commencing proceedings for an offence of gross indecency. This offence, by its definition, only concerned men.

*Court:* The Court compared the present-day conditions to those when the legislation was originally enacted. It outlined the increased understanding and resultant tolerance of homosexual behaviour, as demonstrated by the fact that the majority of the Contracting States do not treat, or deem it necessary to treat, such behaviour as criminal. Further, in recent years, Northern Ireland had not prosecuted such behaviour. This did not appear to have had a detrimental effect on the moral standard of Northern Ireland, nor had there been a call to strengthen such criminal law. The Court concluded that, without more, the interference with Art 8 could not be justified.

## B v France
## (1992) 16 EHRR 1

*Facts:* See 2.1(1).

*Court:* The Court accepted the arguments that attitudes have changed, science has progressed and there is an increasing problem relating to transsexualism. However, it also noted that there still existed uncertainty as to the essential nature of transsexualism and the legal situations which result are still extremely complex. Therefore, the argument that the Convention should be seen as a living instrument and interpreted in light of present-day conditions could not provide a basis for the Court to distinguish the present case from previous transsexual case-law as there was not a sufficiently broad consensus between the Contracting States.

## Cossey v United Kingdom
## (1990) 13 EHRR 622

*Facts:* See 2.1(1).

*Commission:* In its consideration of Art 12, the Commission had regard both to the Court's opinion in the *Rees* judgment, where no violation was found, and to its own previous opinion as expressed in the *Rees* report of 12 December 1984. Ten members found no violation of Art 12; five of these members' reasoning was based on the fact there was no separate violation of Art 12 as the impossibility of Rees marrying a person of the female sex was only a necessary consequence of the violation of Art 8 which the Commission unanimously found in that case. However, in light of such cases as *Marckx*, *Johnston* and *Airey*, the Commission now felt that there was a distinction between the approach taken under Art 8 to de facto family life, irrespective of its legal status and the right under Art 12 for two persons of opposite sex to be united in a formal, legally recognised union. In the applicant's case, the Commission found a factual distinction between it and previous transsexual cases in that Miss Cossey had a male partner wishing to marry her. In these circumstances, Miss Cossey should have had the right to conclude a marriage recognised by UK law with the man she chose to be her husband.

*Court:*   The Court found that whether a person has the right to marry depends not on the existence in the individual case of such a partner or a wish to marry, but on whether or not he or she meets the general criteria laid down by law. The present case was held not to be materially distinguishable on its facts from the *Rees* case. Although some Contracting States would now regard as valid a marriage between a person in Miss Cossey's situation and a man, the Court held that the developments to date did not evidence any general abandonment of the traditional concept of marriage.

However, as regards Art 8, the Court did go on to consider whether it should depart from its previous decisions on the grounds that the Convention should reflect societal changes and remain in line with present-day conditions. The Court referred again to the *Rees* judgment where it was pointed out that there was a need to keep appropriate legal measures for transsexuals under review, having regard particularly to scientific and societal developments. The Court noted that it had been informed of no significant scientific developments that had occurred subsequent to the *Rees* case. The surrounding reports – in connection with the Resolution adopted by the European Parliament on 12 September 1989 and Recommendation 1117 (1989) which seek to harmonise laws and practices in this area – showed the same degree of diversity as at the time of the *Rees* decision. Therefore, a departure from the Court's earlier decision was not necessary to ensure that present-day conditions were reflected in the interpretation of Art 8.

# SW v United Kingdom; CR v United Kingdom
## (1995) 21 EHRR 363

*Facts:*   SW was found guilty of raping his wife in 1991 and CR pleaded guilty to the attempted rape of his wife in 1990. Prior to 1990, as a matter of common law, a husband had been immune from prosecution for the rape of his wife on account of the consent to sexual intercourse that was thought to be inherent in the marriage contract. By the time of conviction, the immunity had disappeared. SW submitted that the immunity still applied at the date of the offence he was alleged to have committed. The trial judge, in the case of CR, ruled that the implied consent could be withdrawn by agreement which could be shown by surrounding circumstances, such as non-cohabitation. The applicants complained that there had been a violation of Art 7 in that they had been found guilty of the crime of rape even though at the time they had committed the act, that act did not constitute a crime.

*Commission:*   The Commission was of the opinion that it is compatible with Art 7 for existing elements of an offence to be clarified or adapted to new circumstances or developments in society insofar as this can reasonably be brought under the original concept of the offence. The constituent elements of the offence may not, however, be essentially changed to the detriment of the accused and any progressive development by way of interpretation must be reasonably foreseeable, with the assistance of appropriate legal advice, if necessary. In a common-law system, therefore, the courts may exercise their customary role of developing the law through cases but, in doing so, may not exceed the bounds of reasonably foreseeable change. In applying the above principles to both the cases, the Commission was of the opinion that there had been no violation of Art 7(1). Due to the well-documented developments in case-law, the

Commission found it inconceivable that either applicant believed that the course of action he embarked upon was lawful.

*Court:* The Court unanimously agreed with the opinion of the Commission. Further, it held that the essentially debasing character of rape is so manifest that the result of the decisions on UK domestic law cannot be said to be at variance with the object and purpose of Art 7, namely to ensure that no one should be subjected to arbitrary prosecution, conviction or punishment. Moreover, the abandonment of the unacceptable idea of a husband being immune against prosecution for rape of his wife was in conformity not only with a civilised concept of marriage but also, and above all, with the fundamental objectives of the Convention, the very essence of which is respect for human dignity and human freedom.

## (2)  CHANGING INTERPRETATIONS IN THE LIGHT OF SUBSEQUENT PRACTICE

### Soering v United Kingdom

### (1989) 11 EHRR 439

*Facts:* The applicant was a German national detained in an English prison pending extradition to Virginia, in the USA, to face charges of murder. A warrant ordering the applicant's surrender to the USA had been signed by the Secretary of State in 1988. This had remained unexecuted while the Commission and Court considered the case. In the meantime, the applicant had been moved to a prison hospital due to his dread of extreme physical violence and homosexual abuse from other inmates in death row. There were objective fears that he may have attempted suicide. The applicant claimed, inter alia, breaches of Arts 3 (the 'death-row phenomenon' amounted to inhuman and degrading treatment) and 6(3)(c) (the trial would be unfair due to the lack of legal aid in Virginia to pursue appeals).

*Commission:* The Commission held that the extradition of a person to a country where he risks the death penalty does not in itself raise an issue under either Art 2 or Art 3.

*Court:* The Court paid particular attention to the written comments of Amnesty International, which had argued that the evolving standards in Western Europe regarding the existence of the death penalty made it necessary to consider the death penalty as an inhuman and degrading punishment within the meaning of Art 3. The Court disagreed, due to the fact that the Convention must be read as a whole. The drafters would not have intended Art 3 as generally prohibiting the death penalty as this would have nullified one of the qualifications to the right to life contained within Art 2(1). However, after recognising the Convention as a living instrument which must be interpreted in the light of present-day conditions, the Court was prepared to consider the subsequent practice of penal policy within the Contracting States. There appeared to be an abolition of capital punishment. The Court accepted that this could be taken as establishing an agreement between the Contracting States to abrogate the exception provided for under Art 2(1), thereby allowing Amnesty International's argument above. However, the Court held that the existence of the Sixth Protocol which provides for the abolition of the death penalty in peacetime evidenced the

intention of States to amend the Convention text by the normal method, therefore
Amnesty International's argument must fail.

*Notes:*   The Court went on to hold that its above finding did not necessarily mean that
the circumstances relating to a death sentence can never give rise to an issue under
Art 3. Present-day attitudes in the Contracting States to capital punishment are
relevant for the assessment whether the acceptable threshold of suffering or
degradation has been exceeded.

## (3)   RIGHTS NOT CREATED

### Johnston v Ireland

### (1986) 9 EHRR 203

*Facts:*   See 2.2(2).

*Court:*   In response to the applicants' claims that Art 12 contained a guarantee of a
right to have the ties of marriage dissolved by divorce as well as a right to marry, the
Court held that it cannot, by means of an evolutive interpretation, create a right that
was not included therein at the outset, particularly where the omission was deliberate.
The Court pointed to the fact that divorce was not intended to be included within the
scope of the Convention by referring to the Seventh Protocol, Art 5, where Contracting
States did not take the opportunity to extend the obligations of States to provide for
dissolution of marriage.

*Note:*   Although the Court held that rights could not be created in the way argued for,
it did hold in this case that rights could be implied, where not expressly set out. In
holding that Art 8 had been violated as regards the third applicant, the Court implied
into the right to 'respect' for family life the right of the child to be integrated into his
family from the moment of birth.

## (4)   IMPLIED RIGHTS

### Golder v United Kingdom

### (1975) 1 EHRR 524

*Facts:*   The applicant was a prisoner who was identified by a prison officer as being
involved in a serious disturbance. He was segregated from other prisoners and told that
disciplinary proceedings may be brought against him. The prison officer withdrew his
allegation and the applicant was returned to his ordinary cell. The incident and its
outcome were recorded in his prison record. The following year, the applicant was
refused permission to consult a solicitor about possible libel proceedings against the
prison officer. The applicant alleged violations of Arts 6(1) and 8.

*Commission:*   The Commission held that the refusal to allow the applicant to consult
a solicitor with a view to commencing legal proceedings amounted to the violation of
Arts 6(1) and 8.

*Court:* The Court held that it was called upon to decide whether Art 6(1) is 'limited to guaranteeing in substance the right to a fair trial in legal proceedings which are already pending, or does it in addition secure a right of access to the courts for every person wishing to commence an action in order to have his civil rights and obligations determined?'. This raises the question of how the Convention should be interpreted. The government, the Commission and the Court were prepared to consider that the Court should be guided by Arts 31 and 33 of the Vienna Convention, 1969. Article 31 states that the process of interpretation of a treaty is a unity, a single, combined operation. The Court therefore held that the terms of Art 6(1), taken in their context, provide reasons to think that the right of access to a court is included among the guarantees set forth. Further, Art 31(2) of the Vienna Convention states that the preamble to a treaty forms an integral part of the context. The Court identified the most significant passage in the Preamble to the European Convention as being that European countries have a 'common heritage of political traditions, ideals, freedom and the rule of law'. Particular significance was given to the 'rule of law' by both the Commission and Court, and the Court found that 'in civil matters one can scarcely conceive of the rule of law without there being a possibility of having access to the courts'.

## 2.4   POSITIVE OBLIGATIONS OF THE STATE

### Marckx v Belgium

### (1979) 2 EHRR 330

*Facts:* See 2.1(2).

*Court:* In finding a violation of Art 8, the Court held that, although Art 8 is primarily of a negative undertaking, it may also impose upon the State positive obligations inherent in an effective 'respect' for family life. Therefore, when considering its domestic legislation as regards the family, in this case in respect of an unmarried mother and her child, the State must act in a manner calculated to allow those concerned to lead a normal family life. The Court enlarged upon this when holding that 'respect' for a family life implies an obligation for the State to act in a manner calculated to allow these ties to develop normally.

### Abdulaziz, Cabales and Balkandali v United Kingdom

### (1985) 7 EHRR 471

*Facts:* See 2.1(2).

*Court:* The Court held that although the essential object of Art 8 is to protect the individual against arbitrary interference by the State, there may be positive obligations inherent in an effective 'respect' for family life. The Court had regard for the diversity of practices amongst the Contracting States and therefore recognised them as having a wide margin of appreciation in this area. The extent of a State's obligation to admit to its territory relatives of settled immigrants will, therefore, vary according to the particular circumstances of the persons involved. The Court held that the duty imposed by Art 8 cannot be considered to extend to a general obligation on the part of a

Contracting State to respect the choice by married couples of their matrimonial residence and to accept the non-national spouses for settlement in that country.

## Soering v United Kingdom
## (1989) 11 EHRR 439

*Facts:*   See 2.3(2).

*Commission:*   The applicant claimed that Art 3 entailed an obligation not to put a person in a position where he will or may suffer such treatment or punishment at the hand of other States. Further, an individual may not be surrendered out of the 'protective zone' of the Convention without the guarantee that the safeguards which he would enjoy are as effective as the Convention standard. In response, the UK government denied such a positive obligation, saying that it should not be held responsible for acts which occur outside its jurisdiction. Alternatively, Art 3 should only apply to cases where such treatment or punishment is certain, imminent and serious. The Commission favoured the applicant saying that a person's deportation or extradition may give rise to an issue under Art 3 of the Convention where there are serious reasons to believe that the individual will be subjected, in the receiving State, to treatment contrary to Art 3.

*Court:*   The Court stressed the territorial limit of the Convention as outlined in Art 1, where Contracting States are required to secure the Convention rights and freedoms within their own jurisdiction. This could not be read as justifying a positive obligation on the Contracting States not to surrender individuals unless satisfied that the conditions awaiting him in the country of destination are in full accord with each of the safeguards of the Convention. However, the Court went on to hold that the finding of no positive obligation in this context did not absolve the Contracting Parties from all responsibility under Art 3. The abhorrence of torture is recognised in the separate United Nations Convention Against Torture and Other Cruel, Inhuman or Degrading Treatment or Punishment, in particular Art 3, 'no State Party shall ... extradite a person where there are substantial grounds for believing that he would be in danger of being subjected to torture'. The Court held that the fact that it is a separate Convention does not mean a similar obligation is not inherent within the European Convention. Further, it would be compatible with the values of the Convention that such an obligation exist. Therefore, extradition may give rise to positive obligations under Art 3 where there is a real risk of being subjected to torture or to inhuman or degrading treatment or punishment in the requesting country.

## Plattform 'Ärzte für das Leben' v Austria
## (1988) 13 EHRR 204

*Facts:*   Plattform 'Ärzte für das Leben' was an association of doctors who campaigned against abortion and sought to change Austrian legislation. It held two demonstrations in 1980 and 1982 which were disrupted by counter-demonstrations despite police presence. The Plattform organisers had feared that incidents might occur and had therefore changed their route in consultation with the local authorities immediately prior to the first demonstration. The police representatives did not refuse to provide protection, but stated that it would be impossible to prevent counter-demonstrators from disrupting the demonstrations. Counter-demonstrators did gather and were not dispersed by the police, and disruptions did occur. Plattform claimed that the police had failed to provide sufficient protection for the demonstration and claimed, inter alia, breaches of Arts 11 and 13.

*Commission:* The Commission held that the complaint under Art 11 was inadmissible as being manifestly ill-founded but at the same time considered it to be arguable for the purposes of establishing a breach of Art 13. It held that Art 11 impliedly required the State to protect demonstrations from those wishing to interfere with or disrupt them. However, it unanimously held there to be no breach of Art 13, the State having provided adequate protection.

*Court:* The Court agreed with the Commission that despite Art 11 being declared inadmissible, it was still arguable for the purposes of Art 13. This necessarily led the Court to interpret Art 11. Whilst recognising that a demonstration may annoy or give offence to persons opposed to the ideas or claims that it is promoting, the participants must be able to demonstrate without fearing physical violence. Therefore, genuine and effective freedom of peaceful assembly was not guaranteed by a purely negative duty of State non-interference. The Court found that, in some circumstances, Art 11 requires positive measures to be taken, even in the sphere of relations between individuals. However, this duty does not extend to an absolute guarantee of protection; it is an obligation as to measures to be taken and not as to results to be achieved. The Court held that the Austrian authorities did not fail to take reasonable and appropriate measures. Further, as there was no arguable claim that Art 11 was violated, Art 13 does not apply.

# Edwards v United Kingdom
## (2002) 35 EHRR 19

*Facts:* Christopher Edwards died in custody from wounds inflicted by a prisoner sharing his cell. Although both prisoners exhibited signs of serious mental illness prior to detention, a member of the prison health care service considered that they were fit to be detained and saw no reason to admit either prisoner to the health care centre. Due to a shortage of space, they were placed in the same cell. When the assailant pleaded guilty to manslaughter by reason of diminished responsibility, the inquest into the killing was closed. A non-statutory inquiry by the authorities into the care and treatment of Christopher Edwards found a 'systematic collapse' of protective mechanisms which should have operated to protect him from the violent acts of another prisoner sharing his cell, and identified a series of shortcomings in the transmission of information by agencies involved in this case. However, the applicants were advised that, in the light of the findings, there were no civil remedies available to them. The applicants complained that there was a breach of a positive obligation by the authorities to protect the life of their son who was killed by another prisoner while in police custody.

*Court:* Recalling that Art 2(1) directs the State not only to refrain from intentional and unlawful killing, but also to take appropriate steps to safeguard lives, the Court considered that in some circumstances Contracting States incurred a positive obligation to protect individuals from the criminal acts of others. This obligation should not impose an impossible or disproportionate burden on the authorities. Before a positive obligation can arise, it is necessary to establish that the authorities knew or ought to have known that there was a real and immediate risk to life, and that they failed to take reasonable measures to avoid the risk. The Court considered that in this case the inadequate nature of the screening process and the failure of the agencies involved in this case to pass on information to the prison authorities disclosed a breach of an obligation to protect life which is guaranteed by Art 2. Furthermore, the absence of an inquest into the killing, together with the fact that the inquiry was held in private and had no power to compel witnesses to attend, resulted in a breach of the procedural obligation to carry out an effective investigation. Although the form of investigation may vary according to the circumstances, any deficiency in procedure that undermines its ability to establish the cause of death or the persons responsible will risk falling short of the required standard. In addition, the inquiry did not provide the applicants with an appropriate means of obtaining an enforceable award of compensation for the damage suffered as a consequence of their son's death. In the Court's opinion, this is an essential element of a remedy under Art 13 which guarantees the right to an effective remedy before a national authority.

## Keenan v United Kingdom
## (2001) 33 EHRR 38

*Facts:*  The applicant's son committed suicide while in custody. Prior to being sentenced to a short period of imprisonment for assault, Mark Keenan was diagnosed as exhibiting signs of paranoid schizophrenia and had a history of frequent episodes of deliberate self-harm. On admission, he was sent to the health care centre for observation and assessment. Attempts to transfer him to an ordinary prison cell failed and he remained in the health care centre. Although he had seen a visiting psychiatrist, a prison doctor who was unqualified in psychiatry amended his medication. Following an incident in which two prison officers were assaulted, he received an additional 28 days in prison with 7 days' loss of association and exclusion from work in a segregation unit, which involved incarceration for 23 hours each day. Although prisoners in this unit received a daily visit from a doctor, the prison chaplain and the governor, contact with staff was minimal. Soon after being transferred to the segregation unit, he was found hanging from the bars of his cell. The inquest jury returned a verdict of death by misadventure. The applicant complained that the authorities failed in their responsibility to protect her son's right to life by not properly assessing him prior to his suicide, and that although segregating prisoners did not in itself amount to ill-treatment, the State had a duty closely to monitor vulnerable prisoners to ensure that they did not suffer unduly. Furthermore, there was no effective national remedy to determine the liability of the authorities for any alleged mistreatment, or for providing compensation.

*Court:*  Where it is established that the authorities knew or ought to have known that there was an immediate risk to life, there is a positive obligation to take protective measures. The obligation to protect the vulnerable is particularly onerous. In this case, the Court was called on to consider the extent to which Contracting States incur an obligation to prevent persons from self-harm. The Court was satisfied that the prison authorities knew that Mark Keenan was a suicide risk and considered whether the prison authorities did all that was reasonably expected of them having regard to the nature of the risk. The Court was unanimous in finding that by placing him under medical supervision the authorities had responded reasonably and had not acted contrary to Art 2. However, the lack of effective monitoring of his condition and the lack of informed psychiatric input into his assessment and treatment was not compatible with the standard required in respect of the mentally ill. Accordingly, the majority of the Court found a breach of Art 3. The Court noted that it was common ground that the inquest failed to provide a remedy for determining liability and was not persuaded that civil proceedings for negligence provided an effective redress for the applicant's complaints. Accordingly, the Court was unanimous in holding that there had been a breach of Art 13.

## Akkoc v Turkey
## (2002) 34 EHRR 51

*Facts:*   Although the Administrative Court had eventually quashed a penalty imposed as a disciplinary sanction in respect of an article published in a newspaper, the applicant maintained that her right under Art 10 had been infringed. Her punishment had been one year's suspension of promotion as a teacher. Further, she claimed that she had been tortured while in police custody and had been intimidated in respect of her application to the Commission. Prior to release from detention, she was taken to see a doctor at the State hospital who signed a report indicating that she had not suffered injury while in custody. She alleged that the examination involved the doctor asking, in the presence of police officers, whether she had any complaints or wanted a medical examination. She was then taken before a public prosecutor, where she reported her ill-treatment and said she had signed a statement under pressure. He ordered her release.

*Commission:*   In its report, the Commission expressed the unanimous opinion that there had been a violation of Arts 10 and 2. It found the applicant to be an honest and credible witness whose evidence was supported by the report from the Ankara Treatment Centre of the Human Rights Foundation. The evidence of the doctor was considered to be unreliable and the medical examination cursory.

*Court:*   The Court is primarily a supervisory body and subsidiary to national systems designed to protect human rights. Contracting States bear the primary burden of conducting an effective investigation into allegations of an interference with Convention rights and have an obligation to provide compensation. In this case, the Court noted that the applicant had used the means available to redress the interference with her right to freedom of expression. Although accepting that the length of time involved in seeking redress was considerable, a period of 5 years and 9 months, the Court considered that in the context of the Turkish legal system this was not sufficiently excessive to deprive the domestic procedures of their efficacy. Accordingly, the Court held that the applicant could no longer claim to be a victim of an interference with her right to freedom of expression. However, accepting the findings of the Commission concerning the applicant's ill-treatment, which involved electric shocks, hot and cold water treatment and blows to the head, the Court found that she was a victim of very serious and cruel suffering which could be characterised as torture. The

Court endorsed the Commission's comments with respect to the importance of independent and thorough examinations of detainees. It considered that:

> 'Such examinations must be carried out by a properly qualified doctor, without any police officer being present and the report of the examinations must include not only the detail of any injuries found but the explanations given by the patient as to how they occurred and the opinion of the doctor as to whether the injuries are consistent with those explanations. The practices of cursory and collective examinations illustrated by the present case undermines the effectiveness and reliability of this safeguard' (para 118).

The Court was satisfied that in the circumstances the questioning of the applicant about her application to the Commission amounted to a form of illicit and unacceptable pressure which hinders the exercise of the right of individual petition.

## Burdov v Russia
## Application No 59498/00, unreported

*Facts:* The applicant complained that failure by a national court to execute final judgments in his favour was incompatible with Art 6(1) and Art 1 of the First Protocol of the Convention. The applicant had taken part in emergency operations at the site of the Chernobyl nuclear plant and suffered illness due to excessive exposure to radioactive emissions. The State authorities informed him that payments awarded for compensation could not be paid due to lack of funding.

*Court:* In finding for the applicant, the Court emphasised that it was not open to a State authority to cite financial difficulties as a reason for failing to honour a judgment debt. The execution of a judgment must be regarded as an integral part of the trial for the purposes of the fair trial requirement enshrined in Art 6. Failure to ensure the applicant obtained compensation payments awarded by a court constituted a breach of Art 6 and amounted to an interference with the applicant's right to peaceful enjoyment of his possessions, which is guaranteed by Art 1 of the First Protocol.

## Kilic v Turkey
## (2001) 33 EHRR 58

*Facts:* The applicant was the brother of a journalist, Kemal Kilic, who was killed while working for the newspaper *Ozgur Gundem*, which had its head office in Istanbul, and whose staff had been subject to constant harassment. Mr Kilic had written to the Governor of Sanliurfa, where he was based, requesting protection. The Governor's office replied to the effect that there had been no attacks in the area, and that the request for protection was refused. Mr Kilic was assassinated on 18 February 1993. An investigation was launched, and a suspect was charged with participation in the killing. The suspect was convicted of other offences, but not of the killing. The Commission declared the applicant's complaints admissible, the applicant relying on Arts 2, 6, 10, 13 and 14 of the Convention.

*Court:* The Court unanimously held that there had been a violation of Art 2, and by six votes to one that the Government had failed to protect the life of Mr Kilic in violation of Art 2. There had also been a violation of Art 13. The Court did not consider it necessary to deal with the question whether there had been violations of Arts 6, 10 and 14. The Court was critical of the failure of the Governor of Sanliurfa to appear before the Commission to give evidence notwithstanding the fact that the government was requested to obtain his attendance on two occasions. The Court observed that it was of the utmost importance for the effective operation of the system of individual petition that, as well as applicants having unfettered access to the Convention organs, 'States should furnish all necessary faculties to make possible a proper and effective examination of applications' (para 52).

In respect of Art 2 the Court held that the Article obliges States to 'take appropriate steps to safeguard the lives of those within its jurisdiction' (para 62). However, the difficulties of policing modern societies are such that 'the scope of the positive obligation must be interpreted in a way which does not impose an impossible or disproportionate burden on the authorities' (para 63). In the present case the Court was convinced that at the time he made his request for protection, Mr Kilic was 'at particular risk of falling victim to an unlawful attack. Moreover, this risk could in the circumstances be regarded as real and immediate' (para 66). The authorities should have been aware of the risk, and although criminal law sanctions were in place and were supervised by the courts in the region where Mr Kilic was killed, the Court noted that these had on a number of instances been found to be unsatisfactory. These defects 'undermined the effectiveness of criminal law protection in the region during the period relevant to this case ... this permitted or fostered a lack of accountability of members of the security forces for their actions which, as the Commission stated in its report, was not compatible with the rule of law in a democratic society respecting the fundamental rights and freedoms guaranteed under the Convention' (para 75). In the circumstances of the case the Court found that the authorities had failed to take reasonable measures to protect the life of Mr Kilic against a real and immediate risk. The Court further found that the investigation into the killing was not effective, and that this too was in breach of Art 2. The same facts led to a finding of a breach of Art 13.

## Ozgur Gundem v Turkey

## (2001) 31 EHRR 49

*Facts:* The applicant, *Ozgur Gundem*, was a daily newspaper based in Istanbul, with a national circulation of up to 45,000 copies. It was forced to close following a string of attacks against its personnel and property. In particular, seven staff members were killed in circumstances originally regarded as 'unknown perpetrator' killings. Some protective measures were taken by the authorities. In December 1993 the police conducted a search of the applicant's office in Istanbul, taking into custody during the process all persons in the building. Documents and archives were seized. Charges were brought against the editor and other staff members alleging that they were members of the PKK and had rendered it assistance. Numerous prosecutions were brought against the newspaper and editor alleging that offences had been committed by the publication of various articles. These led to many convictions, carrying sentences of fines, prison terms and orders of confiscation of issues of the newspaper or the closure of the newspaper for periods of 3 days to one month.

*Court:*   The applicants complained that the Turkish authorities had breached Art 10, having forced the paper to cease publication by a series of attacks and legal steps. The Convention imposes positive obligations on States to give effect to the rights granted under it. In the present case the authorities failed to respond adequately to the attacks made on the newspaper and its staff, and had failed 'in the circumstances, to comply with its positive obligation to protect *Ozgur Gundem* in the exercise of freedom of expression' (para 46). The police operation in which the offices were searched constituted a serious interference with the applicants' freedom of expression. While the measure was in accordance with the law, it was disproportionate to the aim of preventing crime and disorder. In particular, there was no justification given for the detention of all those in the building 'including the cook, cleaner and heating engineer' (para 49) nor for the seizure of the newspaper's archives, documentation and library. The operation was not necessary for the implementation of any legitimate aim. The legal measures taken against the newspaper constituted an interference with the freedom of expression and many could not be justified as 'necessary in a democratic society'. Accordingly, the Court was unanimous in finding that there had been a breach of Art 10.

## 2.5   THE RIGHT TO LIFE

### LCB v UK

### (1999) 27 EHRR 212

*Facts:*   The applicant was born in 1966 and was later diagnosed as having leukaemia. Her father had been present during four nuclear tests between 1957 and 1958. She claimed, inter alia, that failure by the national authorities to warn her parents of the possible risk to her health caused by her father's participation in the nuclear tests, and its failure to monitor her father's radiation dose levels, gave rise to violations of Art 2 (right to life).

*Court:*   The Court held that the State could only have been required to warn the applicant's parents and monitor her health if it appeared likely that irradiation of her father might have engendered a real risk to her health. It was relevant that it had not been established with certainty that the applicant's father had in fact been exposed to dangerous levels of radiation. No evidence was produced to show that, at the time, he had reported symptoms indicating exposure to high levels of radiation. Furthermore, the Court was not satisfied that a causal link had been established between the exposure of a father to radiation and leukaemia in a child subsequently conceived. In the light of the information available to the national authorities at the time, it was not reasonable to expect the State to take the action suggested by the applicant. Accordingly, there had been no violation of Art 2.

### Paton v United Kingdom

### (1980) 3 EHRR 408

*Facts:*   The applicant was told by his estranged wife that she was pregnant and was going to have an abortion. He applied for an injunction to prevent the abortion, but this was denied on the basis that 'in English law the foetus has no legal rights until it is born and has a separate existence from its mother, and that the father of the foetus, whether or not he is married to the mother, has no legal right to prevent the mother from having an abortion'. The abortion was carried out and the applicant alleged breaches of Arts 2, 5, 6, 8 and 9.

*Commission:* The Commission found that the applicant could be regarded as a 'victim' for the purposes of the Convention since 'a potential father is so closely affected by the termination of his wife's pregnancy that he may claim to be a victim'. Since the abortion had already taken place, no domestic remedies could be relevant. There was a recognition that the issue of whether, and at which stage of pregnancy, a foetus has a right to life is a complex one. Although Art 2 guarantees that 'everyone' has a right to life, the Commission found that, as a matter of construction of the Convention, it could apply only to those who have already been born. There were three options available to the Commission: to exclude the foetus from the protection of Art 2 altogether; to recognise a limited right to life of the foetus; or to recognise an absolute right to life of the foetus. The last option was quickly rejected, since the 'life of the foetus is intimately connected with, and cannot be regarded in isolation of, the life of the pregnant woman. If Art 2 were held to cover the foetus and its protection were seen as absolute, an abortion would have to be considered as prohibited even where the continuance of the pregnancy would involve a serious risk to the life of the pregnant woman'. The Commission then decided that it did not have to consider whether a foetus has a limited right to life since Art 2(1) has an implied limitation which justifies an early abortion in order to protect the mother's life or health. The Commission considered, inter alia, American, German and English law on the point of when life begins, and found that each State has a different rule, with further variations between civil and criminal law. Because the issue is so sensitive and depends to such a degree upon the different legal, moral, ethical and religious factors in each Contracting State, the Commission was not prepared to choose one such rule above the others. Therefore, the application was found to be inadmissible.

# Salman v Turkey

## (2002) 34 EHRR 17

*Facts:* The applicant claimed that her husband's death in custody was directly related to ill-treatment amounting to torture which occurred during police interrogation. She relied on the fact that the authorities had failed to give a plausible explanation for marks and injuries found on her husband's body. Further, she claimed that the marks were consistent with the application of 'falaka', which was considered by the European Committee for the Prevention of Torture to be a prohibited form of ill-treatment, and a blow to the chest. Further, she complained that the authorities had failed to conduct an effective investigation into the circumstances of his death. The government disputed these allegations and requested that the Court dismiss the case as inadmissible on account of the applicant's failure to exhaust domestic remedies. Alternatively, it was argued that the evidence did not support the applicant's complaints.

*Commission:* The Commission was unanimous in finding that there had been a breach of Article 2, in respect of the death of the applicant's husband while in custody.

Furthermore, it was found that he had been tortured and that there was no provision for an effective investigation to determine the liability of the authorities for any alleged mistreatment.

*Court:* The Court stressed that Art 2, which safeguards the right to life and sets out the limited circumstances when killing is justified, must be considered to be one of the most fundamental provisions in the Convention. Taken together with Art 3, which prohibits the use of torture, it enshrines one of the basic values in a democracy. Given the importance of the protection afforded by Art 2, the Court subjects any deprivation of life to careful scrutiny. The obligation to protect life is particularly onerous in the case of persons in custody who are considered to be in a particularly vulnerable position. When a person in good health dies in police custody, the burden to provide a satisfactory account for his treatment during detention rests with the authorities. Strong presumptions of fact will arise in respect of the cause of death. In this case, the Court was not satisfied that the government could give a satisfactory account of the injuries found on the body. Further, the Court reaffirmed that the obligation to protect the right to life requires by implication that there should be an effective official investigation into the circumstances surrounding a death resulting from violence allegedly inflicted by State agents. In addition to identifying the probable cause of death, a post mortem examination can provide an accurate record of any signs of ill-treatment or injury. In this case, the defects in the investigation undermined any attempt to determine the extent of police responsibility. Observing that the Convention attached a special stigma to torture, the Court was satisfied, on the basis of the evidence adduced, that the nature and degree of ill-treatment in this case, and the strong inference that it occurred during police interrogation, gave rise to a finding that the applicant's husband had been subjected to torture and died as a consequence.

## Edwards v United Kingdom
## (2002) 35 EHRR 19

*Facts:* See 2.4.

*Court:* Recalling that Art 2(1) directs the State not only to refrain from intentional and unlawful killing, but also to take appropriate steps to safeguard lives, the Court considered that in some circumstances Contracting States incurred a positive obligation to protect individuals from the criminal acts of others. This obligation should not impose an impossible or disproportionate burden on the authorities. Before a positive obligation can arise, it is necessary to establish that the authorities knew or ought to have known that there was a real and immediate risk to life, and that they failed to take reasonable measures to avoid the risk. The Court considered that in this case the inadequate nature of the screening process and the failure of the agencies involved in this case to pass on information to the prison authorities disclosed a breach of an obligation to protect life. Furthermore, the absence of an inquest into the killing together with the fact that the inquiry, which was held in private and had no power to compel witnesses to attend, resulted in a breach of the procedural obligation to carry out an effective investigation. Although the form of investigation may vary according to the circumstances, any deficiency in procedure that undermines its ability to establish the cause of death or the persons responsible will risk falling short of the required standard. In addition, the inquiry did not provide the applicants with an appropriate means of obtaining an enforceable award of compensation for the damage suffered as a consequence of their son's death. In the Court's opinion, this is an essential element of a remedy under Art 13 which guarantees the right to an effective remedy before a national authority.

## Pretty v United Kingdom

## (2002) 35 EHRR 1

*Facts:* The applicant, who was suffering from motor neurone disease, an incurable degenerative illness, submitted that the refusal by the Director of Public Prosecutions to grant her husband immunity from prosecution if he assisted her suicide amounted to a violation for her rights under Arts 2, 3, 8, 9 and 14 of the Convention. She argued that in providing a right to choose whether or not to live, Art 2 protected the individual's right to self-determination in relation to matters of life and death.

*Court:* The Court was not persuaded that the right to life could be interpreted as involving a negative aspect. Although some Convention rights have been interpreted in this manner (for example Art 11 confers a right not to join an association), the Court could not accept that Art 2 conferred the right to die. Observing that Convention jurisprudence has consistently acknowledged the obligation on the State to protect life, the Court was unanimous in holding that the refusal to permit assisted suicide did not violate Art 2. Furthermore, in rejecting her claim that the prohibition resulted in inhuman and degrading treatment for which the State incurred responsibility, the Court did not accept that Art 3 could be interpreted as imposing a positive obligation on the State. Although not prepared to accept that the applicant's claim constituted an infringement of her right to respect for private life, the Court considered that the refusal by the DPP to give an undertaking not to prosecute the applicant's husband was not disproportionate and could be justified as necessary in a democratic society. The applicant's claim did not involve a religion or belief but reflected her commitment to the principle of personal autonomy, which although relevant to her claim under Art 8 did not infringe Art 9. In rejecting her argument that legislation prohibiting assisted suicide discriminated against persons who were physically unable to take their own lives, the Court was of the opinion that there was objective and reasonable justification for not seeking to draw a distinction between persons who were able and those who were unable to commit suicide unaided. Accordingly, the Court was unanimous in finding that the current legislative regime in the UK did not violate the applicant's Convention rights.

## McKerr v United Kingdom; Jordan v United Kingdom; Kelly v United Kingdom; Shanaghan v United Kingdom

## (2002) 34 EHRR 20

*Facts:* The applicants complained that the excessive use of force by members of the Royal Ulster Constabulary (RUC) amounted to a violation of Art 2. In each case the applicants alleged that the RUC had been involved in the unlawful killing of their relatives and that there had been a failure to comply with the procedural requirements under Art 2 to provide an effective investigation into the circumstances of their deaths.

*Court:*   The text of Art 2 demonstrates that it covers not only intentional killing but also situations where it is permitted to use force which may result in unintended killing. The Court observed that:

> 'Any use of force must be no more than "absolutely necessary" for the achievement of one or more of the purposes set out in sub-paragraphs (a) to (c). This term indicates that a stricter and more compelling test of necessity must be employed from that normally applicable when determining whether state action is "necessary in a democratic society" under paragraphs 2 of Articles 8 to 11 of the Convention. Consequently, the force used must be strictly proportionate to the achievement of the permitted aims' (para 104).

The obligation to protect life requires by implication that there must be some form of effective investigation when individuals have been killed by force. The purpose of an investigation is to ensure that domestic laws which protect the right to life are implemented and, in cases involving State agents, to ensure accountability. Although it was not the function of the Court to specify in detail the procedures to be adopted for an examination into the circumstances of a death, to meet the requirements of Art 2 an investigation should be independent, effective, prompt and involve an element of public scrutiny. Further, the next of kin should be involved to an appropriate extent. Notwithstanding the need to take account of legitimate interests such as national security or the protection of material relevant to other investigations, an investigation must meet the procedural requirements of Art 2. Holding that the inquest and a civil action failed to strike the right balance, the Court found a violation of Art 2.

*Note:*   Having consulted the parties, the President of the Chamber decided that in the interests of the proper administration of justice, the proceedings in respect of these cases should be conducted simultaneously.

## Streletz, Kessler and Krenz v Germany
## (2001) 33 EHRR 31

*Facts:*   The three applicants were convicted of offences following the reunification of Germany relating to events that took place before that reunification. The applicants occupied senior positions in the State apparatus and the Socialist Unity Party and were held to be responsible, with others, for various steps taken fully to protect the State border in order to deter entry and exit. In particular, they were responsible for ensuring that border violators were arrested or annihilated. Following their convictions the applicants unsuccessfully appealed. Before the Court the applicants relied on Art 7.

*Court:*   The courts had first found the applicants guilty on the basis of the criminal law applicable in the GDR at the time the offences were committed, but then applied the more lenient law of the FRG when sentencing the applicants. This was consistent with the principles set out in the Unification Treaty of 31 August 1990. The applicants argued that they had acted in accordance with the law of the GDR. The Court found that this was not the case, and in particular that the respect for the need to preserve human life was enshrined in the constitution of the GDR as well as various legislative

Acts. There was no doubt that the applicants bore individual responsibility for the acts in question. It was foreseeable that the acts could one day lead to prosecution, and the applicants, because of the very senior position that they held in the State, 'could not have been ignorant of the GDR's constitution and legislation, or of its international obligations and the criticisms of its border-policing regime that had been made internationally' (para 78). Finally, the Court held that:

'. . . a state practice such as GDR's border-policing policy, which flagrantly infringes human rights and above all the right to life, the supreme value in the international hierarchy of human rights, cannot be covered by the protection of article 7(1) of the Convention' (para 87).

Accordingly, the Court found that Art 7 had not been violated.

*Note:*   In the case of *Gast and Popp v Germany* (2001) 33 EHRR 37 the Court dealt with a complaint to the effect that proceedings for espionage taken against them following German unification exceeded a reasonable length of time. In this case the Court held that Art 6(1) had not been violated.

## NHS Trust A v M; NHS Trust B v H

## Family Division, [2001] 2 WLR 942

*Facts:*   In each case patients were in a persistent vegetative state and the evidence was that it would not be in the best interests of the patients to continue with artificial nutrition and hydration treatment. With the support of relatives of the patients, and hospital staff, the applicant NHS Trusts sought a declaration from the Court to the effect that, pursuant to Sch 1 to the HRA 1998, it was not unlawful to discontinue feeding.

*Held:*   The principles laid down in *Airedale NHS Trust v Bland* [1993] AC 789 need to be reconsidered in the light of the entry into force of the HRA 1998. Articles 2, 3 and 8 of the Convention were relevant in this respect. The patients in both cases were alive, as the brain stem remained intact, and were therefore protected by Art 2. The intention of the withdrawal of treatment was to bring about the patients' death, or to shorten their lives. The Court had not yet dealt with the issue of the withdrawal of artificial nutrition and hydration to patients in a persistent vegetative state, and the Court therefore had to determine the position by reference to other, entirely different, situations. The analysis of the issues by the House of Lords in *Bland* appeared to be consistent with the law of the Convention, and the conclusion to be drawn was that 'an omission to provide treatment by the medical team will . . . only be incompatible with article 2 where the circumstances are such as to impose a positive obligation on the state to take steps to prolong a patient's life' (para 31). The judgment related only to situations in which treatment was being discontinued, and was not relevant to acts by doctors or other members of the health services which might have the effect of shortening a patient's life.

## Re A (Children) (Conjoined Twins: Surgical Separation)
## Court of Appeal, [2001] 2 WLR 480

*Facts:*   J and M were conjoined twin girls, both of whom would die if they were not separated. Separation, however, would lead inevitably to the death of M. The parents of the twins were devout Roman Catholics and opposed the separation, which was supported by the relevant medical staff. At first instance, following an application by the hospital, the judge held that, although regard must be had to the parents' wishes, the interest of J in a relatively normal life outweighed that of her short life if she remained conjoined. The proposed operation was found not to be an unlawful positive act, but rather represented the withdrawal of M's blood supply, and could therefore be carried out.

*Held:*   The operation could lawfully be carried out. In the present case the medical staff faced a conflict of duties: they were under a duty to M not to operate, because to do so would kill her; and they were under a duty to J to operate, because not to do so would kill her. Where the issue raised related to the sanctity of life 'the law must allow an escape through choosing the lesser of the two evils':

> 'Faced as they are with an apparently irreconcilable conflict, the doctors should be in no different position from that in which the court itself was placed in the performance of its duty to give paramount consideration to the welfare of each child. The doctors must be given the same freedom of choice as the court has given itself and the doctors must make that choice along the same lines as the court has done, giving the sanctity of life principle its place in the balancing exercise that has to be undertaken. The respect the law must have for the right to life of each must go in the scales and weigh equally but other factors have to go into the scales as well' (at p 535).

In any event, the proposed operation would not offend the sanctity of life principle. The reality in this case was that M was killing J and 'how can it be just that [J] should be required to tolerate that state of affairs' (at p 536). The

> '... unique circumstances for which this case is authority ... are that it must be impossible to preserve the life of X without bringing about the death of Y, that Y by his or her very continued existence will inevitably bring about the death of X within a short period of time, and that X is capable of living an independent life but Y is incapable under any circumstances, including all forms of medical intervention, of viable independent existence' (at p 537).

*Note:*   This case was heard 10 days before the entry into force of the HRA 1998. The Court found that there was nothing in the HRA 1998 which would call for a different answer to the issue (see p 537 of the judgment).

## 2.6   TERRITORIAL APPLICATION
## Al-Adsani v United Kingdom
## (2002) 34 EHRR 11

*Facts:*   The applicant alleged that he had been tortured in Kuwait by agents and officers of the Government of Kuwait, and brought proceedings for compensation in the English courts. The High Court ordered that his claim be struck out on the ground that the State Immunity Act 1978 granted immunity to foreign governments for acts committed outside their jurisdiction. The applicant argued that the prohibition on torture had acquired the status of a jus cogens norm in international law, taking precedence over treaty law and other rules of international law. On the ground that the alleged torture took place outside the jurisdiction, the government argued the complaint did not fall within Art 1, which requires Contracting States to ensure that everyone within the jurisdiction benefits from the rights and freedoms set out in the Convention.

*Court:* Noting that in *Soering v United Kingdom* (1989) 11 EHRR 439 it was acknowledged that Art 3 had some limited extraterritorial application, the Court was satisfied that liability may result from a decision to expel an individual where there were substantial grounds for believing that the person concerned faced a real risk of torture or inhuman or degrading treatment. In this case, however, the Court noted that the applicant did not suggest that torture took place within the jurisdiction of the UK or that the UK authorities were involved in any way. While accepting that the prohibition on torture had achieved the status of a peremptory norm in international law, the Court observed that the issue in this case was not the criminal liability of an individual for alleged acts of torture, but the immunity of a State in a civil action for damages in respect of acts of torture.

# Cyprus v Turkey
## (2002) 35 EHRR 30

*Facts:* The applicant Government (Cyprus) alleged, with respect to the situation that had existed in Cyprus since the start of Turkey's military operations in northern Cyprus in July 1974, that the Government of Turkey had continued to violate the Convention notwithstanding the adoption by the Commission of reports under former Art 31 of the Convention in 1976 and 1983 and the adoption by the Committee of Ministers of the Council of Europe of resolutions relating to these. Cyprus invoked Arts 1–11 and 13 of the Convention, as well as Arts 14, 17 and 18 read in conjunction with Arts 1–11 and 13. Turkey argued that Cyprus had no locus standi to bring the application as it was not the lawful government of the Republic of Cyprus.

*Court:* The Court first reiterated the position it reached in *Loizidou v Turkey* (1996) 23 EHRR 513 to the effect that in accordance with international practice and in particular resolutions of the United Nations that the Republic of Cyprus has remained the sole legitimate government of Cyprus and on that account their locus standi as the government of a High Contracting Party cannot be in doubt (para 61). Turkey also disputed its liability under the Convention for the allegations set out in the application. It claimed that the acts and omissions complained of were imputable solely to the Turkish Republic of Northern Cyprus (TRNC) which was an independent State. The Court held that Turkey had general responsibility under the Convention for the policies and actions of the TRNC, and that:

> '. . . having effective overall control its responsibility cannot be confined to the acts of its own soldiers or officials in northern Cyprus but must also be engaged by virtue of the acts of the local administration which survives by virtue of Turkish military and other support.

It follows that, in terms of Article 1 of the Convention, Turkey's "jurisdiction" must be considered to extend to securing the entire range of substantive rights set out in the Convention and those additional Protocols which she has ratified, and that violations of those rights are imputable to Turkey' (para 77).

The Court argued further that:

'In the above connection, the Court must have regard to the special character of the Convention as an instrument of European public order (*ordre public*) for the protection of individual human beings and its mission, as set out in Article 19 of the Convention, "to ensure the observance of the engagements undertaken by the High Contracting Parties" . . . Having regard to the applicant Government's continuing inability to exercise their Convention obligations in northern Cyprus, any other finding would result in a regrettable vacuum in the system of human-rights protection in the territory in question by removing from individuals there the benefit of the Convention's fundamental safeguards and their right to call a High Contracting Party to account for violation of their rights in proceedings before the Court' (para 78).

*Note:*   The Court also dealt at length with substantive issues relating to the alleged breaches of the various provisions cited by Cyprus which related mainly to Greek-Cypriot missing persons, of whom there were alleged to be 1485 at the time the application was heard. The Court found that there was an ongoing breach of Arts 2 and 5. In relation to the violations of rights of displaced persons to respect for their home and property the Court found an ongoing violation of Art 8, Art 1 of the First Protocol and Art 13.

# Chapter 3

# THE LEGAL PROCESS IN GENERAL

## 3.1  ACCESS TO A COURT

### Golder v United Kingdom

(1979–80) 1 EHRR 524

*Facts:*  The applicant was placed in solitary confinement and given notice that disciplinary proceedings might be brought against him following his alleged involvement in a serious prison disturbance. He complained that he had been denied the opportunity to consult a solicitor with a view to bringing legal proceedings against a prison officer who had allegedly insulted him. This denial amounted to a breach of Art 6(1).

*Commission:*  In its report, the Commission expressed the unanimous opinion that there had been a violation of Art 6(1).

*Court:*  The Court held that the right of access to a court is an element which is inherent in the right protected by Art 6(1). It noted that, although Art 6 does not state in express terms that there is a right of access to the courts or tribunals, the Convention includes in its preamble reference to the rule of law. In civil matters 'one can scarcely conceive of the rule of law without there being the possibility of having access to a court' (para 34). Furthermore, the Court considered it was inconceivable that Art 6(1) would set out in detail procedural guarantees without providing the right of access to a court. 'The fair, public and expeditious characteristics of judicial proceedings are of no value at all if there are no judicial proceedings' (para 35). However, the right to the courts is not absolute and it may be subject to appropriate limitations. The Court refused to elaborate on a general theory of appropriate limitations, but considered whether, on the facts of this case, the limitation on the right of access violated the Convention. It held that the refusal of the Home Secretary to allow the applicant to consult a solicitor with a view to instituting proceedings resulted in an infringement of his right to go before a court and was a violation of Art 6(1).

*Note:*  The Prison Rules in force at the time were amended to allow a prisoner to institute civil proceedings or to consult a solicitor about instituting such proceedings.

## (1)  IN THE DETERMINATION OF A CRIMINAL CHARGE

### Adolf v Austria

(1982) 4 EHRR 313

*Facts:*  The prosecuting authorities commenced an investigation into an allegation that the applicant had committed an assault. The proceedings were eventually terminated under a provision of the Austrian Penal Code. The applicant claimed that the proceedings were criminal in nature, notwithstanding contrary classification in Austrian law. The government submitted that the procedure in question was designed to 'decriminalise' certain trivial acts and at no time could the applicant be considered as being 'charged with an offence' under Austrian law.

*Court:* In order to determine whether the applicant has been 'charged with a criminal offence', the Court must examine the nature of the proceedings in question. The words 'criminal charge' in Art 6 bear an autonomous meaning, independent of the categorisation applied under domestic law. In view of the nature of these proceedings the applicant had been subject to a criminal charge and Art 6 was applicable.

## (2)  IN THE DETERMINATION OF CIVIL RIGHTS AND OBLIGATIONS

### Ashingdane v United Kingdom

### (1985) 7 EHRR 528

*Facts:*  Following his conviction by a criminal court, the applicant was committed to a mental hospital and placed in a secure special hospital. The Home Secretary eventually ordered his transfer to a local psychiatric hospital; however, his move was delayed due to industrial action by hospital staff. National legislation provided that, in the absence of an allegation of bad faith or negligence, the authorities could not be sued in respect of a refusal to comply with this order. The applicant complained that the effect of this legislation was to prevent him challenging before the courts the lawfulness of his prolonged detention in a secure hospital, and resulted in a breach of Art 6(1).

*Commission:*  The Commission expressed the opinion, by 11 votes to 2, that there had been no breach of Art 6(1).

*Court:*  The Court noted that the right to a court may be relied upon by anyone who considers, on arguable grounds, that there has been an unlawful interference with the exercise of his civil rights. The right of access to a court is not absolute and may be subject to limitations at the discretion of the national authority. However, these limitations should be for a legitimate aim and should be reasonably proportionate to the aim and must not restrict or reduce access in such a way or to such an extent that the very essence of the right is impaired. The Court was of the opinion that, although this legislation was designed to partially restrict mental patients from bringing a case before the courts, it was intended to reduce the risk of unfair harassment of those responsible for their case. Accordingly, this was a legitimate aim which did not 'transgress the principle of proportionality' (para 59), and thus there was no breach of Art 6(1).

### Air Canada v United Kingdom

### (1995) 20 EHRR 150

*Facts:*  The Customs and Excise authorities issued a notice to all airline operators at Heathrow and Gatwick warning of the imposition of penalties if illegal imports were found on their aircraft. The applicant's aircraft was seized when custom officers found a consignment of cannabis resin on board. The airline was informed that it would be returned on payment of £50,000. In the event of a challenge to the seizure, the authorities were required to take proceedings for forfeiture. The applicant company complained that it had been subjected to a criminal penalty and, alternatively, that the seizure amounted to a determination of the company's civil rights.

*Commission:*   The Commission found that the seizure of the aircraft and the subsequent payment of £50,000 did not involve the determination of a criminal charge and did not bring into play Art 6. The payment of money for the return of the aircraft was to be seen as a measure limiting the harm caused to the applicant company, and could not be regarded as a 'penalty'. Similarly, confiscation orders of this kind do not amount to criminal charges within the scope of Art 6.

*Court:*   As regards the determination of a criminal charge, the Court agreed with the Commission. The Court noted that, with regard to the determination of the company's civil rights, judicial proceedings could be brought. The applicant did not institute these proceedings, and the Court declined to examine in the abstract whether the scope of judicial review would satisfy Art 6(1).

## Pellegrin v France

## (2001) 31 EHRR 26

*Facts:*   The applicant was dismissed from his employment in the Ministry of Co-operation and Development on the grounds that he had undertaken public finance work.

*Court:*   In determining the applicability of Art 6 to public servants, the Court should adopt a functional criterion based on the nature of the employee's duties and responsibilities. Accordingly, the Court would ascertain whether the applicant's post entailed direct or indirect participation in the exercise of the powers conferred by public law and duties designed to safeguard the general interests of the State or of other public authorities.

*UNITED KINGDOM CASES*

## R (on the application of B) v Head Teacher of Alperton Community School

## High Court, QBD [2001] EWHC Admin 229, [2001] ELR 359

*Facts:*   The claimants argued that the provisions governing schools exclusions and admissions appeals were in breach of Art 6 of the Convention as the panel members could be appointed, paid and trained by the Local Education Authority (LEA) or Governing Body, and were therefore not independent.

*Held:*   Following case-law from the Convention authorities it did not appear that the right to education could be characterised as a civil right such that Art 6 was applicable to disputes. A finding of misconduct amounting to a serious breach of discipline leading to exclusion clearly affects the reputation of a child, but the issue in the present case was that of whether an Independent Appeal Panel (IAP), dealing with an exclusion decision, determined the civil right to a reputation. The court held that Art 6(1) was not applicable to IAP exclusion proceedings as:

> '... the civil law right to the enjoyment of reputation is not infringed in the course of proceedings (a) not directly decisive of reputation and (b) where the potentiality for damage has been recognised by proper procedural protection ... [and] An IAP is concerned to determine whether reinstatement should be ordered. The governing provisions are contained within a statutory disciplinary code applicable to schools, having the object of regulating, in the public interest, the proper and efficient provision of education' (para 57).

An IAP does not determine a criminal charge. 'Although expulsion is significant it does not lead to a denial of access to the educational system, nor does it constitute the determination of a criminal charge' (para 58).

## (3)   CIVIL RIGHT MUST EXIST IN NATIONAL LAW

### Powell and Rayner v United Kingdom

### (1990) 12 EHRR 355

*Facts:*   The applicants owned properties near Heathrow Airport and complained of disturbance from aircraft noise. Section 76(1) of the Civil Aviation Act 1982 provided for a statutory bar to bringing an action in nuisance in respect of aircraft noise. They complained that their right to access to the courts in civil matters had been violated.

*Commission:*   The Commission rejected the complaint as manifestly ill-founded on the ground that the applicants had no civil right under English law to compensation for unreasonable noise nuisance caused by aircraft, other than that caused by aircraft flying in breach of aviation regulations.

*Court:*   The Court considered that as the applicants' grievance was directed at the limitation of liability in s 76(1), which did not bring into play Art 6(1), there was no violation of a Convention right. The effect of s 76(1) was to exclude liability in certain circumstances, with the result that the applicants could not claim to have a substantive right under English law to obtain relief for exposure to aircraft noise in those circumstances. Therefore, there was no civil right recognised under domestic law to attract the application of Art 6(1).

*LIMITATIONS ON CIVIL RIGHTS*

### Fayed v United Kingdom

### (1994) 18 EHRR 393

*Facts:*   The three applicants were brothers who acquired ownership of the House of Fraser. Prior to the takeover, the applicants took steps to promote their reputation in the press, which led to acceptance of their bona fide status in government circles. This was later considered to be crucial to their acquisition of the company. The government appointed two inspectors to investigate the takeover and a report was published which was unfavourable to the applicants. The brothers complained that the report had determined their civil right to honour and reputation and had denied them effective access to a court in determination of this civil right.

*Commission:*   The Commission considered that the inspectors' role was investigative rather than determinative and would only constitute evidence of the inspectors' opinion in any proceedings. It would be for the courts to determine the actual facts and legal consequences. Thus, although this type of inquiry could lead to civil or criminal proceedings being brought against the company, the report itself did not determine civil or criminal liability. Accordingly, Art 6(1) was not applicable to the proceedings before the inspectors because they did not determine the applicants' civil rights or obligations within the meaning of the Convention. It was noted that the right to enjoy a good reputation and the right to have determined before a tribunal the justification of attacks upon the reputation must be considered to be civil rights within the meaning of Art 6(1). Any civil claim in defamation brought against the inspectors would be met with a defence of privilege. The Commission considered that this defence amounted to a restriction on effective access to court. However, the Commission was of the opinion that safeguards of abuse of privilege could be enforced by way of judicial review. 'Whilst judicial review does not provide complete protection against possibly erroneous conclusions by Inspectors, it does, in the Commission's view provide sufficient guarantees for persons affected by the report, which are proportionate to the general public interest in inquiries of the present kind' (para 75). Thus, the applicants' inability to sue the inspectors in defamation did not impair the essence of the applicants' right to access to a court. The Commission expressed the opinion, by 10 votes to 3, that there was no violation of Art 6(1).

*Court:*   The Court held that the national authorities had not exceeded their margin of appreciation to limit the applicants' access to a court under Art 6(1). The Court had particular regard to the safeguards which existed in relation to the investigation and concluded that a reasonable relationship of proportionality existed between the freedom of reporting accorded to the inspectors and the legitimate aim pursued in the public interest. Article 6(1) had, therefore, not been violated.

*Note:*   The right to a court extends only to disputes over civil rights and obligations which can be said to be recognised under domestic law. The Convention enforcement bodies may not create, by way of interpretation of Art 6(1), a substantive civil right which has no legal basis in the State concerned. However, it would be inconsistent with the rule of law in a democratic society or with the basic principle underlying Art 6(1) if a State could, without restraint or control by the Convention enforcement bodies, remove from the jurisdiction of the courts a whole range of civil claims or confer immunities from civil liability on large groups or categories of persons.

## (4)   LIMITATIONS ON ACCESS TO A COURT

*FAILURE ON THE PART OF THE APPLICANT*

# Hennings v Germany

# (1993) 16 EHRR 83

*Facts:*   Following a dispute with a ticket collector, the applicant was questioned by the Railway Police and refused to make a statement. A report was submitted to the Public Prosecutor's office and a letter sent to the applicant informing him of the charge. The letter set out the procedure for payment of a fine in lieu of a formal prosecution. As no fine was paid by the due date, a penal order was issued which imposed a fine for the original offence and a further offence of dangerous assault which was not included in the original letter. The applicant was not at his home when the postman called to deliver the penal order. A note was left at the applicant's address informing him of the need to collect the penal notice and explaining that a failure to do so could have adverse legal consequences. The applicant failed to lodge an objection to the order within the one-week time-limit prescribed by national law, and a final judgment was entered. The applicant claimed he did not have a key to his letterbox and could not get access to his mail. An application to reinstate the proceedings was dismissed. The applicant complained that the short time-limit and the failure to serve him personally resulted in a violation of Art 6(1) in that he was denied effective access to a court.

*Commission:*   The right of access to a court is not absolute but can be subject to implied limitations. The Commission noted that procedural measures which provide for a waiver of the right to a full trial can have advantages for the accused, who may prefer not to be tried in public. However, it should be possible to revoke the waiver and bring about a normal trial. The Commission considered that strict conditions must govern the serving of the penal order. There must be provision for review if persons, through no fault of their own, fail to object to the order within the time-limit. In this case, the Commission noted that although the time-limit for filing an objection was rather short, national law provided for reinstitution whenever the person concerned was not at fault in failing to lodge an objection. In the absence of evidence of no fault, the Commission was not satisfied there had been a violation of Art 6(1).

*Court:*   The Court held that the authorities could not be held responsible for barring the applicant's access to a court because he failed to take necessary steps to ensure receipt of his mail. Accordingly, there was no violation of Art 6(1).

*LIMITATION PERIOD*

# Stubbings and Others v United Kingdom

# (1996) 23 EHRR 213

*Facts:*   The applicant alleged that her adoptive father and his son had sexually abused her over a period of years, which caused her to experience severe psychological problems. Several years later, following treatment by a psychiatrist, she realised that her problems might be connected to the earlier abusive behaviour. She commenced proceedings against her adoptive father and his son seeking damages for the assault. Her claim was dismissed by the national courts on the basis that it was time-barred under the Limitation Act 1980 which fixed a 6-year limitation period for claims based on breach of duty. She complained that her right to access to a court, guaranteed by Art 6, had been violated

*Court:* The Court referred to its case-law and confirmed that Art 6(1) gives the right to institute proceedings before a court in civil matters, but that this right was subject to limitations. States enjoyed a margin of appreciation, but must ensure that any limitation did not unduly restrict or reduce the right of access to a court, and the limitation must pursue a legitimate aim and be proportionate. Limitation periods served the legitimate aim of ensuring legal certainty and finality, which gave a measure of protection to defendants from old claims which might be difficult to defend. In the opinion of the Court, a 6-year limitation period was not unduly short. It was proportionate to the legitimate aim. In this case, the applicant had had 6 years from her eighteenth birthday to commence her claim. Accordingly, the Court was satisfied that the very essence of the applicant's right of access to a court was not impaired and there had been no violation of the Convention.

## Luisa Diamantina Romero de Ibanez and Roberto Guillermo Rojas v United Kingdom

Application No 58692/00, unreported

*Facts:* The applicants were the parents of Argentinean conscripts killed as a result of the sinking of the *General Belgrano* in May 1982. They claimed that the decision to torpedo a battleship during the Falklands conflict in 1982 amounted to a violation of their sons' right to life.

*Court:* The Court held that proceedings in Argentina, which ended in March 2000, did not constitute domestic proceedings within the meaning of the Convention, which requires that applications must be submitted within 6 months of a 'final decision'. In the absence of a decision of a court in the United Kingdom, the relevant date was the date of the incident itself which was in 1982. Accordingly, the Court found this application inadmissible on the basis that it had been submitted out of time.

## COMPETING PUBLIC INTEREST CONSIDERATIONS

## Tinnelly and McElduff v United Kingdom

(1998) 27 EHRR 249

*Facts:* Two firms tendering for public works contracts in Northern Ireland had both had bids rejected after submitting the lowest tenders. Following an appeal by the first firm to the Fair Employment Agency for Northern Ireland (FEA), the Secretary of State for Northern Ireland issued certificates under s 42 of the Fair Employment (Northern Ireland) Act 1976, to the effect that the decision not to grant the contracts was 'an act done for the purpose of safeguarding national security or the protection of public safety and order'. The FEA brought an action for judicial review of the certificates, and the Fair Employment Commission was called upon to make a ruling on the basis of a certificate issued in respect of the other case. In the first case, the Secretary of State issued a public interest immunity certificate preventing discovery of documents sought by the plaintiff. In the second case, the applicants withdrew their challenge to the Secretary of State's decision, having been told that the s 42 certificate was determinative of the issue and that their case would be rejected. The applicants argued that the issue of certificates that were conclusive blocked their access to courts, and denied them the right to a fair trial.

*Court:* The Convention could not be displaced by the ipse dixit of the executive, even if national security considerations constituted a highly material aspect of the case. Further, the government had not demonstrated to the Court that it would be impossible to modify the proceedings in such a way as to better balance the interests of the applicants and national security.

## PUBLIC POLICY

# Osman v United Kingdom
## [1999] 1 FLR 193

*Facts:* The husband of the first applicant was shot and killed, and the second applicant shot and seriously wounded, by his former teacher who had formed a disturbing attachment to him. Following a number of attacks on the applicants' property, complaints were made to the police. The teacher eventually pleaded guilty to charges of manslaughter on grounds of diminished responsibility. The applicants began a civil action in negligence against the police which was struck out on the ground that the statement of claim disclosed no reasonable cause of action. Relying on the case of *Hill v Chief Constable of West Yorkshire* [1988] 2 All ER 238, the Court of Appeal held that no action could be taken against the police for negligence in the investigation of crime for reasons of public policy.

*Court:* The applicants complained, inter alia, that the decision of the Court of Appeal to dismiss their action for negligence against the police for reasons of public policy amounted to a restriction on their right of access to a court. The Court found that the failure to permit the applicants' action to proceed to trial was a disproportionate restriction on the right of access to a court and amounted to a violation of Art 6. The ruling in *Hill* amounted to the grant of immunity to the police for their acts and omission during the investigation and suppression of crime. The Court held that:

> 'it must be open to a domestic court to have regard to the presence of other public interest considerations which pull in the opposite direction to the application of the rule. Failing this, there will be no distinction made between degrees of negligence or of harm suffered or any consideration of the justice of a particular case.'

# Clunis v United Kingdom

## [2001] HRCD 987

*Facts:* The applicant claimed that a refusal to consider his civil claim on public policy grounds without any examination of the merits denied him access to a court. He had been convicted of manslaughter on the grounds of diminished responsibility and detained under the Mental Health Act 1983. At the time of the killing, he was receiving treatment for a serious psychiatric illness and was under the care of the local health authority. Following the publication of an official report into the incident which seriously criticised his treatment and care, he brought an action in negligence against the responsible authorities. The Court of Appeal found that his case at common law was barred on public policy grounds and did not accept that Parliament, in enacting the after-care provisions of the Mental Health Act 1983, intended that a local authority should be exposed to liability. This matter has been communicated to the government under Arts 6, 8 and 13.

# Devenney v United Kingdom

## (2002) 35 EHRR 24

*Facts:* The applicant argued that the issue of a certificate under s 42 of the Fair Employment (Northern Ireland) Act 1976 amounted to a disproportionate restriction on his right of access to a court. Having been dismissed from employment as a waiter in a Belfast hotel, the applicant lodged a complaint with the Fair Employment Tribunal submitting that he had been unlawfully discriminated against on the grounds of religious belief or political opinion. On presentation of a s 42 certificate issued by the Secretary of State for Northern Ireland, the tribunal concluded that it had no jurisdiction to consider the applicant's complaints in relation to his dismissal and the manner of his dismissal. The issue of a s 42 certificate was considered to be conclusive proof that dismissal was necessary to protect the public or to safeguard national security, which meant that there could be no independent scrutiny to determine whether the applicant was justified in his claim that he had been unfairly dismissed.

*Court:* Observing that the right to institute civil proceedings is not absolute and may in some circumstances be subject to limitations, the Court emphasised that any restriction on access to a court must be justified. Although security considerations in respect of employees in public buildings could legitimately result in limitations on the right of access to a court, it was necessary to establish that the severity of the restriction imposed on the applicant was justified. The Court noted that in *Tinnelly and McElduff v United Kingdom* (1998) 27 EHRR 249, it reached the conclusion that issuing a s 42 certificate effectively amounted to a removal by the executive of the court's jurisdiction. The situation in Northern Ireland did not necessarily rule out the introduction of special judicial procedures which would meet the Art 6(1) requirements of independence and impartiality. The appointment of an independent adjudicator would increase public confidence. In this case, the Court was not persuaded that the government had identified any new elements in this case which would persuade it to depart from its conclusion in *Tinnelly*. Accordingly, issuing a s 42 certificate amounted to a disproportionate restriction on the applicant's right of access to a court.

# Devlin v United Kingdom
## (2002) 34 EHRR 43

*Facts:*   The applicant, a Catholic and a member of the Irish National Foresters, was refused employment as an administrative assistant in the Northern Ireland Civil Service on national security grounds. He complained that the issue of a certificate under s 42 of the Fair Employment (Northern Ireland) Act 1976 preventing him taking his case to an employment tribunal amounted to a disproportionate restriction on his right of access to a court.

*Court:*   In finding for the applicant, the Court noted that there was no independent scrutiny of the facts which led to the issue of the s 42 certificate, and no evidence was ever presented as to why the applicant was considered a security risk. The severity of the restriction imposed by the s 42 certificate was tantamount to the removal of the court's jurisdiction by executive ipse dixit which was not mitigated by other available mechanisms of complaint. Accordingly, the Court unanimously held that in the present case the restriction on the applicant's right to a court was disproportionate and in breach of Art 6.

## STATE IMMUNITY

# Al-Adsani v United Kingdom
## (2002) 34 EHRR 11
# Fogerty v United Kingdom
## (2002) 34 EHRR 12
# McElhinney v Ireland
## (2002) 34 EHRR 13

*Facts:*   The applicants claimed that the doctrine of State immunity acted to prevent them from pursuing claims in domestic courts. Alleging that he had been tortured in Kuwait by agents and officers of the Government of Kuwait, the applicant in *Al-Adsani* brought proceedings for compensation in the English courts. The High Court ordered that his claim be struck out on the ground that the State Immunity Act 1978 granted immunity to foreign governments for acts committed outside their jurisdiction. The applicant in *Fogerty* claimed that an attempt to bring proceedings against her former employer, the US government, was frustrated by the principle of State immunity, and in *McElhinney* an action for damages against a British soldier and the British government was set aside by the Irish High Court on the ground that the applicant was not entitled to bring an action against a member of a foreign sovereign government.

*Court:*   Refusing to accept the government's submission that these claims had no legal basis in domestic law since the doctrine of State immunity extinguishes substantive rights, the Court observed that State immunity should not be seen as qualifying a substantive right, but as a procedural bar on a national court's power to determine the right. In considering whether these restrictions on access to a court were compatible with Art 6, the Court was required to determine whether any limitation was in pursuit of a legitimate aim and was proportionate to the aim pursued. Observing that sovereign immunity is a rule of international law developed from the principle that one State shall not be subject to the jurisdiction of another State, the Court was satisfied that granting sovereign immunity in civil proceedings pursues the legitimate aim of complying with international law to promote and good relations between States through the respect of another State's sovereignty. In assessing whether the restrictions were proportionate to this aim, the Court referred to the Vienna Convention on the Law of Treaties which requires that the Convention should, so far as is possible, be interpreted in harmony with other rules of international law, including those relating to the grant of State immunity. Accordingly, measures reflecting generally recognised rules of international law could not in principle be regarded as imposing disproportionate restrictions on the right of access to a court.

## 3.2  ACCESS TO LEGAL ADVICE

### Murray v United Kingdom

### (1996) 22 EHRR 29

*Facts:*  The applicant, who lived in Northern Ireland, complained, inter alia, that he was denied access to a solicitor after arrest. He was arrested and detained under the United Kingdom Prevention of Terrorism (Temporary Provisions) Act 1989 for allegedly aiding and abetting false imprisonment of a Provisional Irish Republican Army informer. The applicant was cautioned according to the terms of Art 3 of the Criminal Evidence (Northern Ireland) Order, SI 1988/1987 (NI 20), which provided for inferences to be drawn from a failure to mention facts when questioned. He refused to answer questions and indicated that he wished to consult a solicitor. In finding the applicant guilty, the judge indicated that he had drawn strong inferences from the fact that he had failed to answer police questions and had refused to testify.

*Commission:*  The applicant's rights of defence were adversely affected by the restrictions on his access to a solicitor. These restrictions were not in conformity with his right to a fair trial under Art 6(1) and his right to legal assistance under Art 6(3)(c).

*Court:*  In accordance with its usual approach, the Court declined to give an abstract analysis of the problem and confined itself to the facts of the case. Although the right to legal advice was not set out explicitly in the Convention, in some circumstances Art 6 requires that the accused be allowed access to a lawyer during the preliminary stages of an investigation. The Court was of the view that the scheme contained in the 1988 Order was such that it was of paramount importance for the rights of the defence that an accused had access to a lawyer at the initial stages of the police interrogation. Thus, denying the applicant access to a lawyer at a point where his defence rights could well be irretrievably prejudiced amounted to a violation of Art 6.

# Brennan v United Kingdom

## (2002) 34 EHRR 18

*Facts:* The applicant complained that the circumstances under which he was questioned violated his right to a fair trial. Having been arrested in connection with terrorist offences, the applicant was denied access to a solicitor during the initial period in police custody and was not allowed to have his solicitor present during police interviews, or to see his solicitor in private. He argued that the use at trial of damaging admissions made prior to receiving legal advice deprived him of the right to a fair trial.

*Court:* Refusing to speculate as to whether the outcome of the applicant's trial would have been any different if he had been allowed to consult his solicitor in private, the Court observed that the applicant did not make any incriminating admissions during interviews conducted in the absence of a solicitor. Further, no inferences were drawn from any statements or omissions made during the initial interviews. However, the presence of an officer during the applicant's first consultation with his solicitor did infringe his right to an effective exercise of his defence rights. Although finding no reason to doubt the good faith of the police in insisting that a police officer remain during the legal consultation, the Court found no compelling reason for the imposition of this restriction. Accordingly, there was a violation of Art 6.

## 3.3 LEGAL AID

### (1) FREE REPRESENTATION

# Pakelli v Federal Republic of Germany

## (1983) 6 EHRR 1

*Facts:* The applicant appealed against his conviction for offences under the Narcotics Act. The lawyer who represented him at trial was unable to represent him at the appeal because he had previously represented the applicant's accomplice. The applicant was unable to pay for the services of another lawyer and could not return to Germany to represent himself. The respondent government disputed that the applicant was indigent and submitted that Art 6(3)(c) did not require the free provision of legal representation when the applicant was able to represent himself. He complained that the refusal by the authorities to appoint another lawyer amounted to a violation of Art 6(3)(c).

*Commission:* The Commission considered that the personal appearance of the applicant would not have compensated for the absence of his lawyer. Even if the applicant had been able to return to Germany, without the services of a legal practitioner he could not address the complicated legal issues. It expressed the unanimous opinion that the applicant had been the victim of a violation of the Convention.

*Court:* The Court was satisfied that the applicant could not pay for a lawyer. It held that an indigent person charged with a criminal offence is entitled under the Convention to free legal representation when the interests of justice so require. Accordingly, there was a violation of Art 6(3)(c).

# McVicar v United Kingdom

## (2002) 35 EHRR 22

*Facts:* The applicant, a journalist, complained that the unavailability of legal aid in defamation proceedings operated to deprive him of a fair trial. Following the publication of an article suggesting that the athlete Linford Christie regularly used performance-enhancing drugs, an action for defamation was brought against the journalist, the editor and the publishing company. Due to his inability to obtain legal aid or to pay legal fees, the journalist was required to represent himself for the greater part of the proceedings. In addition, he claimed that the exclusion of evidence at trial, the requirement that he bear the burden of proving that allegations made in the article were true, the order for costs against him and an injunction restricting future publication of the allegations breached his right to freedom of expression, which is guaranteed by Art 10.

*Court:* The Court recalled that in order to comply with fair trial guarantees set out in Art 6(1), which include the right of effective access to a court and the right to present an effective defence, Contracting States must on occasion provide legal assistance. However, whether compliance with this provision requires access to free legal representation will depend upon the specific circumstances of the case. While acknowledging the physical and emotional strain resulting from defending a High Court action of this type, which attracted intense media attention, the Court observed that the applicant was a well-educated journalist capable of formulating a cogent argument. The Court was satisfied that the rules relating to the exclusion of evidence were clear and unambiguous and should have been understood by the applicant. Further, the outcome of a libel action 'turned on the simple question of whether or not the applicant was able to show on the balance of probabilities that the allegations at issue were substantially true' (para 55). Thus, the Court did not accept that the law of defamation was sufficiently complex to require a person in the applicant's position to need legal advice. Consequently, the inability of the applicant to claim legal aid did not prevent him from effectively presenting his defence and did not render the proceedings unfair. Given the gravity of the allegations, the Court considered the requirement that the applicant prove that they were substantially true on the balance of probabilities, and the granting of an injunction, amounted to a justified restriction on his freedom of expression under Art 10(2).

## (2) FACTORS TO BE CONSIDERED WHEN AWARDING LEGAL AID

### *COMPLEXITY OF LEGAL ISSUES*

# Granger v United Kingdom

## (1990) 12 EHRR 469

*Facts:* The Supreme Court Legal Aid Committee of the Law Society of Scotland refused to grant the applicant legal aid to appeal against his conviction for perjury on the basis that there appeared to be no substantial grounds for an appeal. There was no provision for this decision to be reconsidered. The refusal of legal aid precluded the instruction of counsel and because solicitors have no right of audience in the High Court of Justiciary, the applicant represented himself. His appeal was unanimously rejected. He complained that there had been a violation of his right to legal assistance as provided by Art 6(3)(c).

*Court:*   The Court considered that the sole issue in this case was whether the interests of justice required that the applicant be given free assistance. This must be determined in the light of the case as a whole. It noted that at some stage during the appeal it became apparent that one of the grounds of appeal raised an issue of complexity and importance. When this situation arose, the authorities that have the overall responsibility for ensuring the fair conduct of the proceedings should have been able to reconsider the refusal of legal aid. The Court considered that it would have been in the interests of justice for free legal assistance to be given to the applicant when the legal complexity became apparent. Accordingly, the applicant's right had been infringed.

## Duyonov v United Kingdom
## Application No 36670/97, unreported

*Facts:*   The applicants' complaint related to the absence of legal aid for proceedings before the Privy Council. Having decided to leave Georgia to seek political asylum, they arranged and paid for travel to Canada. However, they were put ashore in Gibraltar whereupon they promptly surrendered to the immigration authorities and applied for asylum. The Governor of Gibraltar issued an order under s 59(1) of the Immigration Control Ordinance for their removal from Gibraltar and ordered their detention pending removal. Following a series of appeals, the applicants' request for legal aid to appeal to the Privy Council was rejected on the ground that legal aid was not available for these proceedings. Noting that cases which came before the Privy Council generally involved complex matters of law, the Chief Justice was of the opinion that legislation which denied the applicants legal assistance to present their appeal failed to conform to the obligations imposed by the Convention. Following a friendly settlement in which the UK government agreed to pay the applicants £5000 to cover pecuniary and non-pecuniary damage and costs, the case was struck out of the list.

### RISK OF LOSS OF LIBERTY

## Benham v United Kingdom
## (1996) 22 EHRR 293

*Facts:*   The applicant failed to pay his community charge and was required to appear before the court for an inquiry into the reasons for his failure to pay and an assessment of his means. The magistrates found that his failure to pay was due to culpable neglect and issued a warrant for his committal to prison. He complained that a failure to provide him with legal representation infringed his rights under the Convention. Although the magistrates had a discretion to appoint a solicitor to appear for him, he was not entitled to free legal representation as of right.

*Court:* Where the applicant's liberty was at stake, it was in the interests of justice to provide him with legal representation. In addition, this case involved complex issues of law. Although the applicant had access to legal advice prior to the hearing, the failure to provide him with legal representation amounted to a violation of Art 6(3)(c).

## 3.4   FAIR TRIAL

### (1)   ADEQUATE INFORMATION

## Chichlian and Ekindjian v France
## (1989) 13 EHRR 553

*Facts:* The applicants were charged with offences relating to the Customs Code and 'infringement of the legislation and the regulations governing financial relations with foreign countries'. Although the CFI acquitted them, the authorities appealed successfully and they received a suspended term of imprisonment. They stated that they had no knowledge of the customs authorities' appeal until the hearing and complained that they did not have adequate time and facilities to prepare their defence and that the authorities failed to inform them promptly of the nature and cause of the accusations against them.

*Commission:* The Commission expressed the unanimous opinion that there had been a breach of Art 6(3)(c).

*Court:* Taking account of the friendly settlement reached between the respondent government and the applicants, the Court did not consider the issue further. However, the Court noted that it was open to it to disregard the settlement for reasons of public policy.

## Steel v United Kingdom
## (1999) 28 EHRR 603

*Facts:* The applicants were arrested and charged with conduct likely to cause a breach of the peace. They all complained, inter alia, that they had not been given sufficient details of the allegations against them.

*Commission:* The Commission considered that there had been no violation in respect of Art 6(3)(c).

*Court:* The Court considered that the charge sheets given to the applicants contained sufficient information for the purposes of Art 6(3)(c). Accordingly, there had been no breach of this provision.

## Mattoccia v Italy
## [2001] EHRLR 89

*Facts:* The applicant was convicted of rape. The official notification of the offence stated that 'he forced R. who is mentally handicapped to have sexual intercourse with him, in Rome, in November 1985'. No further details were added. He complained that the charge brought against him was too vague and imprecise in that the time and place of the offence were not specified. Further, essential information was repeatedly contradicted and amended during the course of the trial.

*Court:* Recalling that Art 6(3) represents particular aspects of the right to fair trial, the Court noted the need for the accused to be promptly informed of relevant facts. In criminal matters the provision of detailed information concerning the factual and legal basis of the charges is an essential prerequisite of a fair trial. While the amount of detail will vary from case to case, the adequacy of information must be assessed in the light of the Convention, which confers on everyone the right to have adequate time and facilities for the preparation of their defence. The Court was satisfied that in this case the prosecuting authorities did not convey to the applicant all the available material. While the Court acknowledged that rape trials raise very sensitive issues and that cases involving the very young or mentally handicapped often cause prosecuting authorities and the courts serious evidential difficulties, it considered that in this case the defence was confronted with exceptional difficulties. The information provided pre-trial was sufficiently vague to deprive the applicant of an opportunity to defend himself in a practical and effective manner. Accordingly, the Court found a violation of Art 6(3)(b).

## Zoon v The Netherlands
### Application No 29202/95, unreported

*Facts:* The applicant complained that an abridged judgment of the CFI provided insufficient information to decide whether to appeal. For example, it did not list the items of evidence which formed the basis of the conviction. In order to obtain the fully reasoned judgment, the applicant needed to lodge an appeal. This would expose him to the possibility that the Court of Appeal might impose a higher sentence. The respondent government submitted that in order to meet the requirement that a copy of the judgment be made available within 14 days following the close of the trial, it was common practice to provide an abridged version.

*Court:* The Court declined to express a general view of the practice followed in the Netherlands and confined itself to the facts of this case. Noting that in Dutch criminal procedure an appeal involves a rehearing of the case and is not directed against the judgment of the lower court, the Court was satisfied that defence rights were not unduly affected by the absence of a complete judgment. Accordingly, there had been no violation of Art 6(3)(b).

## (2)   CONDUCT OF THE JUDGE
### Kraska v Switzerland
### (1994) 18 EHRR 188

*Facts:* The applicant was prosecuted for practising medicine without authorisation. Although he was acquitted on the basis that the indictment was defective, a subsequent request for authorisation was refused and he appealed against this decision. A member of the Federal Court allegedly expressed a view on the applicant's appeal without having had the opportunity to examine the case file. The judge indicated that he wanted to read the entire public law appeal statement but could not do so because of time constraints. The applicant complained that his right to a fair trial had been violated.

*Commission:* In the Commission's opinion a party is not effectively heard where a judge participates in the case without having acquainted himself with all the material which he regards as relevant to the outcome of the case. Accordingly, the applicant did not receive a fair trial in the determination of his civil rights within the meaning of Art 6(1).

*Court:* The Court was required to decide whether the contested proceedings, considered as a whole, were fair within the meaning of the Convention. It noted that the effect of Art 6(1) 'is, inter alia, to place the "tribunal" under a duty to conduct a proper examination of the submissions, arguments and evidence adduced by the parties, without prejudice to its assessment of whether they are relevant to its decision' (para 30). The Court has stressed on many occasions that it is important that proceedings are seen to be fair. However, in this case the Court was satisfied that there was no evidence that the members of the tribunal failed to examine the appeal with due care before making their decision. Thus, there was no violation of Art 6(1).

# CG v United Kingdom
## (2002) 34 EHRR 31

*Facts:* The applicant complained that excessive, unjustified intervention by the trial judge disturbed defence counsel's concentration, diverted the jury's attention and prevented her from presenting her version of events coherently. Further, any unfairness caused by judicial misconduct during the trial was not remedied by the appeal proceedings. Following her conviction for theft, the applicant appealed on the grounds that the judge had consistently interrupted and hectored defence counsel both during cross-examination of a key prosecution witness and during the applicant's examination-in-chief, making it impossible for her to give evidence in a coherent manner. While acknowledging that the trial judge did 'enter the arena' more frequently than could be justified, sometimes without justification, and that the summing up was short, on occasion inaccurate, and 'somewhat laconic', the Court of Appeal did not consider the conviction to be unsafe for the purposes of the relevant statutory provisions and dismissed the appeal.

*Court:* Convention jurisprudence establishes that in determining issues of fairness for the purposes of Art 6, the Court is required to consider the proceedings as a whole, including any decisions made by the appellate courts. Considerable weight is given to the assessment by the national appellate court which is well placed to determine whether the domestic proceedings were unfair. Although the judge's interruptions occurred at a critical stage of the proceedings, at no point did the judge prevent defence counsel from developing his line of argument and he was permitted to make a closing speech to the jury without unjustified interruption. While observing that judicial intervention in this case was excessive and undesirable, the Court considered that the proceedings did not breach the principle of fairness guaranteed by Art 6. Further, although the Court of Appeal looked into whether the conviction was unsafe rather than unfair, the Court was satisfied that the trial judge's conduct was sufficiently scrutinised during the appeal process for the purposes of Art 6.

In a dissenting opinion, Judge Loucaides considered it relevant to note the respective roles of judges in common-law and civil-law systems, and to bear in mind the inequality between counsel and the presiding judge. This judge did not bear the responsibility of carrying out an investigation into the facts and although he was permitted to seek clarification on specific matters, the questioning of witnesses fell within the competence of counsel for the parties. In taking on the task of questioning key witnesses, the judge exceeded his role and hampered the task of the defence to the extent that there had been a breach of the principle of a fair hearing. Further, the unfairness of the trial was not remedied by the appellate court which concerned itself with the safety of the conviction rather than the issue of unfairness.

## UNITED KINGDOM CASES

## Director General of Fair Trading v Proprietary Association of Great Britain and Proprietary Articles Trade Association

### Court of Appeal, [2001] UKCLR 550

*Facts:* In the process of a trial brought on the basis of the Resale Prices Act 1976 before the Restrictive Practices Court (RPC) it emerged that one of the non-judicial members of the court, Dr Rowlatt, had, during the course of the case, approached the firm Frontier Economics seeking employment. Frontier Economics were engaged by one of the parties in the case to provide expert evidence to the court. The appellants argued that Dr Rowlatt should recuse herself from further participation in the trial. The RPC judged that the test to be applied was that of whether the appellants had 'legitimate grounds for fearing a lack of impartiality, however slight the justification', and found that that was not the case here.

*Held:* The court first examined the leading case of *R v Gough* [1993] AC 646, noting that the case, which had attempted to resolve some of the former conflict in the law, had not met with universal approval. It was felt that the approach taken was out of step with the approach taken in Scotland, as well as a number of Commonwealth countries, and possibly the jurisprudence of the Convention. Following the entry into force of the Human Rights Act 1998 the Court therefore took the opportunity to review the position. The Court held that:

> 'a modest adjustment of the test in *Gough* is called for, which makes it plain that it is, in effect, no different from the test applied in most of the Commonwealth and in Scotland. The court must first ascertain all the circumstances which have a bearing on the suggestion that the judge was biased. It must then ask whether those circumstances would lead to a fair-minded and informed observer to conclude that there was a real possibility, or a real danger, the two being the same, that the tribunal was biased' (para 85).

## (3)  EFFECTIVE AND ACCESSIBLE PROCEDURE
## McGinley and Egan v United Kingdom
## (1998) 27 EHRR 1

*Facts:*   The applicants had both been refused a war pension in respect of medical conditions allegedly caused by their exposure to high levels of radiation. They complained, inter alia, that by withholding documents which would have assisted them in ascertaining whether there was any link between their health problems and exposure to radiation, the authorities denied them the right to a fair hearing.

*Court:*   The Court considered that when a government engages in hazardous activities which could adversely affect the health of those involved, the State is required to establish an 'effective and accessible procedure' enabling applicants to 'seek all relevant and appropriate information'. However, in this case, r 6 of the Pension Appeals Tribunals Rules 1981 provided such a procedure which the applicants failed to use, and accordingly there was no infringement of Art 6.

## (4)  IMPARTIALITY AND INDEPENDENCE
## Lauko v Slovakia
## [1998] HRCD 838
## Kadubec v Slovakia
## (2001) 33 EHRR 41

*Facts:*   In both cases, the applicants were found to have committed offences against public order under the Minor Offences Act 1990 by the Local Office, an administrative body charged with carrying out local State administration under the control of the government. Following unsuccessful appeals to the District Office, the applicants brought their complaints to the Constitutional Court. In *Lauko*, the applicant's complaint that the administrative bodies had not been impartial was dismissed as manifestly ill-founded, and his request for a review of its decision was rejected. In *Kadubec*, the court rejected the applicant's complaint on the basis that he failed to instruct a lawyer to represent him in the proceedings as required by the Constitutional Court Act.

*Court:*   The Court was called upon to consider, inter alia, whether the prosecution and punishment of minor offences could be assigned to administrative bodies without infringing the applicants' right to a fair hearing. It was noted that the offences for which the applicants were convicted were not characterised under domestic law as 'criminal'. Although this is of relevance in determining whether Art 6(1) is applicable, the Court is required to examine the nature of the offence and the severity of the penalty incurred. In both cases, the Court found that the nature of the legal provision infringed and the deterrent and punitive purpose of the penalty imposed was sufficient to show that the offences were criminal in nature. The Court then moved on to consider whether the applicants had received a fair hearing before an independent tribunal. In order to determine whether an administrative body was independent of the executive, the Court considered it was necessary to 'examine the manner of appointment of its members and the duration of their term of office, the existence of guarantees against outside pressures and the question whether the body presents an appearance of independence'. Having taken these factors into consideration, the Court was satisfied that the Local and District Offices could not be considered to be independent of the executive within the meaning of Art 6(1). Administrative bodies could adjudicate in minor matters without infringing Art 6(1) provided there was an opportunity to challenge the decision before an independent and impartial tribunal. In this case, the applicants were unable to have the decisions of the Local and District Offices reviewed and thus had been denied the right to a fair hearing.

## O'Hara v United Kingdom
## (2002) 34 EHRR 32

*Facts:* The applicant, a prominent member of Sinn Fein, was arrested under the Prevention of Terrorism Act (Temporary Provisions) Act 1984 and detained for questioning for 6 days. He was eventually released without charge. Under s 12(1)(b) of this Act, police officers were empowered to arrest without warrant persons suspected of involvement in the commission, preparation or instigation of acts of terrorism. This provision also allowed for an extended period of detention. The arresting officer gave evidence that, prior to arrest, he had been given information by a senior officer that the applicant was suspected of having committed a terrorist offence. O'Hara complained that his arrest and detention were not based on reasonable suspicion, as required by Art 5, but were motivated by malice on the part of the police. Furthermore, he argued that the police justified abuse of their power of arrest by hiding behind references to anonymous informants.

*Court:* The Court noted that 'the exigencies of dealing with terrorist crime cannot justify stretching the notion of "reasonableness" to the point where the safeguard secured by Article 5(1)(c) is impaired' (para 35). It was incumbent upon the respondent government to satisfy the Court that an arrest was based upon reasonable suspicion. Although accepting that suspected terrorists could be detained on the basis of information not disclosed to the suspect, or produced in court on the ground of public interest, the Court observed that it was necessary for the respondent government to furnish sufficient information to establish that an arrest was based on reasonable suspicion. However, the standard imposed by Art 5(1)(c) does not require the police to have sufficient evidence to bring charges at the time of arrest. Indeed, the purpose of detention under this provision was to confirm or dispel the suspicion that formed the basis for the arrest. The Court noted that in proceedings before the domestic court, the applicant did not challenge the good faith of the arresting officers and did not suggest that the arrest was an arbitrary abuse of power by the police. He did not ask questions as to what was said at the briefing nor did he make any requests for disclosure in relation to documentary evidence. Being satisfied that the level of suspicion was sufficient to satisfy the requirements of Art 5, and that it was based on specific information, the Court was unanimous in holding that there was no violation of Art 5(1). Furthermore, the Court found that the approach taken by the domestic courts did not remove the accountability of the police for arbitrary arrest nor conferred on the police any impunity with regard to arrests conducted on the basis of confidential information. However, with regard to the length of time spent in detention, the Court was unanimous in finding a violation. Having regard to the case-law of the Convention, the Court noted that a period of detention in excess of 4 days was not compatible with the requirement of prompt judicial control. Furthermore, because his detention was in accordance with domestic law the applicant had no enforceable right to compensation, which was in breach of Art 5(5).

## McGonnell v United Kingdom
## (2000) 30 EHRR 289

*Facts:* The case arose out of a long-running planning dispute in Guernsey, during the course of which various applications made by the applicant were dismissed, and the applicant was further convicted by the magistrates' court for changing the use of a shed without permission. A final appeal was dismissed by the Royal Court, comprising the Bailiff and seven jurats, in 1995. The Bailiff, a professional judge, is the senior judge of the Royal Court, and has various constitutional functions in the government of Guernsey. In 1993 a challenge had been made to the participation of the Bailiff as a judge in the Royal Court. The Court of Appeal found that the Bailiff could properly discharge both his judicial and constitutional functions (*Bordeaux Vineries Ltd v States Board of Administration* (1993) Guernsey). The applicant rested his case on Art 6.

*Court:* In the present case the concepts of independence and objective impartiality were closely linked. There was no suggestion that the Bailiff was subjectively prejudiced or biased when he heard the applicant's planning appeal, but the applicant did argue that the Bailiff was subjectively biased or prejudiced. The Bailiff had had personal involvement with the planning matters at the heart of the applicant's case on two occasions, and had also played more than a merely ceremonial role in carrying out his constitutional functions. The Court found that 'any direct involvement in the passage of legislation, or of executive rules, is likely to be sufficient to cast doubt on the judicial impartiality of a person subsequently called on to determine a dispute over whether reasons exist to permit a variation from the wording of the legislation or rules at issue' (para 55). It followed in the present case, therefore, that there had been a breach of Art 6.

## De Haan v The Netherlands
## (1998) 26 EHRR 417

*Facts:* The applicant worked at a dry cleaners in the Netherlands, and in 1989 developed physical complaints which caused her to take sick-leave for months at a time. She was in receipt of sick-pay from the Occupational Association for the Chemical Industry (OACI) under the Health Insurance Act. In 1990 the applicant was informed that according to information given to the OACI she was no longer unfit for work and would therefore not receive any further payments. An appeal was lodged before the Appeals Tribunal under the Presidency of Judge S. The appeal was dismissed and a further appeal was made. Judge S was the President of the Chamber of the Appeals Tribunal constituted to hear the further appeal, and did not withdraw from the case. A further, unsuccessful, appeal to the Central Appeals Tribunal relied on Art 6, the argument being made that the Appeals Tribunal had lacked objective impartiality.

*Court:*   It was not contested that Art 6 was applicable. The decisive feature of the case was that Judge S presided over a tribunal called upon to decide on an objection against a decision for which he himself was responsible. It was also considered to be relevant that the tribunal was composed of a professional judge assisted by two lay judges. The Court found, against this background, that the applicant's fears regarding bias were objectively justified, and held that Art 6 had been breached.

## Kingsley v United Kingdom

## (2001) 33 EHRR 13

*Facts:*   This case concerned the impartiality of a statutory body which had made an adverse finding in relation to the applicant prior to the proceedings against him. The applicant was chief executive of a company which owned six casinos in London. The Gaming Board of Great Britain revoked his certificate to hold a management position in the gaming industry. He alleged that panel members were already committed publicly and privately to views which made a fair hearing impossible. This was compounded by the fact that the Board did not provide the applicant with reasons for its decision. His application for judicial review of the decision claimed, inter alia, that the Board was biased against him. The High Court applied a test based on whether there was a real danger of injustice as a result of bias. In concluding that there was no real risk, the court noted that even if there had been unconscious bias the doctrine of necessity applied because the Board was the only body with the jurisdiction to make a decision. In refusing the applicant's request for leave to appeal, the Court of Appeal confirmed the High Court's application of the doctrine of necessity.

*Court:*   In holding unanimously that the applicant had been denied the right to a fair hearing, the Court considered that the Gaming Board did not present the necessary appearance of impartiality and that the subsequent judicial review failed to remedy this defect.

## Jordan (Stephen) v United Kingdom

## (2001) 31 EHRR 6

*Facts:*   The applicant complained that his pre-trial detention and the preliminary stages of the court-martial proceedings against him violated Art 5. He argued that his commanding officer and other officers with decision-making power as regards his detention were too closely connected to the prosecution of the case against him to be regarded as independent.

*Court:*   The Court was of the opinion that, at the relevant time, the provisions governing the prosecution and pre-trial detention of accused members of the armed forces violated Art 5. The power and position of the applicant's commanding officer were such that he could not be regarded as independent of the parties.

## Morris v United Kingdom

## (2002) 34 EHRR 52

*Facts:* The applicant brought a series of complaints arising from the general structure of the court-martial system in the UK. In particular, he submitted that both a court and a 'reviewing authority' which comprised of army officers hearing disciplinary charges brought by the army could not constitute an impartial and independent tribunal for the purposes of Art 6(1). He argued that his commanding and defending officer, the Higher Authority, the Army Court Service, the prosecuting authority and the officers who formed the tribunal were all controlled by the Adjutant General, who was himself directly subordinate to the Defence Council. In addition, he complained about the conduct of the defending officer in his case and the fact that he had been denied access to free legal advice. The government argued that changes introduced by the Armed Forces Act 1996 rendered the court-martial system compatible with the Convention.

*Court:* The Court noted that the 1996 Act had introduced a range of safeguards into the court-martial system. For example, the posts of convening officer and confirming officer had been abolished, and their original roles separated. The presence of the legally qualified civilian judge advocate acted as an important procedural guarantee as did the rules regarding eligibility for selection to a court martial. Further, the function of adjudicator and prosecutor had been separated. Under the 1996 Act, the initial decision whether to bring a prosecution is taken by a senior officer, the Higher Authority, who makes the decision whether a case sent by the commanding officer should be dealt with summarily, referred to the prosecuting authority, or not pursued. The role of prosecutor is performed by the Army Prosecuting Authority which applies similar criteria to those used by the Crown Prosecution Service in civilian cases when making the decision to prosecute. The judge advocate is a civilian lawyer appointed by the Lord Chancellor. Decisions are reached by a majority vote and reasons for sentence are given in open court. There is a right of appeal against conviction and sentence. Accordingly, having examined the new procedures, the Court found no substance in the applicant's general complaint in relation to the relationship between the Defence Council and the Adjutant General. However, the two serving officers who sat on the applicant's court martial had not been appointed for any fixed period of time and, although the ad hoc nature of their appointment did not by itself render the court martial incompatible with the independence requirements of Art 6, it increased the need for the presence of safeguards against outside pressures. The Court considered there were insufficient safeguards to exclude the risk of pressure being brought to bear on these officers. Noting that these officers were relatively junior and remained subject to army discipline, the Court emphasised that there was no statutory bar or other rules which protected them from army influence. The Court considered that the 'reviewing authority', which is a non-judicial body with the power to quash the applicant's conviction, did not meet the requirements of Art 6(1). Further, in this case these flaws were not corrected by the applicant's subsequent appeal to the Court Martial Appeal

Court. Thus the applicant's misgivings about the independence of the court martial had been objectively justified and the Court was satisfied that in respect of some of the applicant's complaints there had been a violation of Art 6(1). However, the Court found that the requirement that an individual pay a contribution towards his legal costs did not violate Art 6(3).

## (5)   TRIAL WITHIN A REASONABLE TIME

### Partington v Greece

### (1998) unreported

*Facts:*   The applicant, a British national, was sentenced to death by the Criminal Court of Thessaloniki following his conviction for murder. On appeal, his sentence was commuted to life imprisonment and he was transferred to the UK under the Council of Europe Convention on the Transfer of Sentenced Persons. He complained that the length of the proceedings, which lasted almost 8 years, was unreasonable and infringed his rights under Art 6.

*Court:*   In assessing the reasonableness of the length of proceedings, the Court took account of the complexity of the case and the conduct of the applicant. Although this case involved some complexity, having regard to the serious nature of the offence and the applicant's grounds of appeal which involved points of law, the Court found that the delay could not be justified. It was noted that, although the delay was caused, in part, by the conduct of the applicant, there were several periods of inexcusable inactivity by the Thessaloniki Court of Appeal. Given the importance of what was at stake for the applicant, it was not reasonable for him to be subjected to an excessive delay and accordingly there had been a breach of Art 6(1).

### Ferrantelli and Santangelo v Italy

### (1996) 23 EHRR 288

*Facts:*   The applicants were arrested on 13 February 1976 and committed for trial for murder on 23 January 1978. Following an allegation that the police had extracted confessions by force, the committal was annulled and the court ordered a new investigation. The accused were committed for trial on 11 March 1980 and acquitted on the basis of reasonable doubt on 10 February 1981. There followed a succession of appeals which ended on 8 January 1992 with a judgment from the Court of Cassation. They complained that the length of proceedings brought against them was excessive and infringed Art 6.

*Commission:*   The Commission expressed the unanimous opinion that there had been a violation in respect of the applicants' complaint.

*Court:*   The Court acknowledged that although the case was complex and each stage of the proceedings had progressed at 'a regular pace', the applicants had not been convicted with final effect until 16 years after their arrest, which was an excessive length of time and amounted to a violation of Art 6.

# IJL, GMR and AKP v United Kingdom
## (2001) 33 EHRR 11

*Facts:* The applicants had been convicted of offences relating to the acquisition of the Distillers Company by Guinness and jointly tried with the chairman of the company, Ernest Saunders. They complained that their right to a fair trial had been violated in a number of respects, namely: the use made at trial of transcripts of pre-trial interviews obtained under compulsion; the refusal by the prosecution to disclose documents relevant to their defence; improper collusion between the prosecution and other agencies and the unreasonable length of the criminal proceedings. Following the decision in *Saunders v United Kingdom* (1996) 23 EHRR 313, the government conceded that there had been a violation of Art 6(1) in respect of a similar complaint in relation to the use made of transcripts of interviews taken under statutory compulsion.

*Court:* Finding that the length of trial could be explained in terms of the considerable complexity of the case, the Court found no violation in relation to the alleged non-disclosure and delay. In *Saunders*, the Court considered that the use at trial of statements made to DTI inspectors under compulsory powers was a violation of the applicant's right against self-incrimination under Art 6 and saw no reason to reach a different conclusion in this case. However, noting that it was not within the Court's province to substitute its own assessment of the facts for that of the domestic court, and observing that the Court of Appeal had examined at length and rejected the allegations that there had been improper collusion, the Court took the view that co-operation between DTI inspectors and other agencies did not violate Art 6(1). While recalling that the right to adversarial trial requires that the prosecution and the defence must be given the opportunity to have knowledge of and comment upon evidence adduced by the other party, the Court observed that all the material relied on by the applicants was disclosed to them prior to proceedings in the Court of Appeal. The fact that the defence had access to all the relevant material before the final appeal was sufficient to remedy the initial failure to disclose and distinguished this case from *Rowe and Davis v United Kingdom* (2000) 30 EHRR 1.

# Dede and Others v Turkey
## Application No 32981/96, unreported

*Facts:* In 1981, the applicants were arrested and placed in custody, accused of belonging to an illegal organisation. Although released from custody, the applicants were still awaiting trial in December 1995. They complained that a period in excess of 14 years amounted to a breach of the right to trial within a reasonable time.

*Court:* The Court was unanimous in finding a violation of Art 6(1).

## (6)   DOUBLE JEOPARDY

### Fischer (Franz) v Austria

### [2001] HRCD 341

*Facts:*   The applicant was found guilty of a range of traffic offences relating to an incident in which a cyclist was killed, including the offence of driving while under the influence of alcohol. He was later convicted of causing death by negligence when intoxicated. He complained that this second conviction violated his right not to be tried or punished twice for an offence for which he had been convicted, which is guaranteed by Art 4 of the Seventh Protocol.

*Court:*   The Court was unanimous in finding a violation of this provision.

## (7)   JURY BIAS

### Remli v France

### (1996) 22 EHRR 253

*Facts:*   The applicant, a French citizen of Algerian origin, attempted to escape from prison and was charged, together with an accomplice, with the homicide of a guard. During the trial, a juror was overheard making a racist remark. The court refused to take formal note of the remark and the applicant was sentenced to life imprisonment. He claimed that he had not had a hearing by an impartial tribunal, that he had suffered discrimination on the ground of racial origin, and that he had no effective remedy in domestic law.

*Commission:*   The Commission considered that the only point at issue was any violation of Art 6(1). The applicant had argued that 'one cannot regard as impartial a court called upon to try two persons of a particular race, which includes in its number a person who has openly disclosed, before the hearing, that he is a racist'. The Commission agreed and found that sufficient doubt had been cast upon the court's impartiality to find a violation of Art 6(1).

*Court:*   In relation to the alleged violation of Art 6(1), the Court found that it was not necessary to prove that any racist remark had been made by a juror. The domestic court's failure to take note of the serious allegation that such a remark had been made was in itself a breach of Art 6(1). The accused's fear that his trial would not be impartial was objectively justified by the domestic court's dismissal of the allegation without even examining the evidence that the remark had been made.

'Article 6(1) of the Convention imposes an obligation on every national court to check whether, as constituted, it is an impartial tribunal within the meaning of that provision where, as in the present case, this is disputed on a ground which does not appear to be manifestly devoid of merit.' The domestic court had not made such a check, and so the applicant had no remedy in national law; hence there was a breach of Art 6(1). However, in relation to the claim of racial discrimination, the Court accepted the government's assertion that, since the applicant had not complained of racial discrimination in the national courts, he had not exhausted domestic remedies. Thus, the Court was unanimous in holding that there had been no violation of Art 14.

# Gregory v United Kingdom
## (1997) 25 EHRR 577

*Facts:* The applicant, who was black and a British citizen, was tried for robbery. During jury deliberations, a note was passed to the judge by the jury which stated: 'Jury showing racial overtones. One member to be excused'. The judge consulted prosecution and defence counsel and it is unclear whether defence counsel asked for the jury to be discharged. The jury was recalled and the judge gave a further direction that, inter alia, 'any thoughts or prejudices of one form or another, for or against anybody, must be put out of your minds . . . It is the evidence alone which decides the case'. The jury found the applicant guilty by a 10:2 majority. He sought leave to appeal against his prison sentence on the basis that the trial judge should have considered discharging at least one member of the jury on the basis of racial prejudice. The Court of Appeal interpreted the note as meaning that 'one member of the jury felt that there was a general overtone of racial comment which was unacceptable and not, as the applicant is suggesting, one member of the jury being so racially prejudiced as to be unable to give proper consideration to the matters before him'. Although the judge could have discharged any or all of the jury for bias, he would have needed evidence of actual bias which had a real danger of affecting the mind of the juror or jurors.

The applicant alleged violations of Arts 6 and 14. The Commission's opinion was that neither provision had been violated.

*Court:* Dealing first with the allegation that the applicant had been denied a fair trial, the Court stated that public confidence in the fairness of criminal proceedings is vital, and that impartiality of trials must be shown from both a subjective and an objective viewpoint. The trial judge's decision to redirect rather than discharge jurors had not been shown to be wrong, and the redirection was clear and forceful:

> 'While the guarantee of a fair trial may in certain circumstances require a judge to discharge a jury it must also be acknowledged that this may not always be the only means to achieve that aim. In circumstances such as those in issue, other safeguards, including a carefully worded redirection to the jury, may be sufficient.'

Thus there was no violation of Art 6(1). The applicant's second allegation was that the trial judge and appeal court had treated racial bias less seriously than they would have treated any other type of bias, citing cases where juries had been discharged for less serious allegations of bias. The Court, however, found that this allegation did not give rise to any separate issue under Art 14, and so there was no violation.

*Note:* This case demonstrates the common treatment of discrimination cases as falling to be discussed under another right or freedom. Article 14 is rarely discussed in its own right as a primary issue of a case. Judge Foighel gave a dissenting opinion in favour of finding a breach of Art 6(1) by reason of discrimination. He argued that:

> 'the members of the jury are given no advance warning on how they are to address an unexpected occurrence of racism within the jury . . . it is of the utmost importance that remedies should be in place to enable a trial judge to ensure that the decision of the jury is

not tainted with any objective suspicion of bias ... a speech from a judge – a redirection – cannot dispel racial prejudice within a jury, if such prejudice exists. The only safeguard which could have been offered by the trial judge in this case was to discharge part or the whole of the jury, or at least to have conducted a more probing enquiry into the effect of the note on the jury's deliberations.'

## Sander v United Kingdom
## (2001) 31 EHRR 44

*Facts:* The applicant complained that he had been denied a hearing before an impartial tribunal because there was subjective bias on the part of some jurors at his trial. Following a complaint by a member of the jury that other jurors had made openly racist remarks and jokes, the trial judge called the jury back into court to discuss the matter. One juror indirectly admitted that he had made comments which could be interpreted as racist. Having received assurances by the jury as a whole that they would reach a verdict solely according to the evidence and without racial bias, the judge rejected the defence application to discharge the jury.

*Court:* In finding for the applicant, the Court emphasised that it is fundamentally important that the courts inspire public confidence. This requires the tribunal to be both objectively and subjectively impartial. Emphasising that the eradication of racism must be seen as a common goal for all Contracting States, the Court considered the allegations made by the complainant to be a very serious matter. The Court found that the judge's warning to the jury and assurances given by jurors were insufficient to remedy the situation. Although discharging the jury is not always the only means to achieve a fair trial, there are situations where this is an appropriate course of action. In this case, the Court considered that the judge should have reacted in a 'more robust manner' to rule out doubt about the impartiality of the tribunal.

## 3.5   EVIDENCE

### (1)   ADMISSIBILITY OF EVIDENCE

## Schenk v Switzerland
## (1988) 13 EHRR 242

*Facts:* The applicant complained that the unauthorised recording of a private telephone conversation, and its subsequent use in evidence, violated his right to a fair trial. The Swiss government did not dispute that the recording was obtained unlawfully, but submitted that the public interest in establishing the truth in the matter of a serious criminal offence justified its use in evidence. It sought to distinguish between the case of prosecuting authorities using unlawful means to obtain evidence and the case of an unlawful act by an individual who hands over the evidence to the authorities.

*Commission:* The Commission considered that this complaint came within the scope of the concept of fair trial. It noted in this case that not all the rights of the defence had been disregarded and reached the conclusion, by 11 votes to 2, that there had been no violation of Art 6(1).

*Court:* Whilst Art 6 guarantees the right to a fair trial, it does not lay down any rules on the admissibility of evidence, which is primarily a matter for regulation under domestic national law. The majority of the Court held that it could not 'exclude as a matter of principle and in the abstract that unlawfully obtained evidence of the present kind may be admissible' (para 46). The function of the Court was to ascertain whether the trial as a whole was fair. The applicant had been given the opportunity to challenge the authenticity of the recording and to cross-examine the persons allegedly involved in the making of the recording. In arriving at its decision that the use of the recording did not deprive the applicant of a fair trial, the Court attached weight to the fact that it was not the only evidence on which the applicant's conviction was based.

*Note:* In a joint dissenting opinion, Judges Pettiti, Spielmann, De Meyer and Carrillo Salcedo considered that compliance with the law when obtaining evidence is not an abstract or formalistic requirement. 'No court can, without detriment to the proper administration of justice, rely on evidence which has been obtained not only by unfair means but, above all, unlawfully. If it does so, the trial cannot be fair within the meaning of the Convention' (p 269). Thus, in confining itself to the particular facts of the case, the Court had limited the scope of its judgment.

## *ADMISSIBILITY OF UNLAWFULLY OBTAINED EVIDENCE*

# Chinoy v United Kingdom

## (1998) unreported

*Facts:* The USA requested the applicant's extradition from the UK under the terms of an Extradition Treaty (United States of America (Extradition) Order 1976, SI 1976/2144). The evidence adduced by the US government included transcripts and tapes of telephone conversations recorded in France. Although the transcripts used in court related solely to business matters, recordings were made of conversations between the applicant and his family. The applicant submitted that the recordings were made without the knowledge of the French authorities, in breach of French sovereignty and without recourse to mutual legal assistance provisions. The English court refused to exercise its discretion to exclude the evidence under s 78 of the Police and Criminal Evidence Act 1984 (PACE). The applicant was committed to prison to await a warrant for his surrender. He complained that the use of unlawfully obtained recordings of telephone conversations violated his rights as guaranteed by Art 8. He also submitted that the unlawfulness of the transcripts tainted the lawfulness of his detention and amounted to a violation of Art 5.

*Commission:* Although there was conflicting evidence as to the lawfulness under French law of the recording of conversations relating to business matters, the Commission considered the application on the basis that the applicant's committal to prison was made on the basis of unlawfully obtained evidence. The issue with regard to Art 8 was limited to whether the *use* made of the recordings disclosed a lack of respect for the applicant's private and family life, his home or his correspondence. The Commission noted that the conversations were recorded without the consent of the UK authorities, and in open court reference was limited to conversations relating to business matters. Accordingly, in respect of Art 8, the Commission found this application to be manifestly ill-founded. The Convention contains no express or implied requirement that evidence obtained unlawfully under domestic law is inadmissible. The Commission considered whether the applicant's detention in this case could be considered arbitrary. There was no indication that the domestic court's decision to admit the transcripts breached national procedural and substantive rules. Accordingly, the decision to allow the prosecution to rely on unlawfully obtained evidence complied with national rules and could not be considered as arbitrary. Thus, the applicant's complaint that his detention was in breach of Art 5 was also manifestly ill-founded.

## Khan v United Kingdom
## (2001) 31 EHRR 45

*Facts:*    The applicant argued that a tape recording of a conversation acquired by the use of a listening device attached to a private house without the knowledge of the owners or occupiers was obtained in violation of his right to privacy. He also complained that the use at trial of evidence obtained in breach of a right guaranteed by the Convention was incompatible with the requirements of fairness guaranteed by Art 6. Following a refusal by the trial judge to exercise his discretion to exclude evidence of the tape recording, the applicant pleaded guilty to drug-related offences. In dismissing the appeal, the House of Lords held that there was no right to privacy in English law and at common law relevant evidence obtained irregularly was admissible, notwithstanding it having been obtained by the use of a covert listening device. The court went on to say that although evidence obtained in violation of a right guaranteed by the Convention was relevant to the exercise of the judge's discretion to exclude evidence under s 78 of PACE, it was not a determinative factor. Although their Lordships considered that the lack of a statutory system regulating the use of surveillance devices by the police was 'astonishing', they were not prepared to overrule the trial judge's decision on admissibility. The government accepted that the listening device did interfere with the applicant's right to privacy, but denied it amounted to a breach of Art 8 on the ground that the regulation of police surveillance operations met with the requirement that any interference must be in accordance with the law and necessary in a democratic society for the prevention of crime.

*Court:*    The Court noted that the phrase 'in accordance with law' refers not merely to compliance with domestic law, but requires that the domestic rules be compatible with the rule of law. In the context of intrusive police surveillance, domestic rules must provide protection against arbitrary interference with an individual's rights under Art 8. The Court was unanimous in finding that the Home Office Guidelines of 1984, the rules applicable at the relevant time, were neither legally binding nor sufficiently accessible to the public and were consequently inadequate to meet the requirements of Art 8. Although the applicant did not suggest that the requirement of fairness guaranteed by Art 6 necessitated the automatic exclusion of evidence obtained in breach of Art 8, he argued that a conviction obtained *solely* on the basis of evidence obtained in consequence of the unlawful acts of prosecuting authorities is contrary to the rule of law and incompatible with Art 6. In considering this issue, the Court stated that its primary function was to determine whether the applicant's trial as a whole was fair, and not to rule whether evidence of this type must, as a matter of principle, be excluded. Acknowledging that the tape recording was, in effect, the only evidence tendered for the prosecution, the Court considered it of relevance that there was no suggestion that this evidence was unreliable. Where there was no risk of unreliability, the need for the court to look for supporting evidence was less important. In rejecting the applicant's claim, the Court noted that he had had ample opportunity to challenge the authenticity of the recording and the domestic courts had a discretionary power under s 78 of PACE to exclude the evidence if they considered its admission would render the trial unfair. The applicant also claimed that if a breach of Art 8 did not satisfy the requirements of s 78 of PACE, then national law failed to provide an effective remedy to enforce the substance of the rights and freedoms guaranteed by the Convention. Considering this element of the applicant's claim related to the breach of Art 8, the Court noted that the criminal courts were called on to consider the admissibility of evidence and not to assess whether any interference with the applicant's right to privacy was in accordance with the law, and further had no power to grant relief. In holding that Art 13 had been violated, the Court rejected the government's submission that it was open to the applicant to lodge a complaint with the Police Complaints Authority. It noted the role played by the Secretary of State in appointing and dismissing members of this body, and considered the system failed to meet the required standard of independence to ensure protection against abuse of authority.

## PG and JH v United Kingdom
### [2001] HRCD 707

*Facts:* The complaint concerned the monitoring and recording of conversations by means of a covert listening device which was placed in the home of one of the applicants; the monitoring of calls made on the applicant's telephone; and the use of listening devices to obtain voice samples while the applicants were at a police station. In addition, the applicants complained that the non-disclosure of evidence relating to the authorisation of the listening device, the hearing of oral evidence by the judge in private, the use in evidence of information obtained from the listening device at the applicant's home, and the manner in which voice samples were obtained amounted to a violation of Art 6.

*Court:* The Court held unanimously that using a covert listening device to record conversations in the applicant's home was a violation of Art 8. Acknowledging that this case was similar to *Khan v United Kingdom* (2001) 31 EHRR 45, the majority of the Court was satisfied that the use in evidence of material obtained in this manner did not violate the right to a fair trial. Observing that the government accepted that police surveillance of the applicant's apartment was not in accordance with the law existing at the time, and noting that there was no statutory scheme to regulate the use of listening devices at the police station, the Court was satisfied that Art 8 had been violated on both occasions. However, the monitoring of telephone calls was considered to be necessary in a democratic society and thus did not violate Art 8. In rejecting the applicants' complaint in respect of non-disclosure, the Court observed that the entitlement to disclosure of relevant evidence is not an absolute right. In any criminal proceedings there may be competing interests, such as national security or the need to protect witnesses or keep secret police methods of criminal investigation. In this case the Court was satisfied that the defence was kept informed and allowed to participate as far as was possible without disclosing sensitive material; defence questions were put to the prosecution witness by the judge in chambers; non-disclosed evidence was not used as part of the prosecution case; and the need for disclosure was monitored by the judge throughout the proceedings. In further rejecting the applicants' submission that the use at trial of the taped evidence obtained in breach of Art 8 amounted to breach of fair trial rights, the Court observed that the tape recording of conversations was not the only evidence against the applicants: the prosecution called 45 witnesses and incriminating evidence was found at the address of one of the applicants and in the car which the applicants were driving. The applicants had been given the opportunity to challenge both the authenticity and the use of the tape. Further, the domestic court retained the discretionary power to exclude evidence if it formed the view that its admission would give rise to substantive unfairness. In rejecting the argument that the manner in which the voice samples were obtained infringed the privilege against self-incrimination, the Court observed that voice samples could be considered as akin to blood, hair or other physical or objective specimens used in forensic analysis to which this privilege did not apply.

## UNITED KINGDOM CASES

## Attorney General's Reference (No 3 of 1999)
### House of Lords, [2001] 2 WLR 56

*Facts:*　The prosecution relied solely upon DNA evidence which was considered by the trial judge to be inadmissible. Despite what the Court of Appeal later described as 'compelling evidence', the judge directed an acquittal.

*Held:*　There is no general principle that unlawfully obtained evidence is inadmissible either in Commonwealth jurisdictions or in Convention jurisprudence. However, their Lordships acknowledged that in some Commonwealth jurisdictions the discretion to exclude unfairly obtained evidence is wider than in England. The Canadian courts will exclude evidence obtained in breach of the Canadian Charter if its admission is likely to bring the administration of justice into disrepute. Australian courts recognise a judicial discretion in which the competing demands of the public interest in the prevention of crime must be weighed against fairness to the accused, and in New Zealand evidence obtained in breach of the Bill of Rights was subject to exceptions created by the overriding demands of justice. Any remedy for unlawfulness in England is to be found in s 78(1) of PACE. This provision permits courts to interpret the fairness of the proceedings as a wide concept which extends to the circumstances in which the evidence was obtained. Lord Hutton observed that in exercising the discretion under s 78, the interests of the victim and the public must be considered as well as the interests of the accused.

## (2)   DISCLOSURE OF EVIDENCE

# Edwards v United Kingdom

## (1992) 15 EHRR 417

*Facts:*   Following the applicant's conviction for robbery and burglary, a complaint was made about the conduct of the investigating officers. It became apparent during an internal police inquiry that the police had not made available to the defence certain items of evidence. The case was eventually referred to the Court of Appeal under the Criminal Appeal Act 1968. The prosecution refused a defence application for disclosure of the results of the inquiry on the grounds of public interest immunity. The defence did not challenge this decision and did not seek to cross-examine the investigating officers on their failure to disclose the evidence. Although the Court of Appeal was critical of the police officer's failure to disclose the evidence, it considered that the admission of this evidence at trial would not have altered the verdict.

*Court:*   The Court considered that for the purposes of Art 6(1), the prosecution was required to disclose all material evidence for or against the accused. The issue of procedural fairness requires the Court to assess the proceedings in their entirety, including the appeals process. In this case, the Court of Appeal consideration of the undisclosed evidence had rectified the defect and the Court held, by a majority of 7 votes to 2, that there was no violation of Art 6. In arriving at its decision, the Court noted that the applicant had failed to make use of procedures which would have enabled him to challenge the decision not to disclose the report of the inquiry and to cross-examine the police officers.

*Note:*   The Court did not consider whether there could be an exception to the principle of full prosecution disclosure on the grounds of public interest. In a dissenting opinion, Judge Pettiti took the view that public interest immunity could never justify non-disclosure of relevant evidence in criminal proceedings. He considered that procedural fairness required the court to have access to all the relevant evidence and not merely to provide the defence with a procedural mechanism to obtain it.

# Rowe and Davis v United Kingdom

## (2000) 30 EHRR 1

*Facts:*   The applicants complained that the withholding of relevant prosecution evidence on public interest grounds without informing the trial judge resulted in an infringement of their rights under Art 6(1). On appeal, counsel for the prosecution had sought an ex parte hearing on the matter of disclosure, or, if inter partes, requested that defence counsel undertake not to discuss what took place with either their instructing solicitor or the appellants. Defence counsel refused to give such an undertaking and the hearing proceeded ex parte. At the substantive appeal, before a differently constituted court, defence counsel was permitted to make submissions as to the factors weighing in favour of disclosure. However, having inspected the disputed documents, which were not shown to the defence, the court decided in favour of non-disclosure. Leave to appeal to the House of Lords was refused.

*Court:* In its judgment, the Court noted that its function was not to decide whether non-disclosure was strictly necessary since, as a general rule, it is for national courts to assess the evidence before them. Its task was to determine whether the proceedings complied with the requirements of adversarial proceedings, that there was equality of arms between prosecution and defence and that there existed adequate safeguards to protect the interests of the accused. Observing that Art 6(1) requires, in principle, that the prosecution should disclose all relevant evidence in their possession, in some cases it may be necessary to withhold certain evidence so as to preserve the fundamental rights of another. Thus the entitlement to disclosure of relevant evidence is not an absolute right; in any criminal proceedings there may be competing interests, such as national security or the need to protect witnesses or keep secret police methods of investigation which must be weighed against the rights of the defence. However, Art 6(1) limits restrictions on defence rights to measures which are strictly necessary and only where any difficulties caused to the defence were sufficiently counterbalanced by the procedures followed by the courts. The Court considered that a procedure whereby the prosecution assesses whether it is in the public interest to keep information secret without any scrutiny of the evidence by the trial judge could not comply with the applicants' rights under the Convention. The trial judge is in the best position to decide whether the undisclosed evidence will cause the defence insurmountable difficulties. In this case, the proceedings before the Court of Appeal failed to rectify the unfairness caused at trial. Accordingly, the Court held that there was a violation of Art 6.

# Jasper v United Kingdom

## (2000) 30 EHRR 441

# Fitt v United Kingdom

## (2000) 30 EHRR 441

*Facts:* The applicants complained that a failure to disclose relevant evidence on the grounds of public interest immunity undermined their right to a fair trial. In both cases the prosecution had made an ex parte application to the judge for an order authorising non-disclosure of evidence. However, in these cases the defence was notified that an application was to be made, permitted to make representations to the trial judge and outline the case for the defence. Furthermore, in the case of *Fitt*, the defence was informed of the nature of the information and on one occasion provided with an edited summary of it. In both cases, the trial judge decided in favour of non-disclosure.

*Court:* Equality of arms between the prosecution and the defence is recognised as lying at the heart of the right to a fair trial. In *Fitt*, the Court said at paras 44–45:

> 'It is a fundamental aspect of the right to a fair trial that criminal proceedings, including the elements of such proceedings which relate to procedure, should be adversarial and that there should be equality of arms between the prosecution and the defence. The right to an adversarial trial means in a criminal case, that both prosecution and the defence must be given the opportunity to have knowledge of and comment on the observations filed and the evidence adduced by the other party (see the *Brandstetter v Austria* judgment of 28 August

1991, Series A no. 211, paragraphs 66, 67). In addition Article 6 paragraph 1 requires, as indeed does English law, that the prosecution authorities should disclose to the defence all material evidence in their possession for or against the accused (see [*Edwards v United Kingdom* judgment of 16 December 1992, Series A no. 247-B,] paragraph 36). However, as the applicant recognised the entitlement to disclosure is not an absolute right. In any criminal proceedings there may be competing national interests, such as national security or the need to protect witnesses at risk of reprisals or keep secret police methods of investigation of crime, which must be weighed against the rights of the accused (see, for example, the *Doorson v The Netherlands* judgment of 26 March 1996, *Reports of judgments and Decisions 1996–11*, paragraph 70). In some cases it may be necessary to withhold certain evidence from the defence so as to preserve the fundamental rights of another individual or to safeguard an important interest. However, only such measures restricting the rights of the defence which are strictly necessary are permissible under Article 6 paragraph 1 (see *Van Mechelen and others v The Netherlands* judgment of 23 April 1997, Reports 1997–111, paragraph 58). Moreover, in order to ensure that the accused receives a fair trial, any difficulties caused to the defence by a limitation on its rights must be sufficiently counterbalanced by the procedures followed by the judicial authorities.'

In these cases, the Court was satisfied that the defence had been permitted to participate in the decision-making process 'as far as was possible' without revealing the material which the prosecution sought not to disclose. The fact that the need for disclosure was at all times being assessed by the trial judge provided an important safeguard in that it was the judge's duty throughout the trial to monitor the fairness or otherwise of the evidence being withheld. Accordingly, the Court was satisfied in both cases that the domestic trial court had applied standards which were in conformity with Art 6 and held by 9 votes to 8 that there had not been a violation of the Convention.

# IJL, GMR and AKP v United Kingdom
# (2001) 33 EHRR 11

*Facts:* See 3.4(5).

*Court:* Finding that the length of trial could be explained in terms of the considerable complexity of the case, the Court found no violation in relation to the alleged non-disclosure and delay. In *Saunders,* the Court considered that the use at trial of statements made to DTI inspectors under compulsory powers was a violation of the applicant's right against self-incrimination under Art 6 and saw no reason to reach a different conclusion in this case. However, noting that it was not within the Court's province to substitute its own assessment of the facts for that of the domestic court, and observing that the Court of Appeal had examined at length and rejected the allegations that there had been improper collusion, the Court took the view that co-operation between DTI inspectors and other agencies did not violate Art 6(1). While recalling that the right to adversarial trial requires that the prosecution and the defence must be given the opportunity to have knowledge of and comment upon evidence adduced by the other party, the Court observed that all the material relied on by the applicants was disclosed to them prior to proceedings in the Court of Appeal. The fact that the defence had access to all the relevant material before the final appeal was sufficient to remedy the initial failure to disclose and distinguished this case from *Rowe and Davis v United Kingdom* (2000) 30 EHRR 1.

# Atlan v United Kingdom
## (2002) 34 EHRR 33

*Facts:* At their trial for importing cocaine, the applicants claimed that a man known as Rudi Steiner, whom they believed to be a Customs and Excise informer, planted a suitcase containing drugs on them. However, there was no evidence to connect the suitcase with Steiner and under cross-examination customs officers repeatedly refused to accept or deny the use of an informer. Throughout the proceedings the prosecution denied possessing any undisclosed material. Four years after their conviction, the applicants discovered new evidence relating to Steiner. Having been informed of this discovery, the prosecution revealed to the defence that, contrary to earlier statements, unused material did exist in evidence. At an ex parte hearing, the Court of Appeal ruled that the interests of justice did not require disclosure of this evidence and dismissed the application for leave to appeal. The applicants complained that prosecution failure to lay evidence before the trial judge which would have allowed him to rule on the question of disclosure deprived them of the right to a fair trial. The government did not seek to deny that the repeated denials by the prosecution relating to unused material, and their failure to inform the trial judge of the truth, was unfair and could not be consistent with the requirements of Art 6. However, the issue before the Court was whether the ex parte procedure before the Court of Appeal was sufficient to remedy this unfairness.

*Court:* Referring to the judgment in the case of *Rowe and Davis v United Kingdom* (2000) 30 EHRR 1, the Court considered that the trial judge is best placed to decide whether or not the non-disclosure of public interest immunity material would be unduly prejudicial to the defence. Although the nature of the undisclosed evidence was never revealed, the Court considered that the sequence of events raised a strong suspicion that it concerned Steiner, his relationship with Customs and Excise, and his role in the investigation. The Court was unanimous in holding that the failure by the prosecution to place this evidence before the judge amounted to a violation of Art 6.

# Garcia Alva v Germany
## Application No 23541/94, judgment of 13 February 2001, unreported

*Facts:* The applicant was a Peruvian national living in Berlin. In 1993 preliminary investigations were initiated against the applicant, who was suspected of being engaged in drug trafficking. He was questioned by police, and an authority was issued for his arrest. The applicant's defence counsel applied for permission to have access to the criminal files, but full access was denied on the grounds that to grant access would be to endanger ongoing investigations. Later the continued detention of the applicant was ordered, with the relevant court relying in part on statements made by K. Neither the applicant nor his counsel were given access to the record of K's questioning. An appeal by the applicant was dismissed and he relied unsuccessfully on Art 5(4) of the Convention. In July 1994 the applicant was convicted of aiding and abetting drug trafficking and was sentenced to 4 years' imprisonment.

*Court:* 'Equality of arms is not ensured if counsel is denied access to those documents in the investigation file which are essential in order effectively to challenge the lawfulness of his client's detention' (para 39). The contents of the contested file appeared to have played a key role in the decision of the District Court to extend the period in which the applicant was detained on remand. While some information was given to the applicant's counsel, and while the Court recognised the need for criminal investigations to be conducted efficiently, the partial disclosure of information in the present case was not sufficient to ensure observance with the requirements of Art 5. The Court therefore found that Art 5 had been violated.

*Note:* The cases of *Schops v Germany* (Application No 25116/94) and *Lietzow v Germany* (Application No 24479/94) dealt with the same issue, albeit on different facts, and judgment in the same terms was given on the same date.

## UNITED KINGDOM CASES

# R v Stratford Justices, ex parte Imbert

## Divisional Court, [1999] 2 Cr App R 276

*Facts:* See 2.1(2).

*Held:* Although emphasising that the jurisprudence of the Strasbourg Court did not lay down 'any rules with regard to, and certainly has not made mandatory, pre-trial disclosure of the order contended for in the present application' (at p 286), Buxton LJ considered that in all but exceptional cases it was desirable that prosecution witness statements be served on the defence. In dismissing the application, Buxton LJ noted that Art 6 does not provide an absolute right to pre-trial disclosure but provides the right to a fair trial. He observed that the Court 'strongly warns that criminal proceedings must be assessed as a whole, and stands against the contention advanced in our case that failure to give disclosure at a particular stage of those proceedings must necessarily render them unfair' (at p 289).

## (3) DISCLOSURE OF DOCUMENTS

# Bendenoun v France

# (1994) 18 EHRR 54

*Facts:* The applicant, a French national resident in Switzerland, dealt in precious stones and works of art. As a result of administrative proceedings, he was fined for customs and tax irregularities and was also sentenced to imprisonment by the French criminal courts for tax evasion. He appealed against the fine and against the conviction on the basis that the whole of the customs file had not been disclosed. He alleged that the failure to provide him with access to his file prevented him from having access to all the facts on which the case against him was based. Accordingly, he complained that this prevented him from identifying facts which could have assisted in his defence and was an infringement of the adversary principle.

*Commission:* The Commission considered that since the applicant did not have access to the whole of the file, which was available to the opposing side, he was deprived of the opportunity to contest matters in it or to make use of the information in it to support his case. This placed him at a disadvantage *vis-à-vis* the tax authorities which resulted in a violation of Art 6(1).

*Court:* The Court considered that the administrative proceedings were criminal in nature notwithstanding their classification as non-criminal in domestic law. However, during the administrative proceedings the authorities had relied only on documents which had been disclosed to the applicant and the applicant and his lawyer had had access to the relevant information in the criminal proceedings. He was aware of the content of most of the documents he claimed had not been disclosed. Accordingly, the Court considered that the failure to produce documents did not infringe the rights of the defence or the principle of equality of arms.

## Foucher v France
## (1997) 25 EHRR 234

*Facts:* The applicant was summoned to appear before a police court on a minor criminal charge and decided to conduct his own defence. The public prosecutor denied his request for access to the criminal dossier on the basis that the documents contained in it could not be released to a private individual. He was eventually sentenced to a fine of FF 3000. He complained that the refusal amounted to a violation of defence rights and was an infringement of the principle of equality of arms.

*Court:* One of the features of a fair trial was that each party must be afforded a reasonable opportunity to present his case in conditions that did not place him at a disadvantage to his opponent. The Court noted that under the terms of the Convention and domestic law, the accused was entitled to conduct his own defence. The nature of the evidence in this case required the applicant to have access to his case file and to obtain a copy of the documents contained within it in order to challenge the evidence against him. As a consequence of the prosecutor's refusal to release the material, the applicant had been unable to prepare adequately his defence. Accordingly, he had not been afforded equality of arms as required by Art 6.

## Kuopila v Finland
## (2001) 33 EHRR 25

*Facts:* The applicant was a Finnish art dealer who acquired for resale a painting attributed to a famous Finnish artist. An allegation was made by the original owner of the painting, and it appeared following a police investigation that the painting had been sold but that the moneys received had not been passed on to the original owner. The applicant was charged with various offences, including fraud, under the Criminal Code. The applicant was subsequently convicted of all the charges brought against her. The applicant had during the course of the proceedings questioned the authenticity of the painting, and when an appeal was made to the Court of Appeal she requested that it have the painting examined. A report prepared for the Court suggested that the painting was not authentic, but the Court considered that this was irrelevant to the criminal charges. The Court of Appeal did not let the applicant know about the report, and upheld the conviction without inviting the applicant to make further comments. A further appeal failed, and the applicant served 20 months in prison. A complaint to the Parliamentary Ombudsman resulted in a critical statement relating to the failure of the Court of Appeal to disclose the existence of the report.

*Court:* The applicant invoked Art 6, and the Court noted that 'under the principle of equality of arms, as a feature of the wider concept of a fair trial, each party must be afforded a reasonable opportunity to present one's case in conditions that do not place him at a disadvantage *vis-à-vis* his opponent' (para 37). The prosecutor was able to present his comments on the report to the Court, but the applicant was not, and 'procedural fairness required that the applicant too should have been given an opportunity to assess the relevance and weight of the supplementary police report' (para 38). The Court was unanimous in finding that Art 6 had been breached.

## 3.6   EXAMINATION OF WITNESSES

### Unterpertinger v Austria

### (1986) 13 EHRR 175

*Facts:* The applicant complained that his rights to a fair trial had been violated in that he had been denied the opportunity to question witnesses. He claimed that his criminal conviction was based exclusively on the basis of statements made to the police by his former wife and stepdaughter which had been read out at the hearing. They asserted their right under Art 152(1)(1) of the Austrian Code of Criminal Procedure to refuse to testify on the basis that they were close relatives of the accused. The applicant was thus prevented from questioning them on their statements. Although he was able to comment on the statements during the hearing, the court refused to admit evidence which challenged the credibility of the witnesses.

*Court:* Whilst the reading of the statements was not in itself inconsistent with Art 6, the use made of them as evidence must not infringe the rights of the defence. The Court was satisfied that the applicant's conviction was based mainly on the written statements of the witnesses and that the lack of opportunity to challenge their evidence significantly curtailed his right to a fair trial.

## (1)   USE OF WRITTEN STATEMENTS

### Kostovski v The Netherlands

### (1989) 12 EHRR 434

*Facts:* The applicant was convicted of robbery on the basis of statements taken from anonymous witnesses. The statements had been taken by the police and heard by an examining magistrate in the absence of the applicant and his lawyer. Neither of the witnesses appeared before the trial court. The government accepted that the conviction was based 'to a decisive extent' on the statements of these witnesses. The applicant complained that he was denied the opportunity to question directly the witnesses against him and thus was prevented from challenging their evidence.

*Court:* Although the admissibility of evidence is primarily a matter for regulation by domestic law, the Court was required to consider whether the use made of the evidence infringed the applicant's right to a fair trial. In principle, all evidence should be produced in the presence of the accused at a public hearing. However, the use of written statements obtained at the pre-trial stage is not in itself inconsistent with Art 6 provided the rights of the defence are respected. These rights require that the accused be given an adequate and proper opportunity to challenge and question a witness against him at some stage in the proceedings. At no stage during these proceedings could the witnesses be questioned directly by or on behalf of the applicant. Furthermore, the trial court did not have an opportunity to observe their demeanour under questioning and was thus prevented from forming an impression of their reliability. The difficulties facing the defence were compounded by the fact that the anonymity of the witnesses was preserved. The Court held that in the circumstances of this case, the applicant was denied the right to a fair trial.

## FAILURE TO PROVIDE AN OPPORTUNITY TO CONFRONT WITNESS AND THE RIGHTS OF DEFENCE

### Saidi v France

### (1994) 17 EHRR 251

*Facts:*   The applicant maintained that his conviction for drug offences was based solely on identification evidence. There was no additional prosecution evidence. He complained that the refusal of the judicial authorities to organise a confrontation with the prosecution witnesses who had identified him, deprived him of a fair trial.

*Commission:*   The Commission noted that the conviction was based on statements obtained prior to trial and that these statements were from persons implicated in drug-related activities. It expressed the opinion, by 13 votes to 1, that there had been a violation of Art 6(1) and (3)(d).

*Court:*   The Court expressed concern that neither at the stage of the investigation nor during the trial was the applicant able to examine or have examined the witnesses who identified him. It was of the opinion that in this case the lack of any opportunity to confront the prosecution witnesses deprived the applicant of a fair trial. Although it noted the difficulties involved in securing evidence in relation to offences of drug trafficking, these considerations did not restrict the rights of the defence guaranteed by Art 6. Accordingly, the Court was unanimous in holding that there had been a violation of Art 6(1) and (3)(d).

## (2)   ANONYMOUS WITNESSES

### Kostovski v The Netherlands

### (1989) 12 EHRR 434

*Facts:*   The applicant was convicted of robbery on the basis of statements taken from anonymous witnesses. The applicant complained that he was denied the opportunity to question directly the witnesses against him and thus was prevented from challenging their evidence.

*Commission:* The Commission expressed the unanimous opinion that there had been a violation of Art 6(3)(d).

*Court:* Although, in principle, all the evidence must be produced in the presence of the accused at a public hearing, the use of written statements as evidence is not in itself inconsistent with the right to a fair trial, provided the rights of the defence are respected. These rights require that the accused be given an adequate and proper opportunity to challenge and question a witness against him at some stage in the proceedings. The difficulties facing the defence were compounded by the fact that the anonymity of the witnesses was preserved. The Court held that in the circumstances of this case the limitation placed on the rights of the defence was irreconcilable with the guarantees contained in Art 6 and, accordingly, the applicant had been denied the right to a fair trial.

# Doorson v The Netherlands
# (1996) 22 EHRR 330

*Facts:* The applicant complained that reliance by the trial court on the evidence of anonymous witnesses violated Art 6(1). He had been identified by six anonymous witnesses and was eventually convicted of drug trafficking offences. During the course of the preliminary investigation, the judge heard the evidence of two anonymous witnesses in the absence of the applicant's lawyer. His case was referred back to the investigating judge by the appeal court. Although counsel for the applicant was given the opportunity to question the witnesses, they were permitted to remain anonymous. The investigating judge was aware of the identity of the witnesses and the Court of Appeal noted that it treated their evidence with the necessary caution and circumspection.

*Court:* The admissibility of evidence is primarily a matter for regulation by domestic law and as a general rule it is for domestic courts to assess the evidence before them. Although using the evidence of anonymous witnesses was not necessarily incompatible with Art 6, the Court acknowledged that it presented the defence with additional difficulties. Although a conviction should not be based solely on the statements of anonymous witnesses, the Court's task was not to give a ruling as to whether statements of witnesses were properly admitted as evidence, but rather to ascertain whether the proceedings as a whole were fair. The principles of a fair trial required the interests of the defence to be balanced against those of witnesses called to testify. Evidence obtained from witnesses under conditions in which the rights of the defence cannot be secured to the extent normally required by the Convention must be treated with extreme care. The Court was satisfied that in the circumstances of this case there was no violation of Art 6.

# Visser v The Netherlands
# [2002] HRCD 65

*Facts:* The applicant's original conviction was based on a statement taken by the police from an anonymous witness. Domestic legislation permitted the identity of a witness to be withheld from the defence, provided the investigating judge examined the witness and was satisfied that the witness was reliable and anonymity was justified. The Dutch Supreme Court quashed the conviction on the ground that the manner in which the facts had been established did not comply with domestic law. The case was referred back to the Court of Appeal and an investigating judge was instructed to interview the witness under oath. In interview, the witness was asked to confirm the statement made to the police in 1988 in which s/he had given reasons for remaining anonymous. Defence counsel was invited to submit questions to the judge in advance of the hearing but heard the interview from a different room. The court reinstated the applicant's conviction. The applicant complained that the use in evidence of a statement taken from an anonymous witness unacceptably restricted defence rights and violated his right to a fair trial

*Court:*     Strasbourg jurisprudence establishes that the use of statements made by anonymous witnesses will not necessarily violate the Convention. Nevertheless, evidence obtained from witnesses under conditions in which the rights of the defence could not be protected to the extent normally required by the Convention must be treated with extreme caution. When assessing whether the procedures followed in the questioning of an anonymous witness were sufficient to counterbalance the difficulties caused to the defence, due weight must be given to the extent to which the anonymous testimony had been decisive in convicting the applicant. The greater the weight of the evidence, the more important it is to ensure that procedures are in place to offset any difficulties caused to the defence. In examining whether the use of anonymous testimony could be justified in this case, the Court noted that the investigating judge's report did not indicate how he had assessed whether it was necessary for the witness to remain anonymous and the Court of Appeal did not conduct an examination into whether there were serious and well-founded reasons for the continued anonymity of the witness. In these circumstances the Court could not be satisfied that the interests of the witness in remaining anonymous could justify limiting the rights of the defence. Accordingly, the proceedings as a whole were considered to be unfair and in violation of Art 6. In the light of this decision, the Court did not proceed to examine whether the procedures put in place by the judicial authorities would sufficiently offset any difficulties facing the defence.

## UNITED KINGDOM CASES

# HM Advocate v Smith (Peter Thompson)
## High Court of Justiciary, 2000 SCCR 910

*Facts:*     An application to allow police officers to give their evidence anonymously was allowed.

*Held:*     Although allowing witnesses to remain anonymous was not necessarily incompatible with the right to a fair trial, the High Court of Justiciary held that anonymity of police officers could be justified only where it was strictly necessary to ensure operational effectiveness and where the court was satisfied that defence rights had been respected.

*POLICE WITNESSES*

# Van Mechelen and Others v The Netherlands

## (1997) 25 EHRR 647

*Facts:* The applicants were convicted of attempted manslaughter and robbery. They complained that their convictions were based primarily upon the evidence of anonymous witnesses.

*Commission:* The Commission noted that Art 6 does not grant the accused an unlimited right to attendance of witnesses in court; it is the responsibility of domestic courts to decide whether it is necessary or advisable to hear a witness. The applicants were suspected of having committed serious offences involving violence, including the attempted murder of police officers. An independent and impartial investigating judge had heard the unidentified witnesses and there was ample opportunity to challenge the evidence. In addition, the applicants' convictions did not solely rest on the statements made by the unidentified witnesses. The Commission was of the opinion that, on balance, the proceedings against the applicants could not be regarded as unfair and accordingly there was no violation of Art 6.

*Court:* The Court drew a distinction between police officers as witnesses and disinterested witnesses or victims, in that police officers are frequently required to give evidence in court. Accordingly, the use of anonymous police officers as witnesses should be resorted to only in exceptional circumstances. Less restrictive measures should be used wherever possible. In this case, the Court was not satisfied that it was necessary to resort to such extreme limitations on the right of the accused to have the evidence against them given in their presence. The Court was of the opinion that there had been a violation of Art 6.

# 3.7   EXECUTION OF JUDGMENTS

## Hornsby v Greece

## (1997) 24 EHRR 250

*Facts:* The applicants were graduates from the UK. The second applicant applied to the Greek Minister of Education for authorisation to establish a private school in Greece. She was refused on the grounds that authorisation could only be granted to Greek nationals. A complaint was lodged with the European Commission alleging a breach of the EC Treaty of Rome 1957. This was upheld by the ECJ. A subsequent attempt to obtain authorisation was refused on the original grounds, although the authorities indicated that the law was under review. The applicants appealed to the Supreme Administrative Court which set aside the decision. However, further applications were also turned down or ignored. The applicants complained that the refusal to comply with the Supreme Court's decision resulted in a violation of Art 6(1).

*Commission:* The Convention provides guarantees against actions by State authorities which could thwart the protection afforded by the courts. The right to access to a court would be rendered illusory and theoretical if the authorities could refuse to comply with court decisions in disputes involving the determination of civil rights and obligations. The Commission was of the opinion that there had been a violation of Art 6(1) in that the applicants had been deprived of effective judicial protection.

*Court:* The Court noted that it would be inconceivable that Art 6 should describe in detail procedural guarantees without protecting the implementation of judicial decisions. Execution of a judgment should be regarded as an integral part of the 'trial' for the purposes of Art 6. The protection afforded by Art 6 extended to the execution of judgments as well as access to a court and the conduct of proceedings. Failure by the authorities to take the necessary steps to comply with an enforceable judicial decision deprived the applicants of any effective protection guaranteed by Art 6(1). Accordingly, there was a violation of the Convention.

## 3.8   NON-INTERFERENCE WITH CONVENTION PROCESSES

### Petra v Romania

### (2001) 33 EHRR 5

*Facts:* The applicant was serving a prison sentence for murder in Romania, and his wife wrote to the Commission to complain that he had not had a fair trial. Subsequent correspondence between the applicant and the Commission was interfered with by the prison authorities. His correspondence was routinely opened, and many letters sent by both the applicant to the Commission, and the Commission to the applicant, did not arrive. The applicant relied on Arts 8 and 25.

*Court:* The Court was unanimous in finding that both Articles had been breached. The regulations relating to the interception of prisoners' mail did not satisfy the requirements of accessibility contained in Art 8 and Romanian law did not indicate with reasonable clarity the scope and manner of exercise of the discretion conferred on the public authorities. The Court did not therefore consider it necessary to consider whether the other elements of Art 8 were satisfied. In respect of Art 25 the Court recalled 'that it is of the utmost importance for the effective operation of the system of individual petition instituted by article 25 that applicants or potential applicants should be able to communicate with the Commission without being subject to any form of pressure from the authorities to modify or withdraw their complaints' (para 43). The applicant had twice been threatened by the Aiud prison authorities when he had asked to write to the Commission, and had been told that 'The Council of Europe is at Aiud and nowhere else'. These actions were contrary to the requirements of Art 25.

*Note:* Article 25, referred to in this case, is now Art 34.

# Akkoc v Turkey

## (2002) 34 EHRR 51

*Facts:* The applicant claimed that she had been tortured while in police custody and had been intimidated in respect of her application to the Commission.

*Court:* The Court was satisfied that in the circumstances the questioning of the applicant about her application to the Commission amounted to a form of illicit and unacceptable pressure which hinders the exercise of the right of individual petition.

# Part 2
# CRIMINAL LAW

# Chapter 4

# GENERAL PRINCIPLES OF CRIMINAL LAW

## 4.1 MEANING OF 'CRIMINAL CHARGE'

### Schmautzer v Austria

### (1995) 21 EHRR 511

*Facts:* The applicant was convicted of failing to wear a seat belt, an offence under the Austrian Road Traffic Act, and was ordered to pay a fine. Under Austrian law, this offence was classified as 'administrative'. The applicant complained that he had been denied the right to a hearing before a tribunal, as required under Art 6, in the determination of a criminal charge against him. He considered that the regulatory offence should be classified as criminal rather than administrative.

*Commission:* In finding that the proceedings in this case determined a 'criminal charge' within the meaning of the Convention, the Commission took account of the fact that failure to comply with this regulation resulted in the possibility of imprisonment. The Commission noted that the Court is required to apply the same test for the applicability of Art 6 to regulatory offences as to other types of proceedings.

*Court:* In order to determine whether the administrative criminal offence gave rise to a 'criminal charge', the Court considered it necessary to ascertain whether or not the provision defining the offence was considered 'criminal' in domestic law. The Court was satisfied that although the nature of the offence and the procedures followed fell within the administrative sphere, they were nevertheless criminal in nature. The Court considered it relevant that the offence was described as an administrative *offence* and an administrative *criminal* procedure. Furthermore the Court, agreeing with the Commission, noted that the financial penalty was accompanied by an order for the applicant's committal to prison in the event of his defaulting on payment. These factors taken together were sufficient to establish that the offence should be classified as criminal for the purposes of the Convention and Art 6 applied.

### Campbell and Fell v United Kingdom

### (1984) 7 EHRR 165

*Facts:* Whilst serving a sentence of imprisonment for terrorist offences, the applicants were involved in prison disturbances which led to disciplinary proceedings being brought against them. Following proceedings before the Board of Prison Visitors, they were convicted of disciplinary charges and lost a range of privileges and a period of remission. The applicants alleged that the proceedings before the Board involved, effectively, the determination of a 'criminal charge' and accordingly they should have been afforded a hearing which complied with the requirements of Art 6.

*Commission:*   In assessing whether the charges were criminal or disciplinary, the Commission considered that generally the State is entitled to deal with a breach of rules designed to maintain prison order under disciplinary law. The loss of privileges was a disciplinary penalty affecting the prisoners' status within the prison. However, the loss of remission, with the consequence that the applicants' release date was significantly prolonged, went beyond what could fairly be considered 'disciplinary' and fell within the criminal sphere. Accordingly, the proceedings before the Board are required to satisfy the requirements of Art 6.

*Court:*   The Court acknowledged that in order to maintain prison discipline, the authorities needed to establish a special disciplinary regime to deal as quickly and effectively as possible with misconduct by prison inmates. Nevertheless, the guarantee of a fair hearing was one of the fundamental principles of a democratic society. In determining whether these proceedings were criminal or disciplinary, the Court emphasised that the meaning of 'criminal' is autonomous under Art 6. Although Contracting States are entitled to draw a distinction in national law between disciplinary and criminal matters, this classification was not decisive for the purposes of the Convention. 'If the Contracting States were able, at their discretion, by classifying an offence as disciplinary instead of criminal, to exclude the operation of the fundamental clauses of Arts 6 and 7, the application of these provisions would be subordinated to their sovereign will. A latitude extending thus far might lead to results incompatible with the object and purpose of the Convention' (para 68). Accordingly, the Court was entitled to consider the nature of the proceedings and, taking account of the gravity of the offences charged and the nature and severity of the penalty risked by the applicants, the Court was of the opinion that Art 6 was applicable.

*Note:*   The Prison Department announced that legal representation would be made available for proceedings before the Board of Visitors and that its decisions would be made public (Resolution DH (86) 7 of 27 June 1986).

# Quinn v Ireland
## (2000) 29 EHRR CD 234

*Facts:*   The applicant had been arrested in connection with serious terrorist offences and questioned under domestic legislation, which required him to give an account of his movements. Failure to provide information amounted to an offence under s 52 of the Offences Against the State Act 1939. He complained that his conviction for refusing to answer questions amounted to a violation of the right to a fair trial. The government argued that Art 6 did not apply to the applicant's complaints because at the time of questioning he had not been formally charged. Furthermore, as no proceedings were taken out against him for a substantive offence he could not complain of a violation of procedural guarantees provided by Art 6. Relying on *Funke v France* (1993) 16 EHRR 297, *Saunders v United Kingdom* (1996) 23 EHRR 313 and *Murray v United Kingdom* (1996) 22 EHRR 29, he argued that once he was arrested and questioned he was 'charged' within the autonomous meaning of that term in Art 6. If he could not rely on Art 6 rights because he had not been charged under Irish law, the guarantees provided by Art 6 would be rendered ineffective.

*Court:* In rejecting the government's submission, the Court recalled that for the purposes of Art 6 a person is 'charged' when his situation has been 'substantially affected'. Since failure to answer questions could lead to a penalty of 6 months' imprisonment, the proceedings had reached the point where he would be 'substantially affected' and therefore 'charged' for the purposes of Article. However, although charged within the meaning of Art 6 when questioned, no criminal proceedings as regards those charges were pursued against him. As a consequence it was arguable that in the absence of substantive criminal proceedings he could not claim to have been the victim of a violation of the procedural guarantees provided by Art 6. The Court emphasised that the Convention should be interpreted in such a way as to guarantee rights which are practical and effective as opposed to theoretical and illusory. Applying this approach to this case the Court noted that if he was he was unable to invoke Art 6, the lack of substantive proceedings against him 'would exclude any consideration under Art 6 of his complaint that he had been, nevertheless, already punished during the earlier criminal investigation for having defended what he considered to be his rights guaranteed by Art 6 of the Convention' (para 45). In the circumstances, the Court found that the applicant could invoke Art 6 in respect of his conviction and imprisonment under s 52 of the 1939 Act. The Court was satisfied that the degree of compulsion imposed on the applicant by the application of s 52 destroyed the essence of the privilege against self-incrimination and the right to remain silent which could not be justified by security and public order concerns.

# Heaney and McGuinness v Ireland

## (2001) 33 EHRR 12

*Facts:* The applicants were charged with membership of an unlawful organisation contrary to s 21 of the Offences Against the State Act 1939. Although acquitted of this charge, they were convicted of failing to provide information contrary to s 52 of the Offences Against the State Act 1939. They argued that s 52 must be read as including the right to refuse to provide such information, and, relying on Art 6 rights, complained that the conviction for refusing to answer questions amounted to a violation of the right to a fair trial. The government argued that since Art 6 provides protection of a procedural nature for the determination of a criminal charge, the applicants could not rely on Art 6 to challenge the offence under s 52 of the 1939 Act. Furthermore, both were acquitted of the substantive charge and could not therefore rely on Art 6 rights.

*Court:* Finding for the applicants, the Court observed that 'if the applicants are unable to invoke Article 6, their acquittal in the substantive proceedings would exclude any consideration under Article 6 of their complaints that they had been, nevertheless, already punished prior to the acquittal for having defended what they considered to be their rights guaranteed by Article 6 of the Convention' (para 45). Accordingly, notwithstanding their acquittal, the applicants could invoke Art 6 in respect of their conviction and imprisonment for failing to provide information under s 52. In addition, the Court found that the degree of compulsion imposed on the applicants by the application of s 52 destroyed the essence of the privilege against self-incrimination and the right to remain silent. Furthermore, the security and public order concerns of the government could not justify a provision which effectively extinguished the rights guaranteed by Art 6.

## [2001] JB Crim LR 748

[2001] Crim LR 748

*Facts:* Relying on Art 6, the applicant complained that proceedings which obliged him to produce incriminating documents failed to comply with procedural requirements under the Convention. According to s 131(1) of the Decree of the Federal Council, persons liable to pay taxes were obliged to co-operate with the tax authorities, in particular to submit accounts, documents and other receipts which could be relevant when determining taxes. A disciplinary fine was imposed on the applicant for failing to submit documents relating to his source of income. Following his continued refusal to produce the documents, a second disciplinary fine was imposed. The applicant submitted that the proceedings at issue in this case involved both the imposition of a supplementary tax and tax evasion proceedings. The calculation of the supplementary tax was the basis for determining the amount of the fine imposed for the tax evasion. He argued that while the supplementary tax part of the proceedings did not give rise to Art 6, the tax evasion proceedings amounted to criminal proceedings within the meaning of Art 6, which provided the applicant with a privilege against self-incrimination. The government argued that the proceedings in this case were of a sui generis nature and outside the scope of Art 6.

*Court:* Convention jurisprudence establishes that there are three criteria to be taken into account when deciding whether a person was 'charged with a criminal offence' for the purposes of Art 6. These are the classification of the offence under national law, the nature of the offence, and the nature and degree of severity of the penalty. Previous authority established that proceedings which resulted in a fine for the criminal offence of tax evasion invoked Art 6. In the present case, the proceedings served several purposes. First, they established whether tax was due, and if necessary imposed both a supplementary tax and a fine for tax evasion. The Court was satisfied that any penalty imposed for tax evasion was intended as punishment rather than as pecuniary compensation. In the Court's opinion, whatever other purposes the proceedings served, by enabling the imposition of a 'not inconsiderable' fine, they amounted to the determination of a criminal charge and invoked Art 6.

## 4.2 BURDEN OF PROOF AND PRESUMPTION OF INNOCENCE

### Salabiaku v France

(1988) 13 EHRR 379

*Facts:* The applicant was charged with the criminal offence of illegal importation of narcotics and a customs offence of smuggling prohibited goods. The Customs Code provided for the presumption of criminal liability for persons found in possession of prohibited goods. The Court of Appeal set aside his conviction for the first offence on the grounds that the facts alleged against him were not sufficiently proven. However, the court upheld this conviction for the customs offence. The applicant complained that the way in which the Customs Code had been applied to him was incompatible with Art 6(1) and (2) of the Convention. By placing upon him an 'almost irrebuttable presumption of guilt' his right to a fair trial and his right to be presumed innocent until proven guilty had been violated.

*Court:* The purpose of Art 6 is to protect the right to a fair trial and in particular the right to be presumed innocent, which enshrine the fundamental principle of the rule of law. Although the Convention does not prohibit presumptions of law or fact, it requires States to confine them within reasonable limits which take into account the importance of what is at stake and maintain the rights of the defence. The domestic court had drawn a distinction between the criminal offence and the customs offence and had given the applicant the benefit of the doubt in respect of the criminal offence, thus 'showing scrupulous respect' for the presumption of innocence. With regard to the second offence, the domestic court took account of the fact that the applicant had been warned by an airline official not to take possession of the goods unless he was sure they belonged to him. The court inferred that by failing to do so and by having in his possession a trunk containing a quantity of cannabis he committed the offence of smuggling prohibited goods. The Court was satisfied that the domestic courts had not resorted automatically to the presumption of guilt, but inferred from the fact of possession a presumption which was not subsequently rebutted by the applicant. Thus, the French court had not applied the Customs Code in a way which conflicted with the presumption of innocence.

# Phillips v United Kingdom
## 11 BHRC 280

*Facts:* The applicant complained that the application of the statutory assumption under the Drug Trafficking Act 1994 violated his right to be presumed innocent. Following his conviction for being involved in the importation of a large quantity of cannabis resin contrary to s 170(2) of the Customs and Excise Management Act 1979, he was sentenced to 9 years' imprisonment. Section 4(3) of the 1994 Act empowers a court to assume that all property held by a person convicted of a drug trafficking offence within the preceding 6 years represented the proceeds of drug trafficking. During the means inquiry conducted under s 2 of the 1994 Act the applicant declined to be interviewed. However, at the confiscation hearing he gave evidence and called witnesses. Applying the statutory presumption, the judge assessed that the applicant had benefited to the extent of £91,400 and made a confiscation order for this amount. Failure to comply with the order would result in an additional 2 years' imprisonment. In reviewing recent domestic case-law, the Court noted that in *HM Advocate v McIntosh* [2001] UKHRR 463, the Privy Council held unanimously that Art 6(2) did not apply to confiscation proceedings, which are part of the sentencing process and do not involve the accused being 'charged with a criminal offence'.

*Court:* The Court declined to examine in abstracto the compatibility with the Convention of the provisions of the Drug Trafficking Act 1994. The Court's function in this case was to determine whether the application of a presumption offended the basic principles of a fair procedure inherent in Art 6. Observing that the purpose of the procedure under the 1994 Act was to enable the national court to assess the amount of the confiscation order and did not involve the accused facing any further charge, the Court found by five votes to two that Art 6(2) did not apply to confiscation proceedings. Although the applicant did not invoke Art 6(1) in his original application, this issue was raised at the hearing. The Court reiterated that the statutory assumption was not applied in order to facilitate a finding that the applicant was guilty of an offence, but was used to enable the national court to assess that amount at which the confiscation order should be fixed. The procedure under the 1994 Act was not without its safeguards. The assessment was conducted in public by a court with a judicial procedure and the applicant had the opportunity to adduce documentary and oral evidence. Furthermore, the assumption could be rebutted if the defendant could show on the balance of probabilities that he had acquired the property by other means, and the trial judge retained a discretion not to apply the assumption if it gave rise to a serious risk of injustice. While the Court considered that an issue relating to the fairness of the procedure might arise in circumstances where the amount of a confiscation order was based on hidden assets, having considered the facts of this case the Court found that the application of the relevant provisions of the 1994 Act was confined within reasonable limits, given the importance of what was at stake, and was unanimous in holding that the operation of the statutory assumption did not violate the notion of a fair hearing.

## Heaney and McGuinness v Ireland
## (2001) 33 EHRR 12
## Quinn v Ireland
## (2000) 29 EHRR CD 234

*Facts:*    The applicants had been arrested in connection with serious terrorist offences and questioned under s 52 of the Offences Against the State Act 1939, which required them to give an account of their movements. In the first case the applicants refused to answer any questions, and in the second the applicant denied any involvement in criminal activity and refused to answer questions about his movements. In both cases the applicants complained, inter alia, that their convictions for refusing to answer questions amounted to a violation of the right to a fair trial.

*Court:*    Recalling that for the purposes of Art 6 a person is 'charged' when their situation has been 'substantially affected', the Court rejected the government's submission that this provision did not apply because at the time of questioning the applicants had not been formally charged. The Court acknowledged that the right to silence and the right not to incriminate oneself are not absolute rights. However, in these cases the Court was satisfied that the degree of compulsion destroyed the very essence of the applicants' privilege against self-incrimination, and held that in both applications there had been an infringement of the right to a fair trial. Observing that in *Saunders v United Kingdom* (1996) 23 EHRR 313 the Court rejected the submission that the complexity of the case and the public interest in the investigation of serious offences could justify departure from basic principles of fair trial, the Court found that the public order concerns of the Irish government could not justify 'a provision which extinguishes the very essence of the applicant's right to silence and against self-incrimination guaranteed by Article 6(1) of the Convention' (*Heaney and McGuinness*, para 58, *Quinn*, para 59). Accordingly, the Court was unanimous in holding that there had been a violation of the applicants' right not to incriminate themselves and, given the close link between the rights guaranteed by Art 6(1) and the presumption of innocence, there was also a violation of Art 6(2).

## Telfner v Austria
## (2002) 34 EHRR 7

*Facts:* The applicant complained that in drawing adverse inferences from the applicant's refusal to make a statement to the police and in speculating about the possibility of his guilt, which was not supported by any evidence, the Austrian criminal courts had acted in disregard of the presumption of innocence. It was alleged that the applicant had been driving a car which struck a pedestrian causing minor injuries. When charged, the applicant stated that he had not been driving the car at the relevant time and refused to make further comment.

*Court:* Although recalling that it is for national courts to assess the evidence, Art 6(2) requires that members of the court do not start with the preconceived idea that the accused committed the offence. Although legal presumptions are not in principle contrary to Art 6, the burden of proof must rest with the prosecution and the accused is entitled to be given the benefit of any doubt. The Court noted that the Silz District Court concluded that the circumstances of the case led 'to the sole, and unequivocal conclusion that only the accused could have committed the offence; presumably he refused to make a statement because he was under the influence of alcohol, but there is no evidence for that finding'. Observing that where the prosecution had established a prima facie case the drawing of commonsense inferences from the accused's silence is compatible with the Convention, the Court was not satisfied that the case against this applicant called for an explanation from him. In the absence of a prima facie case, requiring the applicant to provide an explanation effectively shifted the burden of proof from the prosecution to the defence. Further, speculating about the possibility that the applicant was under the influence of alcohol contributed to the impression that the court had a preconceived view of the applicant's guilt. Accordingly, the Court was satisfied that there had been a violation of Art 6(2).

## *UNITED KINGDOM CASES*

## R v DPP, ex parte Kebilene
## House of Lords, [1999] 4 All ER 801

*Facts:* The respondents were charged under s 16A of the Prevention of Terrorism (Temporary Provisions) Act 1989 which, they argued, reversed the legal burden of proof and was therefore in conflict with the presumption of innocence and in breach of Art 6(2).

*House of Lords:* Although a reversal of the legal burden of proof on a matter central to the wrongdoing alleged against the defendant would violate Art 6(2) of the Convention, it was arguable that this provision did not reverse the legal burden, but merely placed an evidential burden on the defendant. Statutory provisions which partially reverse the burden of proof are not necessarily inconsistent with the Convention. Lord Hope of Craighead considered that Convention cases showed that 'although Article 6(2) is in absolute terms, it is not to be regarded as imposing an absolute prohibition on the reverse onus clauses, whether they be evidential (presumptions of facts) or persuasive (presumptions of law). In each case the questions will be whether the presumption is within reasonable limits' (at 847).

*Note:* Responding to this decision, Parliament enacted the Terrorism Act 2000 which in s 118(1) and (2) provides that the reverse onus of proof is satisfied if the person adduces evidence which is sufficient to raise an issue with respect to the matter unless the prosecution can prove the contrary beyond reasonable doubt.

# R v Lambert; R v Ali; R v Jordan

## House of Lords, [2001] UKHL 37, [2001] 3 WLR 206

*Facts:* Following his conviction for possession of a controlled drug with intent to supply contrary to s 5(3) of the Misuse of Drugs Act 1971, the appellant complained, inter alia, that placing a legal burden on him to prove that he neither believed nor suspected that the substance in his possession was a controlled drug was incompatible with Art 6(2). The basis of this submission is that requiring the defence to prove lack of knowledge shifts the burden of proof and undermines the presumption of innocence.

*Held:* The Court observed that in order for reverse onus provisions in respect of drugs offences to be Convention compliant, they must satisfy the criterion of proportionality. Provided the overall fairness of a criminal trial is not compromised, presumptions of fact or law will not necessarily violate Art 6(2). Accepting that the State bears the burden of demonstrating that a derogation from a Convention right is both legitimate and proportionate, the majority of the court considered that in the context of drug offences, imposing a legal burden on the defence is a disproportionate means of addressing the legislative goal of easing the task of the prosecution. Satisfied that the reverse onus provisions in the 1971 Act were not Convention compliant, the court observed that it was possible to construe these provisions as imposing only an evidential burden on the defence 'without doing violence to the language or to the objective of the section' (para 17). Support for this viewpoint was found in judgments of the Canadian Supreme Court (*R v Oakes* (1986) 26 DLR (4th) 200; *R v Whyte* (1988) 51 DLR (4th) 481; *R v Downey* [1992] 2 SCR 10; *R v Osolin* [1993] 4 SCR 595), and the South African Constitutional Court (*State v Mbatha* [1996] 2 LRC 208; *State v Manamela* [2000] 5 DLR 65). Lord Hutton rejected the view of the majority and considered that the threat posed by drugs to the welfare of society was so grave that 'the transfer of onus satisfied the test that it had a legitimate aim in the public interest and that there was a reasonable relationship of proportionality between the means employed and the aims sought to be realised' (para 98).

# Lynch (Stuart) v DPP

## Divisional Court, [2001] EWHC Admin 882, unreported

*Facts:* The defendant was charged with having a bladed weapon in a public place contrary to s 139 of the Criminal Justice Act 1988. Under this provision, it is a defence to prove that there was a good reason or lawful authority for having a bladed article in a public place. He submitted that this provision was contrary to Art 6.

*Held:* Whether reverse onus provisions are Convention compliant will depend, in part, upon the court's assessment of whether a fair balance has been struck between the public interest and the rights of the individual. The court observed that offences under s 139 were distinguishable from those under s 28 of the Misuse of Drugs Act 1971, in that it was necessary for the prosecution to prove the article was in the defendant's possession. There was a strong public interest in bladed articles not being carried in public without good reason and it was not offensive to the rights of the individual to require them to establish, on the balance of probabilities, a good reason for carrying the article. Parliament was entitled to deter the carrying of bladed articles in public by placing the burden on the carrier without compromising Art 6. The exercise of a reverse onus was proportionate and within reasonable limits.

# HM Advocate v McIntosh

## Privy Council, [2001] 3 WLR 107

*Facts:* Following the petitioner's conviction for a drug trafficking offence under s 4(3)(b) of the Misuse of Drugs Act 1971, the prosecutor applied for a confiscation order under the Proceeds of Crime (Scotland) Act 1995. The court was invited to make assumptions that property either held by him or transferred to him since his conviction or since a date 6 years before being indicted was received by him in connection with the offence of drug trafficking.

*Privy Council:* The Privy Council held unanimously that Art 6(2) did not apply to confiscation proceedings, which are part of the sentencing process and do not involve the accused being 'charged with a criminal offence'. Observing that the right contained in Art 6(2) was not an absolute right and thus could be subject to permissible limitations, the court considered that the statutory assumptions introduced by the Proceeds of Crime (Scotland) Act 1995 were justifiable encroachments on the presumption of innocence.

# R v Rezvi

## House of Lords, [2002] UKHL 1, [2002] 2 WLR 235

*Facts:* The appellant submitted that a confiscation order imposed under Part VI of the Criminal Justice Act 1988 did not accord with his rights under the Convention.

*Held:* In dismissing the appeal, the court was satisfied that confiscation proceedings under the 1988 Act were not incompatible with the Convention. Noting with approval the opinion of the Court in *Phillips v United Kingdom* (2001) Crim LR 817, the court was satisfied that the provisions in the 1988 Act were a proportionate response to the problem they were designed to address and represented a fair balance between the interests of the individual and the public. However, when considering an application for an order the trial judge must avoid any serious or real risk of injustice. If there was such a risk, the court should not make an order.

## R v Benjafield

## House of Lords, [2002] UKHL 2, [2002] 2 WLR 235

*Facts:* This appeal concerned, inter alia, a challenge to the compatibility of reverse burden provisions imposed by the Drug Trafficking Act 1994 with Art 6(1) of the Convention. The appellant submitted that a confiscation order imposed under s 4(3) of the 1994 Act was incompatible with his rights under the Convention. Although this case did not invoke Art 6(2), in that confiscation proceedings did not constitute a criminal charge, the appellant was entitled to the procedural guarantees provided by Art 6(1).

*Held:* Despite some material differences in the confiscation procedures under the Criminal Justice Act 1988 and the 1994 Act, the court was satisfied that the reasoning used in *R v Rezvi* [2002] UKHL 1, [2002] 2 WLR 235 applied to this case with equal force. In dismissing the appeal, the court found that the 1994 Act had as its objective the public interest, and that the measures introduced by this legislation were 'rationally connected with the furtherance of this objective. The procedure devised by Parliament is a fair and proportionate response to the need to protect the public interest. The critical point is that under the 1994 Act, as under the Criminal Justice Act 1988, the judge must be astute to avoid injustice. If there is or might be a serious or real risk of injustice, he must not make a confiscation order' (para 8). In this case the court found that the judge misdirected himself by considering whether on the balance of probabilities there had been 'any risk of injustice' to the appellant. The court noted that the judge must avoid 'any real risk'. However, the court was satisfied that no injustice or prejudice resulted from the misdirection.

## 4.3 PRIVILEGE AGAINST SELF-INCRIMINATION

### (1) COMPULSORY DISCLOSURE OF DOCUMENTS

#### Funke v France

#### (1993) 16 EHRR 297

*Facts:* French customs authorities attempted to compel the applicant to produce documents which might provide them with evidence to commence a prosecution. His refusal to disclose the documents resulted in a court order for the production of his bank statements and the imposition of a pecuniary sanction. The applicant claimed that his conviction for refusing to produce self-incriminating documents violated his right to a fair trial and was in breach of the principle of the presumption of innocence.

*Commission:* The Commission considered, by seven votes to five, that neither the obligation to produce bank statements nor the imposition of pecuniary penalties offended the principle of a fair trial. This conclusion was reached mainly on the basis of the special features of the investigation procedures in business and financial matters.

*Court:* The Court was of the opinion that the customs authorities were using their powers of search and seizure to engage in a fishing expedition to obtain documents which they did not know for certain to exist. It was noted that the authorities were prepared to use financial penalties to compel the applicant to provide evidence of offences he had allegedly committed because the authorities were unable, or unwilling, to obtain them by some other means. The special nature of customs regulations did not justify the infringement of the right of a person charged with a criminal offence to remain silent and not to contribute to incriminating himself. The court held, by eight votes to one, that there had been a violation of Art 6(1).

*Note:* The French customs authorities have altered their practice and the jurisprudence of the *Conseil Constitutionel* has changed, resulting in the communication of documents to customs officials being subject to certain guarantees.

# JB v Switzerland
## [2001] Crim LR 748

*Facts:* Relying on Art 6, the applicant complained that proceedings which obliged him to produce incriminating documents failed to comply with procedural requirements under the Convention. According to s 131(1) of the Decree of the Federal Council, persons liable to pay taxes were obliged to co-operate with the tax authorities, in particular to submit accounts, documents and other receipts which could be relevant when determining taxes. A disciplinary fine was imposed on the applicant for failing to submit documents relating to his source of income. Following his continued refusal to produce the documents, a second disciplinary fine was imposed. He submitted that the information required amounted to a 'fishing expedition' on the part of the authorities. When he refused to supply the information, he was punished with a fine contrary to Art 6(1). The authorities were required to prove any criminal conduct and he was entitled to remain silent. The government submitted that the applicant was not obliged to incriminate himself since the authorities were already aware of the information.

*Court:* The Court considered that the authorities were attempting to compel the applicant to submit the documents which would have provided information as to his income, observing that the Federal Court in its judgment:

> '. . . referred to various obligations in criminal law obliging persons to act in a particular way in order to be able to obtain his conviction, for instance by means of a tacograph installed in lorries, or by being obliged to submit to a blood or urine test. In the Court's opinion, however, the present case differs from such material which, as the Court found in the *Saunders* case, had an existence independent of the person concerned and was not, therefore, obtained by means of coercion and in defiance of the will of that person' (para 68).

In refusing to accept that documents should necessarily be classified as having an existence independent of the will of the applicant, the Court was satisfied that the imposition of fines for refusing to submit documents amounted to an infringement of the privilege against self-incrimination.

## (2)   STATEMENTS OBTAINED BY COERCION

## Saunders v United Kingdom

## (1996) 23 EHRR 313

*Facts:*   The applicant complained that the use in criminal proceedings of answers compulsorily obtained from him in a non-judicial investigation violated his right not to incriminate himself. He had been the Chief Executive Officer of Guinness plc when the company bought Distillers plc in April 1986, following a takeover battle with the Argyll Group plc. During an investigation into the activities of the company, he had been legally obliged to answer questions put to him by Department of Trade and Industry (DTI) inspectors acting under statutory powers provided by s 432 of the Companies Act 1985. Failure to answer these questions could lead to a financial penalty or a prison sentence. The applicant was subsequently convicted of offences involving false accounting, theft and conspiracy. At this trial the prosecution had been allowed to adduce in evidence incriminating statements made during his interviews with the DTI inspectors.

*Commission:*   The Commission was of the opinion that the admissions contained in the interviews must have exerted additional pressure on the applicant to give testimony during the trial rather than remain silent. It considered that the privilege against self-incrimination formed an important element in safeguarding individuals from oppression and coercion and was linked to the principle of the presumption of innocence. The general requirements of fairness contained in Art 6 apply to criminal proceedings in respect of all types of criminal offences. In this case the incriminating evidence obtained from the applicant under compulsion was a 'not insignificant' part of the evidence against him at trial. The Commission, by 14 votes to 1, declared the complaint admissible and expressed the opinion that the applicant had been denied a fair hearing in violation of Art 6(1). At the hearing before the Court, the Commission emphasised that even denials of guilt in the face of incriminating questions could be highly damaging to the defence.

*Court:*   The Court stressed that the right not to incriminate oneself, like the right to silence, was a generally recognised international standard which lay at the heart of the notion of a fair procedure under Art 6 of the Convention. This right was linked to the presumption of innocence. The Court rejected the government's submission that the complexity of corporate fraud and the public interest in the successful prosecution of those responsible justified a marked departure from one of the basic principles of a fair procedure. Similarly, the Court rejected the argument that procedural safeguards requiring the trial judge to exclude admissions which might be unreliable or might have been obtained by oppressive means, and the discretionary power to exclude evidence if its admission would have an adverse effect on the fairness of the proceedings (see ss 76 and 78 of PACE), provided a defence in this case, since they had not prevented the use of the statements in subsequent criminal proceedings. Whether the applicant's rights had been infringed in this case depended upon the use made of his statements at trial. The Court was satisfied that the prosecution had used them in a manner which was intended to cast doubt in the minds of the jury as to the applicant's honesty. The Court held, by 16 votes to 4, that there had been a violation of Art 6(1).

*Note:*   The right not to incriminate could be violated by the use of any statement obtained from the accused by compulsion and was not limited to the use of incriminating statements. However, the Court considered that material obtained under compulsion, but which had an existence independent of the accused, such as breath, blood and urine samples, could be used in criminal proceedings without infringing the accused's rights under the Convention. The Court noted that this complaint was confined to the use made at trial of the statements which the applicant had given to the inspectors under legal compulsion. The administrative investigation by the inspectors was not a judicial procedure and thus was not subject to the guarantees provided by Art 6(1).

## UNITED KINGDOM CASES

## R v Hertfordshire County Council, ex parte Green Environmental Industries Ltd

## House of Lords, [2000] 2 WLR 373

*Facts:*   The appellant had refused to provide information to a local waste regulation authority on the ground that his answers might incriminate him or lead to the discovery of evidence which could be used in a criminal prosecution.

*Court:*   The court observed that Convention jurisprudence did not cast doubt upon the validity of provisions which compel persons to answer questions during a pre-trial investigation. Finding that s 71(2) of the Environmental Protection Act 1990 impliedly excluded self-incrimination as a reasonable excuse for refusing to answer questions which could be used in a criminal prosecution, their Lordships were unanimous in rejecting the appellant's argument that this provision was contrary to Art 6. Lord Hoffmann observed that 'the judgment of the European Court is perfectly clear. It said that it was casting no doubt upon the propriety of the use of compulsory powers at the examination stage. . . . European jurisprudence under Article 6(1) is firmly anchored to the fairness of the trial and is not concerned with extrajudicial inquiries. Such impact Article 6(1) may have is upon the use of such evidence at a criminal trial. . . . The *Saunders* case is therefore no authority for allowing the appellants to refuse to answer'. He noted that the legislative changes introduced as a consequence to *Saunders* did not apply to the provision under discussion, 'presumably because it contains no express provision that answers are to be admissible and therefore leaves the discretion [to exclude evidence] under section 78 unimpaired'.

## Attorney-General's Reference (No 7 of 2000)

## Court of Appeal, [2001] EWCA Crim 888, [2001] 1 WLR 1879

*Facts:* The defendant was adjudicated a bankrupt in 1997. In a bankruptcy questionnaire he indicated that in the 2 years preceding his bankruptcy, he had lost money by gambling. He provided the Official Receiver with documents relating to his estate, which included evidence of his gambling, as required by s 291 of the Insolvency Act 1986. Failure to comply with this provision would have rendered him liable to be sentenced to imprisonment for contempt of court. He was eventually charged under s 362 of the 1986 Act with having 'materially contributed to, or increased the extent of, his insolvency by gambling'. At a pre-trial hearing the judge ruled that the Crown could not produce documents relating to his gambling activities on the ground that their admission would infringe his right to a fair trial. At the invitation of the Crown, the trial judge directed an acquittal.

*Held:* While noting that Convention jurisprudence is at variance on the issue, the court considered it jurisprudentially sound to draw a distinction between statements obtained under compulsory powers, and evidence obtained under compulsion but which had an existence independent of the will of the accused. Accordingly, the court held that the use by the Crown of documents delivered up under compulsory powers in criminal proceedings against a bankrupt for an offence under the Insolvency Act 1986 was not contrary to Art 6.

## (3)   RIGHT TO REMAIN SILENT

## Murray v United Kingdom

## (1996) 22 EHRR 29

*Facts:* The applicant, who lived in Northern Ireland, complained, inter alia, that he was deprived of the right to silence in criminal proceedings. He was arrested and detained under the United Kingdom Prevention of Terrorism (Temporary Provisions) Act 1989 for aiding and abetting the false imprisonment of a Provisional IRA informer. The applicant was cautioned according to the terms of Art 3 of the Criminal Evidence (Northern Ireland) Order 1988, SI 1988/1987 (NI 20), which provided for inferences to be drawn from a failure to mention facts when questioned. He refused to answer questions and indicated that he wished to consult a solicitor. In finding the applicant guilty, the judge indicated that he had drawn strong inferences from the fact that he had failed to answer police questions and had refused to testify.

*Commission:* The complaints were declared admissible, but the Commission found no indication that the applicant was deprived of his right to silence nor was his right to the presumption of innocence violated. The provisions of the 1988 Order 'constitute a formalised system which aims at allowing common sense implications to play an open role in the assessment of evidence'. However, the applicant's rights of defence were adversely affected by the restrictions on his access to a solicitor. These restrictions were not in conformity with his right to a fair trial under Art 6(1) and his right to legal assistance under Art 6(3)(c).

*Court:* In accordance with its usual approach, the Court declined to give an abstract analysis of the problem and confined itself to the facts of the case. It held, by 14 votes to 5, that the drawing of reasonable inferences from silence did not amount to a violation of Art 6. If the circumstances clearly called for an explanation, the tribunal was entitled to take into account the accused's silence when assessing the persuasiveness of the evidence adduced by the prosecution. The Court noted that in European States not bound by formal rules of evidence, domestic courts could take into account relevant circumstances, including the manner in which the accused conducted his defence. Provided there was no compulsion to give evidence, a statute specifically permitting the drawing of inferences did not shift the burden of proof from the prosecution to the defence. Although the right to legal advice was not set out explicitly in the Convention, in some circumstances Art 6 requires that the accused be allowed access to a lawyer during the preliminary stages of an investigation. The Court was of the view that the scheme contained in the 1988 Order was such that it was of paramount importance for the rights of the defence that an accused had access to a lawyer at the initial stages of the police interrogation. Thus denying the applicant access to a lawyer at a point where his defence rights could well be irretrievably prejudiced amounted to a violation of Art 6.

## Averill v United Kingdom
## (2001) 31 EHRR 36

*Facts:* The applicant alleged, inter alia, that the refusal to allow him any access to a solicitor during the first 24 hours of interrogation in police custody, and the absence of a solicitor during his interview, was incompatible with his rights guaranteed by Art 6. In this case the judge acknowledged that he had drawn very strong inferences from the applicant's silence during police questioning.

*Court:* The Court considered that a refusal to allow an accused, who had been cautioned, to consult with a lawyer during the initial period in custody could irretrievably prejudice the rights of the defence. Noting that in this case the judge did invoke the applicant's silence during interview against him, the Court considered that as a matter of fairness access to a lawyer should have been granted before the interrogation began. Consequently, the decision to deny access to a solicitor was in breach of Art 6. However, while it would be incompatible with the right to a fair trial to base a conviction solely or mainly on an accused's silence, in appropriate circumstances silence could be taken into account when assessing the persuasiveness of other evidence adduced by the prosecution. The Court noted that the trial judge was not obliged to draw adverse inferences from silence, but did so in the exercise of his discretion and provided detailed reasons for his decision. Furthermore, the Court of Appeal scrupulously reviewed the reasons given by the trial judge and endorsed his decision. Accordingly, the Court was satisfied that in this case the drawing of adverse inferences by the trial judge did not exceed the limits of fairness required by Art 6.

# McGee v United Kingdom

## Application No 28135/95, unreported

*Facts:* The applicant claimed that he had been compelled to incriminate himself before he had received legal advice and that it was only after he had signed a confession that he was allowed to see a solicitor. Following his arrest, he had been detained in Castlereagh Police Office whereupon he made a specific request to see a solicitor. The applicant argued that the austerity of the conditions of his detention and his virtual solitary confinement was intended to be psychologically coercive and conducive to break down any resolve he had to remain silent.

*Court:* The Court examined the findings and recommendations of the European Committee for the Prevention of Torture and Inhuman or Degrading Treatment and Punishment in respect of the treatment of detainees in Castlereagh and noted that the Committee's concerns and criticisms were reflected in other public documents. Finding for the applicant, the Court considered that procedural fairness required that he should have been given access to a solicitor during the initial stages of interrogation as a counterweight to the intimidating atmosphere in Castlereagh which was designed to sap the applicant's will and make him confide in his interrogators. The Court held that to deny access to a lawyer for over 48 hours in a situation where the rights of the defence were prejudiced was incompatible with the rights of the accused under Art 6.

# Heaney and McGuinness v Ireland

## (2001) 33 EHRR 12

# Quinn v Ireland

## (2000) 29 EHRR CD 234

*Facts:* The applicants had been arrested in connection with serious terrorist offences and questioned under domestic legislation, which required them to give an account of their movements. In the first case the applicants refused to answer any questions, and in the second the applicant denied any involvement in criminal activity and refused to answer questions about his movements. In both cases the applicants complained, inter alia, that their convictions for refusing to answer questions amounted to a violation of the right to a fair trial guaranteed by Art 6(1).

*Court:* Recalling that for the purposes of Art 6 a person is 'charged' when their situation has been 'substantially affected', the Court rejected the government's submission that this provision did not apply because at the time of questioning the applicants had not been formally charged. In finding that the degree of compulsion destroyed the very essence of the applicants' privilege against self-incrimination, the Court held that in both applications there had been an infringement of the right to a fair trial. Observing that in *Saunders v United Kingdom* (1996) 23 EHRR 313 the Court rejected the submission that the complexity of the case and the public interest in the investigation of serious offences could justify departure from basic principles of fair trial, the Court found that the public order concerns of the Irish government could not justify a provision which extinguished the applicants' right to silence guaranteed by Art 6(1). Accordingly, the Court was unanimous in holding that there had been a violation of the applicants' right not to incriminate themselves and, given the close link between the rights guaranteed by Art 6(1) and the presumption of innocence, there was also a violation of Art 6(2).

## Condron v United Kingdom

## (2001) 31 EHRR 1

*Facts:* Acting on their solicitor's advice, the applicants remained silent during interview. When giving evidence at trial, they gave this as the reason for their refusal to answer police questions and were subjected to cross-examination on the nature of the advice. Although the judge drew the jury's attention to the explanation offered, he left them with the impression that even if satisfied as to the plausibility of the applicants' account, they still had the option to draw inferences from silence. Although critical of the judge's direction, the Court of Appeal was satisfied that the convictions were safe. The applicants complained that the decision of the trial judge to leave the jury with the option of drawing adverse inferences from their silence in the police station deprived them of the right to a fair trial within the meaning of Art 6.

*Court:* The Court noted that in the context of trial by jury, the right to silence is not an absolute right and drawing inferences from silence cannot by itself be considered as incompatible with the requirements of Art 6. In *Murray v United Kingdom* (1996) 22 EHRR 29, the Court had discussed the need to strike a balance between the right to silence and the circumstances in which an adverse inference could properly be drawn from silence. Provided appropriate safeguards were in place, the accused's silence, in situations which called for an explanation, could be taken into account when assessing the persuasiveness of the prosecution case. Nevertheless, the right to silence lies at the heart of the notion of a fair trial, and a conviction based solely or mainly on the accused's refusal to answer questions or to give evidence would be incompatible with the fairness provisions. The Court rejected any suggestion that cross-examination on the content of a solicitor's advice raised fair trial issues. Confining its discussion to s 34 of the Criminal Justice and Public Order Act 1994, the Court was aware that this provision had been the subject of 'much interpretation' by the domestic courts. It entrusted a properly directed jury with the task of deciding whether or not to draw inferences from silence. Observing that in this case the appellate court considered the judge's direction to the jury to be unsatisfactory, the Court held that, as a matter of fairness, it was necessary to make clear to the jury that if they were satisfied with the explanation given, it was inappropriate to draw an adverse inference from the applicants' silence in the police station. It is of relevance that in *Murray* the tribunal of fact was an experienced judge who was obliged to explain the reasons for his decision to draw inferences and the weight attached to them. In the absence of any obligation to deliver a reasoned verdict, it was impossible to ascertain what weight, if any, the jury gave to the applicants' silence. In the absence of any mechanism to assess the weight attached to inferences, the judge's direction was crucial. The Court was satisfied that the warning given to the jury not to base a conviction solely on the accused's silence was an insufficient safeguard to rectify the judge's deficient direction on inferences. This defect, which could not be remedied by the appeals process, deprived the applicants of a fair trial.

## Telfner v Austria

## (2002) 34 EHRR 7

See **4.2**.

### UNITED KINGDOM CASES

## Brown v Stott

## High Court of Justiciary, 2000 SLT 379
## Privy Council, [2001] 2 WLR 817

*Facts:* In response to police questioning, the respondent had admitted driving and was subsequently prosecuted for driving after consuming excess alcohol. It was submitted for the respondent that leading evidence at trial of her admission made under s 172 of the Road Traffic Act 1988 for an offence under s 5 of the Act violated her right to a fair trial.

*High Court of Justiciary:* See 2.1(2).

*Held:* Overturning the decision of the High Court of Justiciary, the Privy Council was unanimous in its opinion that the Procurator Fiscal could adduce the respondent's answers to police questions without infringing her privilege against self-incrimination. Referring to the high incidence of death and injury on the roads, and noting the public interest in the enforcement of road traffic legislation, Lord Bingham considered that s 172 constituted a proportionate response to the problem of maintaining road safety. Furthermore, given the need to attain a balance between conflicting interests, he was not persuaded that the use at trial of the respondent's answers to questions obtained as a consequence of this provision compromised her right to a fair trial. Observing that Strasbourg jurisprudence establishes the need to strike a balance between the general interests of the community and the personal rights of the individual, the Privy Council considered that the Convention provides for a graduation of rights which depend upon the seriousness of the criminal charge or the circumstances of the case. While acknowledging that the overall fairness of the criminal trial must not be compromised, and noting the influential decision of *Saunders v United Kingdom* (1996) 23 EHRR 313, the Privy Council considered that treating the privilege against self-incrimination as an absolute right could not be reconciled with Art 6 and Strasbourg jurisprudence. Accordingly, a limited qualification of the rights contained within Art 6 was acceptable provided any limitation was 'reasonably directed by national authorities towards a clear and proper public objective and if representing no greater qualification than the situation calls for'.

# Chapter 5

# INVESTIGATION

## 5.1   ENTRY, SEARCH AND SEIZURE

### (1)   INTERFERENCE WITH PRIVACY

## McLeod v United Kingdom
## [1998] 2 FLR 1048

*Facts:*   Police officers entered the applicant's house in order to prevent a breach of the peace whilst her ex-husband removed property from the former matrimonial home. At the time of entry, the police were informed that the applicant was not at home. She complained that the entry into her home by police officers amounted to a violation of her right to respect for her private life and home. The respondent government accepted that the entry constituted an interference with the right to respect for private life and home, but submitted that it was in accordance with the law and was necessary to prevent disorder.

*Court:*   The Court was satisfied that the common-law power of the police to enter private premises on the grounds of an anticipated breach of the peace was defined with sufficient precision for it to be in 'accordance with the law' as required by Art 8. In addition, the aim of the power enabling the police to enter premises to prevent a breach of the peace was a legitimate one for the purposes of Art 8. The applicant submitted that the justification for the entry had to be made by reference to the degree of risk that existed at the time the police entered the property. In this case the Court was satisfied that the risk of harm to persons or property was insufficient to be considered 'necessary in a democratic society'. It went on to consider whether the police officers' entry into the applicant's premises struck a fair balance between the applicant's rights under Art 8 and the prevention of crime and disorder. The Court was of the opinion that on being informed that the applicant was not present, the police officers should have realised that the risk of disorder was small and should not have entered the house. The means employed by the police officers in this case were disproportionate to the legitimate aim pursued and, accordingly, there had been a violation of Art 8.

### (2)   INTERFERENCE WITH CORRESPONDENCE

*SEIZURE OF DOCUMENTS*

## Miailhe v France
## (1993) 16 EHRR 332

*Facts:*   The applicant complained that the search of his premises and the seizure of nearly 15,000 documents by French customs officials violated his right to respect for his private and family life, his home and his correspondence. The search and seizure was in accordance with domestic law and was carried out as part of an investigation into alleged offences of tax evasion and exchange–control offences.

*Commission:*   The Commission found that the search and seizure constituted an interference with the exercise of the applicant's rights under Art 8(1). It went on to consider whether this interference was justified under Art 8(2), which permits some restriction on the exercise of these rights, provided the restriction was 'in accordance with the law' and 'necessary in a democratic society' in a legitimate interest. The Commission pointed out that an interference cannot be regarded as 'in accordance with the law' within the meaning of Art 8(2) unless it has some basis in domestic law. Furthermore, the legal rules which conferred on the customs authorities a power to search premises and seize documents must be sufficiently accessible and foreseeable. In this case, the Commission was satisfied that the relevant French law satisfied these criteria. The Commission found that the interference in question was for the purposes of a legitimate interest, namely the economic well-being of the country and the prevention of crime. The measures taken by the authorities formed part of the normal procedures used to prevent tax evasion and did not go beyond what was necessary in a democratic society. The Commission accepted the government's submission that house searches and the seizure of documents were the only means available to the authorities to gather physical evidence to secure a conviction and prevent capital outflows and tax evasion. It found, by 11 votes to 7, that in this case there had been no violation of Art 8.

*Court:*   The Court recognised that in order to obtain sufficient evidence to secure a conviction, it may be necessary for law enforcement agencies to conduct searches and seize relevant material. However, domestic law and practice must afford adequate and effective safeguards against abuse by the authorities. In this case, the court was satisfied that the powers enjoyed by customs officials were too wide, 'in particular, they had exclusive competence to assess the expediency, number, length and scale of inspections'. Furthermore, in the absence of any requirement of a judicial warrant, the restrictions and conditions provided for in law appeared 'too lax and full of loopholes for the interferences in the applicants' right to have been strictly proportionate to the legitimate aim pursued'. In finding that there had been a violation of Art 8, the Court emphasised that, although Contracting States have a certain margin of appreciation in assessing the need for an interference, this must go hand in hand with supervision by the institutions of the Convention. The exceptions provided for in Art 8(2) must be narrowly interpreted. It noted that the seizures made on the applicants' premises were 'wholesale and, above all, indiscriminate, to such an extent that the customs considered several thousand documents to be of no relevance to their inquiries and returned them to the applicants'. The Court held, by eight votes to one, that there had been a breach of Art 8.

# Cremieux v France
## (1993) 16 EHRR 357

*Facts:* In the course of a criminal investigation, customs officers seized documents relating to the applicant's business transactions. The applicant claimed that, in addition to documents relating to his business, the authorities took possession of private papers and correspondence. The respondent government accepted that the search and seizure amounted to an interference but argued that it was the only means available to the authorities for investigating offences of tax evasion and the illegal removal of large amounts of capital out of the jurisdiction. The applicant complained that the search and seizure made by customs officers at his home and at his other addresses infringed his right to respect for his home, his private life and his correspondence. Between 27 January 1977 and 26 February 1980, customs officers carried out 83 separate house searches and seizures at his home and other premises.

*Commission:* The Commission accepted the government's submission that the power to search for and seize documents was necessary in the investigation of exchange control regulations. It noted that the legal provision under which these searches and seizures were carried out contained a variety of procedural protections against arbitrary treatment, including a guarantee of judicial scrutiny. This was welcomed by the Commission as providing a check on the possible abuse of power by the public authorities. When dealing with matters affecting the economic well-being of the country, the State 'should be allowed a margin of appreciation large enough to take into account the fact that the international judge has a duty to respect the policy decisions of the national authorities'. The Commission found that the interference by the customs authorities did not exceed what could be regarded as necessary in a democratic society and consequently did not result in a violation of Art 8.

*Court:* The Court acknowledged that the unlawful transfers of capital abroad could damage the economic well-being of States. Furthermore, States now faced serious difficulties due to the scale and complexity of banking systems, the scope of international investment and the easing of border controls. The Court accepted that it might be necessary to provide the authorities with sufficient powers to conduct house searches and seize evidence of exchange control offences in order to prosecute those responsible. However, the relevant legislation and practice must afford adequate and effective safeguards against abuse. In this case, the customs authorities were given very wide powers: 'in particular, they had exclusive competence to assess the expediency, number, length and scale of inspections'. Furthermore, in the absence of any requirement of a judicial warrant, the restrictions and conditions on entry, search and seizure provided for by the national rules 'appear too lax and full of loopholes' to meet the requirements of the Convention. The Court held, by eight votes to one, that there had been a breach of Art 8.

*Note:* The Budget Acts of 30 December 1986 and 29 December 1989 amended Art 64 of the French Customs Code. All home searches, except those carried out in connection with an in flagrante delicto procedure, have to be authorised in advance by a reasoned order of the president of the *Tribunal de grande instance* or a judge designated by him.

## 5.2   SURVEILLANCE

### (1)   INTERCEPTION OF TELEPHONE CALLS

## Klass and Others v Federal Republic of Germany

## (1978) 2 EHRR 214

*Facts:*   The applicants claimed that German legislation which permitted the authorities to open letters and listen to telephone conversations violated their rights to respect for private life and correspondence. Under this legislation, the person concerned had no right to be informed of the surveillance measures and did not have recourse to the courts when the measures were terminated.

*Commission:*   In its report, the Commission noted that the surveillance measures permitted by this legislation amounted to an interference with the exercise of the rights protected by the Convention. Although not specifically mentioned in Art 8(1), it considered that telephone calls are covered by the notion of 'private life' and 'correspondence'. In previous cases, the Court acknowledged that some compromise between the requirements for defending a democratic society and individual rights is inherent in the system of the Convention. The Commission expressed the opinion, by 12 votes in favour, with 1 abstention, that the present case did not disclose a violation of Art 8.

*Court:*   The respondent government did not deny that the surveillance procedures involved an interference with the exercise of a right protected by the Convention, but submitted that the interference was justified by the terms of Art 8(2). Judicial notice was taken of the fact that democratic societies were under threat from highly sophisticated forms of espionage and terrorism which could, on occasion, justify the need to resort to covert methods of surveillance. Nevertheless, the Court emphasised that secret surveillance was 'tolerable under the Convention only in so far as strictly necessary for safeguarding the democratic institutions'. States did not enjoy unlimited discretion to subject persons to covert surveillance and must provide adequate and effective guarantees against abuse. There must be 'a balance between the exercise by the individual of the right guaranteed to him under paragraph 1 and the necessity under paragraph 2 to impose secret surveillance for the protection of the democratic society as a whole'. The Court carried out a detailed examination of the contested legislation and found that it was in accordance with the law and was satisfied that any interference was justified as being necessary in the interests of national security and/or for the prevention of disorder or crime. It contained procedures to ensure that surveillance was not ordered haphazardly, irregularly or without proper care. The surveillance was subject to a process of review, which was accompanied by procedures which guaranteed the individual's rights. Although in principle it was desirable to entrust supervisory control to a judge, the legislation provided other safeguards which were independent and 'vested with sufficient powers and competence to exercise an effective and continuous control'. The Court considered that failure to inform a person that he had been under surveillance was not in principle incompatible with Art 8(2). The Court was unanimous in finding no violation of Art 8.

# Malone v United Kingdom
## (1984) 7 EHRR 14

*Facts:*  Following his acquittal for dishonestly handling stolen goods, the applicant brought a civil action seeking to establish that the interception of his telephone by the police during the criminal investigation had been unlawful. Although the government consistently denied that the applicant's telephone had been tapped, it conceded that as a suspected handler of stolen goods he belonged to a class of persons liable to have their calls intercepted. At the time, the relevant domestic law and procedure required that the police obtain a warrant issued by the Home Secretary prior to intercepting telephone calls. The applicant complained that the interception of his telephone and his correspondence was in violation of Art 8.

*Commission:*  The Commission noted in its report that the existence of laws and practices in England and Wales which permit and establish a system for effecting secret surveillance of communications amounted in itself to an 'interference ... with the exercise' of the applicant's rights under Art 8 regardless of any measures actually undertaken. Thus, it was necessary to consider whether the measures taken were in accordance with the law. With respect to surveillance, it was important that the law 'should define the circumstances in which an interference may take place with reasonable precision'. The Commission considered that the procedure for the issuing of warrants was regulated by administrative practice and not by rules of law, and similarly, that the scope, form, content and duration of a warrant did not appear to be defined by law. In the Commission's opinion, interceptions could not be considered to be carried out 'in accordance with law' and, by 11 votes, with 1 abstention, decided that there had been a breach of the applicant's rights under Art 8.

*Court:*  The issue to be determined was whether domestic law and practice on the interception of communications was laid down 'with reasonable precision in accessible legal rules that sufficiently indicated the scope and manner of exercise of the discretion conferred on the relevant authorities'. The Court found that the present state of the law in England and Wales governing the interception of communications for police purposes was 'somewhat obscure and open to differing interpretations'. Furthermore, the inherent secrecy surrounding telephone tapping carries with it the danger of abuse by the authorities which could be harmful for democratic society. The Court was satisfied that the interference with the applicant's right to respect for his private life and correspondence was not 'in accordance with the law', and was unanimous in its decision that there had been a violation of Art 8 of the Convention. In view of this conclusion, the Court did not consider whether the national rules provided guarantees against abuse but acknowledged that this type of interference could only be regarded as 'necessary in a democratic society' if the system of surveillance provided adequate guarantees against abuse.

*Note:*  The scope of this case is limited to the question of interceptions carried out by, or on behalf of, the police involved in a general criminal investigation, and does not consider the powers given to other law enforcement agencies such as customs officers or the security services. The Interception of Communications Act 1985, which has been introduced subsequent to this decision, expressly sets out the grounds for the authorised interception of communications on the public telecommunications systems.

## (2)  PRIVATE AND BUSINESS TELEPHONES

## Huvig v France

## (1990) 12 EHRR 528

*Facts:*   In the course of a criminal investigation, the investigating judge authorised the interception of the applicants' private and business telephones. Although there was no statutory provision to permit telephone tapping, the Code of Criminal Procedure empowered a judge to order any necessary investigative measure connected with the prosecution of an offence. The applicants complained that domestic law did not provide sufficient safeguards against arbitrary interference with the rights protected by Art 8.

*Commission:*   Before the Commission, the government listed 17 safeguards provided by French law which related to telephone tapping. Nevertheless, the Commission was of the opinion, by 10 votes to 2, that there had been a breach of Art 8.

*Court:*   The interception of telephone conversations amounted to a serious inter-ference with the exercise of the applicants' right to private life and correspondence. This interference was in breach of the Convention unless it was in accordance with the law and for the purpose of one of the aims referred to in Art 8(2). The expression 'in accordance with the law' required that the interception had some basis in domestic law. It also refers to the quality of the legal rule which must be accessible and foreseeable and must be compatible with the rule of law. The Court was satisfied that the telephone tapping had a legal basis in French law which was sufficiently accessible to the persons affected. However, the nature of this form of intrusion required that the law regulating it must be 'particularly precise'. Although French law provided some valuable safeguards, including the need for a decision by an investigating judge, the Court considered that overall the system lacked sufficient legal certainty and did not afford adequate safeguards against abuse:

> 'For example, the categories of people liable to have their telephones tapped by judicial order and the nature of the offence which may give rise to such an order are nowhere defined. Nothing obliges a judge to set a limit on the duration of telephone tapping. Similarly unspecified are the procedures for drawing up the summary reports containing intercepted conversations; the precautions to be taken in order to communicate the recordings intact and in their entirety for possible inspection by the judge and the defence; and the circumstances in which recordings may or must be erased or the tapes destroyed, in particular where an accused has been discharged by an investigating judge or acquitted by a court' (para 34).

As a consequence, the applicants did not enjoy the minimum degree of protection to which they were entitled under the rule of law in a democratic society. Accordingly, there had been a violation of the Convention.

*Note:*   In relation to common-law systems, the Court has held that the word 'law' in the expression 'prescribed by law' includes statutes and the unwritten common law. In this case the Commission considered that in France only a substantive enactment of general application could amount to law for the purposes of Art 8(2). In continental legal systems, case-law is considered to be a secondary source of law. However, in relation to Art 8(2), the Court has always interpreted the term 'law' in the substantive rather than the formal sense. This interpretation prevents problems arising from differences in the legal systems of the Contracting States. The Court emphasised that case-law plays an important part in the development of the law in continental countries, and to ignore it would be to 'undermine the legal system of the Continental States almost as much as the *Sunday Times* judgement of 26 April 1979 would have "struck at the roots" of the United Kingdom's legal system if it had excluded the common law from the concept of law'. Accordingly, the Court held that with regard to the written law, the term 'law' 'is the legislative enactment as interpreted by the courts in the light of recent case law'.

## (3)   RECORDING OF CONVERSATION WITH A THIRD PARTY

### A v France

### (1993) 17 EHRR 462

*Facts:*   The applicant complained that the recording of her telephone conversation with a third party, at the instigation of the third party, infringed her right to respect for private life and correspondence within the meaning of Art 8. The conversation was recorded by a police officer acting without the authority of either his superior officer or an investigating judge. Although the government conceded that the interception was not in accordance with French law, it contested the applicability of Art 8, in that there had neither been invasion of privacy, as the conversation dealt exclusively with preparations for the commission of a crime, and nor was there interference by a public authority.

*Court:*   A telephone conversation did not lose its character because its content concerned the public interest. Although the authorities did not order the interception, the officer was acting in the performance of his duties as a high-ranking police officer. The Court was satisfied that the authorities were involved to such an extent that the State's responsibility under the Convention was engaged. The interception constituted an interference which was not in accordance with the law and accordingly there was a breach of Art 8.

## (4)   INTERCEPTION OF OFFICE TELEPHONES

### Halford v United Kingdom

### (1997) 24 EHRR 523

*Facts:*   The applicant complained that telephone calls made from her office and from her home had been intercepted. The government accepted that there was a reasonable likelihood that calls made from her office telephone had been intercepted but did not accept that calls made from her home had been intercepted. She complained that the interception amounted to an unjustifiable interference with her right to respect for private life and freedom of expression, contrary to Arts 8 and 10.

*Commission:* The Commission accepted that conversations made on the telephones in the applicant's office fell within the scope of 'private life' and 'correspondence' in Art 8, since the Court in its case-law had adopted a broad construction of these expressions. It was of the opinion, by 26 votes to 1, that there had been violations of Art 8 in relation to the applicant's office telephones and, unanimously, that there had been no violation of Arts 8 or 10 in relation to her home telephones.

*Court:* In rejecting the government's submission that employers should, in principle, be able to monitor calls made by employees on office telephones, the Court decided that telepone calls made from business premises are covered by the notions of 'private life' and 'correspondence' within Art 8. Employees who made calls on an internal telecommunications system operated by their employer should have a reasonable expectation of privacy. In this case, the government conceded that the office calls had been intercepted. The Court was satisfied that the applicant's employer had not given a warning that the calls may be intercepted. Since domestic law did not regulate the interception of calls made on an internal system, it could not be said that the interception was 'in accordance with the law' as required by Art 8. Accordingly, the Court was unanimous in holding that there had been a violation of Art 8 in relation to calls made on the applicant's office telephones. However, the Court was not satisfied that there was sufficient evidence to establish that the calls made from home had been intercepted and thus could find no violation in respect of these calls.

## (5) INTRUSIVE SURVEILLANCE
## Khan v United Kingdom
## (2001) 31 EHRR 45

*Facts:* The applicant argued that a tape recording of a conversation acquired by the use of a listening device attached to a private house without the knowledge of the owners or occupiers was obtained in violation of his right to privacy. He also complained that the use at trial of evidence obtained in breach of a right guaranteed by the Convention was incompatible with the requirements of fairness guaranteed by Art 6. Following a refusal by the trial judge to exercise his discretion to exclude evidence of the tape recording, the applicant pleaded guilty to drug-related offences. In dismissing the appeal, the House of Lords held that there was no right to privacy in English law and at common law relevant evidence obtained irregularly was admissible, notwithstanding it having been obtained by the use of a covert listening device. The court went on to say that although evidence obtained in violation of a right guaranteed by the Convention was relevant to the exercise of the judge's discretion to exclude evidence under s 78 of PACE, it was not a determinative factor. Although their Lordships considered that the lack of a statutory system regulating the use of surveillance devices by the police was 'astonishing', they were not prepared to overrule the trial judge's decision on admissibility. The government accepted that the listening device did interfere with the applicant's right to privacy, but denied it amounted to a breach of Art 8 on the ground that the regulation of police surveillance operations met with the requirement that any interference must be in accordance with the law and necessary in a democratic society for the prevention of crime.

*Court:* The Court noted that the phrase 'in accordance with law' refers not merely to compliance with domestic law, but requires that the domestic rules be compatible with the rule of law. In the context of intrusive police surveillance, domestic rules must provide protection against arbitrary interference with an individual's rights under Art 8. The Court was unanimous in finding that the Home Office Guidelines of 1984, the rules applicable at the relevant time, were neither legally binding nor sufficiently accessible to the public and were consequently inadequate to meet the requirements of Art 8. Although the applicant did not suggest that the requirement of fairness guaranteed by Art 6 necessitated the automatic exclusion of evidence obtained in breach of Art 8, he argued that a conviction obtained *solely* on the basis of evidence obtained in consequence of the unlawful acts of prosecuting authorities is contrary to the rule of law and incompatible with Art 6. In considering this issue, the Court stated that its primary function was to determine whether the applicant's trial as a whole was fair, and not to rule whether evidence of this type must, as a matter of principle, be excluded. Acknowledging that the tape recording was, in effect, the only evidence tendered for the prosecution, the Court considered it of relevance that there was no suggestion that this evidence was unreliable. Where there was no risk of unreliability, the need for the court to look for supporting evidence was less important. In rejecting the applicant's claim, the Court noted that he had had ample opportunity to challenge the authenticity of the recording and the domestic courts had a discretionary power under s 78 of PACE to exclude the evidence if they considered its admission would render the trial unfair. The applicant also claimed that if a breach of Art 8 did not satisfy the requirements of s 78 of PACE, then national law failed to provide an effective remedy to enforce the substance of the rights and freedoms guaranteed by the Convention. Considering this element of the applicant's claim related to the breach of Art 8, the Court noted that the criminal courts were called on to consider the admissibility of evidence and not to assess whether any interference with the applicant's right to privacy was in accordance with the law, and further had no power to grant relief. In holding that Art 13 had been violated, the Court rejected the government's submission that it was open to the applicant to lodge a complaint with the Police Complaints Authority. It noted the role played by the Secretary of State in appointing and dismissing members of this body, and considered the system failed to meet the required standard of independence to ensure protection against abuse of authority.

## PG and JH v United Kingdom
## [2001] HRCD 707

*Facts:* The complaint concerned the monitoring and recording of conversations by means of a covert listening device which was placed in the home of one of the applicants; the monitoring of calls made on the applicant's telephone; and the use of listening devices to obtain voice samples while the applicants were at a police station. In addition, the applicants complained that the non-disclosure of evidence relating to the authorisation of the listening device, the hearing of oral evidence by the judge in private, the use in evidence of information obtained from the listening device at the applicant's home, and the manner in which voice samples were obtained amounted to a violation of Art 6.

*Court:*    The Court held unanimously that using a covert listening device to record conversations in the applicant's home was a violation of Art 8. Acknowledging that this case was similar to *Khan v United Kingdom* (2001) 31 EHRR 45, the majority of the Court was satisfied that the use in evidence of material obtained in this manner did not violate the right to a fair trial. Observing that the government accepted that police surveillance of the applicant's apartment was not in accordance with the law existing at the time, and noting that there was no statutory scheme to regulate the use of listening devices at the police station, the Court was satisfied that Art 8 had been violated on both occasions. However, the monitoring of telephone calls was considered to be necessary in a democratic society and thus did not violate Art 8. In rejecting the applicants' complaint in respect of non-disclosure, the Court observed that the entitlement to disclosure of relevant evidence is not an absolute right. In any criminal proceedings there may be competing interests, such as national security or the need to protect witnesses or keep secret police methods of criminal investigation. In this case the Court was satisfied that the defence was kept informed and allowed to participate as far as was possible without disclosing sensitive material; defence questions were put to the prosecution witness by the judge in chambers; non-disclosed evidence was not used as part of the prosecution case; and the need for disclosure was monitored by the judge throughout the proceedings. In further rejecting the applicants' submission that the use at trial of the taped evidence obtained in breach of Art 8 amounted to breach of fair trial rights, the Court observed that the tape recording of conversations was not the only evidence against the applicants: the prosecution called 45 witnesses and incriminating evidence was found at the address of one of the applicants and in the car which the applicants were driving. The applicants had been given the opportunity to challenge both the authenticity and the use of the tape. Further, the domestic court retained the discretionary power to exclude evidence if it formed the view that its admission would give rise to substantive unfairness. In rejecting the argument that the manner in which the voice samples were obtained infringed the privilege against self-incrimination, the Court observed that voice samples could be considered as akin to blood, hair or other physical or objective specimens used in forensic analysis to which this privilege did not apply.

## UNITED KINGDOM CASES

## R v P

## House of Lords, [2001] 2 All ER 58

*Facts:*    The appellants argued that, as a matter of public policy, transcripts of telephone conversations obtained by intercepting telephones outside the jurisdiction, which by reason of the operation of the Interception of Communications Act 1985 would be inadmissible if obtained in the UK, should not be adduced at trial, whether or not the interception was in accordance with foreign law, and whether or not such evidence would be received in foreign criminal proceedings. The Court of Appeal was satisfied with the trial judge's finding that the foreign law enforcement agencies had acted lawfully throughout the proceedings. The telephone calls, which were recorded by means of an intercept being placed on a telephone in another country, were in accordance with the law of that country, as was the subsequent handing over to the British authorities for the purposes of prosecution. The Court of Appeal reviewed the national authorities and Convention case-law and was satisfied that they provided support for the view that the discretionary power to exclude evidence under s 78 of PACE 'marches hand in hand' with Art 6(1) of the Convention.

*House of Lords:*   In dismissing the appeal, the court observed that the decision of *Khan v United Kingdom* (2001) 31 EHRR 45 demonstrated that the HRA 1998 did not invalidate previous national authority and that s 78 was an appropriate safeguard of the fairness of the trial. It provided a highly persuasive authority in favour of the prosecution case. The critical question for the court in this case was whether the appellants had received a fair trial. The court noted that the European Court of Human Rights emphasised that the defendant was not automatically entitled to have unlawfully obtained evidence excluded merely because it had been obtained unlawfully. Convention case-law established that the fair use of intercept evidence at trial is not a breach of Art 6, even if the evidence was obtained in breach of another right protected by the Convention. When considering whether to exercise the discretion to exclude the intercept evidence under s 78 of PACE, the trial judge is required to apply the same criteria that would be applied when determining fairness under Art 6.

# Chapter 6
# ARREST, DETENTION AND BAIL

## 6.1 MEANING OF DETENTION
### Guzzardi v Italy
### (1980) 3 EHRR 333

*Facts:* The applicant was suspected of involvement in criminal activities linked to the Mafia. He was required to live on a restricted part of a small island and was subjected to constant surveillance by the authorities. He was later moved to a mainland village and was required to report daily to the authorities. He complained, inter alia, that the requirement to live in a restricted area effectively deprived him of his liberty and was in breach of Art 5.

*Court:* Compulsory residence on the small island amounted to a loss of liberty and accordingly his detention was subject to the requirements of Art 5. The residency order in respect of the mainland did not result in the applicant's liberty for the purposes of Art 5.

## 6.2 RIGHT TO 'SECURITY' OF THE PERSON
### Bozano v France
### (1987) 9 EHRR 297

*Facts:* The applicant was convicted in absentia in Italy of serious crimes. The Italian authorities unsuccessfully sought his extradition from France. The French government ordered his deportation from France and he was arrested and taken to the Swiss border and was then extradited to Italy. He complained that his arrest and forcible removal to Switzerland was contrary to Art 5(1) in that it deprived him of his right to liberty and security of the person.

*Court:* The Court considered that the purpose of Art 5 was to protect the individual from arbitrariness which required that any measure depriving an individual of his liberty must be compatible with the purposes of this provision. It noted that Art 5 was concerned with an individual's right to liberty and his right to security of the person. Accordingly, the applicant's abduction by the authorities was neither lawful nor compatible with his right to security of the person. It was really a disguised form of extradition and his detention was not for any of the purposes set out in Art 5.

## 6.3   GROUNDS OF ARREST

### (1)   REASONABLE SUSPICION

# Brogan and Others v United Kingdom

## (1988) 11 EHRR 117

*Facts:*   The applicants were arrested under s 12 of the Prevention of Terrorism (Temporary Provisions) Act 1984 on reasonable suspicion of being involved in the commission, preparation or instigation of acts of terrorism. Within a few hours of arrest, they were cautioned and questioned about their involvement in specific criminal offences. None of the applicants was brought before a judicial authority and they were all subsequently released without charge. They complained that their arrest and detention was not grounded on reasonable suspicion of having committed a criminal offence as required by Art 5(1)(c).

*Commission:*   The purpose of a criminal investigation was to discover the evidence required for a conviction and thus it was not a condition of arrest that the commission of the offence had been established. The reasonable suspicion referred to in this provision does not mean that the person's guilt can be established at the time of arrest. However, if the interrogation does not confirm the suspicion, the detainee will normally be released and not brought before a court. The Commission was unanimous in finding no violation of Art 5(1)(c).

*Court:*   The Court noted that the applicants were all questioned within a relatively short time of their detention and the questioning related to specific offences. Accordingly, it was satisfied that these arrests were based on reasonable suspicion of the commission of an offence within the meaning of Art 5(1)(c). The fact that the applicants were neither charged nor brought before a court did not necessarily mean that the purpose of their detention was not in accordance with Art 5(1)(c). Article 5(1) 'does not presuppose that the police should have obtained sufficient evidence to bring charges, either at the point of arrest or while the applicants were in custody'. The Court could find nothing to suggest that the police acted in bad faith and were satisfied that the applicants' arrest was for the bona fide reason of confirming or dispelling concrete suspicions.

# Fox, Campbell and Hartley v United Kingdom

## (1990) 13 EHRR 157

*Facts:*   The applicants were arrested and detained by the police for up to 44 hours under s 1 of the Northern Ireland (Emergency Provisions) Act 1978. They complained that the basis of their arrest was not 'reasonable suspicion' of having committed a criminal offence as required by Art 5(1), but was for the purpose of interrogation and intelligence gathering.

*Court:*   The Court considered that having a reasonable suspicion 'presupposes the existence of facts or information which would satisfy an objective observer that the person concerned may have committed a criminal offence. What may be regarded as "reasonable" will however depend upon all the circumstances'. It was acknowledged that the investigation and prosecution of terrorist offences presented the authorities with specific problems. Thus, the 'reasonableness' of the suspicion justifying such arrests cannot always be judged according to the same standards as are applied in dealing with conventional crime. However, the Court was of the opinion that the notion of reasonable suspicion could not be stretched to the point 'where the essence of the safeguard secured by Art 5(1)(c) is impaired'. The Court considered that although the arrest and detention of the applicants had been based on an honest suspicion, the government failed to provide sufficient evidence that there had been a 'reasonable suspicion' for the purposes of Art 5(1)(c). Accordingly, there was a violation of Art 5(1).

*Note:* Section 6 of the Northern Ireland (Emergency Provisions) Act 1987, which came into force on 15 June 1987 and was subsequent to the facts of this case, replaced s 11(1) of the Northern Ireland (Emergency Provisions) Act 1978 which had contained no requirement that the suspicions of the arresting officer should be 'reasonable' (Resolution DH (91) 39 of 13 December 1991).

# Murray v United Kingdom
## (1995) 19 EHRR 193

*Facts:* The applicant was arrested by a British army officer under s 14 of the Northern Ireland (Emergency Provisions) Act 1978, allegedly on suspicion of involvement in the collection of money for the purchase of arms for the Provisional IRA in the USA. Under this legislation, a member of the armed forces was empowered to arrest without warrant and detain for up to 4 hours a person whom he or she honestly and genuinely suspected of committing any criminal offence. Despite repeated requests by the applicant, the officer would not disclose details of the nature of the criminal offence allegedly committed. She complained that contrary to Art 5(1)(c) she had not been arrested on reasonable suspicion of having committed a criminal offence. Furthermore, the purpose of her arrest and subsequent detention had not been to bring her before a competent authority but for the purpose of interrogating her with a view to gathering intelligence.

*Court:* The Court's task was to determine whether the national legislation met the objective standard of 'reasonable suspicion' laid down in Art 5(1). Although intelligence gathering is essential in combating terrorist offences, investigating authorities do not have carte blanche to arrest suspects for questioning free from effective control by domestic courts and by the supervisory institutions of the Convention. The existence of reasonable suspicion will depend on the facts of each case. It was relevant, but not decisive, that the 1978 Act provided for an honest and genuine belief, a subjective standard, rather than reasonable suspicion which is an objective standard. The Court noted that the level of suspicion required for arrest and detention was not the same as that needed to justify a conviction or bring a criminal charge and considered that the length of the deprivation of liberty at risk was also relevant. In this case the period of detention was limited to a maximum of 4 hours. The Court found that there were sufficient facts or information which provided a plausible and objective basis for suspicion that the applicant may have committed a criminal offence. Accordingly, the Court was satisfied that she was arrested and detained on 'reasonable suspicion'.

## 6.4   LENGTH OF PRE-TRIAL DETENTION

### (1)   DETENTION BEFORE CHARGE

## Brogan and Others v United Kingdom

## (1988) 11 EHRR 117

*Facts:*   The applicants complained that their arrest and detention under s 12 of the Prevention of Terrorism (Temporary Provisions) Act 1984 was an infringement of the requirement in Art 5(3) that detainees 'shall be brought promptly' before a judicial authority. A person arrested under s 12 could be detained for a period of 7 days without being brought before a magistrate or other judicial authority.

*Commission:*   The case-law established that a period of 4 days in ordinary cases and 5 days in exceptional cases satisfied the requirement of promptness in Art 5(3). Accordingly, the Commission was of the opinion that the detention of two of the applicants for periods of 5 days and 11 hours and 6 days and 16½ hours was excessively long and in violation of the Convention.

*Court:*   The Court took judicial notice of the special difficulties facing law enforcement agencies involved in the investigation of serious terrorist offences. It accepted that, subject to certain safeguards, it might be necessary to extend the period in which the authorities may keep a suspect in police custody before being brought before a magistrate. However, the degree of flexibility in the notion of promptness was very limited for the purposes of Art 5(3). The Court considered that attaching too much importance to the nature of the offence in order to justify 'so lengthy a period of detention without appearance before a judge' would result in an excessively wide interpretation of the word 'promptly'. As a consequence, the procedural guarantee provided by Art 5(3) would be significantly impaired. The fact that the applicants' detention was for the purposes of protecting the community as a whole from terrorism was insufficient to prevent the Court finding that there had been a violation of Art 5(3).

*Note:*   On the basis of the threat posed by terrorism in relation to Northern Ireland, the UK government decided that the special arrest and detention provisions were necessary and should remain in place. Accordingly, the Secretary General of the Council of Europe was notified of the UK's intention to derogate from Art 5(3) (Resolution DH (90) 23 of 24 September 1990). This took effect from 23 December 1988 and ended on 23 March 1989.

### (2)   DETENTION PENDING TRIAL

## Wemhoff v Federal Republic of Germany

## (1968) 1 EHRR 55

*Facts:*   The applicant was arrested and charged with offences relating to breach of trust and remanded in detention for a period in excess of 3 years pending trial. He complained that the length of time spent in custody exceeded the 'reasonable time' requirement contained in Art 5(3) of the Convention.

*Commission:*   The Commission found that the expression 'reasonable time' was 'vague and lacking in precision' and required evaluation in the light of the following seven criteria: the actual length of detention; the nature of the offence; material moral or other effects on the detainee; conduct of the accused; difficulties in the investigation of the offence; the manner in which the investigation was conducted; and the conduct of the judicial authorities concerned. Although no criticism could be made of the conduct of the case by the judicial authorities, the Commission attached particular importance to the actual length of detention and expressed the opinion, by seven votes to three, that Art 5(3) had been violated.

*Court:*   The Court did 'not feel able' to adopt the Commission's approach, and considered that it must 'judge whether the reasons given by the national authorities to justify continued detention are relevant and sufficient to show that detention was not unreasonably prolonged' (para 12). The reasons given in this case related to the complex nature of the case and fear that the applicant would suppress evidence. The Court was satisfied that these reasons justified the applicant's continued remand in custody, and concluded that unless the exceptional length of the proceedings was due to a fault on the part of the authorities there was no breach of the obligations imposed by Art 3.

## MB v Switzerland
## Application No 28256/95, unreported

*Facts:*   The applicant, who had at one time admitted that she was a member of a terrorist organisation, complained that her request for release from detention was decided with insufficient haste to comply with Art 5(4), which guarantees detainees not only the right to institute proceedings to challenge the lawfulness of detention but also the right to a speedy decision. Having withdrawn her admission, she requested release from detention on the ground that there was no evidence against her and requested access to the case file. A period of 34 days passed from the time the court confirmed her detention to the service of the Federal Attorney's decision to dismiss her request.

*Court:*   The requirement that decisions must be taken 'speedily' must be determined in the light of the circumstances of each case. Although noting that the applicant was detained in connection with serious offences, the Court considered that the issues relating to the applicant's request for release were straightforward. Further, the fact that Switzerland had chosen a two–tier structure to consider release from detention on remand, which may take more time than a simple process, did not justify undue delay. It was for the State to organise its judicial system in such a way as to comply with the requirements of the Convention. In this case the Court was unanimous in holding that the overall duration of the proceedings was excessive and in breach of Art 5(4).

## Szeloch v Poland
## Application No 33079/96, unreported

*Facts:*   The applicant complained, inter alia, that his detention on remand for a period of 4 years and 3 months was unreasonably long. He submitted that the main reason for his lengthy pre-trial detention, which was used to establish whether he was responsible for sexually abusing children, was effectively a punitive measure. The government argued that his detention was based on a firm suspicion and was subject to regular review by a judge. Furthermore, the applicant's continued detention was justified on the grounds of the complexity of the case, which involved very serious offences, and that there was a real risk that the applicant would interfere with witnesses.

*Court:* Although lawful detention must be based on reasonable suspicion, after a lapse of time it is no longer by itself a sufficient reason for continued detention. The Court considered it necessary to examine whether the grounds given by the national authorities justified the applicant's continued remand in custody. Finding an absence of concrete facts to support the government's submission, the Court was of the view that the grounds relied on 'can not be deemed, as is required by case law, relevant and sufficient throughout the applicant's pre-trial detention' (para 92). Furthermore, the Court noted that the national court did not address the applicant's request to consider other forms of pre-trial remand. Accordingly, the Court found a violation of Art 5.

## 6.5   PROCEDURE 'PRESCRIBED BY LAW'

### Steel v United Kingdom

### (1999) 28 EHRR 603

*Facts:*   The applicants had all been arrested and charged with conduct likely to cause a breach of the peace. Although not categorised as a criminal offence in domestic law, it was not disputed that breach of the peace was an offence within the meaning of Art 5(1). Following a finding that the case against her was proved, the first-named applicant was committed to prison for 28 days when she refused to be bound over to keep the peace. The second applicant also refused to be bound over and was committed to prison for 7 days. The third, fourth and fifth applicants were detained by the police for 7 hours but the proceedings against them were withdrawn when the prosecution decided not to call any evidence. They all complained, inter alia, that their arrest and detention had not been 'prescribed by law' as required by Art 5(1) and was a disproportionate interference with their right to freedom of expression. In addition, it was argued that the first and second applicants' detention for non-compliance with a court order amounted to a serious interference with their right to freedom of expression.

*Court:*   The Court rejected the applicants' argument that the provision under which they were detained was too vague to allow them 'to foresee to a reasonable degree' the legal consequences of their behaviour. It was satisfied that the concept of breach of the peace had been sufficiently clarified by the English courts to permit a person to be detained if it was reasonably feared that they would cause harm to persons or property or provoke others to violence. Having examined the evidence, the Court found that the police were justified in fearing that the first and second applicants might provoke others to violence but the behaviour of the other applicants had been entirely peaceful. Accordingly, there was no infringement in respect of the arrest and detention of the first two applicants but there had been a breach in respect of the others. Although the first and second applicants' detention amounted to an interference with their right to freedom of expression, in the circumstances it was not disproportionate, bearing in mind the importance in a democratic society of maintaining the rule of law.

# Hashman and Harrup v United Kingdom

## (2000) 30 EHRR 241

*Facts:* The applicants were bound over by the Gillingham magistrates to keep the peace and be of good behaviour. On appeal, the Crown Court held that, although their conduct did not amount to a breach of peace, it was contra bonos mores, and bound them over. The applicants alleged a violation of Art 10 in that the concept of contra bonos mores, which is defined as behaviour that is 'wrong rather than right in the judgment of the majority of contemporary fellow citizens', is too broadly defined to comply with the requirement that any interference with freedom of expression must be 'prescribed by law'.

*Court:* The Court held, by 16 votes to 1, that the order binding over the applicants not to behave contra bonos mores was too vague and imprecise to comply with Art 10(2). Restating the principle that a norm cannot be regarded as a 'law' unless it is formulated with sufficient precision to enable the citizen to regulate his conduct, the Court considered that the provision to bind over a person to be of good behaviour was insufficiently well defined. An individual may not be able to identify the type of behaviour which would breach the order of the court.

# 6.6 DETENTION OF MINORS

## Bouamar v Belgium

## (1987) 11 EHRR 1

*Facts:* The applicant complained that his detention in a remand prison on nine separate occasions with a view to his being committed to a suitable institution was not justified under the terms of Art 5(1)(d). Under this provision, minors may be detained only for the purposes of educational supervision or to bring them before a competent legal authority.

*Commission:* The Commission noted that detention under Art 5(1) must be for one of the categories of arrest or detention listed in sub-paragraphs (a) to (f). Belgian legislation provided for the provisional detention of minors for a period not exceeding 15 days if it proved 'materially impossible to find an institution capable of receiving the minor immediately'. The legislation was intended as an urgent measure and came within the scope of Art 5(1)(d), but the manner in which it was applied was not compatible with the Convention. The Commission noted that this case did not concern an individual placement but involved nine successive periods, each lasting 15 days, and that at the time there was no custodial institution capable of receiving the applicant.

*Court:* The Court emphasised that it was for domestic courts to interpret and apply domestic law and in principle it was not for the Court to express a view on the Belgian system. Article 5(1)(d) does not preclude an interim custody measure being used as a preliminary to a regime of supervised education provided the imprisonment is swiftly followed by an educational programme. In reality, the applicant was detained in a remand prison in conditions of virtual isolation and without the assistance of staff with educational training. The Court was not prepared to accept that his detention could not be regarded as furthering any educational aim, and was in breach of Art 5(1).

## 6.7  DETENTION OF THE MENTALLY ILL

### Winterwerp v The Netherlands

### (1979–80) 2 EHRR 387

*Facts:*  The applicant was committed to a psychiatric hospital by the direction of the local burgomaster under an emergency procedure in 1968. He had previously received voluntary treatment following an accident in which he had suffered severe brain damage. Six weeks later, on his wife's application, he was confined to the same hospital under an order made by the District Court. On his wife's application, and later at the request of the public prosecutor, the commitment order was renewed from year to year. At the time of the application the most recent renewal order was made in 1977. The applicant relied on both Arts 5 and 6.

*Court:*  There was no dispute that the applicant had been deprived of his liberty within the meaning of Art 5(1). The applicant argued that his detention did not meet the requirements embodied in the words 'lawful detention of persons of sound mind'. 'Sound mind' is not a term which is defined in the Convention, and 'it is a term whose meaning is continually evolving, as research in psychiatry progresses, an increasing flexibility in treatment is developing and society's attitude to mental illness changes, in particular so that a greater understanding of the problems of mental patients is becoming more widespread' (para 37). The relevant Netherlands legislation did not appear to be inconsistent with the wording of Art 5, and a person detained under it, the Court found, 'in principle falls within the ambit of Art 5(1)' (para 38).

The Court then considered whether the detention could be characterised as 'lawful'. The evidence submitted to the courts in the present case indicated that the applicant showed schizophrenic and paranoiac reactions, was unaware of his condition, and had committed some fairly serious acts without being aware of their consequences. Various attempts at his rehabilitation had failed. The Court found therefore that the confinement was lawful, and that the procedure under which the detention was implemented was also lawful.

The applicant further argued that Art 5 encompassed, for any person of unsound mind, the right to appropriate treatment in order to ensure that they were not detained longer than absolutely necessary. The Court held that the Article did not give rise to a positive right of treatment.

The Court found that Art 5(1) had not been breached. However, the Court was still obliged to consider whether Art 5(4) had been breached. Neither the burgomaster nor the public prosecutor could be regarded as possessing the characteristics of a court. Although the District Court was clearly a court, the intervention of such a body would satisfy the requirements of Art 5(4) only where 'the procedure followed has a judicial character and gives to the individual concerned guarantees appropriate to the kind of deprivation of liberty in question' (para 57). The Court found that that was not the case here, holding that:

'... it is essential that the person concerned should have access to a court and the opportunity to be heard either in person or, where necessary, through some form of representation ... Mental illness may entail restricting or modifying the manner or exercise of such a right ... but it cannot justify impairing the very essence of the right. Indeed, special procedural safeguards may prove called for in order to protect the interests of persons who, on account of their mental disabilities, are not fully capable of acting for themselves' (para 60).

Here, the applicant was never associated in the proceedings leading to the various detention orders made against him, and was not heard by the courts, nor given the chance to argue his case. The Court found that the procedures in the present case did not meet the requirements of Art 5(4). The Court concluded:

'To sum up, the various decisions ordering or authorising Mr Winterwerp's detention issued from bodies which either did not possess the characteristics of a "court" or, alternatively, failed to furnish the guarantees of judicial procedure required by Art 5(4); neither did the applicant have access to a "court" or the benefit of such guarantees when his requests for discharge were examined, save in regard to his first request which was rejected by the Regional Court ... Mr Winterwerp was accordingly the victim of a breach of article 5(4)' (para 67).

*Note:* See also *Winterwerp v The Netherlands No 2* (1982) 4 EHRR 228 where the Court dealt with the issue of just satisfaction.

# Riera Blume and Others v Spain

## (2000) 30 EHRR 632

*Facts:* The applicants were members of a religious sect, the *Centro Esoterico de Investigaciones* who, following an investigation ordered by a judge, were arrested. They were then released into the custody of their families at an hotel where they were detained in separate rooms for 3 days under the supervision of psychiatrists for 'deprogramming' as it was feared that their behaviour could be erratic and dangerous, and that they might be suicidal. On their release all the applicants immediately lodged a criminal complaint alleging, inter alia, false imprisonment, and offences against the exercise of personal rights. Proceedings were initiated, but the accused were subsequently acquitted on the grounds that the acts complained of had been prompted by a philanthropic and well-intentioned motive. This verdict was upheld on appeal, and the Constitutional Court refused to intervene on the grounds that there was no fundamental right to have a person convicted.

*Court:* The applicants based their claim on Art 5 and the Court was unanimous in holding that there had been a breach of the Convention. In order to determine whether someone has been deprived of their liberty the starting point must be the concrete situation, and account must be taken of a whole range of criteria (see eg *Engel v Netherlands (No 1)* (1979–80) 1 EHRR 647). It was not disputed that the judge had given oral instructions to the police to hand the applicants over to their families and had suggested that it would be as well to intern them in a psychiatric centre. The applicants were kept in secured rooms under constant supervision, and were, during this time, questioned by an official. The Catalan police and the authorities played a significant role in the detention of the applicants, for which there was no legal basis. Accordingly Art 5 had been breached.

## UNITED KINGDOM CASES

## R v Mental Health Review Tribunal; Secretary of State for Health, ex parte KB and Others

### QBD, Administrative Court, [2002] EWHC Admin 639, unreported

*Facts:* Applications for judicial review of the process under which reviews of detention under the Mental Health Act 1983 were lodged. In each case hearings arranged by the Mental Health Review Tribunal were repeatedly delayed, and delays were increasing over time. The patients affected argued that the delays constituted breaches of Art 5 of the Convention, and that their cases were representative of a general failure in the system.

*Held:* Questions relating to the administration of justice generally, and in particular financial resourcing, did not fall to be considered by the courts (see eg Lord Bridge in *R v Secretary of State for the Environment, ex parte Hammersmith & Fulham London Borough Council* [1990] 3 All ER 589: 'what is the appropriate level of public expenditure and public taxation is, and always has been, a matter of political opinion'). However, where issues were raised in relation to the application of Art 5 the Court had jurisdiction to review the compatibility of the relevant processes with that provision. In the present cases the requirements that a hearing be held within a reasonable time were breached, and the Secretary of State must have been aware that delays were occurring, or were likely to occur. The applications were allowed.

## Re F (Adult Patient)

### Court of Appeal, [2000] UKHRR 712

*Facts:* The High Court had agreed to hear a claim for declaratory relief in respect of T, a mentally incapacitated female adult, in respect of whom the local authority was seeking a declaration to the effect that T be kept in local authority care. There was evidence of systematic neglect and sexual abuse while T was within the family home. T's mother at first consented to her being placed in care, but later withdrew that consent. The mother appealed, relying in part on Arts 5 and 8 of the Convention.

*Held:* The Mental Health Act 1959 did not make sufficient provision in respect of adults who were not able to look after themselves, as was recognised by the House of Lords in *Re F (Mental Patient – Sterilisation)* [1990] 2 AC 1, and in those cases the common-law doctrine of necessity could be invoked. In doing so, account had to be taken of the fundamental rights guaranteed by the Convention, Art 5 of which permitted the detention of persons of unsound mind. The respect for family life provided for in Art 8 did not invalidate this provision, but required a proper balance to be drawn up. It was inherent in Art 8 that the courts and local authorities had a duty to protect persons where they were not able properly to protect themselves, as was the case here.

# 6.8   RIGHT TO COMPENSATION FOR UNLAWFUL ARREST

## Brogan and Others v United Kingdom

## (1988) 11 EHRR 117

*Facts:*   The applicants were arrested and detained under s 12 of the Prevention of Terrorism (Temporary Provisions) Act 1984. The Court found that two of the applicants had been arrested and detained without charge for an excessively long period, in breach of Art 5(3) of the Convention. They claimed that domestic law did not provide an enforceable right to compensation.

*Court:*   The UK government did not dispute that it was not open to the applicants to seek compensation before the Northern Ireland courts on the basis that their detention was in violation of rights guaranteed by the Convention. Accordingly, the applicants did not have an enforceable right to compensation as required by Art 5(4).

## Thynne, Wilson and Gunnell v United Kingdom

## (1990) 13 EHRR 666

*Facts:*   The applicants had been convicted of serious criminal offences and sentenced to discretionary life sentences. Their release was dependent upon a recommendation from the Parole Board. They complained that the lack of regular judicial scrutiny of the lawfulness of their detention was in breach of Art 5(4) and that domestic law did not provide an enforceable right to compensation for the alleged breach.

*Court:*   The Court found no reason to depart from its previous decisions that the Parole Board did not satisfy the requirements of Art 5(4), thus there had been a breach of Art 5(4). The government did not deny that this violation could not give rise to an enforceable claim for compensation before the domestic courts. Accordingly, there had been a violation in respect of Art 5(5).

# 6.9   BAIL

## (1)   REASONS FOR REFUSAL OF BAIL

*LEGISLATIVE PROHIBITION*

## Caballero v United Kingdom

## (2000) 30 EHRR 643

*Facts:*   The applicant complained that his automatic pre-trial detention under s 25 of the Criminal Justice and Public Order Act 1994, which resulted in the automatic denial of bail pending trial, constituted a breach of Art 5(3). Furthermore, he did not have an enforceable right to compensation within the meaning of Art 5(5).

*Commission:*   The Commission found that in enacting s 25 of the 1994 Act the legislature had effectively removed judicial control of pre-trial detention. Observing that judicial control of interference by the executive with an individual's liberty was an essential feature of the guarantees embodied in Art 3, which is designed to minimise the risk of arbitrariness in the pre-trial detention of accused persons, the Commission concluded that there had been a breach of Art 5(3). The Commission also noted that Mr Caballero's detention complied with domestic law and that he did not have a domestic remedy for detention which violated Art 5(3). It concluded therefore that there had been a violation of Art 5(5).

## SBC v United Kingdom
## (2002) 34 EHRR 21

*Facts:* The applicant had been convicted in 1978 of manslaughter and sentenced to 3 years' imprisonment. In 1996, he was arrested on suspicion of incest, rape and indecent assault. He claimed that the application of s 25 of the Criminal Justice and Public Order Act 1994, which resulted in the automatic denial of bail pending trial, constituted a breach of Art 5(3). Furthermore, he did not have an enforceable right to compensation within the meaning of Art 5(5). Although the government was prepared to concede that there had been a violation of Art 5(3) and (5), the Court considered that the circumstances of this case required further examination of the issues arising under Art 5.

*Court:* The Court recalled that in *Caballero v United Kingdom* (2000) 30 EHRR 643 it considered that in order to comply with Art 5 the executive must not fetter the power of a judge to grant bail. After consideration of the facts, the Court considered there to be no material difference between the relevant facts of *Caballero* and the present case. Accordingly, the Court unanimously held that there had been a violation of Art 5 and that the finding of a violation in itself constituted sufficient just satisfaction for any non-pecuniary damage suffered by the applicant.

*Note:* Section 25 of the 1994 Act has now been amended by s 56 of the Crime and Disorder Act 1998 which provides:

> 'In sub-section (1) of section 25 of the 1994 Act (no bail for defendants charged with or convicted of homicide or rape after previous conviction for such offences), for the words "shall not be granted bail in those proceedings" there shall be substituted the words "shall be granted bail in those proceedings only if the court or, as the case may be, the constable considering the grant of bail is satisfied that there are exceptional circumstances which justify it".'

## *FAILURE TO APPEAR*

## Stögmüller v Austria
## (1979–80) 1 EHRR 155

*Facts:* The applicant was arrested and detained for a total of 2 years and 7 weeks pending trial. He was refused bail on the grounds that he might commit further offences or abscond. He complained that his continued detention was in breach of Art 5(3).

*Court:* The Court noted that the danger of the accused absconding was not established just because it was possible or easy for him to cross the border; a requirement that he surrender his passport would have addressed this problem. In order to justify a refusal to grant bail on the basis of failing to appear, there should be 'a whole set of circumstances, particularly, the heavy sentence to be expected or the accused's particular distaste of detention, or the lack of well established ties in the country'. The court would then have reason to suppose that the consequences and hazards of flight would seem to the accused to be a lesser evil than continued imprisonment. In this case the Court was not satisfied that the danger of the applicant absconding was sufficient to justify keeping him in detention. Accordingly, the length of his detention pending trial was unreasonable and in violation of Art 5(3).

## INTERFERENCE WITH THE COURSE OF JUSTICE

## Wemhoff v Federal Republic of Germany

## (1979–80) 1 EHRR 55

*Facts:* The applicant was remanded in custody pending trial for offences relating to breach of trust and denied bail. One of the reasons given by the authorities to justify continued detention was the existence of a danger that, if released, the applicant would suppress important evidence. He complained that his continued detention in custody violated Art 5(3).

*Court:* The reasonableness of the applicant's continued detention must be assessed in each case by reference to its special features. The Court must judge whether the reasons given by the national authorities to justify continued detention are relevant and sufficient to show that detention is not unreasonably prolonged. With regard to the existence of a danger of suppression of evidence, the Court considered this to be a relevant factor and that the anxiety of the German court was justified in view of the nature of the offences and the complexity of the case. Accordingly, the applicant's continued detention was not in breach of Art 5(3).

## RISK OF FURTHER OFFENCES

## Toth v Austria

## (1992) 14 EHRR 551

*Facts:* The applicant was arrested and remanded in custody for a period of 2 years, 1 month and 2 days before he was convicted and sentenced. One of the reasons given by the authorities to justify his continued detention was the danger that he might commit further offences while on bail. He complained that his continued detention pending trial was in violation of Art 5(3).

*Commission:* The Commission noted that the Austrian courts provided evidence of the applicant's previous convictions for similar offences and that he was unemployed. It accepted that in reaching its decision to continue his remand in custody, the domestic court could reasonably conclude that there was a risk of the applicant committing further offences. However, the Commission questioned whether, as the detention continued and the grounds for refusing bail diminished, there was sufficient justification for continued detention. Having regard to the overall length of detention and the lack of diligence by the authorities, the Commission found that the remand in detention exceeded a reasonable time within the meaning of Art 5(3).

*Court:* The Court must judge whether the grounds cited by the national authorities continued to justify detention. Where the grounds for continued detention are relevant and sufficient, the Court must also ascertain whether the national authorities exercised due diligence in the conduct of the proceedings. The Court shared the Commission's view that 'the national courts could reasonably fear that the applicant might commit further offences but considered that the proceedings had not been conducted with due expedition'. Consequently, there had been a violation of Art 5(3).

# Chapter 7

# SENTENCING AND PUNISHMENT

## 7.1 RELEASE ON LICENCE AND TARIFF SENTENCING
### Weeks v United Kingdom
### (1987) 10 EHRR 293

*Facts:* The applicant, who had been sentenced to life imprisonment for robbery, was released on licence. Following his involvement in a number of minor offences, the Home Secretary ordered that his licence be revoked. The Parole Board considered his case and confirmed his recall to prison. There followed a series of releases on licence and recalls to prison, and eventually the applicant moved to France in breach of the conditions of his licence. He complained that his detention was no longer justified under Art 5(1)(a) and that contrary to Art 5(4) he had been unable to challenge the lawfulness of his recall before a court.

*Court:* In order to justify detention under Art 5(1)(a), there must be a sufficient causal link between the conviction and the deprivation of liberty. The Court rejected the applicant's submission that the requisite causal link between the objectives of the sentencing court as regards his loss of liberty, and the decision to recall had been broken. The appropriateness of the original life sentence was not the subject of these proceedings; however, the Court noted that, under English law, his liberty was at the discretion of the executive for the rest of his life. In this case the Court was required to examine the sufficiency of the grounds on which the applicant's recall was ordered, but noted that national authorities were better placed to assess the evidence in any particular case. The Court was of the opinion that the decision of the national authorities remained within the bounds of the margin of appreciation and thus his recall did not violate Art 5(1). Accordingly, the applicant's recall to prison and the period of subsequent detention were not incompatible with the Convention.

*Note:* Life sentences are now imposed only in the most serious of cases and therefore it is unlikely that a similar problem would arise in the future.

### Hussain v United Kingdom
### (1996) 22 EHRR 1

*Facts:* The applicant was convicted of murder and sentenced to detention during Her Majesty's pleasure. The decision whether to recommend release after he had served the punitive part of his sentence was made by the Parole Board. He complained that under current regulations he was unable to have his continued detention reviewed by a court as required by Art 5(4).

*Commission:* The Commission noted the distinction between mandatory and discretionary life sentences. The latter was developed to deal with mentally ill and unstable offenders and served a preventative rather than a punitive purpose. The condition of these offenders was subject to change and the decision to continue their detention required review by a body satisfying the requirements of Art 5(4). The case-law established that the Parole Board did not satisfy these requirements. Although a new Parole Board had been instituted with the power to make decisions and hold oral hearings in some cases, with respect to this applicant it still had no decision-making power and could not be regarded as a body satisfying the requirements of Art 5(4). Consequently, the Commission found that there had been a violation of the Convention.

*Court:* The Court considered whether detention during Her Majesty's pleasure should be classed as a discretionary or mandatory life sentence and concluded that, on balance, it was comparable to a discretionary life sentence. Accordingly, the applicant is entitled under Art 5(4) to have his detention reviewed periodically by a court. The newly constituted Parole Board did not have sufficient powers to satisfy the requirements of Art 5(4). Consequently, the applicant was denied the opportunity to bring his case before a court with the necessary procedural guarantees to satisfy this provision.

## Oldham v United Kingdom

## (2001) 31 EHRR 34

*Facts:* The applicant, a discretionary life prisoner who had been released on licence and recalled to prison complained, inter alia, that a 2-year delay between Parole Board reviews was unreasonable. He was convicted of manslaughter on grounds of diminished responsibility in 1970 and sentenced to life imprisonment. Medical evidence adduced at the trial indicated that he suffered from a mental abnormality induced by alcohol. He was released on licence subject to the condition that he should undergo treatment for his alcohol problem. Following an assault on his partner, he was recalled to prison and his licence revoked. While in prison he attended a variety of courses related to alcohol awareness and anger management. Although his initial application to the Parole Board in 1996 for release was rejected, in 1998 the Board acknowledged a significant progress in his condition and recommended his release. In practice, review hearings took place at intervals of 2 years or less at the discretion of the Secretary of State. The government submitted that in this case 2 years was a reasonable interval between hearings.

*Court:* The issue to be determined is whether the time interval between reviews complies with Convention case-law. This requires that national courts not only reach a decision 'speedily' but also, where an automatic review of detention exists, make decisions at regular intervals. The Court recognised the need for a flexible system of review which took account of the personal circumstances of the prisoner. Although it is not the Court's function to determine the maximum period of time between reviews, in earlier cases the Court and the Commission had accepted periods of less than one year between reviews and rejected periods of more than one year. The Court acknowledged that both the Secretary of State and the Parole Board had the power to bring forward the date of review which introduced some flexibility into the system. However, noting that the applicant in this case had no such power to seek an earlier review, the Court held unanimously that 2 years was excessive and infringed Art 5(4).

## Hirst v United Kingdom
### [2001] HRCD 577

*Facts:* The applicant was sentenced to life imprisonment for manslaughter in 1980 and a tariff period set at 15 years. Due to concerns about his dangerousness and risk of escape, he was initially sent to a high security prison. Having successfully completed an anger management course, his behaviour improved significantly and in 1993 he was transferred to a Category B prison. In December 1994, 5½ months after the expiry of the tariff period, the Parole Board's Discretionary Lifer Panel (DLP) decided it would not be safe to release the applicant, but recommended transfer to an open prison. His continued detention was subsequently reviewed by the DLP in October 1996 and July 1998 and a further review fixed for July 2000.

*Court:* The Court noted that in order to comply with Art 5(4), a competent court must reach its decision 'speedily' and, where an automatic review of the lawfulness of detention had been instituted, its decisions must follow at reasonable intervals. Observing that although the review procedure in the present case had some flexibility in that the DLP and the Secretary of State could bring forward the review date, the Court noted that the applicant in this case could not apply for a review within a 2-year period. Holding unanimously that the undue delay between review procedures carried out by the Parole Board in respect of the applicant's continued detention amounted to a breach of Art 5(4), which guarantees the right to have the lawfulness of detention decided speedily by a court, the Court was satisfied that delays of 21 months and 2 years were not reasonable.

## T v United Kingdom
### (2000) 30 EHRR 121

*Facts:* Following his conviction for murder, the applicant was sentenced to be detained during Her Majesty's pleasure. The trial judge recommended a tariff period of 8 years to be served to satisfy the requirements of retribution and deterrence. The Lord Chief Justice subsequently increased this to 10 years. Following a decision by the Home Secretary to increase the tariff period to 15 years, the applicant instituted judicial proceedings claiming that this was a disproportionately long period which failed to take account of his need for rehabilitation. The majority of the House of Lords accepted that it was unlawful for the Home Secretary to adopt a policy which treated as irrelevant the progress and development of a child serving this type of sentence. However, their Lordships did not set a new tariff period. In the light of the judgment by the House of Lords, the Home Secretary adopted a new policy in relation to young offenders detained at Her Majesty's pleasure and in future the initial tariff period would be kept under review.

*Court:*   The applicant complained, inter alia, that since his conviction he had had no opportunity to have the continued lawfulness of his detention determined by a judicial body and that tariff fixing by a member of the executive failed to meet the requirements of Art 6. He submitted that, having regard to the fact that he was 11 years old at the time of sentencing, and taking account of the fact that children develop physically, intellectually and emotionally, his tariff period should have been shorter and his continued detention should be kept under review. The Court noted that within the context of Art 5 it was not required to determine the appropriate length of sentence. However, observing that tariff fixing in respect of a sentence at Her Majesty's pleasure amounted to the determination of a sentence, the Court addressed the question whether the applicant should be able to have the lawfulness of his continued detention determined by a body meeting the requirements of Art 5(4). The Court recalled that in *Hussain v United Kingdom* (1996) 22 EHRR 1, the Court held that in respect of sentences at Her Majesty's pleasure, Art 5 required that after the expiry of the tariff period the detainee was entitled to challenge the legality of continued detention 'since its only justification could be dangerousness, a characteristic subject to change' (para 118). The Court noted that since the House of Lords had quashed the tariff set by the Home Secretary no new tariff had been fixed. In the circumstances, the Court was satisfied that the applicant had been deprived of the opportunity to have the lawfulness of his continued detention reviewed by a judicial body and found a breach of Art 5(4). Furthermore, the Court was satisfied that tariff fixing by the Home Secretary for prisoners detained during Her Majesty's pleasure was contrary to Art 6(1) of the Convention.

# Curley v United Kingdom

## (2000) 31 EHRR 14

*Facts:*   The applicant was convicted of murder when he was aged 17 and sentenced to be detained during Her Majesty's pleasure. The tariff part of the sentence, which was set at 8 years, expired in 1987 and he became eligible for release on licence. Although the Parole Board reviewed his case on a number of occasions, the Home Secretary did not order his release until May 1997. He complained that since the expiry of the tariff period, the lawfulness of his detention had not been subject to review by a court offering the necessary judicial guarantees because his release was still dependent upon approval by the Secretary of State.

*Court:*   The Court noted that, in the light of the decision in *Hussain v United Kingdom* (1996) 22 EHRR 1, the government had put in place new procedures which changed the procedure under which the cases of prisoners detained during Her Majesty's pleasure were reviewed by the Parole Board. Thus, during a review, prisoners could be legally represented and could examine and cross-examine witnesses. However, the Parole Board did not have the power to direct the release of a prisoner, which remained the prerogative of the Home Secretary. The Court recalled that Convention case-law establishes that 'prisoners detained during Her Majesty's pleasure are entitled, after the expiry of their "tariff", to have the lawfulness of their continued detention reviewed by a court offering the necessary judicial guarantees, in particular, the power to order release and adversarial proceedings. . . . The applicant's tariff expired in 1987.

Before his eventual release in May 1997, the applicant did not receive a review by a body fulfilling this criteria as the Parole Board, even under the interim arrangements, did not have the power to order the applicant's release' (para 32). Accordingly, the Court was unanimous in holding that this sentence was contrary to Art 5(4).

## Stafford v United Kingdom
## (2002) 152 NLJ 880

*Facts:* The applicant complained that the decision to detain him after the end of the term of his prison sentence for offences of dishonesty was arbitrary in that it bore no relation to the original basis of his detention, which was for an offence of violence. Furthermore, he submitted that as the only basis for his continued detention concerned issues relating to risk and dangerousness, which were susceptible to change, he had a right to have the lawfulness of his detention decided by a body that satisfied the requirements of Art 5(4). The applicant received a mandatory life sentence for murder in 1967. After early release on licence, he was detained for breach of conditions but released again. In 1994, he was convicted of cheque fraud, sentenced to a term of 6 years and his life licence revoked by the Secretary of State. Observing his relatively successful transition from prison to the community without violent re-offending, the Parole Board considered that the risk of serious re-offending was low and rec-ommended his release on licence. Following the Secretary of State's rejection of this recommendation, the applicant challenged the lawfulness of the decision to continue his detention. The House of Lords was satisfied that the Secretary of State did not exceed the extent of his discretionary power.

*Court:* In assessing whether the applicant's continued detention under the original mandatory life sentence was contrary to Art 5(1), the Court found that the mandatory sentence did not impose imprisonment for life as a punishment. Noting that for the purposes of setting the tariff period, domestic law no longer drew a distinction between the different categories of prisoners sentenced to life imprisonment, the Court considered that the tariff period represented the element of punishment. Conse-quently, this applicant had exhausted the punishment element of his original offence at the expiry of the tariff period. Having served his sentence for fraud, his continued detention under the mandatory life sentence could not be justified by his punishment for the original offence of murder. Finding that there was insufficient causal connection between the possible commission of other non-violent offences and the original sentence for murder, the Court could not accept that: 'a decision making power by the executive to detain the applicant on the basis of perceived fears of future non-violent criminal conduct unrelated to his original murder conviction accords with the spirit of the Convention, with its emphasis on the rule of law and protection from arbitrariness' (para 82). Accordingly, the Court found a violation of Art 5(1).

Furthermore, by acknowledging that the tariff was the punishment element of the mandatory life sentence, the Court accepted that setting the tariff was:

> '. . . a sentencing exercise and not the administrative implementation of the sentence of the court as can be seen in cases of early or conditional release from a determinate term of imprisonment. After the expiry of the tariff, continued detention depends on elements of

dangerousness and risk associated with the objectives of the original sentence for murder. These elements may change with the course of time, and thus new issues of lawfulness arise requiring determination by a body satisfying the requirements of Article 5(4). It can no longer be maintained that the original trial and appeal proceedings satisfied, once and for all, issues of compatibility of subsequent detention of mandatory life prisoners with the provisions of Article 5(1) of the Convention' (para 87).

In rejecting the government's submission that the power of the Parole Board to direct the applicant's release was sufficient to comply with the Convention, the Court noted that although it could recommend release, the power to order release lay with the Secretary of State. Accordingly, there was a violation of Art 5(4).

*Note:* In this case the material facts did not differ significantly from the Court's finding in *Wynne v United Kingdom* (1995) 19 EHRR 333, in which it was accepted that the mandatory life sentence constituted punishment for life. Although not bound by the doctrine of precedent, the Court takes the view that 'in the interests of legal certainty, foreseeability and equality before the law that it should not depart, without cogent reason, from precedents laid down in previous cases' (para 68). However, in order to ensure the Convention is interpreted in a manner which ensures individuals receive practical and effective protection, it is necessary to take account of changing conditions and legal developments. In this case the Court considered that it was necessary to reassess the appropriate application and interpretation of the Convention and concluded that the finding in *Wynne* should 'no longer be regarded as reflecting the real position in the domestic criminal justice system of the mandatory life prisoner' (para 79).

## UNITED KINGDOM CASES

# R (Noorkoiv) v Secretary of State for the Home Department and Another

## Court of Appeal, [2002] EWCA Civ 770, [2002] TLR 227

*Facts:* The appellant was sentenced to life imprisonment and a tariff period fixed at 30 months, which expired on 21 April 2001. At a Parole Board hearing on 22 June 2001 it was agreed to continue his detention. His complaint related to the delay between the expiry of the tariff periods and the Parole Board hearing. He submitted that the lawfulness of his detention ceased when his tariff period ended.

*Held:* The Parole Board's current arrangements for determining the status of discretionary and automatic life prisoners infringed Art 5(4). A life prisoner was due for release on the expiry of his tariff period unless he constituted a danger to the public. For administrative reasons, hearings were generally scheduled to take place at the end of the quarter following the expiry of the tariff period. Convention case-law established that any delay in determining whether a prisoner was eligible for release required justification. Lack of resources did not provide the Parole Board with a valid reason for hearing an application after the expiry of the tariff period. Accordingly, it was necessary for a scheme to be devised which allowed the Parole Board to consider an application before the tariff period had ended.

# R v Offen

## Court of Appeal, [2001] 1 WLR 253

*Facts:* The appellant complained that an automatic life sentence imposed under s 2 of the Crime (Sentences) Act 1997 was not compatible with his rights under the Convention.

*Held:* The Court of Appeal held that the imposition of a mandatory sentence under s 2 of the 1997 Act did not breach Art 5 provided the test in respect of 'exceptional circumstances' was applied appropriately. Offences that triggered the automatic life sentence were offences for which a court could pass a discretionary life sentence. In establishing automatic life sentences, Parliament intended to protect the public from persons who presented a real, future risk. However, if the facts revealed that the statutory presumption in favour of a life sentence was misplaced, this would provide exceptional circumstances for the purposes of s 2 of the Act. Accordingly, the court must take care not to impose a life sentence unless satisfied that there was evidence which established the need for this type of preventative measure. Allowing the appeal in this case, the court considered that the appellant did not present a significant risk to the public and thus a life sentence was inappropriate.

# R (Anderson and Taylor) v Secretary of State for the Home Department

## Court of Appeal, [2001] EWCA Civ 1698, (2001) 98(47) LSG 27

*Facts:* The appellants were sentenced to mandatory life sentences for murder and complained that the Home Secretary had fixed a tariff period in excess of that recommended by the judge. It was submitted for the appellants that the fixing of the tariff in the case of a mandatory life sentence was part of the sentencing process and therefore required a judicial determination. They challenged the Home Secretary's decision on the ground that it was incompatible with the fair trial provisions of the Convention for the executive to be engaged in a sentencing exercise. Rejecting this submission, the Divisional Court considered that the mandatory life sentence for murder was an automatic penalty and the setting of the tariff an administrative rather than a sentencing procedure.

*Held:* The court considered the nature of tariff setting in relation to mandatory life prisoners and the current Strasbourg jurisprudence. Although satisfied that the existing mandatory life sentence regime was in fact contrary to Art 6, the court dismissed these appeals on the ground that it was constrained by Convention case-law. The statutory scheme which required the trial judge to fix the tariff for discretionary life prisoners, introduced in response to *Thynne, Wilson and Gunnell v United Kingdom* (1990) 13 EHRR 666, did not apply to mandatory life prisoners. In *V v United Kingdom* (1999) 30 EHRR 121, the Court found that sentences at Her Majesty's pleasure were also contrary to the Convention. Consequently, the Home Secretary could no longer fix the tariff in relation to Her Majesty's pleasure detainees. Although the court was prepared to accept that as a matter of domestic law the setting of a tariff in the case of a mandatory life prisoner could be considered to be part of the sentencing exercise, it noted that in *Wynne v United Kingdom* (1995) 19 EHRR 333, the Court accepted that there was a material difference between a mandatory and a discretionary life sentence. Although noting that this issue would soon be re-examined by the Court in *Stafford v United Kingdom* (above), and predicting that the present regime for implementing mandatory life sentences would be found to breach the Convention, the Court considered that it was required by s 2 of the HRA 1998 to follow current Convention case-law. Rejecting the appellants' case, the court considered that in fixing the tariff period the Home Secretary did not act contrary to the Convention.

## R v Parole Board, ex parte Justin West

## Divisional Court, [2002] EWHC Admin 769, unreported

*Facts:*   The applicant was sentenced to 3 years' imprisonment and released on licence at the halfway point of his sentence. The Secretary of State for the Home Department revoked his licence and ordered his recall to prison. He sought judicial review of a refusal by the Parole Board to grant his appeal against the revocation of his licence. He submitted that the Home Secretary had acted contrary to the Convention.

*Held:*   The sentence imposed by the trial court provided for administrative recall in appropriate circumstances. The process of administrative recall, which was intended to protect the public from risk of re-offending, was not penal in character and did not involve the determination of civil rights and obligations under Art 6(1).

## 7.2   RETROSPECTIVE PUNISHMENT

## Welch v United Kingdom

## (1995) 20 EHRR 247

*Facts:*   The applicant was convicted on five counts relating to drug offences and was sentenced to 22 years' imprisonment. The trial judge imposed a confiscation order pursuant to the Drug Trafficking Act 1986 which came into force after the applicant's arrest, but before his conviction. The applicant complained that the confiscation order amounted to the imposition of a retrospective penalty and was in violation of Art 7.

*Commission:*   There was no clear definition of the term 'penalty' in the context of Art 7 and the Commission conducted an assessment of the measure. It concluded that the confiscation order was not punitive and did not constitute a penalty for the purposes of Art 7.

*Court:*   The Court did not question the domestic court's powers of confiscation, nor was there a dispute concerning the retrospective effect of this order; it was made in respect of offences that had been committed before the provision came into force. The issue for the Court was whether the confiscation order amounted to a 'penalty' within the meaning of Art 7. The concept of 'penalty' is an autonomous concept, and the Court 'must remain free to go behind appearances and assess for itself whether a particular measure amounts to a "penalty"'. Factors to be taken into account include:

whether the measure was imposed following conviction for a criminal offence; the nature and purpose of the measure; its characterisation under national law; the procedures involved in the making and implementation of the measure; and its severity. The Court applied the relevant factors to this case and found a strong indication of a regime of punishment. Taking account of the combination of punitive elements the Court decided the order was a penalty and in breach of Art 7.

*Note:* The 1986 Act was replaced by the Drug Trafficking Act 1994, which came into force on 3 February 1995. A confiscation order is no longer mandatory in all cases. The prosecution can seek an order or the court can proceed of its own motion.

## 7.3   CAPITAL PUNISHMENT

### Soering v United Kingdom

### (1989) 11 EHRR 439

*Facts:*   The United Kingdom sought to extradite a German national from the UK to the USA under the terms of an extradition treaty that had been incorporated into the law of the UK (United States of America (Extradition) Order 1976, SI 1976/2144 and the United States of America (Extradition Amendment) Order 1986, SI 1986/2020). The applicant was accused of committing a murder in Bedford County, Virginia and argued that his extradition would amount to a violation of Art 3. In capital murder cases, the State of Virginia could impose the death penalty which may involve very long periods of time spent on death-row. The applicant accepted that the death penalty did not per se violate the Convention; however, exposure to the 'death-row phenomenon' would amount to inhuman and degrading treatment. The government submitted that the Convention should not be interpreted so as to impose responsibility of a Contracting State for acts which occur outside its jurisdiction. The basis for this argument was that such an interpretation would interfere with international treaty rights and lead to a conflict with the norms of the international judicial process. Further, it would involve adjudication on the internal affairs of a foreign State and its domestic criminal justice system. In support of this argument, the government relied upon traditional principles of extradition which respect the rule of non-inquiry.

*Court:*   The Court was of the opinion that to surrender a person to another State where there were substantial grounds for believing that he would be in danger of being subjected to torture, inhuman or degrading treatment would be a violation of Art 3. Liability was incurred by the extraditing Contracting State 'by reason of its having taken action which has as a direct consequence the exposure of an individual to proscribed ill-treatment'. Furthermore, it was noted that: 'Article 3 enshrines one of the fundamental values of the democratic societies making up the Council of Europe. It is also to be found in similar terms in other international instruments such as the 1966 International Covenant on Civil and Political Rights and the 1969 American Convention on Human Rights and is generally recognised as an internationally accepted standard' (para 88).

*Note:*   Following the issue of a diplomatic note stating that the US authorities would not prosecute the applicant for the offence of capital murder, the applicant was eventually extradited to the USA.

## 7.4  UNACCEPTABLE FORMS OF PUNISHMENT

### (1)  CORPORAL PUNISHMENT

# Tyrer v United Kingdom

# (1978) 2 EHRR 1

*Facts:*  Following his conviction for assault occasioning actual bodily harm, the applicant was sentenced to three strokes of the birch by a juvenile court in the Isle of Man. He complained that this form of punishment was in breach of Art 3 of the Convention.

*Commission:*  In its report, the Commission expressed the opinion, by 14 votes to 1, that judicial corporal punishment was degrading and its infliction on the applicant amounted to a breach of Art 3.

*Court:*  The Court shared the Commission's view that the applicant's punishment did not amount to torture within the meaning of Art 3. Similarly, it could not properly be described as 'inhuman'. Accordingly, the question for the Court was whether the applicant had been subjected to 'degrading treatment'. It considered that for punishment to be 'degrading' 'the humiliation or debasement involved must attain a particular level'. In arriving at its conclusion, the Court was required to take account of the nature and context of the punishment itself and the manner and method of its execution. It noted that judicial corporal punishment was institutionalised violence carried out by the authorities and constituted an assault on 'precisely that which it is one of the main purposes of Art 3 to protect, namely a person's dignity and physical integrity'. The Court did not consider it relevant that the punishment was imposed for an offence of violence. Accordingly, the Court found that judicial corporal punishment amounted to degrading treatment and was in violation of Art 3.

*Note:*  After the Court announced its decision, the Chief Justice of the Isle of Man informed the judges and the courts that judicial corporal punishment was in future to be considered in breach of the Convention.

### (2)  TORTURE AND INHUMAN OR DEGRADING TREATMENT

*DEGREES OF SEVERITY*

# Ireland v United Kingdom

# (1978) 2 EHRR 25

*Facts:*  This case arose out of interrogation techniques used to obtain information from suspected IRA terrorists. The so-called 'five techniques' included wall-standing, hooding and food and sleep deprivation. The complaint alleged that these and other practices to which suspects were subjected amounted to torture and inhuman and degrading treatment contrary to Art 3.

*Commission:*  The Commission emphasised that ill-treatment must reach a minimum level of severity if it is to fall within the scope of Art 3. The assessment of this minimum will be relative and will depend upon factors which include the duration of the treatment, its physical and mental effects and the age, sex and health of the victim. It unanimously expressed the opinion that the combined use of the five techniques amounted to inhuman treatment and torture.

*Court:* The Court noted that Art 3 makes no provision for derogation even in the event of a public emergency threatening the life of the nation. The Court, agreeing with the Commission, considered that the five techniques fell into the category of inhuman treatment, and were also degrading within the meaning of Art 3. It held, by 16 votes to 1, that the use of the five techniques constituted a practice of inhuman and degrading treatment and amounted to a violation of the Convention. The distinction between inhuman treatment and torture derived principally from the intensity of suffering, and, in the opinion of the Court, the special stigma attaching to the term 'torture' required the application of cruel treatment which caused very serious suffering. The Court found, by 13 votes to 4, that the application of the five techniques did not occasion suffering of the particular intensity and cruelty implied by the word 'torture' within the meaning of Art 3.

*Note:* In March 1972, the UK gave a solemn undertaking that the authorities would no longer use the five interrogation techniques.

# Salman v Turkey

## (2002) 34 EHRR 17

*Facts:* The applicant claimed that her husband's death in custody was directly related to ill-treatment amounting to torture which occurred during police interrogation. She relied on the fact that the authorities had failed to give a plausible explanation for marks and injuries found on her husband's body. Further, she claimed that the marks were consistent with the application of 'falaka', which was considered by the European Committee for the Prevention of Torture to be a prohibited form of ill-treatment, and a blow to the chest. Further, she complained that the authorities had failed to conduct an effective investigation into the circumstances of his death. The government disputed these allegations and requested that the Court dismiss the case as inadmissible on account of the applicant's failure to exhaust domestic remedies. Alternatively, it was argued that the evidence did not support the applicant's complaints.

*Commission:* The Commission was unanimous in finding that there had been a breach of Art 2, in respect to the death of the applicant's husband while in custody. Furthermore, it was found that he had been tortured and that there was no provision for an effective investigation to determine the liability of the authorities for any alleged mistreatment.

*Court:* Observing that the Convention attached a special stigma to deliberate inhuman treatment causing very serious and cruel suffering, the Court emphasised that a distinction must be drawn between torture and inhuman and degrading treatment. Referring to Art 1 of the UN Convention against Torture and Other Cruel, Inhuman or Degrading Treatment, it noted that in addition to the severity of the treatment, torture should involve a purposive element. (The UN Convention defines torture in terms of the international infliction of severe pain or suffering with the aim, inter alia, of obtaining information, inflicting punishment or intimidation.) The Court was satisfied on the basis of the evidence adduced, that the nature and degree of ill-treatment in this case, and the strong inference that it occurred during interrogation, gave rise to a finding that the applicant's husband had been subjected to torture. In respect to the death of the applicant's husband, the Court stressed that Art 2, which safeguards the right to life and sets out the limited circumstances when killing is justified, must be considered to be one of the most fundamental provisions in the Convention. Taken together with Art 3, which prohibits the use of torture, it enshrines one of the basic values in a democracy. Given the importance of the protection afforded by Art 2, the Court subjects any deprivation of life to careful scrutiny. The obligation to protect life is particularly onerous in the case of persons in custody, who are considered to be in a particularly vulnerable position. When a person in good health dies in police custody, the burden to provide a satisfactory account for their treatment during detention rests with the authorities. Strong presumptions of fact will arise in respect of the cause of death. In this case, the Court was not satisfied that the government could give a satisfactory account of the injuries found on the body. Further, the Court reaffirmed that the obligation to protect the right to life requires by implication that there should be an effective official investigation into the circumstances surrounding a death resulting from violence allegedly inflicted by State agents. In addition to identifying the probable cause of death, a post mortem examination can provide an accurate record of any signs of ill-treatment or injury. In this case, the defects in the investigation undermined any attempt to determine the extent of police responsibility. Observing that the Convention attached a special stigma to torture, the Court was satisfied on the basis of the evidence adduced, that the nature and degree of ill-treatment in this case, and the strong inference that it occurred during police interrogation, gave rise to a finding that the applicant's husband had been subjected to torture and died as a consequence.

## 7.5    TREATMENT IN PRISON

### Akkoc v Turkey

### (2002) 34 EHRR 51

*Facts:* Although the Administrative Court had eventually quashed a penalty imposed as a disciplinary sanction in respect of an article published in a newspaper, the applicant maintained that her right under Art 10 had been infringed. Her punishment had been one year's suspension of promotion as a teacher. Further, she claimed that she had been tortured while in police custody and had been intimidated in respect of her application to the Commission. Prior to release from detention, she was taken to see a doctor at the State hospital who signed a report indicating that she had not suffered injury while in custody. She alleged that the examination involved the doctor asking, in the presence of police officers, whether she had any complaints or wanted a medical examination. She was then taken before a public prosecutor, where she reported her ill-treatment and said she had signed a statement under pressure. He ordered her release.

*Commission:* In its report, the Commission expressed the unanimous opinion that there had been a violation of Arts 10 and 2. It found the applicant to be an honest and credible witness whose evidence was supported by the report from the Ankara Treatment Centre of the Human Rights Foundation. The evidence of the doctor was considered to be unreliable and the medical examination cursory.

*Court:* The Court is primarily a supervisory body and subsidiary to national systems designed to protect human rights. Contracting States bear the primary burden of conducting an effective investigation into allegations of an interference with Convention rights and have an obligation to provide compensation. In this case, the Court noted that the applicant had used the means available to redress the interference with her right to freedom of expression. Although accepting that the length of time involved in seeking redress was considerable, a period of 5 years and 9 months, the Court considered that in the context of the Turkish legal system this was not sufficiently excessive to deprive the domestic procedures of their efficacy. Accordingly, the Court held that the applicant could no longer claim to be a victim of an interference with her right to freedom of expression. However, accepting the findings of the Commission concerning the applicant's ill-treatment, which involved electric shocks, hot and cold water treatment and blows to the head, the Court found that she was a victim of very serious and cruel suffering which could be characterised as torture. The Court endorsed the Commission's comments with respect to the importance of independent and thorough examinations of detainees. It considered that:

> 'Such examinations must be carried out by a properly qualified doctor, without any police officer being present and the report of the examinations must include not only the detail of any injuries found but the explanations given by the patient as to how they occurred and the opinion of the doctor as to whether the injuries are consistent with those explanations. The practices of cursory and collective examinations illustrated by the present case undermines the effectiveness and reliability of this safeguard' (para 118).

The Court was satisfied that in the circumstances the questioning of the applicant about her application to the Commission amounted to a form of illicit and unacceptable pressure which hindered the exercise of the right of individual petition.

# Price v United Kingdom
## (2002) 34 EHRR 53

*Facts:* In addition to suffering kidney problems, the applicant was four-limb deficient and was confined to a wheelchair. In the course of civil proceedings, she refused to answer questions relating to her financial position and was committed to prison for 7 days for contempt of court. Despite suffering from a severe disability, she was placed in a cell which had not been adapted for the needs of a disabled person. She was initially held in a police station cell and alleged that she was forced to sleep in her wheelchair and was unable to use the toilet since it was higher than her wheelchair and inaccessible. Her custody record showed that she frequently complained of the cold. The nursing record reported that the duty nurse had been unable to lift her off the toilet and had been required to call a male officer who undertook the task of cleaning her and helping her off the toilet. The applicant complained that she was subjected to humiliating treatment and, as a consequence of the inadequate sanitary arrangements, by the time of her release she required catheterisation.

*Court:*   Although there was no evidence of any positive intention on the part of the authorities to humiliate the applicant, the Court considered that detaining a severely disabled person in conditions where she is dangerously cold and unable to go to the toilet or keep clean without difficulty constituted degrading treatment contrary to Art 3. The Court considered it significant that the documentary evidence submitted by the government indicated that the police and prison authorities were unable to cope adequately with the applicant's special needs. Accordingly, the Court was unanimous in finding a violation of Art 3.

## UNITED KINGDOM CASES

## Napier v The Scottish Ministers

## Scottish Court of Session, [2002] UKHRR 308

*Facts:*   A prisoner on remand in HM Prison Barlinnie in Glasgow sought to challenge the conditions under which he was detained on the ground that they were sufficiently inadequate to be contrary to Art 3 of the Convention, and were thus unlawful by virtue of s 6(1) of the Human Rights Act 1998. His complaint related to overcrowding; inadequate light, ventilation and exercise; and lavatory arrangements which involved the process known as 'slopping out', which required prisoners to empty vessels used for urine and faeces. He produced in evidence a report which stated that these conditions exacerbated an existing medical condition. In addition to damages, he requested a transfer to an alternative location with detention arrangements which did not breach his Convention rights. Although accepting that the petitioner had established a prima facie case, the respondents did not accept that there was in this case a breach of Art 3.

*Held:*   The court noted that the problem of detention conditions in Barlinnie was 'a long-standing one, and that the complete solution is as far away now (five years) as it was in 1994' (para 15). In granting the petitioner's request, the court refused to accept that the fact that other prisoners might seek a similar order, or that it would be difficult or impracticable to relocate all the other remand prisoners, constituted a good reason for refusing the petitioner an interim order. Observing that the respondents had conceded that he had established a prima facie case, the court considered that the petitioner was entitled to have his case decided on its merits and ordered his transfer within 72 hours.

## 7.6   DEATH IN CUSTODY

## Edwards v United Kingdom

## (2002) 35 EHRR 19

*Facts:*   Christopher Edwards died in custody from wounds inflicted by a prisoner sharing his cell. Although both prisoners exhibited signs of serious mental illness prior to detention, a member of the prison health care service considered that they were fit to be detained and saw no reason to admit either prisoner to the health care centre. Due to a shortage of space, they were placed in the same cell. When the assailant pleaded guilty to manslaughter by reason of diminished responsibility, the inquest into the killing was closed. A non-statutory inquiry by the authorities into the care and treatment of Christopher Edwards found a 'systematic collapse' of protective mechanisms which should have operated to protect him from the violent acts of another prisoner sharing his cell, and identified a series of shortcomings in the transmission of information by agencies involved in this case. However, the applicants were advised that, in the light of the findings, there were no civil remedies available to them. The applicants complained that there was a breach of a positive obligation by the authorities to protect the life of their son who was killed by another prisoner while in police custody.

*Court:* Recalling that Art 2(1) directs the State not only to refrain from intentional and unlawful killing, but also to take appropriate steps to safeguard lives, the Court considered that in some circumstances Contracting States incurred a positive obligation to protect individuals from the criminal acts of others. This obligation should not impose an impossible or disproportionate burden on the authorities. Before a positive obligation can arise, it is necessary to establish that the authorities knew or ought to have known that there was a real and immediate risk to life, and that they failed to take reasonable measures to avoid the risk. The Court considered that in this case the inadequate nature of the screening process and the failure of the agencies involved in this case to pass on information to the prison authorities disclosed a breach of an obligation to protect life which is guaranteed by Art 2. Furthermore, the absence of an inquest into the killing, together with the fact that the inquiry was held in private and had no power to compel witnesses to attend, resulted in a breach of the procedural obligation to carry out an effective investigation. Although the form of investigation may vary according to the circumstances, any deficiency in procedure that undermines its ability to establish the cause of death or the persons responsible will risk falling short of the required standard. In addition, the inquiry did not provide the applicants with an appropriate means of obtaining an enforceable award of compensation for the damage suffered as a consequence of their son's death. In the Court's opinion, this is an essential element of a remedy under Art 13 which guarantees the right to an effective remedy before a national authority.

## Keenan v United Kingdom
## (2001) 33 EHRR 38

*Facts:* The applicant's son committed suicide while in custody. Prior to being sentenced to a short period of imprisonment for assault, Mark Keenan was diagnosed as exhibiting signs of paranoid schizophrenia and had a history of frequent episodes of deliberate self-harm. On admission, he was sent to the health care centre for observation and assessment. Attempts to transfer him to an ordinary prison cell failed and he remained in the health care centre. Although he had seen a visiting psychiatrist, a prison doctor who was unqualified in psychiatry amended his medication. Following an incident in which two prison officers were assaulted, he received an additional 28 days in prison with 7 days' loss of association and exclusion from work in a segregation unit, which involved incarceration for 23 hours each day. Although prisoners in this unit received a daily visit from a doctor, the prison chaplain and the governor, contact with staff was minimal. Soon after being transferred to the segregation unit, he was found hanging from the bars of his cell. The inquest jury returned a verdict of death by misadventure. The applicant complained that the authorities failed in their responsibility to protect her son's right to life by not properly assessing him prior to his suicide, and that although segregating prisoners did not in itself amount to ill-treatment, the State had a duty to closely monitor vulnerable prisoners to ensure that they did not suffer unduly. Furthermore, there was no effective national remedy to determine the liability of the authorities for any alleged mistreatment, or for providing compensation.

*Court:*   Where it is established that the authorities knew or ought to have known that there was an immediate risk to life, there is a positive obligation to take protective measures. The obligation to protect the vulnerable is particularly onerous. In this case, the Court was called on to consider the extent to which Contracting States incur an obligation to prevent persons from self-harm. The Court was satisfied that the prison authorities knew that Mark Keenan was a suicide risk and considered whether the prison authorities did all that was reasonably expected of them having regard to the nature of the risk. The Court was unanimous in finding that by placing him under medical supervision the authorities had responded reasonably and had not acted contrary to Art 2. However, the lack of effective monitoring of his condition and the lack of informed psychiatric input into his assessment and treatment was not compatible with the standard required in respect of the mentally ill. Accordingly, the majority of the Court found a breach of Art 3. The Court noted that it was common ground that the inquest failed to provide a remedy for determining liability and was not persuaded that civil proceedings for negligence provided an effective redress for the applicant's complaints. Accordingly, the Court was unanimous in holding that there had been a breach of Art 13.

## Akdeniz v Turkey
### Application No 23954/94, unreported

*Facts:*   The applicants alleged that their relatives had disappeared after they had been detained by the security forces and could be presumed dead. They submitted that under Art 2, the authorities were obliged to provide a plausible explanation as to what happened to their relatives and to hold an effective investigation into the circumstances of the deaths. Adopting the conclusions of the Commission, the applicants further submitted that the conditions of detention amounted to inhuman and degrading treatment. They also complained that they had been summoned and questioned by the police and public prosecutors about their application to the Commission which amounted to a serious interference with the exercise of their right of individual petition and was in breach of former Art 25(1), now replaced by Art 34.

*Commission:*   The Commission declared the application admissible. In its report, it expressed the opinion that there had been a violation of Arts 2 and 3 in respect of the missing relatives and a violation of Arts 5 and 13. Furthermore, the State had failed to comply with its obligations under former Art 25.

*Court:*   Accepting the facts as established by the Commission, the Court found that there was a presumption that 11 men who disappeared after being held in detention by the security forces were dead. In the absence of a satisfactory account by the authorities of what happened during this period of detention, these deaths are attributable to the

Turkish government. Further, despite the weight of evidence, the public prosecutors did not take steps to discover the whereabouts of the men and demonstrated a reluctance to pursue any lines of inquiry concerning the involvement of the security forces. Accordingly there was a violation of Art 2. The Court was also satisfied that there was sufficient evidence to show that the treatment suffered by the applicants' relatives reached the threshold of inhuman and degrading treatment contrary to Art 3. Further, in view of the Court's reasoning and finding in respect to Art 2, the Court was satisfied that the applicants' relatives had been detained in complete disregard of the safeguards contained in Art 5. Regarding the submission that the authorities interfered with the applicants' right of petition, the Court reiterated that 'it is of the utmost importance for the effective operation of the system of individual petition that applicants should be able to communicate freely with the Convention organs without being subjected to pressure by the authorities to withdraw or modify their complaints' (para 118). However, whether contacts by the authorities amount to improper practices must be determined in the light of the circumstances of each case. Being satisfied that in this case there was undue interference by the authorities, the Court found that the respondent government failed to comply with its obligations under the former Art 25.

## UNITED KINGDOM CASES

## Wright & Another v Secretary of State for the Home Department
## High Court, [2001] EWHC Admin 520, unreported

*Facts:*   The relatives of man who died as a result of a severe asthma attack while in police custody alleged that his treatment prior to death was in breach of Art 2 or 3 of the Convention, and that there had been a failure to carry out a proper investigation into his death. The deceased had had a long history of serious asthma. On the evening of his death, he told a fellow prisoner that he needed medical assistance. By the time help arrived, he had stopped breathing and was transferred to hospital whereupon he was certified dead. An inquest returned the verdict of death by natural causes. On reading a newspaper article which stated that the medical practitioner assigned to the prison had been suspended and that he had previously been found guilty of serious professional misconduct, the claimants' concerns about the deceased's medical treatment were reinforced. Their civil action in negligence resulted in the defendant admitting liability.

*Held:*   The court observed that during the inquest there was no suggestion that the medical treatment given in prison was inadequate or that the medical staff lacked the necessary competence. Further, it noted that as a consequence of the defendant's admission of liability there was no cross-examination or testing of expert evidence and no determination of any specific allegations of negligence. Acknowledging that it was arguable that the treatment of the prisoner did result in a breach of Arts 2 and 3, the court found that the inquest and the civil proceedings did not comply with the procedural obligations imposed by Art 2. In cases involving State authorities, there must be some form of effective official investigation which ensures accountability for deaths occurring under their responsibility. Although the form of investigation may vary, it should have procedures whereby it is possible to establish the cause of death and the persons responsible. In respect of the defendant's continuing breach of the procedural obligations under Art 2, the court ordered the Secretary of State to set up an independent investigation into the circumstances of the death. Leave to appeal was granted. The court noted that if this situation was to be avoided in the future 'steps should be taken to ensure that, in every case where Article 2 of the convention may be engaged, the coroner's inquest complies with the procedural obligations arising under that Article' (para 68).

*Note:*  The court noted that in *Keenan v United Kingdom* (2001) 33 EHRR 38, in which it was also alleged that death resulted from a failure by the authorities to comply with its obligations under Arts 2 and 3, the applicant did not complain of a breach of the procedural obligation imposed by Art 2. The court suggested that the reason for this omission was because the Strasbourg Court could grant a remedy for a breach of Art 13, which requires national authorities to provide an effective remedy for breaches of Convention rights, an option not open to the High Court under the HRA 1998.

## R (Amin) v Secretary of State for the Home Department
### High Court, [2001] EWHC Admin 719, unreported

*Facts:*  The claimants alleged that the Secretary of State had failed to hold an open and public investigation into the circumstances of the death of Zahid Mubarek, who was killed by a racist, violent prisoner while in custody.

*Held:*  The court considered that the criminal trial of the assailant and the internal inquiry held by the Prison Service, which did not establish the reasons for placing the two prisoners in the same cell, did not constitute an effective inquiry for the purposes of Art 2. Accordingly, the claimants were entitled to a declaration that a public investigation be held at which they would have the opportunity to cross-examine key witnesses.

## R v DPP, ex parte Manning
### Divisional Court, [2001] QB 330

*Facts:*  The applicants' brother died of asphyxia while in police custody. Despite the inquest jury returning a verdict of unlawful killing, the Director of Public Prosecutions decided not to prosecute prison officers who had been responsible for conducting a forcible search of the deceased immediately before his death. The applicants sought judicial review of this decision on the ground that no adequate reasons for the decision were given and that the reasons which were given were unsustainable. The evidence presented at the inquest suggested that the death resulted from the manner in which a police officer had held the prisoner's head. Following a police investigation into the incident, the papers were sent to the Crown Prosecution Service. A senior caseworker concluded that although there was a prima facie case against the officer, there was no realistic chance of establishing that excessive force had been used deliberately, rather than as an attempt to restrain the deceased, who had been struggling. Accordingly, there was insufficient evidence to justify a prosecution.

*Held:*  The court was satisfied that neither domestic law nor the Convention imposed an absolute and unqualified obligation on the DPP to give reasons for a decision not to prosecute. However, the court acknowledged that the right to life is the most fundamental of all human rights and that the power to derogate is very limited. It was accepted that death resulting from violent acts by persons employed by the State must raise profound concerns which required a thorough investigation. Observing that in this case the deceased's family had been represented at the inquest, the Divisional Court considered that 'the holding of an inquest in public by an independent judicial official, the coroner, in which interested parties are able to participate must in our view be regarded as a full and effective enquiry' (para 33). However, Lord Bingham observed that where the inquest jury returns a verdict of unlawful killing, the Strasbourg Court expects that a plausible explanation would be given for a decision not to prosecute. He considered that in the absence of compelling grounds for not giving reasons the DPP should account for the decision not to prosecute in order to show that solid grounds existed for what might appear to be a surprising or even inexplicable decision. Although ordering the DPP to reconsider the decision not to prosecute, the Divisional Court emphasised that the effect of this decision 'is not to require the Director to prosecute. It is to require reconsideration of the decision whether or not to prosecute. On the likely or proper outcome of that reconsideration we express no opinion at all'.

## Orange v Chief Constable of West Yorkshire
## Court of Appeal, [2001] EWCA Civ 611, [2001] 3 WLR 736

*Facts:* The plaintiff's husband, who had been arrested for being drunk and disorderly, committed suicide while in a police cell by hanging himself from a horizontal bar with his belt. She alleged that the police were negligent in failing to remove the belt and by placing him in a cell which contained a dangerous suspension point. The county court judge dismissed the claim on the ground that in the absence of evidence to suggest that the deceased posed a suicide risk, no duty of care was owed to protect him from self-harm.

*Held:* It was accepted that the police owe a duty to any person in their custody to take reasonable steps to ensure that person's health and safety. Acknowledging that there was an increased risk of suicide amongst people in custody, the authorities had a general duty of care to identify whether a detainee presented a suicide risk. If a detainee is known to be a suicide risk, the police have an obligation to pass on this information to the prison authorities. In this case, the court was satisfied that the police had taken reasonable steps to assess the suicide risk. In the absence of evidence to suggest that the plaintiff's husband presented a risk to himself or to any other person, the police had not been negligent in permitting him to keep his belt. Although the cell did not comply with recommendations set out by the Home Office, placing the prisoner in this cell did not amount to a breach of a duty of care owed to the deceased.

*Note:* Although the Court of Appeal referred to the judgment in *Keenan v United Kingdom* (2001) 33 EHRR 38, and see above, it did not consider that this decision 'in any way affects the conclusion that we have come to as to the scope of the appropriate duty of care in common law. If anything, it confirms our view that the special and unusual duty is one which is only owed where the authorities know, or ought to have known, of a suicide risk in an individual prisoner's case' (para 47).

# Chapter 8

# SUBSTANTIVE CRIMINAL ISSUES

## 8.1 DEFINITION OF A CRIMINAL OFFENCE

### Kokkinakis v Greece

### (1993) 17 EHRR 397

*Facts:* The applicant, a Jehovah's Witness, had been arrested more than 60 times for proselytism, and had been imprisoned several times. The circumstances of the most recent case were that he and his wife were invited into a woman's home and began a discussion with her. Her husband called the police and the applicant and his wife were convicted of the criminal offence of proselytism. The applicant alleged breaches of Arts 7, 9 and 10 in relation to his criminal conviction.

*Commission:* The relevant issue was whether the vagueness of the wording of the offence of proselytism infringed Art 7. A criminal offence must be clearly described by the law creating it. Although the wording in the relevant statute was vague and created a very broad actus reus, Greek courts interpreted the legislation in a clear and consistent manner and so there was no breach in this respect (11:2 votes). The Court agreed with this aspect of the Commission's opinion.

## 8.2 DOUBLE JEOPARDY

### Gradinger v Austria

### 23 October 1995, unreported

*Facts:* The applicant caused a car accident in which a cyclist was killed. A blood test showed that he had a blood alcohol level of 0.8 grams per litre. He was tried and convicted of causing death by negligence. The trial court considered whether he should be sentenced for the more serious offence of causing death by negligence while under the influence of drink, but relied upon a medical report which stated that he could not have exceeded the prescribed alcohol limit for that offence. However, 2 months later the applicant was sentenced for another offence, driving under the influence of drink. The second court relied upon a second medical report which found that the applicant's blood alcohol level must have exceeded 0.95 grams per litre at the time of the accident, since the blood test was carried out later at a hospital where he was receiving treatment for his injuries. Domestic appeals upheld both convictions and produced yet another confusing medical report which found a third potential blood alcohol level. The applicant argued that Art 6 had been breached since, inter alia, the second sentence had been imposed by an administrative tribunal rather than an 'independent and impartial tribunal'. The Commission gave a unanimous opinion that there had been such a breach, and further that there had been a breach of Art 4 of the Seventh Protocol.

*Court:*   The Court dealt quickly with the allegation in relation to Art 6(1), accepting both the applicant's and the Commission's view that the second conviction was for a criminal offence within the sense of Art 6(1); although 'the offences in issue and the procedures followed in the case fall within the administrative sphere, they are nevertheless criminal in nature'. The fine imposed as a sentence had a prison sentence attached as a default measure and the only right of appeal was to a Constitutional Court, and so the decision taken to convict him of the second offence denied him of access to an impartial tribunal. Hence there had been a violation of Art 6.

In relation to the double jeopardy point, the Court agreed that Art 4 of the Seventh Protocol had been violated. The 'aim of Art 4 of Protocol No 7 is to prohibit the repetition of criminal proceedings that have been concluded by a final decision'. Since the applicant had been acquitted of the aggravated offence of causing death by negligence whilst under the influence of drink at his first trial, he could not later be sentenced for another offence with the same key elements. The government had argued that the two offences in question had different aims and were different in nature; one was 'designed to penalise acts that cause death and threaten public safety' and the other 'to ensure a smooth flow of traffic'. The Court found that, although the differences did exist, the only important factor for the present issue was whether both convictions related to the same conduct. Since the two offences related to the same core conduct, that of driving under the influence of drink, the second conviction was a violation of the double jeopardy rule.

*Note:*   The UK has not ratified the Seventh Protocol and has no clear plans to do so; nor is the double jeopardy rule enshrined within the HRA 1998. However, the issue of double jeopardy has recently become an intensely topical one, especially since the Macpherson inquiry into the murder of Stephen Lawrence started a debate as to whether the common-law rule should be abolished. The Convention rule is relatively similar to that at English criminal law, although English law applies the rule slightly more in favour of the accused and the Convention allows slightly wider exceptions.

## 8.3   MARITAL RAPE

## SW v United Kingdom; CR v United Kingdom

## (1995) 21 EHRR 363

*Facts:*   The first applicant and his wife still cohabited, but had separate bedrooms. When his wife threatened to leave him, the applicant forced her to leave the marital home. When, with police help, she returned, the applicant had sex with her by force. He was convicted of rape.

The second applicant had been convicted of attempted rape and assault on his estranged wife, who had left the marital home and returned to live with her parents. The couple intended to divorce, but the applicant broke into his in-laws' home and attempted to have sex with his wife by force.

At the time of each of the offences, the marital rape exemption still existed. This ancient rule held that a husband could not be found guilty of rape of his wife, since the marriage contract gave him a right to have sex with her and she was thereby deemed to consent. The rule was overturned in 1991 by the Court of Appeal in *R v R* [1991] 4 All ER 481, which was decided after the applicants' offences were committed but before they stood trial. The applicants alleged a violation of Art 7 by their conviction and sentencing for conduct which, at the time of its commission, was not a criminal offence.

*Commission:* The Commission found that there had been no violation of Art 7 in respect of either applicant. In CR's case, the applicant could have foreseen that his conduct would be classified as criminal since the case-law was developing rapidly in that direction. Recent cases had held that the marital rape exemption did not apply where the couple had petitioned for divorce or obtained a judicial separation. There were comparable situations to that of the applicant, who had agreed to a divorce and whose wife had left the marital home. Thus his criminal liability did not constitute retroactive judicial legislation. In SW's case, although the couple were still technically cohabiting, it was again found to be foreseeable that the marital exemption would be abolished imminently. The Commission found no real difference between the facts of the two cases, even though SW did not fall within any of the exceptions to marital immunity existing at the time of his offence. Reform, first by the courts and then by Parliament in the Criminal Justice and Public Order Act 1994 was predictable and, indeed, almost inevitable at the time of the applicants' assaults on their wives; thus neither applicant could honestly have believed that he was acting lawfully.

However, a dissenting opinion by Mr Loucaides and Mr Nowicki found that *R v R* had dramatically changed the law of rape, with an effect on the applicants. 'It was neither a clarification of the existing elements of the offence in question, nor an adaptation of such elements to new circumstances which could reasonably be brought under the original concept of the offence.' Thus the change in case-law could not have been reasonably foreseeable to the applicant(s) even with the assistance of legal advice.

*Court:* The Court also found that there had been no violation of Art 7. Article 7 is a very important rule of the Convention, and 'should be construed and applied, as follows from its object and purpose, in such a way as to provide effective safeguards against arbitrary prosecution, conviction and punishment'. It requires not only that the criminal law should not be applied retrospectively to the defendant's advantage, but also that the criminal law should be clear and accessible so that 'an individual can know from the wording of the relevant provision and, if need be, with the assistance of the courts' interpretation of it, what acts and omissions will make him criminally liable'. However, judicial interpretation is necessary and 'the progressive development of the criminal law through judicial law-making is a well entrenched and necessary part of legal tradition'. Article 7 cannot 'be read as outlawing the gradual clarification of the rules of criminal liability through judicial interpretation from case to case, provided that the resultant development is consistent with the essence of the offence and could reasonably be foreseen'. Changes in the marital rape immunity rule had been proposed and advocated for some time, and its abolition was widely expected. The Court of Appeal, and later the House of Lords, in the case of *R v R* had done no more than continue a process of dismantling the marital immunity by case-law. 'There was no doubt under the law as it stood on 18 September 1990 that a husband who forcibly had sexual intercourse with his wife could, in various circumstances, be found guilty of rape. Moreover, there was an evident evolution, which was consistent with the very essence of the offence, of the criminal law through judicial interpretation towards treating such conduct generally as within the scope of the offence of rape. This evolution had reached a stage where judicial recognition of the absence of immunity had become a reasonably foreseeable development of the law.' Rape is such a debasing crime that the applicants' convictions were within the spirit of the Convention and the abandonment of the marital immunity rule was an act which showed the fundamental objectives of the Convention, that is 'respect for human dignity and human freedom'. Hence there had been no violation of Art 7 (unanimous).

## 8.4   BLASPHEMOUS LIBEL

### Gay News Ltd and Lemon v United Kingdom

### (1982) 5 EHRR 123

*Facts:*   The applicants had published a sexually explicit poem and illustration of Christ in their magazine. They were convicted of the common-law offence of blasphemous libel. The offence is somewhat obscure, and there was debate as to whether any mens rea was required. The trial judge had directed the jury that there was no requirement that the blasphemy should be intentional. The majority of the House of Lords agreed, although it was accepted that the law was, or had been, unclear. The applicants alleged that there had been a breach of Art 7, since they had been convicted of an offence which either did not exist at the time of the relevant publication, or was based upon legal principles of insufficient clarity.

*Commission:*   The Commission accepted that the common law is idiosyncratic due to its method of development, but stated that any form of judicial law-making must remain within reasonable limits. Courts must not create new, retroactive criminal offences, nor extend existing offences to encompass conduct which was lawful at the time of its commission. However, 'it is not objectionable that the existing elements of the offence are clarified and adapted to new circumstances which can reasonably be brought under the original concept of the offence'. While the law of blasphemous libel lacks clarity, the courts' interpretation of that law in the applicants' case had been reasonable. It was clear that the offence did exist; the lack of clarity related only to the precise nature of the mens rea required: 'the application of a test of strict liability and the exclusion of evidence as to the publisher's and editor's intention to blaspheme did not amount to the creation of new law in the sense that earlier case law clearly denying such strict liability and admitting evidence as to the blasphemous intentions was overruled'. Therefore, the House of Lords had clarified the law rather than changed and expanded it. The Commission also found that the law was accessible to the applicants, who could have foreseen the correct interpretation with appropriate legal advice. Thus, there was no violation of Art 7.

## 8.5   CRIMINAL CONTEMPT OF COURT

### Times Newspapers Ltd and Neil v United Kingdom

### (1993) 15 EHRR CD 49

*Facts:*   This case was part of the *Spycatcher* litigation. The *Sunday Times* printed serialised extracts from *Spycatcher* on 12 July 1987, 2 days before the memoirs were published in the United States. The Attorney-General had obtained injunctions to prevent publication by the *Observer* and *Guardian* newspapers in July 1986, and brought an action for contempt of court against the *Sunday Times*. No action was taken to restrain publication in the USA or Canada. The relevant question was whether newspapers other than those covered by the injunctions were bound by them, with the effect that publication would constitute criminal contempt of court. Before it published the extracts, the *Sunday Times* and its editor had received legal advice, based on a ruling by the Vice Chancellor, that the injunctions did not apply to them and hence they were not in contempt of court. An injunction was obtained against the *Sunday Times* on 16 July 1987, and the applicants were found guilty of criminal contempt of court in 1989. The Court of Appeal was sympathetic to the applicants, but upheld their convictions. The applicants alleged, inter alia, that there had been a violation of Art 7 since, at the time of publication of the extracts, they were not guilty of an offence.

*Commission:*   The Commission dealt with the issue only briefly, finding that the common-law offence of criminal contempt is prescribed by law and its constituent elements were sufficiently clear at the time of publication of the extracts. 'The fact that the established legal principles involved were applied to novel circumstances does not render the offence retroactive in any way.' There had been no extension of the relevant law, and hence there was no violation of Art 7.

## 8.6   RAPE

## Aydin v Turkey

## (1997) 25 EHRR 251

*Facts:*   The applicant, a 17-year-old Kurdish girl, was taken from her village by security forces and held in custody for several days. During that time she was raped, beaten, stripped and humiliated. She and her family attempted to obtain legal redress for these and other incidents, but were unsuccessful and subjected to further ill-treatment and harassment. She alleged breaches of Arts 3, 6, 13 and 25. The Commission found violations of Arts 3 and 6, having conducted a thorough inquiry into evidence to support the allegations of criminal activity by the security services. The government strongly denied the allegations, arguing that the girl's story and those of her family were inconsistent and inaccurate, that rape could not have taken place because there were not many bruises on the girl's body, and that her injuries and lack of virginity could be explained by her having ridden a donkey. The government further argued that, since she had married and had a child within 18 months of the incident, she could not have been raped because a rape victim would be too traumatised to marry. The Commission refuted the government's version of events and found, inter alia, that rape constitutes torture and is therefore a violation of Art 3.

*Court:*   The Court accepted the facts as established by the Commission, and stated that there is no permissible excuse for a violation of Art 3. Torture is the most serious type of violation of that Article, and must be distinguished from inhuman and degrading treatment. The distinction is made to 'allow the special stigma of "torture" to attach only to deliberate inhuman treatment causing very serious and cruel suffering'. Rape in detention 'must be considered to be an especially grave and abhorrent form of ill-treatment given the ease with which the offender can exploit the vulnerability and weakened resistance of the victim. Furthermore, rape leaves deep psychological scars on the victim which do not respond to the passage of time as quickly as other forms of physical and mental violence'. The suffering inflicted upon the applicant and her family must have been caused for the purpose of obtaining information from them and thus the Court found that 'the accumulation of acts of physical and mental violence inflicted on the applicant and the especially cruel act of rape to which she was subjected amount to torture in breach of Article 3' (14:7 votes). The Court also found that the failure to investigate or to take seriously the girl's complaint amounted to serious inadequacies in the criminal investigation process and so Arts 6 and 13 had been violated.

# X and Y v The Netherlands

## (1985) 8 EHRR 235

*Facts:*   The applicants were Mr X and his daughter Y, who lived in a home for children with mental disabilities. When she was 16, Y was raped by the son of the home's director, B, causing great distress and trauma to Y. Mr X filed a criminal complaint on his daughter's behalf, stating her lack of mental capacity to do so herself. The public prosecutor's office decided not to proceed against B if he did not commit a similar offence within 2 years. Mr X appealed against that decision but lost. The Court of Appeal did not consider that a rape charge could be proven, and also stated that by law the girl, being over 16, should have made any complaint herself. Although there are offences of sex with the 'helpless', that term has been restricted to physical incapacity, and other relevant offences required the complaint to be made by the victim. Mr X alleged violations of Art 3 in relation to his daughter and of Arts 8, 13, and 14 in relation to both applicants. The Commission found that there had been a breach of Art 8, but not of Art 3, and that it was not necessary to examine whether Art 14 applied.

*Court:*   Both the applicants and the government had agreed that Art 8 applied to the present case since a person's sex life is within the concept of 'private life'. There are positive obligations on a State to ensure effective respect for family or private life, which 'may include the adoption of measures designed to ensure respect for private life even in the sphere of the relations of individuals between themselves'. Y's rights were insufficiently protected by civil law remedies such as actions for damages and injunctions to prevent further offences: 'This is a case where fundamental values and essential aspects of private life are at stake. Effective deterrence is indispensable in this area and it can be achieved only by criminal law provisions; indeed, it is by such provisions that the matter is normally regulated'. Any other rape victim without mental disability would have had recourse to the criminal law. The existing criminal law did not protect Y's rights, and so there was a violation of Art 8.

The applicants had also argued that the difference of treatment between people with mental disabilities and other categories deserving of special protection against sexual assaults, such as children, was discrimination. The Court, however, did not think it necessary to examine this issue separately. 'An examination of the case under . . . Art 14 is not generally required when the Court finds a violation of one of the former Articles taken alone. The position is otherwise if a clear inequality of treatment in the enjoyment of the right in question is a fundamental aspect of the case, but this does not apply to the breach of Art 8 found in the present proceedings.'

The Court dealt similarly with Art 3, although it accepted that rape fell within the definition of inhuman and degrading treatment.

## 8.7   SELF-DEFENCE, THE PREVENTION OF CRIME AND THE USE OF LAWFUL FORCE

### Klass and Others v Federal Republic of Germany

### (1994) 18 EHRR 305

*Facts:*   The first applicant was stopped outside her flat by police who claimed that she had earlier crossed a red traffic light and that she now smelled of alcohol. She was unable to provide a breath specimen and was told that she would have to attend the hospital for a blood test. A scuffle broke out, during which she was arrested and the blood sample was taken. Two separate medical opinions agreed that she had considerable bruising and would suffer long-term problems with an injured shoulder.

The applicant was charged with obstructing a police officer in the execution of his duty and with driving under the influence of alcohol and, although both of these charges were eventually dismissed, she was later sentenced for a 'regulatory' drink-driving offence. The applicant alleged that her treatment during her arrest constituted inhuman and degrading treatment contrary to Art 3. The Commission found only a violation of Art 3 in relation to the first applicant. Although her arrest had been lawful, the use of force resulting in serious injuries could only be justified if it could be shown that the force used was necessary in order for the police to carry out their lawful duties.

*Court:*   The Court disagreed with the Commission as to the correct interpretation of the facts relating to how the first applicant's injuries were caused, and found that the injuries were equally consistent with either her version of events or that of the arresting officers. Since the domestic courts had seen the witnesses first hand and had an opportunity to assess their credibility, the court decision as to the facts should only be overturned on the basis of very strong evidence. Thus, there was no violation of Arts 3 or 8 in respect of either applicant.

*Note:*   Judge Pettiti gave a long and detailed dissenting opinion in which he argued that since police violence was considered to be a serious problem throughout Europe, and 'the role of the police is to ensure the safety and protection of the public', he believed that Art 3 had been violated. The burden of proof should be upon the police to show that the injuries had been caused by the use of necessary force on their part. 'While the police must intervene to provide the necessary protection and law enforcement, they have to respect fundamental rights when doing so. The basic rule is that the police must protect the individual from any violence and ensure people's physical safety. When called upon to act in regard to serious criminal offences, they are not entitled to use violence other than in circumstances of self defence or forceful resistance, and then the response must be proportionate to the danger.'

# McCann v United Kingdom

## (1996) 21 EHRR 97

*Facts:*   An IRA Active Service Unit was thought to be planning to carry out a terrorist car bomb attack in Gibraltar. SAS officers were carrying out a surveillance operation on one of the suspects, who parked a car then left to meet the two other suspects. An SAS officer suspected that the car might contain a bomb, although he had not made a detailed examination of the inside or underneath of the car. The SAS were ordered to arrest the three suspects, and during an attempt to do so the three suspects were shot dead. The SAS had believed that the suspects were about to detonate a car bomb by remote control. In fact the suspects were unarmed, did not possess any detonating devices, and the car did not contain a bomb. Although a jury returned verdicts of unlawful killing at the inquest, all domestic court actions failed. The applicants alleged a violation of Art 2.

*Commission:*   The government had argued that the force used against the suspects did not exceed that which was absolutely necessary in order to defend the citizens of Gibraltar from unlawful violence. The applicants had alleged that there was a government 'shoot to kill' policy under which the SAS were instructed to kill the suspects; or, alternatively, that the SAS had been negligent and had failed to recognise the suspects' right to life. The Commission found that there was no evidence of any 'shoot to kill' policy, and further that the shooting of the suspects was absolutely necessary in the circumstances as the SAS had perceived them to be at the time. This was due to the perception that a bomb would be detonated by remote control, with resultant death and chaos; against such a perceived threat, the force used by the SAS could not be regarded as disproportionate. Once the SAS were sure that there was a risk of death or serious injury to civilians, they were entitled to act to prevent such harm, regardless of whether the risk was substantial. Thus, there was no violation of Art 2.

*Court:*   The Court also found that there was no evidence of a 'shoot to kill' policy nor of any plan to kill the suspects. The SAS were in a difficult position, having a duty to protect the people of Gibraltar, but also having to respect national and international law on the use of lethal force. The Court had regard to two separate tests. First, was the force used proportionate to the risks perceived and the aim to be achieved? Secondly, was the SAS operation planned and organised in a manner which would minimise the risk of killing the suspects? Since the SAS had honestly believed that the suspects were about to detonate a car bomb, and that it was necessary to use lethal force in order to prevent the detonation, the immediate cause of the deaths was held not to be a violation of Art 2. However, earlier events were seen differently by the Court. The suspects could have been arrested on arrival in Gibraltar if the safety of the people of Gibraltar was really the government's priority. The government should have taken greater care to investigate whether in fact there was a car bomb before authorising the SAS action. Once the SAS were ordered to make the arrests, it was highly likely that any sudden movement by the suspects would cause the SAS to use lethal force against them. Thus, the Court was not convinced that the force used was no more than was absolutely necessary in the defence of a person from unlawful violence, and there was a breach of Art 2.

# Kelly v United Kingdom
## (1993) 16 EHRR CD 20

*Facts:*  Five joyriders in a car in Belfast broke through a military road block in an attempt to escape. The soldiers manning the road block shot at the driver in order to stop the car, and the driver was killed. The driver's father brought an action against the Ministry of Defence for assault and negligence, arguing that the force used was excessive and unreasonable in the circumstances. The trial judge found that the soldiers had reasonably believed that the car contained terrorists who would commit further offences if they were not stopped; thus the force used was justified in order to prevent crime. The applicant claimed that the force used was not justified under Art 2(2)(a), (b), or (c) and thus Art 2 had been breached.

*Commission:*  In discussing whether the force used was 'absolutely necessary', the Commission stated that the use of lethal force is justified only when it is proportionate to the legitimate aim pursued. Relevant factors include: the nature of the aim; the dangers to life and limb inherent in the situation; the degree of risk that the force used might result in loss of life; and all the relevant circumstances surrounding the deprivation of life. In the circumstances, the soldiers' reactions were 'absolutely necessary' for the purpose of effecting a lawful arrest under Art 2(2)(b), since the use of force 'was strictly proportionate, having regard to the situation confronting the soldiers, the degree of force employed in response and the risk that the use of force could result in the deprivation of life'. Thus there was no breach.

## 8.8   CONSENT

# Laskey, Jaggard and Brown v United Kingdom
## (1997) 24 EHRR 39

*Facts:*  This case concerned a group of homosexual men who were convicted of various offences against the person, including wounding and assault occasioning actual bodily harm. The charges related to incidents which spanned a 10-year period, and included 'maltreatment of the genitalia' with a variety of implements, beatings and branding. Some incidents left scarring but there were no permanent disabling injuries and no medical treatment was required. All of the injuries were inflicted with the consent of the 'victim' and conducted in private. The applicants had all pleaded guilty at trial since the trial judge had ruled that the consent of the victim could not provide them with any defence to the charges. Prison sentences were reduced on appeal and the House of Lords upheld the convictions. The applicants alleged breaches of Arts 7 and 8, arguing that their convictions were the result of an unforeseeable interpretation of criminal common law, and additionally that the convictions were an unjustifiable interference with their right to respect for their private lives.

*Commission:*  The Commission found only the Art 8 allegation to be admissible, and found that there had been no violation.

*Court:*  The Court found that, whilst sexual orientation and sexual activity are an aspect of 'private life', a relatively large number of people were involved in the event related to the applicants' convictions and so it was open to question whether the activities could be regarded as part of their 'private' lives. However, the Court was prepared to assume that this requirement had been satisfied. On the question of whether the convictions were necessary in a democratic society, the Court found that:

> 'one of the roles which the State is unquestionably entitled to undertake is to seek to regulate, through the operation of the criminal law, activities which involve the infliction of physical harm. This is so whether the activities in question occur in the course of sexual conduct or otherwise. The determination of the level of harm that should be tolerated by the law in situations where the victim consents is in the first instance a matter for the State concerned since what is at stake is related, on the one hand, to public health considerations and, on the other, to the personal autonomy of the individual.'

The applicants were not convicted on the basis of their private sexual behaviour, but on the basis of the injuries caused and the potential for harm inherent in the activities. The Court found no evidence that the applicants would have been treated differently if they had not been homosexuals (but note that the case of *R v Wilson (Alan)* [1996] 3 WLR 125 appears to do just that). Further, the Court considered the measures taken against the applicants to be proportionate, given that the charges were specimen counts and that the sentences had been reduced on appeal. Hence there was no violation of Art 8 (unanimous).

# Part 3
# IMMIGRATION, DEPORTATION AND ASYLUM

# Chapter 9

# RIGHTS OF IMMIGRANTS AND ASYLUM SEEKERS

## 9.1  RIGHT TO CONTROL ENTRY

### (1)  TO BE EXERCISED IN A NON-DISCRIMINATORY MANNER

**Abdulaziz, Cabales and Balkandali v United Kingdom**

(1985) 7 EHRR 471

*Facts:*  The applicants were women born outside the UK who had legally settled in the UK and had been given the right to remain indefinitely. They each married after coming to the UK and sought permission for their husbands to enter or to remain in the UK. Permission was refused in each case. The applicants claimed that UK immigration rules were discriminatory as to sex and race, and violated the right to respect for family life since the women were being deprived of their husbands. One of the applicants also alleged discrimination on the ground of birth. All three applicants alleged violations of Arts 3 and 8.

*Commission:*  The Commission was of the opinion that the right of a foreigner to enter or remain in a country was not, as such, guaranteed by the Convention, but immigration controls had to be exercised consistently with Convention obligations. Consequently, the exclusion of a person from a State where members of his family were living might raise an issue under Art 8. The Commission also considered whether there had been a breach of Art 14.

The government did not dispute that under national rules it was easier for a man settled in the UK to obtain permission for his non-national spouse to enter or remain in the country for settlement, but claimed that the difference had an objective and reasonable justification. The Commission was of the opinion that the number of husbands accepted for settlement in the UK did not justify a difference of treatment on the ground of sex. Accordingly, there had been discrimination on the grounds of sex. However, the majority of the Commission was of the opinion that there had been no violation with regards to race.

The Commission was of the opinion that a difference of treatment based on the mere accident of birth, without regard to the individual's personal circumstances or merits, constituted discrimination in violation of Art 14.

*Court:*  The Court acknowledged that the extent of the State's obligation to admit relatives of settled immigrants would vary considerably according to circumstances and therefore the State had a wide margin of appreciation. This margin was increased by the fact that, in international law, a State has the right to control the entry of non-nationals. However, the duty imposed by the Convention did not extend to a general obligation on the part of the Contracting State to respect the choice by married couples of the country of their matrimonial residence and to accept the non-national spouses for settlement in that country. Therefore, as the applicants had failed to show any obstacles to establishing family life in their husbands' country, there was no breach of Art 8.

The Court, agreeing with the Commission, held that the advancement of the equality of the sexes is today a major goal in Contracting States which meant that weighty reasons would have to be advanced to justify any difference in treatment. Even if men did have a greater impact on the labour market than women, the Court indicated that this would not be a sufficient reason to justify discrimination on the grounds of sex. Thus, the Court found a violation of Art 14 with respect to sex.

## East African Asians v United Kingdom
## (1973) 3 EHRR 76

*Facts:*    The 31 applicants had all been denied leave to enter or to remain permanently in the UK. Twenty-five of the applicants were citizens of the UK and its colonies, and the other six were British 'protected persons'. The government argued that the refusal was neither degrading treatment under Art 3, nor discriminatory, since the UK is not a party to any Convention right to enter one's own country and the relevant legislation applied to all persons regardless of race. The applicants alleged a violation of Arts 3 and 14.

*Commission:*    The Commission treated racial discrimination as a type of degrading treatment, and hence did not find it necessary to examine Art 14. Deportation of a person could be inhuman or degrading treatment in exceptional circumstances, whether that person is an alien or a citizen. The two groups of applicants were considered separately. The group of 25 citizens alleged that they had been promised free entry and that since their continued residence in East Africa was illegal, they were being rendered stateless and subject to intense hardship. The Commission found that the legislation, which imposed immigration controls on most East African Asian citizens, was racially motivated. The Commission found that 'a special importance should be attached to discrimination based on race; that publicly to single out a group of persons for differential treatment on the basis of race might, in certain circumstances, constitute a special form of affront to human dignity; and that differential treatment of a group of persons on the basis of race might therefore be capable of constituting degrading treatment when differential treatment on some other ground would raise no such question'. Thus, the racial discrimination amounting to degrading treatment violated Art 3.

The second category, the six 'protected persons', were treated differently. They were not British subjects and the relevant legislation did not distinguish between categories of British protected persons on any racial basis. Thus, there was no racial discrimination and hence no degrading treatment in relation to the six applicants.

A further argument of breach of Arts 8 and 14 was made in respect of three of the applicants, whose wives had already been granted permanent residence in the UK. The government argued that the husbands and wives had separated voluntarily and that even where Art 8 does guarantee a right for a family to reside together in a particular place, that place is where the husband, rather than the wife, lawfully resides. The Commission rejected the government's arguments; under the legislation a wife was entitled to join a UK-resident husband, and so the three applicants had been subject to discrimination on the ground of sex in relation to their family lives.

## UNITED KINGDOM CASES

## R v Secretary of State for the Home Department, ex parte Isiko

## Court of Appeal, [2001] UKHRR 385

*Facts:* The Secretary of State took the decision in accordance with the Home Department's policy guidelines on deportation and removal set out in DP3/96 to remove two Ugandan asylum-seekers. The High Court quashed that decision on the grounds that the Secretary of State had failed to carry out the balancing test set out in *R v Lord Saville of Newdigate and Others, ex parte A and Others* [1999] 4 All ER 860. The test applied by the Secretary of State had been that of whether the appellant could demonstrate that there were 'the most exceptional circumstances' justifying their right to remain. Following Art 8 of the Convention the removal would have amounted to a harsh and excessive exercise of power.

*Held:* The application of fundamental rights principles into domestic law and procedures called for a more intrusive form of judicial review than had previously been the case. In particular, the onus was now on the Secretary of State to demonstrate that such rights had not been violated. In the present case, however, the implementation of DP3/96, which could lead to breaches of fundamental rights, was not such as to be unlawful under Art 8. The role of the court remained that of determining whether the decision maker had exceeded the limits of his discretion, and that was not the case here.

## (2)  RESPECT FOR THE FAMILY

## Ahmut v The Netherlands

## (1996) 24 EHRR 62

*Facts:* The first applicant applied for a residency permit for his son from his first marriage. The request was rejected by the Deputy Minister of Justice on the basis that the second applicant did not belong to his father's family in The Netherlands because he had remained with his mother in Morocco and was part of his paternal grandmother's family. The applicant had failed to show that there was no one in Morocco who could take care of him. The applicants claimed that the refusal to grant a residency permit and the subsequent deportation back to Morocco was a violation of Art 8.

*Commission:* The Commission recalled that the Convention did not guarantee a right to enter or reside in a particular country. However, in view of the right to respect for family life ensured by Art 8, the exclusion of a person from a country in which his close relatives reside may raise an issue under this provision. The Commission was of the opinion that the links between the applicants may be regarded as constituting family life within the meaning of Art 8. Therefore, the refusal of a residence permit must be considered as an interference with Art 8. The interference must therefore be justified under Art 8, para 2. The Commission identified the legitimate aim pursued as being the economic well-being of the country. It noted that the Dutch immigration policy established special conditions for the purpose of regulating the labour market and the general restriction of immigration in a densely populated country. However, the Commission also noted that the second applicant was 14 years old and it had not been established how and by whom he would be cared for if returned to Morocco. Further, if the second applicant was expelled from The Netherlands there would be a risk that the ties between the applicants would be weakened or broken. The son had also been living in The Netherlands for the past 5 years without the approval of the Dutch authorities but also without action to expel him. Consequently, the Commission was of the opinion that the expulsion of the second applicant would not achieve a fair balance between the interests of the parties involved. The interference was therefore not necessary in a democratic society as being disproportionate to the legitimate aim pursued. The interference was therefore not justified and Art 8 had been violated.

*Court:* The Court stated that a child who is born as a result of a marital union is ipso iure part of that union and there therefore exists a bond amounting to family life as meant by Art 8. A family life between the applicants was therefore established. The Court held that where immigration is concerned, Art 8 cannot be considered to impose on a State a general obligation to respect immigrants' choice of the country of their matrimonial residence and to authorise family reunion in its territory. Therefore, the facts of the case had to be considered. The Court found that the son had lived in Morocco all his life and had strong links with the linguistic and cultural environment of his country, and also still had family there. The fact that the applicants were living apart was due to the father's conscious decision to settle in The Netherlands rather than return to Morocco. The father had also retained his Moroccan nationality. Therefore, the father was not prevented from maintaining the degree of family life he had opted for, nor was there any obstacle to prevent him returning to Morocco. In these circumstances, the Court held that the respondent State could not be said to have failed to strike a fair balance between the parties' interests. No violation of Art 8 was found.

## 9.2 DETENTION OF ENTRANTS AT BORDER

### Amuur v France

### (1996) 22 EHRR 533

*Facts:* The applicants were Somali nationals seeking refugee status. On arrival at Paris-Orly Airport, they were detained for 20 days and placed under strict police surveillance. Following the refusal by the Minister of the Interior to grant leave to enter, the applicants were sent to Syria. The applicants claimed that their detention was in violation of Art 5.

*Commission:* The Commission held that Art 5 was not applicable to the detention of the applicants. It was of the opinion that the degree of physical constraint could not be described as 'deprivation of liberty'. The Commission drew particular attention to the fact that the applicants could at any time have returned voluntarily to Syria. The transit zone was 'open to the outside' even if it was not open 'on the French side'.

*Court:*   The Court held that detaining aliens in the international zone does indeed involve a restriction upon liberty, but one which is not in every respect comparable to that which obtains in centres for the detention of aliens pending deportation. Such confinement, accompanied by suitable safeguards for the persons concerned, is acceptable only in order to enable States to prevent unlawful immigration while complying with their international obligations, particularly under the Geneva Convention Relating to the Status of Refugees 1951 and the Convention. Above all, such confinement must not deprive the asylum-seeker of the right to gain effective access to the procedure for determining refugee status. The applicants were held in the airport transit zone for 20 days. They were sent back to Syria without being able to make an effective application to the authority having jurisdiction to rule on their refugee status. Further, the mere fact that it is possible for asylum-seekers to leave the country where they wish to take refuge cannot exclude a restriction on liberty. Consequently, the Court concluded that holding the applicants in the transit zone of the airport was equivalent in practice, in view of the restrictions suffered, to a deprivation of liberty.

In deciding whether Art 5(1) had been violated, the Court held that in order to ascertain whether a deprivation of liberty has complied with the principle of compatibility with domestic law, the quality of the law must also be assessed. In respect of foreign asylum-seekers, the domestic law must be sufficiently accessible and precise in order to avoid all risk of arbitrariness. The Court concluded that the French law did not allow the ordinary courts to review the conditions under which aliens were held or to impose a limit on the administrative authorities as regards the length of time for which they were held. It did not provide for legal, humanitarian and social assistance, nor did it lay down procedures and time-limits for access to such assistance so that asylum-seekers like the applicants could take the necessary steps. Consequently, the Court held that the French legal rules did not guarantee the applicants' right to liberty and there had been a breach of Art 5.

## 9.3   ASYLUM

### (1)   RISK OF ILL-TREATMENT

## Hatami v Sweden

## [1998] HRCD 951

*Facts:*   The applicant grew up in the town of Borojerd in Iran. A sister and three brothers had been granted political asylum in Sweden due to their political activities in Iran, although another brother and two sisters remained and lived peaceably in Borojerd. However, the applicant arrived in Sweden and asked for asylum, claiming that he had suffered ill-treatment and torture as result of his political affiliations. He was interrogated briefly and a report was drawn up which the applicant signed, although he could not read, write or understand Swedish and the content was not explained to him. The applicant's request for asylum was rejected on the grounds that the authorities did not find credible his evidence concerning his political activities or the ill-treatment. This conclusion was primarily based on the fact that the applicant's statements, both oral and written, were inconsistent. The applicant claimed that this refusal of asylum and the consequent deportation back to Iran would expose him to a real risk of treatment contrary to Art 3.

*Commission:*   The Commission recalled that Contracting States have the right, as a matter of well-established international law and subject to their treaty obligations including their obligations under the Convention, to control the entry, residence and expulsion of aliens. The right to political asylum is not protected in either the Convention or its Protocols. However, the decision to expel a person may give rise to an issue under Art 3, where substantial grounds have been shown for believing that the person concerned faces a real risk of being subjected to torture or inhuman or degrading treatment or punishment in the receiving country. In such circumstances, Art 3 implies the obligation not to expel the person in question to that country. Further, the activities of the individual in question, however undesirable or dangerous, cannot be a material consideration. The Commission was of the opinion that the inconsistent information was an incorrect basis for the Swedish authorities' decision to refuse asylum. Further, the Commission's own examination disclosed that the inconsistencies which may have occurred did not relate to the applicant's submissions, but rather to the Swedish authorities' inaccurate presentation and interpretation of the case. The Commission also stated that complete accuracy is seldom to be expected by victims of torture. However, the Commission recalled nevertheless that, even if the applicant's version of the events was taken into account, the Commission had also to examine whether the applicant would face a risk of ill-treatment if returned to Iran. The Commission held that evidence had been adduced to establish substantial grounds for believing that the applicant would be exposed to a real risk of treatment contrary to Art 3 of the Convention.

*Court:*   Due to the attainment of a friendly settlement between the Swedish Government and Hatami, the case was struck out of the list.

# Nsona v The Netherlands

## (2001) 32 EHRR 9

*Facts:*   The first and second applicants, Francine Nsona (aged 9) and Bata Nsona were Zairean nationals. Bata had claimed refugee status in The Netherlands in 1989 and had been granted a residence permit. Francine was detained at the airport hotel on arrival in The Netherlands in 1993. Bata applied to the District Court to be appointed as Francine's temporary guardian, but was later refused. The President of the Regional Court of The Hague found no compelling reasons on the basis of which Francine should be allowed to reside in The Netherlands. Francine travelled alone back to Zaire, after which Bata applied for a provisional residence visa for her but was refused. The first applicant, Francine, complained that her expulsion, and the conditions under which the expulsion order was carried out, constituted inhuman treatment contrary to Art 3 of the Convention. Both applicants claimed that Francine's expulsion violated their right to respect for family life as guaranteed by Art 8.

*Commission:* The applicants complained that Francine's unaccompanied return to Zaire, the Dutch authorities' failure to make adequate arrangements for her to be met on arrival there and the failure to guarantee her care and welfare in Zaire amounted to treatment contrary to Art 3. The Commission recalled that Contracting States have the right, as a matter of well-established international law and subject to their treaty obligations, including those based on Art 3, to control the entry, residence and expulsion of aliens. The expulsion of an alien by a Contracting State may give rise to an issue under Art 3 where substantial grounds have been shown that the person concerned faced a real risk of being subjected to treatment contrary to Art 3. The Commission further recalled that a treatment has to reach a certain level of severity before it can be considered to breach Art 3. The Commission considered that in this particular case, the first applicant's expulsion must have involved a certain hardship and cannot be considered as having been carried out with due concern to the relevant factors, but it did not reach the level of severity necessary for Art 3 to be applicable.

As regards Art 8, the applicants claimed that they were barred from developing a family life. They argued that an interference with a new family life may also be contrary to Art 8. The Commission noted that the applicants' family relationship had remained unsubstantiated. Consequently, there had been no violation of Art 8.

*Court:* The Court agreed with the findings of the Commission. As regards Art 3, the Court did draw attention to the haste with which the Dutch authorities gave effect to their decision to remove Francine and their willingness to hand over responsibility for her welfare as soon as she had left the Dutch territory in view of her age. However, this did not reach the level sufficient to make Art 3 applicable. Consequently, there was no violation of Art 3. As regards Art 8, the Court drew attention to the deceit which the applicants had initially employed when Francine arrived in The Netherlands. The Court held that in view of this, the Dutch authorities cannot be blamed for refusing to accept the applicants' claims of family ties which were unsubstantiated. Consequently, there had been no violation of Art 8.

# Vilvarajah v United Kingdom
## (1991) 14 EHRR 248

*Facts:* The five Tamil applicants had sought asylum in the UK after experiencing ill-treatment in Sri Lanka which included heavy beatings, random shootings, indiscriminate bombing, loss of belongings, deprivation of food, detention, electric shock treatment and threat of life. After considering the applications under normal immigration procedure, namely whether the applicants had a well-founded fear of persecution for the purposes of the 1951 Refugee Convention, the UK rejected the requests. After continuing to suffer ill-treatment in Sri Lanka, the applicants sought judicial review of the refusals of asylum and also complained that the refusals violated, inter alia, Art 3. They were granted exceptional leave to enter.

*Commission:* The Commission identified the main issue as being whether the applicants' removal to Sri Lanka was in breach of Art 3 of the Convention because it exposed them to a real risk of torture or inhuman or degrading treatment in that country. The Commission referred to *Soering v United Kingdom* (1989) 11 EHRR 439, which confirmed that Contracting States have an obligation under Art 3 not to send people to countries where there are substantial grounds for believing that they would be in danger of being subjected to treatment proscribed by Art 3. Although *Soering* concerned extradition, the Commission was of the opinion that the same criteria applies to any forced removal of a person to a country where he faced a real risk. Therefore, although the Contracting State is not directly responsible for acts of the receiving State, what happens to the asylum seeker on return cannot be wholly ignored as it may cast light on whether the risk has been rightly or wrongly assessed by the Contracting State. Given the information available at the relevant dates, late 1987 and early 1989, the Commission held, by a vote of 7 to 7, with a casting vote by the President, that there had been no violation of Art 3.

*Court:* The Court emphasised that the right to political asylum is not contained in either the Convention or its Protocols. However, it is established that the expulsion by a Contracting State of an asylum seeker may give rise to an issue under Art 3 where substantial grounds have been shown for believing that the person concerned faced a real risk of being subjected to torture or to inhuman or degrading treatment or punishment in the country to which he was returned. In deciding this, the Court held that it must assess the issue by having regard to all the material placed before it. It may have regard to information which comes to light subsequent to the expulsion which could be of value in conforming or refuting the appreciation that has been made by the Contracting State or the well-foundedness or otherwise of an applicant's fears. The ill-treatment must attain a minimum level of severity if it is to fall within the scope of Art 3. The Court held that the evidence did not establish that the applicants' personal position was any worse than the generality of other members of the Tamil community. There was a possibility that they may be detained and ill-treated but a mere possibility is not sufficient to give rise to a breach of Art 3. Accordingly, the Court held by 8 votes to 1 that there had been no violation of Art 3.

## (2)   COLLECTIVE EXPULSION OF ASYLUM SEEKERS

### Conka v Belgium

### (2002) 34 EHRR 54

*Facts:* The applicants' request for political asylum in Belgium was refused and they were ordered to leave the territory within 5 days. Subsequent applications for legal aid to seek judicial review of this decision and for a stay of execution were dismissed. Several months later, the Belgian police issued a notice requiring their attendance at a police station. The notice indicated that the reason for attendance was to enable files relating to their application for asylum to be completed. On arrival, the applicants were served with warrants for their arrest and ordered to leave the territory. They were detained in a transit centre with many other refugees of Romany origin until their expulsion to Slovakia.

*Court:* While accepting that in some circumstances it may be necessary for the authorities to use subterfuge to counter criminal activities, the Court held that deliberate acts designed to mislead asylum seekers in order to make it easier to deprive them of their liberty was incompatible with Art 5(1). Furthermore, failure to inform the applicants' lawyer in time to lodge an appeal prior to expulsion amounted to a violation of Art 5(4), which provides that persons deprived of their liberty are entitled to take proceedings to assess the lawfulness of detention. Additionally, in this case the procedures taken to detain and deport a large number of persons of the same origin did not afford sufficient guarantees to demonstrate that the personal circumstances of each individual had been taken into account. Thus it was not possible to eliminate all doubt that the expulsion might have been collective. Accordingly, the Court was satisfied that the circumstances surrounding the detention and subsequent expulsion of a group of Slovakian nationals of Romany origin infringed the right to liberty and security guaranteed by Art 5, and violated Art 4 of the Fourth Protocol which prohibits the collective expulsion of aliens.

## UNITED KINGDOM CASES

## Sepet and Bulbul v Secretary of State for the Home Department

### [2001] EWCA Civ 681, [2001] INLR 376

*Facts:* The applicants were Turkish Kurdish nationals who objected to performing compulsory military service, and who claimed asylum in the UK. The Secretary of State rejected their claims, and both appealed to special adjudicators. In both cases the adjudicators found that the applicants were 'partial' objectors. They did not object to military service generally, but were specifically objecting to performing military service for the Turkish army as they were opposed to the Turkish Government, and did not want to contribute in any way to operations against the Kurds. A further appeal was made to the Immigration Appeal Tribunal, where the applicants were again unsuccessful. The Tribunal found that in order to be a refugee on the basis of an objection to military service the applicants would first have to establish the reasonable likelihood of some deeply held non-discriminatory conviction, which was not the case. The applicants appealed to the Court of Appeal.

*Held:* The appeal was dismissed. Laws LJ referred to the United Nations Convention Relating to the Status of Refugees 1951 and the Protocol of 1967, in which a refugee is defined in Art 1A as:

'any person who:

. . .

(2) . . . owing to well-founded fear of being persecuted for reasons of race, religion, nationality, membership of a particular social group or political opinion, is outside the country of his nationality and is unable or, owing to such fear, is unwilling to avail himself of the protection of that country;'.

Reference was also made to the *Handbook on Procedures and Criteria for Determining Refugee Status* published in 1979 by the UNHCR. This discussed at some length the position of those claiming refugee status in order to avoid military service, which included at para 171:

'Not every conviction, genuine though it may be, will constitute a sufficient reason for claiming refugee status . . . it is not enough for a person to be in disagreement with his government regarding the political justification for a particular military action.'

The case of *Thlimmenos v Greece* (2001) 31 EHRR 15 was considered in detail in the judgment of Parker LJ, and he concluded that it did not assist the applicants, and the court found that 'the most that can be said of *Thlimmenos v Greece* is that the conception of conscientious objection as a right arising under the [Convention] might live to fight another day; it is not established by the Strasbourg jurisprudence to date' (per Laws LJ at para 176).

In conclusion, the court held that the applicants, who were not absolute conscientious objectors, did not benefit from refugee status.

# Chapter 10

# EXTRADITION AND DEPORTATION

## 10.1 EXTRADITION

### Soering v United Kingdom

### (1989) 11 EHRR 439

*Facts:* The UK sought to extradite a German national from the UK to the USA under the terms of an extradition treaty that had been incorporated into the law of the UK (United States of America (Extradition) Order 1976, SI 1976/2144 and the United States of America (Extradition Amendment) Order 1986, SI 1986/2020). The applicant was accused of committing a murder in Bedford County, Virginia, and argued that his extradition would amount to a violation of Art 3. In capital murder cases the State of Virginia could impose the death penalty which may involve very long periods of time spent on death-row. Capital punishment is permitted under certain conditions by Art 2(1) of the Convention. The applicant accepted that the death penalty did not per se violate the Convention, but he submitted that exposure to the 'death-row phenomenon' would amount to inhuman and degrading treatment, which was prohibited by Art 3. Furthermore, his extradition to the USA would constitute a violation of Art 6(3)(c) because there was no provision in the State of Virginia for him to pursue various appeals. The UK government submitted that the Convention should not be interpreted so as to impose responsibility of a Contracting State for acts which occur outside its jurisdiction. The basis for this argument was that such an interpretation would interfere with international treaty rights and lead to a conflict with the norms of the international judicial process. Further, it would involve adjudication on the internal affairs of a foreign State and its domestic criminal justice system. In support of this argument, the government relied upon traditional principles of extradition which respect the rule of non-inquiry.

*Commission:* The President of the Commission informed the UK government, in accordance with r 36 of the Commission's rules of procedure, that it was desirable, in the interests of the parties and the proper conduct of proceedings, not to extradite the applicant to the USA until the Commission and the Court had had the opportunity to consider the application.

*Court:* The Court was of the opinion that to surrender a person to another State, where there were substantial grounds for believing that they would be in danger of being subjected to torture, inhuman or degrading treatment, would be in violation of Art 3. Liability was incurred by the extraditing Contracting State 'by reason of its having taken action which has as a direct consequence the exposure of an individual to proscribed ill-treatment'. Furthermore, it was noted that: 'Article 3 enshrines one of the fundamental values of the democratic societies making up the Council of Europe. It is also to be found in similar terms in other international instruments such as the 1966 International Covenant on Civil and Political Rights and the 1969 American Convention on Human Rights and is generally recognised as an internationally accepted standard'.

After consideration of the applicant's complaint that his return to the USA would violate his rights under Art 6, the Court was of the opinion that if a fugitive had suffered or risked suffering a 'flagrant denial of a fair trial' in the requesting State, then an extradition may give rise to an application under Art 6. However, in this case, the Court found no issue arising under this provision.

*Note:*   Following the issue of a diplomatic note stating that the US authorities would not prosecute the applicant for the offence of capital murder, the applicant was eventually extradited.

# (1)   DISGUISED EXTRADITION

## Bozano v France

## (1987) 9 EHRR 297

*Facts:*   The applicant was convicted in absentia in Italy of serious crimes. The Italian authorities unsuccessfully sought his extradition from France. The extradition request was vetoed by the French court on the ground that the rights of the defence had not been sufficiently protected by the proceedings in the Italian court. The French government ordered his deportation from France and he was arrested and detained in custody. The file of the case revealed that he was taken immediately, by force, to the Swiss border where he was held in custody until he was handed over to the Italian authorities who had lodged an extradition request with the Swiss authorities. The French courts quashed the deportation order on the grounds that it was an abuse of power. The applicant complained that his arrest, detention and forcible removal to Switzerland was contrary to Art 5(1) in that it deprived him of his right to liberty and security of the person. He submitted that his detention had not been for a purpose provided by Art 5(1)(f).

*Commission:*   The jurisprudence of the Commission and the Court demonstrates that the aim underlying Art 5 is to guard against arbitrary action by the authorities because in a democratic society subscribing to the rule of law, arbitrary detention can never be regarded as 'lawful'. 'Lawfulness' of detention presupposes conformity with domestic law and also must be for a purpose set out in the Convention. In addition, it noted that both the 'ordering and the execution of the measures entailing deprivation of liberty must be lawful' (para 72). It was noted that detention for the purposes of extradition was no longer permitted under French law. The Commission considered it was not required to express a general view on the issue of 'disguised extradition' by means of deportation with regard to the Convention. However, in this case the Commission was satisfied that the applicant's detention had a purpose different from detention with a view to deportation and consequently was in breach of Art 5(1).

*Court:*   The Court considered that the purpose of Art 5 was to protect the individual from arbitrariness which required that any measure depriving an individual of his liberty must be compatible with the purposes of this provision. It noted that the Art 5 was concerned with an individual's right to liberty and his right to security of the person. Accordingly, the applicant's abduction by the authorities was neither lawful nor compatible with his right to security of the person. It was really a disguised form of extradition designed to circumvent the negative ruling of the French court and his detention was not for any of the purposes set out in Art 5. The Court noted that there was a volume of evidence to suggest that the applicant's account of events was true. Accordingly, the Court was satisfied that there was a breach of Art 5(1) of the Convention.

## 10.2   DEPORTATION

### (1)   EVIDENCE REQUIRED IN SUPPORT OF APPLICANT'S CLAIM

### HLR v France

### (1997) 26 EHRR 29

*Facts:*   The applicant was arrested in France whilst travelling from Colombia to Italy and was found in possession of a quantity of cocaine. Following his conviction by a French court, he was sentenced to 5 years' imprisonment and permanently excluded from French territory. The Minister of the Interior issued an order for his deportation to Colombia. The applicant claimed that the source of the risk was not from Colombian authorities but from the threat of reprisals by drug traffickers, who were angry at statements made by him to the French police. Furthermore, the authorities were unable to offer him any guarantee of protection. He claimed that if he were deported to Colombia he would run a serious risk of being treated in a manner contrary to Art 3 of the Convention.

*Commission:*   The Commission informed the French government that it was desirable in the interests of the parties and the proper conduct of proceedings to refrain from deporting the applicant until the application had been considered. In determining whether there was a risk of proscribed treatment, strict criteria must be applied. Making a finding in the applicant's favour did not require that the risk came from the Colombian authorities. In this case, the risk to the applicant came from criminal organisations and, in the opinion of the Commission, it 'appeared more than likely that the Colombian authorities would not be able to give HLR adequate protection'. Accordingly, the Commission found, by 19 votes to 10, that there would be a violation of Art 3 if the applicant were deported to Colombia.

*Court:*   The absolute prohibition on torture or inhuman and degrading treatment applied, irrespective of the applicant's conduct and notwithstanding that the danger emanated from persons or groups who were not public officials. The Court accepted that a State has a duty to provide persons with adequate protection from groups or individuals but accepted that it was not always able to guarantee the total security of persons within its jurisdiction. In cases like this, the applicant was required to demonstrate prima facie evidence that there was a real and serious risk that he would be subjected to the forms of treatment proscribed by Art 3. The Court was of the opinion that the applicant had failed to show that there were substantial grounds for believing that deportation would 'definitely and inevitably place him in a situation where his life or his physical integrity would be threatened'. In the light of this finding, the Court held, by 15 votes to 6, that there would be no violation of Art 3 if the order for the applicant's deportation were to be executed.

*Note:*    This case demonstrates the burden on the applicant to provide sufficient evidence. The Court considered that:

> 'The documents from various sources produced in support of the applicant's memorial provide insight into the tense atmosphere in Colombia, but do not contain any indication of the existence of a situation comparable to his own. Although drug traffickers sometimes take revenge on informers, there is not relevant evidence to show in HLR's case that the alleged risk is real. His aunt's letters cannot by themselves suffice to show that the threat is real. Moreover, there are no documents to support the claim that the applicant's personal situation would be worse than that of other Colombians, were he to be deported.'

Further, the Court was not satisfied that Amnesty International reports revealed that the authorities were incapable of giving him adequate protection.

## (2)   HABEAS CORPUS AND JUDICIAL REVIEW

### Chahal v United Kingdom

### (1996) 23 EHRR 413

*Facts:*    The applicant was a leading figure in the Sikh community in the UK. In 1985, he was detained under the Prevention of Terrorism (Temporary Provisions) Act 1984 on suspicion of involvement in a conspiracy to assassinate the Indian Prime Minister. He was released without charge. In 1986, he was convicted of assault and affray and served concurrent sentences of 6 and 9 months. In 1990, the Home Secretary decided to deport the applicant to India under s 3(5)(b) of the Immigration Act 1971 because his continued presence in the UK was not 'conducive to the public good' for reasons of national security and he was detained pending deportation. In 1990, he applied for political asylum on the basis that he could establish the 'well-founded fear of persecution' test as required under the terms of the United Nations Convention on the Status of Refugees 1951. In 1991, the Home Secretary refused his request for asylum. The applicant applied to the Divisional Court for judicial review of the Secretary of State's decision. The decision to refuse asylum was quashed and referred back to the Home Secretary. However, following re-examination of the case by the Secretary of State, asylum was again refused. The deportation order was also reviewed, but the Home Secretary concluded that it was right to proceed.

Macpherson J, in the Divisional Court, refused the application for habeas corpus on the basis that the Secretary of State had the power to detain any person who was the subject of a deportation order. The applicant also applied for judicial review. The court accepted that the Secretary of State, in arriving at his decision, could take into account factors which he was not obliged to disclose to the court. The applicant complained that his deportation to India would expose him to a real risk of torture or inhuman or degrading treatment in violation of Art 3. In addition, he complained that his detention had been for an excessive length of time and was in violation of Art 5(1) and that he was denied the opportunity to have his detention pending deportation reviewed by a court in violation of Art 5(4).

*Commission:* The Commission noted that, in a case where there were serious doubts as to the likelihood of a person being subjected to treatment of punishment contrary to Art 3, the benefit of that doubt could be given to the deporting State whose national interests were threatened by the person's presence. However, the national interests of the State could not be invoked to override the interests of the individual where there was sufficient evidence to suggest that that he would be subjected to ill-treatment if expelled. The Commission expressed the unanimous opinion that there would be a violation of Art 3 if the applicant was deported to India and that the length of his detention had been excessive and in breach of Art 5(1). The Commission considered it was unnecessary to examine the alleged violation of Art 5(4).

*Court:* The Court decided, by 12 votes to 7, that the order for the applicant's deportation to India would, if executed, give rise to a violation of Art 3. The national interests of the State could not be invoked to override the interests of the individual where there were substantial grounds for believing that he would be subject to ill-treatment if expelled. In determining whether there is a risk, the Court can consider all the evidence before it and obtain further information of its own motion. It held that the prohibition against expulsion in Art 3 cases was absolute irrespective of the applicant's conduct and that his return would amount to a violation of Art 3, notwithstanding the efforts of the Indian authorities to bring about reform. In arriving at its decision, considerable weight was given to reports of Amnesty International and the United Nations' Special Rapporteur on Torture.

With regard to the alleged breach of Art 5, the Court recalled that the deprivation of liberty under Art 5(1) was justified only for as long as deportation proceedings were in progress. If these proceedings were not 'prosecuted with due diligence' then the detention would cease to be permissible under Art 5(1)(f). Although the Court was of the opinion that the length of detention gave some cause for concern, in view of the exceptional circumstances of this case and taking account of the fact that the national authorities had conducted the deportation proceedings with due diligence and that adequate guarantees against arbitrary detention existed, the Court considered that the applicant's detention complied with the requirements of Art 5(1)(f). Accordingly, there had been no violation of Art 5(1). The Court noted that because national security was involved, the domestic courts were not able to review whether the decisions to detain the applicant, and to keep him in detention, were justified on the grounds of national security. The advisory panel that considered his case could not be considered a 'court' within the meaning of the Convention. Although cases involving terrorism and national security raised special problems, the Court was of the opinion that national authorities must still be subject to effective control by the courts. The Court did not consider that proceedings in the UK for habeas corpus and for judicial review satisfied the requirements of Art 5(4) and that there had been a breach of Art 5(4).

## (3)   RISK STEMMING FROM FACTORS OUTSIDE CONTROL OF STATE

# D v United Kingdom

## (1997) 24 EHRR 423

*Facts:*   The applicant, who came from St Kitts, had been refused leave to remain in the UK on compassionate grounds. On his arrival in 1993, he was found to be in possession of a significant quantity of cocaine. He was denied leave to enter the country and given notice that he would be removed within a matter of days. However, he was arrested and subsequently convicted of importing a controlled drug, whereupon he was sentenced to 6 years' imprisonment. Whilst serving his sentence, he was diagnosed as having AIDS and, by mid-1996, his prognosis was poor with a short life expectancy. Shortly before his release on licence, the immigration authorities ordered his removal to St Kitts. He complained, inter alia, that his expulsion would violate Art 3 of the Convention in that he would be deprived of his current medical treatment and, as a consequence, would be exposed to a real risk of dying under the most distressing circumstances which would amount to inhuman treatment.

*Commission:*   The Commission concluded that the removal of the applicant would engage the responsibility of the respondent State under Art 3, even though the risk of being subjected to inhuman and degrading treatment stemmed from factors for which the authorities could not be held responsible. The Commission expressed the opinion, by 11 votes to 7, that the applicant's expulsion would violate Art 3.

*Court:*   The absolute prohibition contained in Art 3 must be respected whether or not the applicant had been given leave to enter the UK. The applicant's physical presence was sufficient for him to be within the jurisdiction of the respondent State within the meaning of Art 1. Furthermore, the protection guaranteed by Art 3 applied 'irrespective of the reprehensible nature of the conduct of the person in question'. The Court was aware of the need to weigh competing public requirements against each other. On the one hand, there is the public interest in removing alien drug couriers from the State's territory. On the other hand, there is the public interest in ensuring all persons received protection from torture or inhuman treatment. The Court noted the gravity of the offence with which the applicant was convicted and was: 'acutely aware of the problems confronting Contracting States in their efforts to combat the harm caused to their societies through the supply of drugs from abroad. The administration of severe sanction to persons involved in drug trafficking, including expulsion of alien drug couriers like the applicant, is a justified response to this scourge'.

The right to expel such persons must be balanced against the absolute prohibition on torture and inhuman or degrading treatment enshrined in the Convention. Where the Court is satisfied there was a real risk that the applicant's removal would be contrary to Art 3, the balance must be in favour of non-expulsion. In this case, the Court considered the applicant's expulsion would amount to a violation of Art 3.

# Bensaid v United Kingdom

## (2001) 33 EHRR 10

*Facts:* The applicant suffered from schizophrenia and claimed that if he were deported to Algeria he would be unable to obtain adequate medication for his condition. He relied on information indicating that terrorist activities made travel dangerous and would add to the strains on his precarious mental balance. The government submitted that the applicant suffered from a mental illness, the effects of which were likely to be long term whether he was in the UK or Algeria. Relying on a letter from an Algerian doctor indicating that the drug taken by the applicant was available in his local hospital which he could receive as an in-patient, the government refuted the claim that the applicant faced a real risk of being subjected to treatment contrary to Art 3.

*Court:* Although Art 3 is more commonly applied where the applicant is at risk from proscribed treatment which emanates from intentionally inflicted acts by public authorities, the Court reserves the right to be flexible and consider other contexts in which a violation of Art 3 may occur. The Court considered that the applicant's claim that he would suffer a deterioration of his condition if returned to Algeria was 'to a large extent speculative'. Although the Court accepted the seriousness of the applicant's condition, it considered that the threshold set by Art 3 was particularly high 'where the case does not concern the direct responsibility of the Contracting State for the infliction of harm' (para 40). The Court did not find that there was a sufficiently real risk that the applicant's removal in these circumstances would be contrary to the standards of Art 3. This case did not disclose the exceptional circumstances of the case of *D v United Kingdom* (1997) 24 EHRR 423, where the applicant had been in the final stages of a terminal illness with no prospect of medical care. Accordingly, the Court found that the implementation of the decision to remove the applicant to Algeria would not violate Art 3.

## (4)   REVIEW OF CURRENT SITUATION IN RECEIVING STATE

# Ahmed v Austria

## (1996) 24 EHRR 278

*Facts:* The applicant complained that his expulsion to Somalia would expose him to the risk of being subjected to treatment contrary to Art 3 of the Convention. He had been granted refugee status by the Austrian authorities on the ground that there was a risk that he would suffer persecution if he were to return to Somalia. Following his conviction for robbery, his refugee status was rescinded. Subsequently, the authorities ordered his deportation on the ground that he constituted a danger to the community.

*Commission:* The Commission attached weight to the fact that the Austrian authorities, in granting him refugee status, had been satisfied that there was a real risk of persecution if he returned to Somalia. It noted that Somalia was still in a state of civil war and that the dangers to which the applicant would have been exposed when he applied for refugee status still existed. The Commission expressed the unanimous opinion that his expulsion to Somalia would expose him to a serious risk of being subjected to treatment contrary to Art 3.

*Court:*   The Court noted that Art 3 'enshrines one of the fundamental values of democratic society, prohibits in absolute terms torture, inhuman and degrading treatment or punishment irrespective of the victim's conduct'. This principle is valid when issues arise under Art 3 in expulsion cases and the activities of the victim cannot be a material consideration. In order to assess the risks to the applicant, the Court was required to assess the current political situation in Somalia. Accordingly, the Court was unanimous in expressing the opinion that the applicant's deportation to Somalia would breach Art 3 for as long as he faced a serious risk of being subjected there to persecution.

# Jabari v Turkey
## (2000) 9 BHRC 1

*Facts:*   The applicant, an Iranian national, alleged that she would face a real risk of ill-treatment and death by stoning if expelled from Turkey and returned to Iran. Further, she alleged that she had been denied an effective remedy to challenge her expulsion. She claimed that she committed adultery while living in Iran and had to leave the country before criminal proceedings were commenced. She entered Turkey illegally and attempted to travel to Canada via Paris using a forged Canadian passport. On arrival in Paris, she was apprehended by the French authorities and returned to Turkey. The Turkish authorities ordered her deportation. Her application for asylum was rejected as it had been submitted out of time. The government questioned the substance of the applicant's fears, submitting that it was significant that she did not claim asylum status when she arrived in Paris. Requests for asylum must be lodged within 5 days of entry into Turkey.

*Court:*   The Court noted that the right to political asylum is not contained in either the Convention or its Protocols. However, it is well established in Convention case-law that expulsion by a Contracting State may give rise to an issue under Art 3 where there are substantial grounds for believing a person would be subjected to ill-treatment in the receiving State. Having regard to the absolute nature of Art 3, 'a rigorous scrutiny must necessarily be conducted of an individual's claim that his or her deportation to a third country will expose that individual to treatment prohibited by Art 3' (para 39). In this case, the Court was not persuaded that the authorities had conducted any meaningful assessment of the applicant's claim. Furthermore, 'the automatic and mechanical application of such a short time-limit for submitting an asylum application was at variance with the protection of the fundamental value embodied in Art 3' (para 40). The Court gave weight to the UNHCR's conclusion on the applicant's claim. Having regard to these considerations, the Court found that there was a real risk of the applicant being subjected to ill-treatment if she returned to Iran. Accordingly, in the event of the decision to deport the applicant to Iran being implemented, there would be a violation of Art 3.

# Hilal v United Kingdom
## (2001) 33 EHRR 2

*Facts:* The applicant claimed that he faced a real and immediate risk of ill-treatment if he was deported to Tanzania. He also argued that Art 3 imposed a positive obligation on the respondent State to investigate his claim that he would be exposed to a real risk of treatment contrary to Art 3 if he returned to Tanzania. Prior to leaving, he had been detained by the authorities on account of his involvement with the Civil United Front (CUF) and badly treated. Reports on the situation in Tanzania demonstrated that there was still active persecution of members of the CUF. The government submitted that the applicant had been found to lack credibility by the Special Adjudicator, which cast overwhelming doubt over whether he had indeed been tortured.

*Court:* The Court recalled that States have the right to control the entry, residence and expulsion of aliens. However, expulsion may give rise to an issue under Art 3 where there are substantial grounds for believing that the person would face a real risk of being subjected to torture or ill-treatment in the receiving State. In these circumstances, Art 3 implies an obligation not to expel the person to that country. The Court accepted that the applicant had been arrested and detained because he was a member of the CUF and that he had been ill-treated during detention. The Court examined the materials provided by the applicant in support of his case and found no basis to reject them. Accordingly, the Court was satisfied that, in the circumstances, the deportation of the applicant to Tanzania would amount to a violation of Art 3.

## *UNITED KINGDOM CASES*

# X v Secretary of State for the Home Department
## [2001] 1 WLR 740

*Facts:* Although a Mental Health Review Tribunal considered it appropriate to permit an asylum-seeker to continue his detention under the Mental Health Act 1983, it would not be a breach of Art 3 if he was returned to Malta, notwithstanding that the level of care would be lower.

# Part 4
# FAMILIES, CHILDREN AND GENDER

# Chapter 11

# FAMILIES

## 11.1 NOTION OF 'FAMILY LIFE' CAN INCLUDE A VARIETY OF RELATIONSHIPS

### (1) NEPHEW

**Boyle v United Kingdom**

**(1994) 19 EHRR 179**

*Facts:* The applicant complained that a refusal by a local authority to allow him access to his nephew, who was subject to a care order, and the absence of any possibility to apply to the court for access, infringed his right to respect for family life. (Prior to the entry into force of s 34(3) of the Children Act 1989, the applicant had no statutory right to apply to the court for contact with his nephew.) The government took the view that the bond between uncle and nephew was insufficient to constitute family life.

*Commission:* The Commission was of the opinion that the relationship between an uncle and nephew could, depending upon the circumstances, fall within the concept of 'family life'. It was significant that the applicant lived in close proximity and had had frequent contact with his nephew. The Commission was satisfied that in this case a sufficient emotional bond had developed between the applicant and the child to fall within the scope of family life. Domestic law did not provide a means whereby the applicant could be involved in decisions affecting his relationship with the child 'to the degree sufficient to provide him with the requisite protection of his interest'. Accordingly, the Commission expressed the opinion, by 14 votes to 4, that there had been a violation of Art 8.

*Court:* The Registrar was advised that s 34(3) of the Children Act 1989 now conferred on any person, who has obtained leave of the court to make an application, the possibility of having the question of contact between the child placed in local authority care and that person determined by a court in proceedings complying with Art 6(1). Accordingly, the Court recorded that a friendly settlement had been reached, the applicant agreed to discontinue his action and the Court agreed to strike the case out of the list.

### (2) GRANDPARENTS

**Bronda v Italy**

**(2001) 33 EHRR 4**

*Facts:* Following reports that her mother was neglecting her parental duties, the applicant's granddaughter had been taken into care and parental rights assigned to the local authority. Subsequently, she was placed with foster-parents and her grandparents were granted three access visits a year. Eventually, the court ruled that the child was available for adoption. The applicants complained that, in failing to return the child to her original family, the authorities had violated their right to private and family life.

*Commission:*   In its report, the Commission expressed the opinion, by 10 votes to 3, that there had been no violation of Art 8.

*Court:*   It was not disputed that a failure to return the child to its original home clearly amounted to an interference with the applicants' right to respect for their family life. Such interference amounts to a violation of Art 8 unless it is in accordance with the law, pursues an aim that is legitimate and is regarded as necessary in a democratic society. The Court noted that the mutual enjoyment by parent and child of each other's company constitutes a fundamental element of family life and that domestic measures hindering such enjoyment amount to an interference protected by Art 8. This principle applies with relations between a child and its grandparents. In determining whether the measures taken by the authorities are necessary, it is of crucial importance to consider what is in the best interests of the child. In the present case, the Court held that a fair balance had to be struck between the child's interest in remaining with her foster-parents and her natural family's interest in having her to live with them. The Court attached special weight to the overriding interest of the child, now aged 14 and who had always indicated a desire to remain with her foster-parents, and concluded that the child's interest outweighed that of her grandparents. Consequently, as the national authorities had not gone beyond their margin of appreciation, there had been no violation of Art 8.

## (3)   SAME SEX RELATIONSHIPS

*UNITED KINGDOM CASES*

## Fitzpatrick v Sterling Housing Association Ltd
House of Lords, [1999] 3 WLR 1113

*Facts:*   The claimant argued he was entitled to succeed to a protected tenancy on the basis of the Rent Act 1977, Sch 1, as he was a member of the family of T (deceased) by virtue of a long-standing homosexual relationship. The Court of Appeal had found that the claimant was not a family member. The claimant appealed, relying in part on Art 8 of the Convention.

*Held:*   The House of Lords held that the concept of family in the Act was a flexible one, subject to ongoing judicial interpretation. In the context of the Act a man and a woman living together in a stable relationship were capable of being members of a family, and there could be no rational basis for withholding that status from same sex relationships. To uphold the appeal was not to usurp Parliament, but was to give effect to the breadth of the meaning of 'family'.

## 11.2   RIGHT TO DIVORCE AND REMARRY

# Johnston v Ireland

## (1986) 9 EHRR 203

*Facts:*   Under the Irish Constitution, the first applicant was unable to obtain a dissolution of his marriage to enable him to marry the second applicant. The first and second applicants had lived together in a stable relationship for several years with their child, the third applicant. They complained that the absence of provision in Ireland for divorce, and the failure to recognise the family life of people living in a family relationship outside marriage, infringed their rights under the Convention. Furthermore, the absence of an appropriate legal regime reflecting the third applicant's natural family ties amounted to a failure to respect her family life.

*Commission:*   The Commission was unanimous in finding that the right to divorce and thus the right to remarry was not guaranteed by the Convention. The fact that Irish law did not confer a recognised family status on the first and second applicants did not give rise to a breach of the Convention. However, the legal regime concerning the status of an illegitimate child under Irish law failed to respect the family life of all three applicants and was in breach of Art 8.

*Court:*   The notion of family in Art 8 is not confined solely to marriage-based relationships and may encompass other de facto 'family' ties where the parties are living together outside marriage. However, the Court was not prepared to interpret Art 8 as imposing a positive obligation on States to establish a special regime for unmarried couples which was analogous to that of married couples. Noting that, in this case, the respondent State had done nothing to prevent the applicants from living together, the Court expressed the view that there had been no interference by the public authorities with the family life of the first and second applicants. However, the Court found that the significant differences in the legal status of legitimate and illegitimate children amounted to a failure to respect the third applicant's family life. As a result of the close and intimate relationship between the third applicant and her parents, all three applicants were affected by this failure. Accordingly, there had been a violation of Art 8 in respect of all applicants.

## (1)   PROHIBITION ON REMARRIAGE

# F v Switzerland

## (1987) 10 EHRR 411

*Facts:*   Following the applicant's third divorce, he was made the subject of an order prohibiting him from remarriage within 3 years. He complained that the prohibition on remarriage violated Art 12, which provides that men and women of marriageable age have the right to marry and found a family. The respondent government sought to distinguish the right to marry from the right to remarry. The exercise of a right to remarry would depend upon the right to divorce, which did not flow from the Convention.

*Commission:*   In its report, the Commission expressed, by 10 votes to 7, the opinion that there had been a violation of Art 12.

*Court:*   If domestic legislation provides for divorce, which the Court accepted was not a requirement of the Convention, Art 12 secures for divorced persons the right to marry without unreasonable restrictions. Although the stability of marriage is a legitimate aim which is in the public interest, compelling a person to take time to reflect upon remarriage was not a sufficient reason to justify the interference with a person's right to marry. The order prohibiting the applicant's remarriage affected the very essence of a right protected by the Convention and amounted to a violation of Art 12.

## 11.3   RIGHTS OF PARENTS

### (1)   BEST INTERESTS OF THE CHILD

## McMichael v United Kingdom

## (1995) 20 EHRR 205, Court; (1993) 15 EHRR CD 80, Commission

*Facts:*   The first applicant was not married to the mother of his son at the time of his birth and was not named on the birth certificate. The child's mother was suffering from a mental illness and, shortly after giving birth, her son was taken from her and placed in the care of the local authority. The first applicant visited his son for a short period, eventually acquiring parental rights when he married the second applicant. However, in the meantime, the child had been placed in the care of foster-parents and released for adoption by the court. The applicants complained that, in depriving them of the care and custody of their child, the national authorities violated their right to private and family life.

*Commission:*   It was not in dispute that the measures taken by the local authority interfered with the applicants' right to private and family life. However, bearing in mind the margin of appreciation accorded to the domestic authorities, this interference was justified as being necessary in a democratic society for the protection of health and for the protection of the rights of others.

*Court:*   The Court held that the decision-making process determining the custody and access arrangements in regards to the child did not afford the requisite protection of the applicants' interests as safeguarded by Art 8. The Court did not consider it appropriate to draw any distinction between the two applicants as regards the extent of the violation.

## Bronda v Italy

## (2001) 33 EHRR 4

*Facts:*   See 11.1(2).

*Court:*   In determining whether the measures taken by the authorities were necessary, the Court considered that it was of crucial importance to consider what is in the best interest of the child. In the present case, the Court held that a fair balance had to be struck between the child's interest in remaining with her foster-parents, and her natural family's interest in having her to live with them. The Court attached special weight to the overriding interest of the child, now aged 14 and who had always indicated a desire to remain with her foster-parents, and concluded that the child's interest outweighed that of her grandparents. Consequently, as the national authorities had not gone beyond their margin of appreciation, there had been no violation of Art 8.

## (2) RIGHTS OF THE NATURAL FATHER

*ACCESS*

# Sahin v Germany; Sommerfeld v Germany; Hoffmann v Germany
## [2002] 1 FLR 119

*Facts:* The applicants were German fathers whose children had been born outside of wedlock but who had acknowledged paternity. Applications were made to the German courts for access orders, but the courts held that it was for the mother, in the exercise of her right of custody, to determine the child's relations with third persons and that the fathers could be granted a right of access by the court only if it could be demonstrated that it was in the interests of the child. In the first case the court found that access would not be in the child's interests as the mother had taken such a strong dislike to the applicant that the child would be put into a situation of antipathy and tensions which would probably considerably affect her well-being. Appeals were unsuccessful. There was a disparity in the domestic law recognised by the Regional Court in that the person with custody in the case of a child born out of wedlock, typically the mother, controlled access. The Federal Constitutional Court refused to entertain the applicants' case.

*Court:* The applicants relied on Arts 8 and 14, and the Court restated the position that Art 8 applies to de facto relationships as well as marriage-based relationships. The bond created at birth between child and parent should not be destroyed by the breakdown of the relationship between the parents. The interference with the right to family life was in accordance with the law, and pursued a legitimate aim. However, the interference should be subject to close examination. In the first case there was insufficient evidence to suggest that the child would have been adversely affected, such that there was a breach of Art 8. In the second case there was also a breach as there had been inadequate consideration of the case. In the third case, however, the domestic courts had given the father adequate opportunity to be heard, and had also listened to the comments of the child such that there was no breach of Art 8. There was a violation of Art 14 in that, under the rules in Germany prior to their being changed, any analysis of the interests under consideration called for a distinction to be made between those situations in which a child was born in wedlock and those in which it was not.

# Glaser v United Kingdom

## (2001) 33 EHRR 1

*Facts:* The applicant complained that the failure by authorities in England and Scotland to enforce effectively his right to contact with his three children, who were living with their mother, resulted in a breach of his right to respect for private and family life. This case involved protracted proceedings relating to access arrangements in which the applicant's former wife refused to comply with access orders and moved the children from England to Scotland without leave of the court.

*Court:* The Court observed that whilst Art 8 includes a right for a parent to have measures taken with a view to his or her being reunited with their children, this obligation is not absolute since the rights and freedoms of all concerned must be taken into account, including the best interests of the child. Where contact with a parent may threaten those interests, it is for national authorities to strike a fair balance. Noting that the main obstacle to the applicant enjoying contact with his children was opposition by his former wife, the Court was satisfied that there was no fundamental defect in existing structures designed to enforce the applicant's rights. Accordingly, the authorities did not fail in their responsibilities to protect the applicant's right to respect for family life. Further, the Court considered, having regard to the particular circumstances of the case, that the overall length of proceedings, which began in 1992, was not excessively long and thus did not violate Art 6(1).

## *ADOPTION*

# Keegan v Ireland

## (1994) 18 EHRR 342

*Facts:* The applicant's illegitimate child was placed for adoption without his knowledge or consent. He applied for custody and instituted proceedings before the court to be appointed as the child's guardian. The application was refused and an adoption order made in respect of the child. He was informed that he had no locus standi in relation to proceedings before the Adoption Board. The applicant maintained that the respondent State failed to respect his family life by facilitating a placement for adoption without his knowledge or consent. Accordingly, there had been a violation of his right to family life and he had been discriminated against in the exercise of these rights when his position was compared with that of a married father.

*Commission:* The Commission was satisfied that the applicant had sufficient links with the child to establish family life, and was of the view that the obstacles created by Irish law to the applicant establishing a relationship with his daughter constituted lack of respect for his family life. The Commission expressed the opinion that there had been a violation of Art 8 and thus it was unnecessary to examine whether he had been the subject of discrimination.

*Court:* The Court considered that the concept of 'family' in Art 8 'is not confined solely to marriage-based relationships and may encompass other de facto "family" ties where parties are living together outside marriage. A child born out of such a relationship is *ipso iure* part of that "family" unit from the moment of his birth and by the very fact of it. There thus exists between the child and his parents a bond amounting to family life even if at the time of birth the parents are no longer cohabiting or if their relationship has then ended'.

In this case, the Court was satisfied that the relationship between the applicant and the child's mother had the hallmark of family life for the purposes of Art 8. The fact that the relationship subsequently broke down did not alter this conclusion more than it would for a couple who were lawfully married and in a similar situation. Furthermore, according to the principles set out by the Court in its case-law, where the existence of a family tie with a child has been established, States must act in a manner calculated to enable that tie to be developed and legal safeguards must be created to ensure the child's integration into the family. The decision to place the child for adoption without the father's knowledge or consent and the subsequent adoption order amounted to an interference with the applicant's right to respect for family life. The Court did not accept that these measures were necessary in a democratic society and was satisfied that there had been a violation of Art 8. In addition, the Court was satisfied that the applicant had no right under Irish law to challenge the decision to place his child for adoption either before the courts or the Adoption Board. Accordingly, there had been a breach of Art 6.

*Note:* Legislation was introduced in Ireland in 1998 to prevent a repetition of these violations and to ensure compliance with Art 53. The Adoption Act 1998 gives natural fathers the right to be consulted in matters of adoption of their children. It sets out a formal procedure for consulting the natural father, if known, or any person who believes that he is a father of a child born out of wedlock, before a child is placed for adoption, so as to allow the father an opportunity to exercise his right to apply for guardianship and/or custody of the child.

## PRESUMPTION OF PATERNITY

# Kroon v The Netherlands
## (1994) 19 EHRR 263

*Facts:* The first and second applicants were the biological parents of the third applicant, who was born while the first applicant was married to another man. Although the applicants did not cohabit, the second applicant contributed to the care and upbringing of the child. They complained that under Dutch law they were unable to obtain recognition of the true paternity of the child. Furthermore, while a married man could deny the paternity of children born during a marriage, it was not open to a married woman to do so.

*Commission:* The Commission expressed the opinion that the fact that it was impossible under Dutch law for anyone but the first applicant's husband to deny paternity, and for the second applicant to recognise the third applicant as his child amounted to a lack of respect for private and family life. Accordingly, the respondent State was in breach of a positive obligation imposed by Art 8.

*Court:*   The Court was satisfied that a bond existed between the applicants which amounted to 'family life,' and thus Art 8 was applicable. The essential object of Art 8 is to protect the individual against arbitrary action by public authorities. Where the existence of a family tie with a child has been established, the State must act in a manner calculated to enable that tie to develop, and legal safeguards must be established which render possible the child's integration into the family. It has been established that the notion of 'family life' is not restricted to marriage-based relationships and can encompass other relationships where parties are living together. Although, as a rule, living together may be a requirement for such a relationship, exceptionally other factors may also serve to demonstrate that a relationship has sufficient constancy to create de facto family ties. In this case, the applicants had established that sufficient ties existed for their relationship to be recognised as 'family life' within the meaning of Art 8. The only way to establish legally recognised family ties between the second and third applicants would require the first and second applicants to marry. The Court was of the opinion that respect for family life requires that biological and social reality prevail over a legal presumption, which may fly in the face of both established fact and the wishes of those concerned without actually benefiting anyone. In this case, the respondent State had failed to secure, for the applicants, respect for their family life. Accordingly, there had been a violation of Art 8.

## PATERNITY LEAVE

## Petrovic v Austria

## (2001) 33 EHRR 14

*Facts:*   The applicant applied for a parental leave allowance so that he could look after his child while his wife continued to work. The employment office turned his application down on the ground that under the Unemployment Benefit Act 1977, only mothers were entitled to receive such payments. The applicant complained that the refusal to grant him parental leave allowance was discriminatory and violated his right to family life.

*Commission:*   In its report, the Commission expressed the opinion that there had been a violation of Art 14 taken together with Art 8.

*Court:*   The Court noted that the allowance paid by the State was intended to promote respect for family life and necessarily affected the way in which the latter was organised as, in conjunction with parental leave, it enabled one parent to stay at home and care for the children. In granting parental leave allowance, States were able to demonstrate their respect for family life and the allowance came within the scope of Art 8. It was not disputed that distributing the allowance to mothers amounted to a difference in treatment on grounds of sex. The Court recalled that Contracting States enjoyed a margin of appreciation in assessing whether and to what extent differences in otherwise similar situations justified different treatment in law. The scope of the margin of appreciation varied according to circumstance and subject matter. The idea of giving financial assistance to either parent in order to allow the parent concerned to remain in the home to care for children was relatively recent. Until recently, welfare measures of this kind had primarily been intended to enable mothers of young children to stay at home and care for very young children. Nowadays, both parents were sharing the caring role and States were moving towards extending welfare measures to fathers. However, there remained a very great disparity between the legal systems of Contracting States in this area. The Austrian authorities' refusal to grant the applicant a parental leave allowance had not, therefore, exceeded the margin of appreciation allowed to them. Consequently, the difference in treatment complained of had not been discriminatory within the meaning of Art 14.

## 11.4 LIFESTYLE

### (1) REFUSAL TO GRANT CUSTODY TO PARENT LIVING IN A HOMOSEXUAL RELATIONSHIP

## Salgueiro da Silva Mouta v Portugal

## (2001) 31 EHRR 47

*Facts:* Following the dissolution of his marriage, the applicant had been living in a stable homosexual relationship. In awarding the applicant's ex-wife custody of their child, the court noted that a homosexual environment could not be considered the healthiest for the child's development. The applicant complained that the appeal court's decision to award custody on the basis of his homosexuality constituted an unjustified interference with his right to respect for family life. Furthermore, it amounted to an interference with his right to respect for his private life in that it was specified that he must hide his homosexuality in his meetings with his daughter.

*Commission:* The Commission declared the application admissible under Art 8.

*Court:* After hearing preliminary arguments in December 1998, the Court declared that the application could not be rejected as being manifestly ill-founded, and that a full hearing on the substance of the case was necessary.

*Note:* Both this and the following two cases are still before the Court at the time of writing. They are included here in recognition of the importance of this chain of cases.

## Frette v France

## [2002] HRCD 91

*Facts:* The applicant, an unmarried homosexual, applied for leave to adopt. He was refused on the grounds that his 'lifestyle' did not appear to provide the necessary safeguards for him to be entrusted with the care of a child. He appealed successfully on the basis that the decision-making authorities had misinterpreted the relevant legislative provisions. The amicus curiae was of the opinion that this decision amounted to introducing a form of discrimination between prospective adopters on the basis of choice of private lifestyle, which the legislature had not intended. The *Conseil d'Etat* quashed this decision and held that, despite the applicant's personal qualities and aptitude for bringing up children, he could not provide the requisite safeguards demanded of someone adopting a child. He complained, inter alia, of interference with his right to respect for his private and family life.

This application has been communicated to the French government under Art 8.

## Cardoso and Johansen v United Kingdom
### Application No 47061/99, unreported

*Facts:* The applicants had cohabited in a stable homosexual relationship since 1981. The first applicant, a Brazilian national, entered into a marriage of convenience in order to remain living with the second applicant, an Australian national with indefinite leave to remain in the UK. In 1996, the first applicant was diagnosed as having an AIDS-related illness, and his Brazilian family indicated that they did not wish to have further contact with him. In 1998, the Secretary of State discovered that he had used a false passport to gain entry to the UK and, having noted that he could obtain treatment in Brazil, ordered that he be removed. The second applicant would not be permitted to join the first applicant in Brazil. The applicants complained that the first applicant's removal would, inter alia, interfere with their right to private and family life.

The application was communicated to the UK government under Art 8.

## 11.5   REGISTRATION OF A FORENAME
### Guillot v France
### RJD, 1996-V, No 19

*Facts:* Following a refusal by the registrar of births, deaths and marriages to accept the forename chosen by the applicants, their child was entered on the register without a forename. The ground for refusal was that the name was not listed in the calendar of saints' days. Furthermore, the forename consisted of two names joined by a preposition. The authorities were prepared to allow the parents to register the child's forename provided they joined the names with a hyphen, thereby avoiding the preposition. The applicants complained that this refusal amounted to a failure to respect their private and family life.

*Commission:* Having attempted unsuccessfully to secure a friendly settlement, the Commission drew up a report and expressed the opinion that there had been no violation of Art 8.

*Court:* Although the Court noted that Art 8 did not contain any explicit provision of forenames, it expressed the opinion that this issue came within the sphere of Art 8. Since forenames were a means of identifying persons within their family and the community, they do concern private and family life and the choice of a child's forename by its parents is a personal, emotional matter. However, in this case, the child used the forename without hindrance and the French authorities had been prepared to allow the parents to register the names using a hyphen. Consequently, the Court did not find the inconvenience complained of by the applicants was sufficient to raise an issue of failure to respect private and family life under Art 8. Accordingly, there had been no violation of the Convention.

## 11.6 LEGITIMATE INTERFERENCE WITH THE RIGHT TO PRIVATE AND FAMILY LIFE

### (1) PUBLIC ORDER AND PREVENTING CRIME

### Moustaquim v Belgium

### (1991) 13 EHRR 802

*Facts:* The applicant, a Moroccan national, had lived with his family in Belgium for about 20 years and had been granted a residence permit. Following his conviction for a substantial series of offences, he was made the subject of a deportation order requiring him to leave Belgium and not return for 10 years. The applicant alleged that his deportation interfered with his family and private life.

*Commission:* In its report, the Commission expressed the opinion, by 10 votes to 3, that the order for deportation was disproportionate because the authorities had not achieved a just balance between the applicant's interest in maintaining a family life and the public interest in the prevention of disorder. Accordingly, there had been a breach of Art 8.

*Court:* The Court was satisfied that the applicant's family life was seriously disrupted by the measure taken against him. However, it did not seek to underestimate the Contracting States' concern to maintain public order, in particular in exercising their right, as a matter of well-established international law and subject to their treaty obligations, to control the entry, residence and expulsion of aliens. Nevertheless, in cases where the exercise of this right interfered with a right protected by Art 8(1), it must be shown to be 'necessary in a democratic society' and must be proportionate to the legitimate aim pursued. In arriving at its decision, the Court noted that the applicant came to Belgium when he was very young, his schooling had been in French, he had little knowledge of the language of his country of origin and his close relatives had been living in Belgium for a long time. The Court was satisfied that, in the circumstances, a proper balance had not been achieved between the interests involved. Accordingly, there had been a violation of Art 8.

### Benrachid v France

### Application No 39518/98

*Facts:* Following his conviction for armed robbery and hostage taking, the applicant, an Algerian national, had been expelled from France where he had lived with his family since he was 7 years old.

*Commission:* The Commission expressed the view that given the age at which the applicant arrived in France and the fact that his family still lived there, the expulsion constituted an interference with his right to private and family life. However, Contracting States had the right to control the entry, and expulsion of non-nationals, provided there was no interference with the right secured by Art 8. It was significant that the applicant had performed his military service in Algeria and thus had some link with that country. In the circumstances, the applicant's expulsion was necessary to pursue the legitimate aim of defending public order and preventing crime.

Accordingly, the measure was not disproportionate and the application was manifestly ill-founded.

## Djaid v France
### Application No 38687/97

*Facts:*   The applicant, an Algerian national, had lived in France with his family since he was a baby and had fathered two French children. Following his conviction for serious drug-related offences, the Court of Appeal ordered his permanent exclusion from France. He complained that the exclusion order violated his right to respect for his private and family life.

*Court:*   The Court considered that the permanent exclusion order amounted to an interference with the applicant's private and family life. However, it was significant that the applicant had chosen to retain his Algerian nationality and did not appear to have demonstrated any intention of taking French nationality. Further, the evidence did not clearly establish whether he had maintained emotional ties with the children whose paternity he had recognised and he had not shown that he was living with someone in a stable relationship. It was of note that the first child was conceived after the exclusion order had been imposed, when the applicant was aware that his position was somewhat unsettled. The Court understood the need for the authorities to be very firm when dealing with people who are involved in the misuse of drugs. Accordingly, in view of the serious nature of the offence, this interference with the applicant's right to private and family life was legitimate and necessary and the application was manifestly ill-founded.

## 11.7   RIGHT OF SPOUSES NOT TO GIVE EVIDENCE AGAINST EACH OTHER IN CRIMINAL INVESTIGATIONS: BREACH OF CONFIDENTIALITY BY AUTHORITIES

### Z v Finland
### (1997) 25 EHRR 371

*Facts:*   The applicant and her husband were both diagnosed as being HIV-positive. During a criminal investigation into sexual offences allegedly committed by the applicant's husband, she invoked her right under Finnish law not to give evidence against her spouse. The public prosecutor obtained disclosure orders from the court. She complained that there had been violations of her respect for private and family life as guaranteed by Art 8 on account of orders imposed on her doctors and psychiatrist to give evidence and disclose information about her in criminal investigations involving her husband; the seizure of her medical records at the hospital where she had been treated and their inclusion in their entirety in the investigation file; the decisions of the competent courts to limit the confidentiality of the trial record to a period of 10 years; and the disclosure of her identity and medical data in the Court of Appeal's judgment.

*Commission:*   In its report, the Commission expressed the unanimous opinion that there had been a violation of Art 8 in that the applicant's rights had been interfered with in a manner which could not be said to be necessary in a democratic society.

*Court:*    It was undisputed that the various measures complained of constituted an interference with the applicant's right to respect for private and family life. In considering whether the measures were proportionate to the legitimate aim pursued, the Court noted that respecting the confidentiality of medical records is a vital principle in the legal systems of all Contracting States. The disclosure of such data can dramatically affect a person's private and family life. This was especially valid as regards the protection of the confidentiality of information about HIV infection, in that potential and actual HIV carriers may be deterred from undergoing tests and seeking medical treatment. At the same time, the Court accepted that the interests of a patient and the community as a whole in protecting the confidentiality of medical data could be outweighed by the public interest in investigation and prosecution of crime and in the publicity of court proceedings, where such interests were shown to be of even greater interest.

The Court noted that, in this case, the questioning of witnesses took place in camera, the transcripts of witness statements were classified as confidential and those involved in the proceedings were under a duty to treat the information as confidential. On balance, the Court was satisfied that the orders requiring the applicant's medical advisers to give evidence and the seizure of her medical records and their inclusion in the investigation file had not given rise to a violation of Art 8. However, the order to make the transcripts of the evidence given to her medical advisers and her medical records accessible to the public in 2002 would, if implemented, constitute a violation of Art 8 and the disclosure of the applicant's identity and medical condition by the Court of Appeal infringed Art 8.

# Chapter 12

# CHILDREN

## 12.1 CARE, CUSTODY AND ACCESS

### (1) LENGTH OF PROCEEDINGS

### Paulsen-Medalen and Svensson v Sweden

### (1998) 26 EHRR 260

*Facts:* The first applicant was the mother of two children, P and J. Following an investigation by the social authorities, the children were provisionally taken into care in 1989 on the ground that there were such deficiencies in their care as to endanger their health and development. The first applicant appealed, but the decision was upheld. The children were placed in separate foster homes. On 20 March 1990, the authorities decided to restrict the applicant's access to a 2½-hour visit in the foster homes every second week. On 27 March 1990, she appealed and although at first instance the decision was quashed, it was eventually upheld and she was refused further leave to appeal. Meanwhile, on 19 June 1990, the authorities restricted her right to speak to J on the telephone to two calls per week and maintained the restrictions on her access. She challenged these decisions but the County Administrative Court upheld them on 3 October 1990. Her first appeal was rejected on 11 January 1991, and her further appeal failed in the Supreme Administrative Court on 28 June 1993.

*Commission:* In relation to the first applicant's complaint about the length of proceedings (3 years and 3 months) which determined the question of access between her and her sons, the Commission found a violation of Art 6(1). In the Commission's opinion, 'proceedings concerning a parent's access to his or her child, who has been placed in public care, require by their very nature to be dealt with urgently'. It found no convincing explanation for the delay from the respondent government.

*Court:* The Court found that the reasonableness of the length of proceedings is to be assessed 'in the light of the complexity of the case and the conduct of the applicant and that of the relevant authorities'. In cases concerning restrictions on access between a parent and a child taken into public care, 'the nature of the interests at stake for the applicant and the serious and irreversible consequences of the taking into care may have on his or her enjoyment of the right to respect for family life require the authorities to act with exceptional diligence in ensuring progress of the proceedings'. It was found that the delay was not due to the applicant's conduct or the complexity of the case but due to the fact that 'the authority concerned could not be said to have acted with the exceptional diligence required by Art 6(1) of the Convention in such cases'. The Court found a violation of Art 6(1) and awarded compensation for moral damage plus legal costs.

# McMichael v United Kingdom

## (1995) 20 EHRR 205, Court; (1993) 15 EHRR CD 80, Commission

*Facts:* In November 1987, the second applicant gave birth to a son, A. At the time, she denied that the first applicant was the father of A, although she later admitted that he was. Due to a recurrence of mental illness in the second applicant, a children's hearing was convened and A was taken to foster-parents. In February 1988, a children's hearing decided that A needed compulsory care. In December 1988, access visits were terminated and this was confirmed at a children's hearing in June 1989. A was adopted in 1993. The applicants had lodged an application with the Commission in October 1989 alleging violations of Arts 6(1), 8 and 14.

*Commission:* The Commission declared admissible the applicants' complaints that they were unable to see confidential reports and documents submitted to the children's hearings and the first applicant's complaints that as a natural father he had no legal rights to custody or to participate in the care proceedings. A violation of Art 8 was found in respect of both applicants and a violation of Art 6(1) in respect of the second applicant. No violation of Art 14 was found.

*Court:* The Court found that Art 6(1) had no application to the first applicant's complaint. Under Scots law, the natural father of a child born out of wedlock, 'did not automatically have parental rights in relation to the child'. The Court noted that documents before the children's hearings were not disclosed to the second applicant or her representative. The Court accepted that 'in this sensitive domain of family law there may be good reasons for opting for an adjudicatory body that does not have the composition or procedures of a court of law'. However, as a general principle, a fair trial means 'the opportunity to have knowledge of and comment on the observations filed or evidence adduced by the other party'. The Court concluded that the second applicant did not receive a fair hearing and a violation of Art 6 was found.

As the facts complained of also had repercussions on a 'fundamental element of the family life of the two applicants', the Court thought it appropriate to examine the facts under Art 8. It concluded that the decision-making process determining custody and access 'did not afford the requisite protection of the applicants' interests as safeguarded by Article 8'. A violation of Art 8 was found in respect of both applicants. No violation of Art 14 was found.

## *UNITED KINGDOM CASES*

# A Health Authority v X (Discovery: Medical Conduct)

## Court of Appeal, [2001] EWCA Civ 2014, [2001] UKHRR 1213

*Facts:* During the course of care proceedings a judge ordered the disclosure of patient records relating to children held by a doctor to the Health Authority in order to allow an assessment of the extent to which Dr X and others had complied with the terms of service of the Health Authority. The order was made only subject to strict conditions, and the Health Authority appealed these conditions, arguing that doctors were under an unqualified obligation to supply patient records in response to Health

Authority requests. At first instance it was held that while patient records were protected under Art 8 of the Convention, disclosure could be required where there was a compelling public interest and where there were adequate safeguards in place to protect patient records from abuse.

*Held:* The strict confidentiality with which such records had to be treated was not absolute and had to be balanced against the public interest. In the present case, where concerns had been raised relating to the administration of the medical system, the public interest in the proper administration of the system outweighed the rights of the individual patients. However, the judge was quite correct to attach conditions to the disclosure of the records. The appeal was dismissed.

## (2)  CHILDREN TAKEN INTO CARE

## TP and KM v United Kingdom

## (2002) 34 EHRR 2

*Facts:*  TP was the mother of the second applicant, KM. The local authority, the London Borough of Newham, suspected that KM was being sexually abused. At a case conference concern was expressed about the home situation, and the inability of TP to protect KM from 'a steady stream of young men'. Later KM disclosed to an interviewer that she had been abused by 'X'. TP's boyfriend shared the same first name as X. The local authority applied and was granted a place of safety order, and a medical examination suggested that abuse might have taken place. After various procedures KM was returned to TP and her boyfriend for a rehabilitation period. It was eventually accepted that TP's boyfriend was not the abuser of KM. The applicants initiated an action in negligence against the local authority and were unsuccessful. The House of Lords upheld the Court of Appeal, which had held that no claim for breach of statutory duty could arise from any alleged right to custody of a child which could give rise to an award for damages.

*Court:*  The applicants' case was based on alleged breaches of Arts 6, 8 and 13 of the Convention. The Court found that Art 6 had not been breached. In relation to the assumption that TP's boyfriend was the abuser, which led to the first decision to take KM into care, the Court found that the mistake was not 'of such a nature as to deprive the decision to take [KM] into care of a legitimate basis' (para 75). However, the failure to disclose a video of KM's interview and its transcript was in breach of Art 8, as the disclosure would have allowed TP to deal quickly with the allegations made. As regards Art 13, the Court found that 'the applicants should have had available to them a means of claiming that the local authority's handling of the procedures was responsible for the damage which they had suffered and obtaining compensation for that damage' (para 109).

## UNITED KINGDOM CASES

## Re S (Minors); Re W (Minors)

## House of Lords, [2002] UKHL 10, [2002] 2 All ER 192

*Facts:* The two cases arose on appeal from the Court of Appeal and related to the extent to which parts of the Children Act 1989 were compatible with the HRA 1998. The Court of Appeal dealt with the extent to which the judiciary could exercise control over the implementation by a local authority of a care plan, the Court ceasing to have jurisdiction once a care order had been made. The Court found that there were instances in which the implementation of a care order could have adverse effects for the child in question, but leave no avenue for judicial intervention. In the cases under consideration it was possible that there had been breaches of rights guaranteed by the Convention. The Court considered that the HRA 1998 required some amendment to the traditional role of the judiciary. The Court of Appeal advanced a new procedure under which certain aspects of the care plan were to be 'starred' at trial, and if a starred aspect was not achieved within a given period the local authority would be obliged to reactivate the process that led to the creation of the plan, allowing the courts an ongoing role in the supervision of the plan.

*Held:* It was necessary to draw a distinction between the compatibility of the primary legislation with the Convention rights and the HRA 1998, and the possibility that in particular cases such rights might be breached. The fact that the latter occurred did not necessarily invalidate the relevant primary legislation. It was for Parliament to remedy defects in primary legislation and the courts could not attribute meanings to Acts which fundamentally departed from them. To do so was to cross the boundary line between interpretation and amendment. In the present case the fact that there might be a violation of Art 8 in the application of the care order system did not invalidate the relevant parts of the Children Act 1989. The government was urged to address the problems raised by the Court of Appeal, but the present system under which once a care order was made the resolution of any uncertainties was a matter for the local authority, remained valid.

## (3)   FAMILY REUNION

## Hokkanen v Finland

## (1994) 19 EHRR 139

*Facts:* In 1985, following the death of his wife, the applicant's 18-month-old daughter, S, was cared for by the wife's parents. They decided not to return S to the applicant and in July 1986 the District Court ordered that S should remain with them, although the applicant was granted access. The grandparents refused to comply with the access arrangements. In January 1987, the applicant was granted custody, but again the grandparents refused to comply and S remained living with them. In November 1990, the grandparents refused to comply with a further access order and, in 1991, succeeded in gaining custody of S. The applicant applied to the Commission in 1992 alleging violations of Arts 6(1), 8, and 13.

*Commission:* The Commission found that the national authorities had failed to make the efforts which could reasonably be expected to enforce the applicant's rights. It concluded that no fair balance was struck between the various interests involved and that the non-enforcement of the applicant's custody rights and non-enforcement of his visiting rights 'amounts to a lack of respect for his family life' in violation of Art 8. No violation of Art 6(1) was found and it was decided that it was not necessary to consider Art 13.

*Court:* The Court found links sufficient to establish family life within the meaning of Art 8 and stated that Art 8 includes a right for the parent to have measures taken with a view to his or her being reunited with the child. This principle also applies where the origin of the provisional transfer of care is a private agreement. However, the Court recalled that the obligation of the national authorities to facilitate reunion is not absolute 'since the reunion of a parent with a child who has lived for some time with other persons may not be able to take place'. It is for the national authorities to strike a fair balance and what is decisive is whether the national authorities have taken all such necessary steps to facilitate reunion as 'can reasonably be demanded in the special circumstances of each case'. The Court concluded that the competent authorities here had not made reasonable efforts to facilitate reunion and that the non-enforcement of the applicant's right of access constituted a breach of his right to respect for his family life under Art 8. However, the Court found that the non-enforcement of the applicant's custody rights and transfer of custody to the grandparents, involved no separate violation of Art 8. The measure was not disproportionate to the legitimate aim of protecting the child's interests. With respect to Art 6(1), the Court concluded that the length of the second custody proceedings did not exceed a 'reasonable time' and it decided that it was not necessary to consider the Art 13 complaint.

# Eriksson v Sweden
## (1989) 12 EHRR 183

*Facts:* C gave birth to her daughter L in February 1978. L was taken into care in March 1978 on the ground that the conditions in her home were unsatisfactory as C had been convicted of handling stolen goods and of possession of narcotics and sentenced to prison. L was placed in a foster home. In May 1980, C applied for the termination of the care of her daughter. This was refused and her appeals were unsuccessful. In January 1983, the Social Council terminated care but prohibited the natural parents from removing L from the foster home. C was granted access to L in the foster home every second month. C's appeals against this were unsuccessful. In December 1984, C and L applied to the Commission alleging violations of Arts 6(1), 8, 13 and Art 2 of the First Protocol.

*Commission:* The Commission found violations of Arts 8 and 6(1) in respect of the complaints of both C and L. No violations of Art 13 or Art 2 of the First Protocol were found.

*Court:* The Court accepted that the prohibition on C from removing L from the foster home, the maintenance of this prohibition for more than 6 years and the restrictions on access amounted to an interference with C's right to respect for family life guaranteed by Art 8(1). The Court then examined Art 8(2) and concluded that whilst the prohibition on removal was in accordance with law, the restrictions on access were not as 'there are no legal provisions on which any such restrictions could be based'. It found that the prohibition on removal and restrictions on access had a legitimate aim in that they protected L's health and rights. However, the Court concluded that the 'severe and lasting restrictions on access combined with the long duration of the prohibition on removal' were not proportionate to the legitimate aims pursued. A violation of Art 8 was found with respect to the prohibition and restrictions on access. In relation to Art 6(1), the Court found that the proceedings concerning the prohibition on removal were not in violation of Art 6(1). However, a violation of Art 6(1) was found, in that C did not have a remedy before a court with regard to the restrictions imposed on her access to L. No violation of Art 2 of the First Protocol or Art 13 was found. For the same reasons given in relation to C's complaint, the Court also found violations of Arts 8 and 6(1) in respect of L.

## Olsson v Sweden (No 2)

## (1992) 17 EHRR 134

*Facts:* The applicants were husband and wife with three children, S, H, and T, who were taken into care in 1980. In 1987, the Supreme Administrative Court held that the public care of the two younger children, H and T, should terminate. However, the Social Council prohibited the applicants, pursuant to s 28 of the Social Services Act, from removing H and T from their respective foster homes. No formal decision with regard to access was taken in connection with this decision and the applicants' appeals against the prohibition were unsuccessful. In their application of 1987 to the Commission, the applicants alleged violations of Arts 6, 8, and 13.

*Commission:* The Commission concluded that the restrictions on the applicants' access to their children were not in accordance with law, as they did not have a sufficient basis in Swedish law as required by Art 8(2). Although the prohibition was in accordance with law, the fact that it was allowed to remain in force for more than 2 years without any meaningful contact between the applicants and their children and 'without any other effective measure to resolve the existing problems being taken' was found not to be necessary in the interests of the children and in violation of Art 8. A violation of Art 6(1) was found in that the applicants did not have access to court to challenge the restrictions on access. However, no violation of Art 6(1) was found with respect to the length of any of the proceedings.

*Court:* The prohibition on removal and restrictions on access were found to be interferences with the applicants' right to respect for family life. Although the prohibition was in accordance with the law, the restrictions on access were not, and a violation of Art 8 was found. With respect to the prohibition, the Court found that its aim, the protection of the children's health and rights and freedoms, was legitimate, and also that it was based on reasons which were relevant. Having regard to the margin of appreciation, the Court concluded that it had not been established 'that the welfare authorities failed to fulfil their obligations to take measures with a view to the applicants being reunited with H and T'. In the Court's view, the prohibition on removal and restrictions on access were based on relevant and sufficient reasons and not in violation of Art 8. With respect to Art 6, a violation was found in that the applicants were not able to have the restrictions on their access reviewed by a court. However, it did not find that the total duration of the proceedings, of over 2 years, was excessive having regard to the complexity of the case.

## (4)  ACCESS TO PERSONAL FILES

### Gaskin v United Kingdom

### (1989) 12 EHRR 36

*Facts:*  The applicant was taken into care in 1960 and boarded out with various foster-parents. The local authority was under a duty to keep records concerning him and his care and, from the age of 18, the applicant attempted to obtain access to these records. Following a change of policy in 1983, some records were disclosed to the applicant, although many contributors refused to waive confidentiality. The law changed in 1989 but was not retrospective. Therefore the applicant could still not obtain all of the records. He applied to the Commission in 1983 alleging violations of Arts 8 and 10.

*Commission:*  The Commission considered that the applicant's case file would contain information concerning highly personal aspects of the applicant's childhood, development and history and thus could constitute his principal source of information about his past and formative years. It concluded that the refusal to allow him access to the file was an interference with his right to respect for his private life which was not justified under Art 8(2). No violation of Art 10 was found.

*Court:*  The Court found that the records contained in the file 'undoubtedly do relate to the applicant's private and family life', therefore the question of access fell within the ambit of Art 8. However, it noted that by refusing the applicant complete access to his file, the UK cannot be said to have interfered with his private or family life, and found that the substance of the complaint was not that the State had acted, but that it had failed to act.

Examining Art 8(2), the Court considered that the confidentiality of the contents of the file served a legitimate aim by protecting the rights of contributors and also of the children in need of care. However, it found that persons in the situation of the applicant have a vital interest, protected by the Convention, 'in receiving the information necessary to know and to understand their childhood and early development'. It accepted that a system like the British one, which made access to records dependent on the consent of the contributor, could in principle be compatible with Art 8. However, the Court concluded that for such a system to be in conformity with the principle of proportionality, an independent authority must finally decide whether access has to be granted in cases where a contributor failed to answer or withheld consent. As no such procedure was available to the applicant, a violation of Art 8 was found.

With respect to Art 10, the Court concluded that it did not embody an obligation on the State concerned to impart the information in question to the individual and no violation of that Article was found.

## (5) DENIAL OF ACCESS TO FAMILY MEMBERS

### Andersson v Sweden

### (1992) 14 EHRR 615

*Facts:* The first applicant's son, R, who was the second applicant, was born in 1974. In 1985, R was taken into public care on the basis of a report indicating that R's health and development were seriously disturbed as a result of his mother's behaviour, and contact between the applicants was prohibited. In 1986, the Social Council placed R in a foster home and the first applicant's appeals against this were unsuccessful. R stayed in the foster home until 1988 when the public care order was terminated. He then went to live with the first applicant. In 1987, the applicants' complaints to the Commission concerning Arts 8 and 13 were declared admissible in respect of the prohibition on access.

*Commission:* The Commission noted that when a child is in care, Art 8 in principle guarantees the parent and child a right of mutual contact and the restrictions on access in the present case constituted an interference with the applicants' right to respect for family life. It found that in view of the lack of the precision of the law itself and of the decisions taken on the basis of the law, the restrictions on the first applicant's telephone contacts and correspondence with the second applicant 'were not ordered in accordance with the law within the meaning of Art 8(2)'. Accordingly, a violation of Art 8 was found. No violation of Art 13 was found.

*Court:* The Court noted that the natural family relationship is not terminated by reason of the child being taken into care and that telephone conversations between family members are covered by the notions of family life and correspondence within the meaning of Art 8. Therefore, there had been an interference with the applicants' right to respect for their family life and correspondence. However, the Court found that the limitations on access, including communication by telephone and correspondence, were in accordance with the law within the meaning of Art 8(2) and had a legitimate aim. But, having regard to all the circumstances of the case, it considered that the aggregate of the restrictions imposed by the social welfare authorities on meetings and communications by correspondence and telephone between the applicants 'was disproportionate to the legitimate aims pursued' and therefore not necessary in a democratic society. A violation of Art 8 was found. No violation of Art 13 was found in respect of either applicant.

### W v United Kingdom

### (1987) 10 EHRR 29

*Facts:* The applicant's youngest child, S, was voluntarily placed in the care of the local authority and, in August 1979, the authority assumed parental rights over S, although it was agreed that S would be returned if his parents overcame their domestic difficulties. In February 1980, it was decided that S should be placed with foster-parents with a view to adoption, and that access should be restricted. This was approved without further reference to the applicant or his wife and their appeals were unsuccessful. The applicant lodged a complaint with the Commission in 1982 alleging violations of Arts 6(1), 8 and 13.

*Commission:* The Commission noted that the procedures applied to restriction or denial of access must be such as to show respect for the parents' family life. Parents should normally have the right to be heard before decisions on such matters are taken and to be fully informed about any important measures taken. Here, the 'applicant and his wife were not consulted ... and the information about such decisions was insufficient and incomplete'. A violation of Art 8 was found and a violation of Art 6(1) was found in that the applicant was denied access to a court for the determination of his access to S.

*Court:* The Court confirmed that the mutual enjoyment by parent and child of each other's company constitutes a fundamental element of family life and that this relationship is not terminated when a child is taken into care. It noted that decisions such as those under consideration must be based on relevant considerations, conducted in a manner that is fair, and involve the natural parents to a degree sufficient to provide them with the requisite protection of their interests. The length of the proceedings may also be relevant. The Court found that the applicant had been insufficiently involved in the decision-making process and that there was no reason for this. Taking into consideration the duration of the wardship proceedings as well, the Court concluded that there had been a violation of Art 8. Finding Art 6(1) applicable, the Court noted that for the purposes of compliance with Art 6(1), the parents must be able to have the authority's decision reviewed by a tribunal which could examine the merits. As the English courts did not satisfy this requirement, a violation of Art 6(1) was also found.

*Note:* See also *B v United Kingdom* (1987) 10 EHRR 87; *H v United Kingdom* (1987) 10 EHRR 95; *O v United Kingdom* (1987) 10 EHRR 82; and *R v United Kingdom* (1987) 10 EHRR 74.

# Olsson v Sweden (No 1)
## (1988) 11 EHRR 259

*Facts:* In 1980, the authorities placed three of the applicants' children, H, T and S, under supervision 'in view of their parents' inability to satisfy their need for care and supervision'. Later that year, the children were taken into care and the applicants' appeals against this decision were unsuccessful. The children were placed in separate foster homes and children's homes and the applicants had varying degrees of access to them. Over the next few years, the applicants' requests for the termination of care were rejected and their appeals unsuccessful. In 1983, the applicants complained to the Commission alleging violations of Arts 3, 6, 14 and Art 2 of the First Protocol.

*Commission:* The Commission confirmed that the decision to take the children into care and the refusal to discontinue care interfered with the applicants' Art 8(1) right to respect for their family life. It also confirmed that Art 8 guarantees parents a right of contact with their children after a care decision. The Commission concluded that the care decisions, in combination with the placement of the children in separate foster homes from each other, and away from the applicants, were in violation of Art 8. No further violations were found.

*Court:* The Court confirmed that the measures were interferences with the applicants' right to respect for their family life and therefore had to fall within Art 8(2). With respect to the taking of the children into care and the refusals to terminate care, the Court noted that the decision to take a child into care is 'an interference of a very serious order' and therefore 'must be supported by sufficiently sound and weighty considerations'. However, having regard to the margin of appreciation, the Court concluded that the Swedish authorities were reasonably entitled to think that it was necessary to take the children into care. With respect to the refusals to terminate care, the Court again found that the authorities had sufficient reasons. However, in relation to the implementation of the care decision, the Court concluded that the placement of H and T 'at so great a distance from their parents and from S must have adversely affected the possibility of contacts between them' and that this situation was compounded by the restrictions on parental access. The Court concluded that the measures taken in implementation of the care decision were not supported by sufficient reasons justifying them as proportionate to the legitimate aim pursued and gave rise to a breach of Art 8. However, no violations of Arts 3, 6, 13, 14 or Art 2 of the First Protocol were found.

## Johansen v Norway
## (1997) 23 EHRR 33

*Facts:* The applicant gave birth to her child, S, on 7 December 1989 and on 13 December 1989 S was provisionally taken into care. In May 1990, it was decided to: take S into permanent care; deprive the applicant of her parental responsibilities; place S in a foster home with a view to adoption; deny the applicant access as from the moment of the child's placement in the foster home; and keep the latter's address secret. The Oslo City Court upheld the decision on appeal and the applicant was refused leave to appeal to the Supreme Court. She lodged a complaint with the Commission in October 1990 alleging violations of Arts 6, 8 and 13.

*Commission:* The Commission found that the measures at issue 'amounted to interferences with the applicant's right to respect for her family life' in violation of Art 8 unless it could be shown that Art 8(2) was satisfied. Although it concluded that the taking into care of S on 13 December 1989 was necessary and based on relevant and sufficient reasons, it found a violation of Art 8 with respect to the decision to deprive the applicant of her parental rights and access.

*Court:* The Court recalled that the mutual enjoyment by parent and child of each other's company constitutes a fundamental element of family life and that domestic measures hindering such enjoyment amount to an interference with the right protected by Art 8. With respect to Art 8(2), it held that, whilst there was a wide margin of appreciation in relation to assessing the necessity of taking a child into care, stricter scrutiny was called for with respect to further limitations. It found that the taking into care of S and the maintenance of the care decision were based on relevant and sufficient reasons for the purpose of Art 8(2). However, with respect to the decision to deprive parental rights and access, the Court stated that taking a child into care 'should normally be regarded as a temporary measure to be discontinued as soon as circumstances permit'. It concluded that the measures in the present case were particularly far-reaching, as they would deprive the applicant of her family life with the child. 'Such measures should only be applied in exceptional circumstances and could only be justified if they were motivated by an overriding requirement pertaining to the child's best interests.'

The Court concluded that the decision depriving the applicant of her parental rights and access to her daughter was not sufficiently justified for the purposes of Art 8(2) and a violation of Art 8 was found.

## (6) DENIAL OF CUSTODY

### Rieme v Sweden

### (1992) 16 EHRR 155

*Facts:* The applicant had a daughter, S, by Mrs J who had custody of S until she was taken into care in 1977 and placed in a foster home. The applicant applied for custody of S in 1978 but withdrew his application. In 1981, he applied for custody again and in 1983 the Court ordered that custody of S be transferred to him. However, the Social Council decided, pursuant to s 28 of the Social Services Act, to prohibit the applicant from removing S from the foster home. The applicant's appeals were unsuccessful. In 1989, the prohibition on removal was terminated. In his application to the Commission in 1986, the applicant alleged violations of Arts 6 and 8. Only the Art 8 aspect of his complaint was declared admissible.

*Commission:* The Commission found an interference with the applicant's right to respect for family life guaranteed by Art 8. It concluded that the Social Council's 'lack of activity' could not be reconciled with its legal duty 'actively to promote a reunion as soon as a prohibition on removal has been issued'. Also, taking into consideration the fact that the applicant had no legal opportunity to successfully develop his access, the Commission concluded that it could not be necessary in a democratic society, irrespective of the margin of appreciation, 'to maintain the prohibition in force for the whole period of more than five years'. A violation of Art 8 was found.

*Court:* The Court concluded that there had been an interference with family life but that this interference was in accordance with law and satisfied a legitimate aim, protecting the health and the rights and freedoms of the child. Taking into account all the factors, the Court concluded that the interests of S, who was a very sensitive, fragile and vulnerable person, outweighed the applicant's interest in being reunited with her and therefore the interference complained of was not disproportionate to the legitimate aims pursued. Having regard to their margin of appreciation, the Court found that the social welfare authorities had relevant and sufficient reasons for keeping the child in the foster home. No violation of Art 8 was found.

## (7) DISCRIMINATION

### Hoffman v Austria

### (1993) 17 EHRR 293

*Facts:* The applicant married Mr S in 1980 and they had two children. The applicant became a Jehovah's Witness in 1983 and left Mr S in 1984. Their divorce was made final in 1986. Following their separation, both the applicant and Mr S applied for parental rights over the children. In 1986, parental rights were granted to Mr S instead of the applicant. The Supreme Court cited the applicant's plans to bring them up according to the principles of Jehovah's Witnesses' teaching as a reason for its decision and was particularly concerned with the possible negative effects of her membership of the Jehovah's Witnesses. The applicant applied to the Commission in 1987 alleging that she had been denied custody of the children on the grounds of her religious convictions in violation of Arts 8, 9, 14 and Art 2 of the First Protocol.

*Commission:* The Commission recalled that Art 8 applies to custody decisions, not only if the children are taken into public care, but also if they concern the award of custody to one of the parents after a divorce or separation, and therefore it was applicable to the facts of this case. The Commission noted that the Supreme Court came to a different decision because the applicant was a member of the Jehovah's Witnesses. Therefore, for discrimination not to be found pursuant to Art 14, objective and reasonable grounds must exist for the distinction. As no justification was established, the Commission concluded that there had been a violation of Art 8 read in conjunction with Art 14. No additional issue was found to arise with regard to Art 9 and no violation of Art 2 of the First Protocol was found.

*Court:* The Court accepted that there had been a difference in treatment and that that difference was on the ground of religion. It noted that such difference in treatment is discriminatory in the absence of an objective and reasonable justification. Although it found the aim pursued by the Supreme Court a legitimate one (the protection of the health and rights of children), it concluded that a distinction based essentially on a difference in religion alone was not acceptable. The Court found no reasonable relationship of proportionality between the means employed and the aim pursued. A violation of Art 8 taken in conjunction with Art 14 was found by 5 votes to 4. It found no separate issue under Art 9 and arguments in relation to the other Articles had been abandoned.

## (8)   CHILDREN OF PRISONERS

### *UNITED KINGDOM CASES*

### R v Secretary of State for the Home Department, ex parte P; R v Secretary of State for the Home Department, ex parte Q

Court of Appeal, [2001] EWCA Civ 1151, [2001] UKHRR 1035

*Facts:* The appellants had challenged the practice of the Prison Service of automatically removing a child of 18 months of age from mothers in prison where the child was born in prison, in accordance with Prison Service Order No 4801. The appellants relied in part on Art 8 of the Convention.

*Held:* The prison authorities were entitled to adopt a policy in this respect, the aim of which was to serve the best interests of the child. However, an automatic policy did not permit individual assessments to be made in relation to specific cases, and it might be the case that the consequences of removal for a particular child would be catastrophic.

Prisoners did not automatically lose the right to respect for their family life by virtue of the fact of their imprisonment, and the Court therefore had to balance the operation of the public interest against the restriction of the right on the person affected. In the present case Q could not be found a suitable placement, and the child was very attached to the mother such that there was sufficient evidence to suggest that Q's case was sufficiently exceptional to justify a departure from the standard policy. P's appeal was dismissed, Q's appeal was allowed and the case was referred back to the prison authorities.

*Note:* P's application for leave to apply to the House of Lords was under consideration at the time of writing.

## 12.2 IMMIGRATION

### (1) FAMILY REUNION

### Ahmut v The Netherlands

### (1996) 24 EHRR 62

*Facts:* The first applicant was born in Morocco in 1945, migrated to The Netherlands in 1986, married a Dutch national and became a Dutch national himself in 1990 whilst retaining his original Moroccan nationality. Two of the children from his first marriage, a son and a daughter, came to The Netherlands from Morocco in 1990 and applied for residence permits which were refused. In 1993, the first applicant and his children lodged an application with the Commission alleging that the failure of the Dutch authorities to grant them residence permits violated their right to respect for their family life contrary to Art 8. The application was declared admissible only with respect to the first applicant and his son.

*Commission:* The Commission found that the refusal of a residence permit 'must be considered as an interference with their right to respect for family life'. In considering whether the interference was justified under Art 8(2), the Commission took into account the facts that the second applicant was a minor, that his mother was dead, and that his father was his closest relative. It found that if the second applicant is expelled from The Netherlands 'there will be a risk that the ties between the applicants will be weakened or broken'. The Commission concluded that the interference was not necessary in a democratic society as being disproportionate to the aim pursued and, therefore, there had been a violation of Art 8.

*Court:* The Court held that a child born of marital union is 'ipso jure part of that relationship; hence, from the moment of the child's birth and by the very fact of it, there exists between him and his parents a bond amounting to family life'. Therefore, Art 8 was applicable. However, the Court confirmed that Art 8 'cannot be considered to impose on a State a general obligation to respect the immigrants' choice of the country of their matrimonial residence and to authorise family reunion in its territory'. It found that the second applicant had strong links with Morocco and that there was no obstacle to the first applicant returning to Morocco. Therefore, in the Court's view, the Dutch government struck a fair balance between the applicants' interests and its own interests in controlling immigration. By 5 votes to 4, no violation of Art 8 was found.

# Gül v Switzerland

## (1996) 22 EHRR 93

*Facts:*   The applicant was a Turkish national who lived with his wife in Switzerland, where he applied for political asylum as a Kurd in 1983 and was granted a residence permit on humanitarian grounds in 1990. He sought permission to bring to Switzerland his two sons who remained in Turkey. This request was rejected and his appeal dismissed. His further appeal to the Swiss Federal Court was declared inadmissible. He complained to the Commission in 1993 that the refusal by the Swiss authorities to allow his two sons to join him was in violation of Art 8.

*Commission:*   With respect to the applicant's son, E, the Commission found a close link as this 'arises naturally from the relationship existing between a minor child and his parents'. The applicant was therefore found to enjoy the protection afforded by Art 8 in respect of family life and the refusal to permit E to join his father was found to be an interference with the applicant's right under Art 8(1). With respect to Art 8(2), the Commission found the interference in accordance with law and with a legitimate aim, the economic well-being of the country. However, it concluded that a fair balance had not been struck between the various interests at stake: 'such financial considerations are not sufficient to justify a permanent separation of a child from its parents'. It found, by 14 votes to 10, a violation of Art 8.

*Court:*   The Court recalled that it followed from the concept of family that a child born of marital union is 'ipso jure part of that relationship'. Therefore, 'from the moment of the child's birth and by the very fact of it, there exists between him and his parents a bond amounting to family life which subsequent events cannot break save in exceptional circumstances'. In considering whether there had been an interference with the applicant's right under Art 8, the Court found that a fair balance must be struck between the competing interests of the individual and the community and 'the State enjoys a certain margin of appreciation'. Article 8 cannot be expected to 'impose on a State a general obligation to respect the choice by married couples of the country of their matrimonial residence and to authorise family reunion in its territory'. It concluded that there were no obstacles to the applicant and his wife developing a family life in Turkey and that E's move to Switzerland would not be the only way for the applicant to develop family life with his son. It concluded that Switzerland had not failed to fulfil the obligations arising under Art 8(1) and that there had been no interference with the applicant's family life in violation of Art 8.

## 12.3   ADOPTION

# Keegan v Ireland

## (1994) 18 EHRR 342

*Facts:*   The applicant's former girlfriend, V, gave birth to their daughter in 1988 and he saw the child only once. During her pregnancy, V made arrangements for the child to be adopted and the child was placed with prospective adopters soon after her birth. The applicant instituted proceedings to be appointed the child's guardian, as this would enable him to challenge the proposed adoption. He also applied for custody. These applications were unsuccessful and an adoption order was made. The applicant complained to the Commission in 1990 alleging violations of Arts 6, 8 and 14.

*Commission:* The Commission found that the applicant's links with the child were sufficient to bring the relationship within the scope of Art 8. It noted that, under Irish law, the natural father is placed at a considerable disadvantage when attempting to obtain guardianship or custody of a child whom the mother has placed for adoption, since his prior consent or knowledge is not required. Further, the test applied as regards guardianship placed the burden on the natural father of establishing that in his care the child would receive a better quality of welfare 'a formidable, if not insuperable obstacle to a successful application'. The Commission found a violation of Art 8 as the applicant's relationship with his daughter had not been given sufficient recognition and protection. The Commission also concluded that as the applicant did not have at his ·disposal a procedure satisfying the requirements of Art 6 in respect of his dispute as to the placement of his daughter for adoption, there had been a violation of Art 6(1). The Commission did not examine Art 14.

*Court:* The Court confirmed that there existed between the child and her parents a bond amounting to family life even if at the time of her birth the parents are no longer cohabiting or their relationship has ended. Therefore, from the moment of the child's birth, there existed between the applicant and his daughter a bond amounting to family life. The Court found that Irish law permitted the applicant's child to be placed for adoption shortly after birth without his knowledge or consent. It noted that 'such a state of affairs not only jeopardised the proper development of the applicant's ties with the child but also set in motion a process which was likely to prove irreversible'. The government having advanced no reasons relevant to the welfare of the child to justify such an approach, the Court found a violation of Art 8. Furthermore, the fact that the applicant had no rights under Irish law to challenge the placement of the child for adoption was found to be in violation of Art 6(1). Article 14 was not examined.

## UNITED KINGDOM CASES

## Re B (A Minor)

House of Lords, [2001] UKHL 70, [2002] 1 WLR 258

*Facts:* An adoption order was made in respect of B in favour of her natural father, and was overturned on appeal. B's mother and father had had a relationship for over a year, and the mother was pregnant at the time the relationship ended, although she did not tell the father. When B was born, she was given up for adoption and placed with foster carers. The identity of the father was discovered and he visited B and made clear his desire to look after her. Eventually an agreement for an adoption order was signed by the mother, at which time she indicated that she did not want to have contact with B in the future. The adoption order would have excluded the mother from future involvement in B's life and the Official Solicitor argued that the adoption order would not operate in the best interests of B. The Court of Appeal held that the adoption of a child by one natural parent would not be granted unless there was sufficient justification for the exclusion of the other parent from the child's life. In so doing the court concluded that the judge at first instance had failed to interpret the Adoption Act 1976 in a way which was consistent with Art 8 of the Convention.

*Held:*    The House of Lords held that in order for the Court of Appeal to substitute its judgment for that of the judge at first instance it had to determine that the judge had misdirected him or herself on a matter of law. In the present case it was not clear that this was the case. In particular, in considering Art 8 of the Convention it had to be borne in mind that the right being considered was primarily that of the child in this case, and s 15(3) of the Adoption Act 1976 did not operate in a way that was inconsistent with the Convention.

## 12.4    REGISTER OF BIRTHS

### (1)    PATERNITY

### Kroon v The Netherlands

### (1994) 19 EHRR 263

*Facts:*    The first applicant and second applicant had a stable relationship from which their son, the third applicant, was born in 1987. At the time of the birth, the first applicant was still married to someone else, although the marriage had broken down and they were later divorced. The third applicant was entered in the register of births as the son of the first applicant and her husband even though the third applicant was the father. The registrar refused the applicants' request to change the register, noting that the first applicant's husband had to bring proceedings to deny paternity before another man could recognise the child as his. The applicants' appeals against this decision were unsuccessful. They applied to the Commission in 1991 alleging violations of Arts 8 and 14.

*Commission:*    The Commission concluded that Art 8 was applicable as, although they did not live together, there was a long-standing relationship between the applicants and it was not disputed that the second applicant was the biological father of the child. It recognised that, in some situations, the right to respect for family life in Art 8 may require that real paternity be legally recognised. Therefore, the impossibility of contesting the paternity of the first applicant's former husband, and of having the second applicant recognised as the father, was in violation of Art 8. No violation of Art 14 was found.

*Court:*    The Court confirmed that the notion of family life in Art 8 may encompass de facto family ties even where the parties were not living together. It also confirmed that there was a bond between the second and third applicants amounting to family life 'whatever the contribution of the latter to his son's care and upbringing'. Article 8 was found to be applicable, implying a positive obligation on the authorities to allow complete legal family ties to be formed between the second applicant and his son. The Court concluded that 'biological and social reality' must prevail over 'a legal presumption . . . which flies in the face of both established fact and the wishes of those concerned without actually benefiting anyone'. A violation of Art 8 was found as The Netherlands had 'failed to secure to the applicants the respect for their family life to which they are entitled'. No violation of Art 14 was found.

# Rasmussen v Denmark
## (1985) 7 EHRR 371

*Facts:* In 1973, the applicant and his wife separated. His wife retained custody of their two children, a boy and a girl, and he was obliged to pay maintenance. In 1975, he challenged the paternity of the girl, but discontinued the proceedings when his wife waived claims for maintenance for the child. Following their divorce, his former wife lodged with the authorities a renewed petition for maintenance and the applicant resumed payments. As a result, the applicant sought leave to institute proceedings out of time to determine the paternity of the child but leave was refused. The applicant applied to the Commission in 1979 alleging sex discrimination in that his former wife had an unlimited right of access to court to challenge his paternity while he did not.

*Commission:* The Commission found that the husband and wife were placed in analogous situations as far as a paternity suit was concerned. It was satisfied that the difference in treatment was due to a desire to prevent the child being placed in a worse position by the institution of paternity proceedings several years after her birth. However, it found no reasonable relationship of proportionality between the means employed and the aim sought to be realised. A violation of Art 14 taken in conjunction with Arts 6 and 8 was found.

*Court:* The Court found Arts 6 and 8 applicable to the facts of the case and, for the purposes of Art 14, found a difference in treatment as between the applicant and his former wife with respect to the possibility of instituting proceedings to contest paternity. It assumed that the difference was made between persons placed in analogous situations. The Court noted that, with respect to Contracting States' legislation regarding paternity proceedings, there was no common ground and, in most, the position of mother and father was regulated in different ways. The Court concluded that the introduction of time-limits for the institution of paternity proceedings was justified by the desire to ensure legal certainty and to protect the interests of the child. Such time-limits were less necessary for wives than for husbands since 'the mother's interests usually coincided with those of the child, she being awarded custody in most cases'. Accordingly, the Court concluded that having regard to their margin of appreciation, the authorities also did not transgress the principle of proportionality. No violation of Art 14 was found.

## *REGISTRATION OF TRANSSEXUAL AS FATHER OF CHILD*

# X, Y and Z v United Kingdom
## (1997) 24 EHRR 143

*Facts:* X, the first applicant, was a female-to-male transsexual who, since 1979, had lived in a permanent and stable union with second applicant, Y, a woman. Z, the third applicant, was born to Y in 1992 as a result of artificial insemination by a donor. The Minister of Health advised X in 1992 that the Registrar-General was of the view that only a biological man could be regarded as a father for the purposes of registration and X was not permitted to be registered as Z's father. The applicants alleged violations of Art 8 and Arts 8 and 14 taken together.

*Commission:* The Commission concluded that, to all appearances, the first applicant was the third applicant's father and that the applicants enjoyed family life within the meaning of Art 8(1) of the Convention. Taking note of the 'trend in Contracting States towards the legal acknowledgement of gender re-assignment' and having regard 'in particular to the welfare of the third applicant and her security within the family unit' the Commission concluded that the absence of an appropriate legal regime reflecting the applicants' family ties 'discloses a failure to respect their family life'. By 13 votes to 5, a violation of Art 8 was found and, in view of this conclusion, Art 14 was not considered.

*Court:* The Court held that the notion of family life in Art 8 was not confined to families based on marriage and may encompass other de facto relationships such as the ties that linked the three applicants. Therefore, Art 8 was applicable.

Although the Court was prepared to accept that there might be positive obligations inherent in an effective respect for private or family life, it noted that 'regard must be had to the competing interests of the individual and of the community as a whole'. The community as a whole 'has an interest in maintaining a coherent system of family law which places the best interests of the child at the forefront'. It concluded that Art 8 imposed no obligation for the State formally to recognise as the father of a child a person who is not the biological father and that this did not amount to a failure to respect family life within the meaning of Art 8. It was held by 14 votes to 6 that there had been no violation of Art 8 and it was not considered necessary to consider the Art 14 complaint.

## (2)   ALTERATION OF BIRTH CERTIFICATE

### Rees v United Kingdom

### (1984) 7 EHRR 429, Commission; (1986) 9 EHRR 56, Court

*Facts:* The applicant was born female and recorded in the register of births as a female. In 1970, after learning that she was a transsexual, the applicant sought treatment, changed her name and had been living as a man ever since. From 1973 onwards, the applicant made a number of requests, including a formal request, to the Registrar-General to secure the alteration of his birth certificate to show his sex as male. The Registrar-General refused to alter the register. The applicant complained to the Commission in 1979 alleging violations of Arts 8 and 12.

*Commission:* The Commission confirmed that Art 8 may impose positive obligations on the State and accepted the applicant's view that sex was one of the essential elements of human personality. It concluded that Art 8 must be understood as protecting an individual against the non-recognition of his changed sex as part of his personality and that 'it must be possible for the individual after the change has been effected, to confirm his/her normal appearance by the necessary documents'. As no reason of public interest was disclosed for the refusal to amend the register, the Commission unanimously found a violation of Art 8. However, no violation of Art 12 was found.

*Court:* The Court also confirmed that there may be positive obligations inherent in an effective respect for private life as the 'mere refusal to alter the register of births or to issue birth certificates ... cannot be considered as interferences'. The Court noted that the notion of respect was not 'clear-cut' and the 'notion's requirements will vary considerably from case to case'. The Court stated that, in determining whether or not a positive obligation exists, a fair balance has to be struck between the general interest of the community and the interests of the individual. Unlike the Commission, the Court found no violation of Art 8. It concluded that the UK was fully entitled, in the exercise of its margin of appreciation, 'to take account of the situation pertaining there in determining what measures to adopt'. The positive obligations arising from Art 8 'cannot be held to extend that far'. With respect to Art 12, the Court found that the right to marry guaranteed by Art 12 'refers to the traditional marriage between persons of opposite biological sex' and that the exercise of this right was subject to the laws of the Contracting States. No violation of Art 12 was found.

## 12.5   ILLEGITIMATE CHILDREN

### (1)   RECOGNITION

### Johnston v Ireland

### (1986) 9 EHRR 203

*Facts:*   The first applicant's marriage broke down in 1965 and he moved in with the second applicant in 1971. Their daughter, the third applicant, was born in 1978. At the time, under the Constitution of Ireland, the first applicant was unable to obtain dissolution of his marriage. He was therefore unable to marry the second applicant and the third applicant had the legal situation of an illegitimate child. The applicants lodged their application with the Commission in 1982 alleging breaches of Arts 8, 9, 12, 13 and 14.

*Commission:*   The Commission found no breach of Arts 8 or 12 in that the right to divorce and subsequently to remarry is not guaranteed by the Convention. Furthermore, it found no breach of Art 8 in that Irish law did not confer a recognised family status on the first and second applicants. However, in relation to the third applicant, the Commission found that, under Irish law, she was not regarded as forming part of the family and that her status, in important respects, was different from that of a child born in wedlock. It concluded that the policy of non-recognition 'of the reality of her family ties, in contradistinction to the legal position of the child born in wedlock, represents a failure by the State to provide a framework for the proper ordering of relations between the third applicant and her parents'. A violation of Art 8 was found but no violations of Arts 9, 12, 13 or 14 were found.

*Court:*   The Court held that a right to divorce could not be derived from Art 12 or from Art 8. Furthermore, no discrimination within the meaning of Art 14 was found and it was concluded that Art 9 was not applicable. In relation to the first and second applicants, no interference with their family life was found: 'Ireland has done nothing to impede or prevent them from living together and continuing to do so ... Article 8 cannot be interpreted as imposing an obligation to establish a special regime for a particular category of unmarried couples'. However, in relation to the third applicant, the Court stated that the normal development of the natural family ties between the first and second applicants and their daughter required 'that she should be placed, legally and socially, in a position akin to that of a legitimate child'. Examining the legal situation of the third applicant, the Court found that it differed considerably from that of a legitimate child and it had not been shown 'that there are any means available to her or her parents to eliminate or reduce the differences'. It concluded that the absence of an appropriate legal regime, reflecting the third applicant's family ties, amounted to a failure to respect her family life in violation of Art 8.

# Marckx v Belgium
## (1979) 2 EHRR 330

*Facts:*   Under Belgian law, no legal bond between an unmarried mother and child resulted from the mere fact of birth and the child was regarded as 'illegitimate'. Therefore, as P was unmarried, she had to make arrangements to 'recognise' her daughter, A, born in 1973, so that she could become A's guardian. However, in order for P to increase A's rights, it was necessary for P to adopt A, which she duly did in 1974. In 1975, P and A made an application to the Commission alleging that the process of recognition and the resulting rights obtained by A were in violation of Arts 3, 8, 14 and Art 1 of the First Protocol.

*Commission:*   The Commission found a breach of Art 8 taken alone and in conjunction with Art 14 with respect to A and breaches of Art 14 taken in conjunction with Art 8 and Art 1 of the First Protocol with respect to P.

*Court:*   The Court noted that Art 8 made no distinction between the legitimate and the illegitimate family and that a single woman and her child are 'one form of family no less than others'. It stated that respect for family life required the existence in domestic law of legal safeguards that render possible, as from the moment of birth, the child's integration in its family. The Court concluded that the legal requirements in relation to 'illegitimate children' were not consonant with respect for family life as these impeded the normal development of such life. A violation of Art 8 was found in relation to P. A violation of Art 8 was also found with respect to A due to the risk that, until the process of recognition was complete, the child remained separated in law from its mother. The distinction between legitimate and illegitimate children was found to lack objective and reasonable justification, and a violation of Art 14 in conjunction with Art 8 was also found in respect of both P and A. The fact that, in certain respects, A never had a legal relationship with P's family was also examined. The Court found that family life included the ties between near relatives such as grandparents and grandchildren and the State should act in a manner calculated to allow those ties to develop. A violation of Art 8 was found with respect to both applicants, as well as a violation of Art 14 taken in conjunction with Art 8. With respect to the legal rights of an illegitimate child and its unmarried mother as regards inheritance, a violation of Art 14 taken in conjunction with Art 8 was found. In relation to Art 1 of the First Protocol, it was confirmed that the right to dispose of property constituted 'a traditional and fundamental aspect of the right to property'. Therefore, limitations on unmarried mothers such as P were discriminatory and in violation of Art 14 taken in conjunction with Art 1 of the First Protocol.

# (2)  RIGHT TO A NAME

## Stjerna v Finland

## (1994) 24 EHRR 194

*Facts:*   The use of surnames is regulated strictly in Finland. The applicant wished to change his surname to an ancestral version, but his request was refused by the local administration for a variety of reasons, allegedly including that one of his ancestors was illegitimate and so the applicant could not prove an unbroken right to use the name. He claimed a breach of Art 8 in conjunction with Art 14, in that the Finnish authorities had failed to respect his private life.

*Commission:*   The Commission was of the opinion that there had been no violation either of Art 8 alone or of Art 8 in conjunction with Art 14. Article 8(1) 'ensures a sphere within which everyone can freely pursue the development and fulfilment of one's personality. The right to develop and fulfil one's personality necessarily comprises the right to an identity and, therefore, to a name'. However, 'respect for private life' is an imprecise term and its meaning will depend on the circumstances. There are good reasons why a State might wish to regulate the use of surnames, particularly where the name in question has specific historical or cultural connotations. Although the applicant's present name gave rise to an unfortunate nickname and was often misspelt, this was not sufficient suffering or inconvenience to trigger Art 8. A right to change surname cannot be considered to be included within the right to respect for private life.

As for Art 14, although discrimination on the grounds of illegitimacy could be the basis of a claim, the Commission found that the applicant had not brought any evidence that his ancestor's illegitimacy was a decisive factor in the refusal to allow the change of surname. Thus, it was impossible to make a comparison against the treatment of a similar case, and so discrimination could not be proven.

*Court:*   The Court found that there was no violation of Art 8. Legal restrictions on the use of names may be justified in the public interest, for reasons such as accurate identification or population registration. There is a wide margin of appreciation under Art 8, and so it is for a State to decide the most appropriate policy in this area. The applicant had shown some inconvenience arising from his present name, but the Court did not consider this to be significant. A difference of treatment is discriminatory only if it has no objective and reasonable justification. The applicant had argued that the refusal to allow the change of name was due at least partly to the illegitimacy of his ancestor, and so based on the discriminatory ground of birth. The Court, however, was not convinced that the illegitimacy had made a difference to the domestic adminis-tration; there was no reason to believe that a hypothetical person with a legitimate ancestor would have been treated differently from the applicant. The reason for the refusal in the applicant's case appears rather to have been that the preferred name had not been used in his family for over 200 years. Thus, there was an objective and reasonable justification for the treatment of the applicant, if in fact it had been discriminatory at all. Hence, there was no violation of Art 8 in conjunction with Art 14.

## (3)   HEREDITARY RIGHTS

### Inze v Austria

### (1987) 10 EHRR 394

*Facts:*   The applicant was born out of wedlock in 1942. His mother died intestate in 1975 and left as heirs the applicant, her husband and her second son who was born in wedlock. The farm that she left to her heirs was subject to special legislation providing that farms of a certain size may not be divided and one of the heirs must take over the entire property and pay off the others, and also that precedence should be given to legitimate children. The applicant argued that, as he was the eldest son, he should take over the farm and challenged the constitutionality of the provision giving precedence to legitimate children. His challenge and subsequent appeals were rejected but he eventually reached a settlement with his half brother. The applicant applied to the Commission in 1979 alleging a violation of Art 1 of the First Protocol taken in conjunction with Art 14.

*Commission:*   By 6 votes to 4 the Commission found a breach of Art 14 read in conjunction with Art 1 of the First Protocol.

*Court:*   The Court found that the facts fell within the ambit of Art 1 of the First Protocol, and that therefore Art 14 was applicable. It noted that 'very weighty reasons would have to be advanced before a difference of treatment on the ground of birth out of wedlock could be regarded as compatible with the Convention'. It was not persuaded by the government's arguments, most of which were based on 'general and abstract considerations'. The Court unanimously found a violation of Art 14 taken together with Art 1 of the First Protocol.

## 12.6   DETENTION

### Bouamar v Belgium

### (1988) 11 EHRR 1

*Facts:*   Pursuant to the Young Person's Welfare Act, on nine occasions, in 1980, it was ordered by the Juvenile Court that the applicant, then aged 16 and a minor, be placed in a remand prison as it was materially impossible to find 'an individual or institution able to accept him immediately'. He was detained for a total of 119 days and his appeals against these orders were unsuccessful. The applicant complained to the Commission alleging violations of Arts 5(1)(d), 5(4), 13 and 14 of the Convention.

*Commission:*   Article 5(1)(d) provides that a minor may be deprived of his or her liberty only for the purpose of 'educational supervision' or for the purpose of 'bringing him before the competent legal authority'. The Commission found that this was not a case of an urgent measure adopted for the specific purpose of finding an institution for educational supervision and therefore the deprivation of liberty was not justified under Art 5(1)(d) and not within the scope of Art 5(1)(b). A violation of Art 5(1) was found. A violation of Art 5(4) was also found in that the Juvenile Court was not a 'court' within the meaning of Art 5(4) and the applicant was not given the opportunity to take proceedings to test the lawfulness of his detention. No violations of Arts 13 or 14 were found.

*Court:* The Court noted that, as the facts did not fall within Art 5(1)(b), it had to be shown that they fell within Art 5(1)(d). The Court rejected the contention that these were lawful detentions for the purpose of bringing the applicant before the competent legal authority. However, the Court stated that the confinement of a juvenile in remand prison 'does not necessarily contravene sub-paragraph (d), even if it is not in itself such as to provide for the person's educational supervision'. The placement does not have to be an immediate one and it is permissible to use an interim custody measure but in such circumstances 'the imprisonment must be speedily followed by actual application of such a regime'. The Court concluded that the detention of the applicant in a remand prison 'in conditions of virtual isolation and without the assistance of staff with educational training cannot be regarded as furthering any educational aim'. A violation of Art 5(1) was found. A violation of Art 5(4) was also found as the applicant's ordinary appeals and appeals on points of law did not have practical effect. No violation of Art 14 was found as the Court considered a difference in treatment of this kind 'does not amount to discrimination'. Article 13 was not considered.

# Nielsen v Denmark
## (1988) 11 EHRR 175

*Facts:* The applicant's parents separated and, as they were not married, only his mother had parental rights over him and he remained with her. In 1979, the applicant refused to return to his mother following a holiday with his father and the authorities placed him in a children's home with the consent of all parties. He ran away from the home to his father who then 'went underground' with him. The father was arrested and the social authorities, with the consent of the applicant's mother, placed the applicant in the Department of Child Psychiatry in the county hospital. Two months later, the applicant went into hiding with his father again but was found and placed in a children's home. Following his mother's request, he was admitted to the State Hospital's child psychiatric ward in September 1983. His appeals against his detention were unsuccessful but he was discharged in March 1984. The applicant applied to the Commission in February 1984, alleging that his placement in the child psychiatric ward was in breach of Art 5(1) and (4).

*Commission:* The Commission noted that, as the chief physician of the child psychiatric ward took the final decision on the question of hospitalisation, the responsibility of the State was engaged. It found a deprivation of liberty within the meaning of Art 5 as the applicant, who was not mentally ill, had been detained in a psychiatric ward and, when he disappeared from the hospital, 'he was found and brought back by police'. It concluded, by 11 votes to 1, that there had been a violation of Art 5(1) and by 10 votes to 2, that there had been a violation of Art 5(4).

*Court:* The Court confirmed that the protection afforded by Art 5 also covers minors, but noted that the decision on the question of hospitalisation was in fact taken by the mother in her capacity as holder of parental rights. Therefore, neither the chief physician's nor the social authorities' involvement in the case altered the mother's position under Danish law as sole person with power to decide on the hospitalisation of the applicant or on his removal from hospital. Therefore, Art 5 was not applicable insofar as it is concerned with deprivation of liberty by the authorities of the State. It concluded that it must be possible for a child like the applicant to be admitted to hospital at the request of the holder of parental rights and that such a situation is not covered by Art 5(1). The Court found by 9 votes to 7 that the hospitalisation of the applicant did not amount to a deprivation of liberty within the meaning of Art 5 but was a responsible exercise by his mother 'of her custodial rights in the interests of the child'.

## UNITED KINGDOM CASES

## W Borough Council v DK and Others
## Court of Appeal, [2001] 2 WLR 1141

*Facts:*   A secure accommodation order was imposed on K, a youth, in June 2000 under the Children Act 1989, s 25. Following a psychiatric investigation, K was found not to be suffering from any mental illness, but was diagnosed as having symptoms consistent with Hyperkinetic Conduct Disorder, such that K was a risk both to himself and to others. It was argued that s 25 of the Children Act 1989 was incompatible with the Convention, and the Court was required to determine whether the detention of liberty entailed in the secure accommodation order was such as to fall within Art 5 of the Convention, and, if so, whether it was lawful.

*Held:*   All parties accepted that Art 5 was applicable, and that 'educational supervision' should not be read so as to be equated only with classroom teaching. In the present case there was no incompatibility of the detention with the requirements of Art 5. It was necessary to draw a distinction between measures taken by a public authority and the legislation on which those measures were based. It could be the case that the former would be incompatible with the Convention and the latter compatible.

## 12.7   SEXUAL ABUSE
### (1)   RIGHT TO BRING PROCEEDINGS
## Stubbings and Others v United Kingdom
## (1996) 23 EHRR 213

*Facts:*   Ms Stubbings, born in 1957, allegedly suffered from sexual abuse as a child and sought to bring legal proceedings in 1987, but the defendants argued that the claim was time-barred under the Limitation Act 1980. The High Court and Court of Appeal held that, as her claim was based on a 'breach of duty', the limitation period for such actions was 3 years, subject to a discretion to extend 'where it would be equitable to do so'. This was to be measured either from the date on which the cause accrued, or from the date on which the plaintiff first knew the injury in question was significant and attributable to the defendants. The High Court found in favour of the defendants, but the Court of Appeal accepted Ms Stubbings' argument that she did not realise she had suffered sufficiently seriously until 1984. On appeal to the House of Lords, this decision was reversed. It was held that 'breach of duty' did not embrace intentionally inflicted injuries and that these were subject to a 6-year limitation period which had expired. Following this decision, others were forced to discontinue similar claims. The applicants complained to the Commission in 1993 that they had been denied access to a court in violation of Art 6(1) and that the difference in rules applied to them and other types of claimant was discriminatory contrary to Art 14.

*Commission:*   The Commission found that it must generally be accepted in the interests of the good administration of justice that there are time-limits. However, finding the applicants in an analogous position to victims of negligently inflicted injury, it concluded that the applicants may be regarded as victims of a difference in treatment as regards the regulation of their access to court in the determination of their claims. It unanimously found a violation of Art 14 in conjunction with Art 6(1).

*Court:*   The Court recalled that Art 6(1) is not absolute, but may be subject to limitations in respect of which States enjoy a certain margin of appreciation. It found no violation of Art 6(1) taken alone. Although finding Art 8 applicable, considering the protection afforded by the domestic law against the sexual abuse of children and the margin of appreciation allowed to States in these matters, the Court concluded that it had not been violated. With respect to Art 14, the Court found that as between the applicants and victims of other forms of deliberate wrongdoing there was no disparity in treatment. Secondly, it found that the victims of intentionally and negligently inflicted harm cannot be said to be in analogous situations for the purposes of Art 14. The Court concluded that there had been no violation of Art 14 taken in conjunction with either Art 6(1) or Art 8.

# Z and Others v United Kingdom
## (2002) 34 EHRR 3

*Facts:*   The applicants were four children in the same family who had suffered severe neglect and ill-treatment at home. The relevant local authority had had this brought to their attention, and over a 4-year period there had been a number of case hearings and meetings to consider the treatment which the applicants received from their parents. The family was first referred to the social services in 1987, but it was not until 1992 that the applicants were taken into care. The applicants brought an action, which was unsuccessful, against the local authority, arguing that it had failed in the duty of care owed to them. The House of Lords rejected their final appeal, finding that no action in negligence or breach of statutory duty lay against the local authority concerning the discharge of its duties relating to the welfare of children under the Children Act 1989 (*X and Others v Bedfordshire County Council* [1995] 3 All ER 353). The applicants relied on Arts 3, 8 and 6.

*Court:*   There had been a breach of Art 3:

> '... the neglect and abuse suffered by the four child applicants reached the threshold of inhuman and degrading treatment. This treatment was brought to the local authority's attention ... it was under a statutory duty to protect the children and had a range of powers available to them, including removal from their home. The children were however only taken into emergency care, at the insistence of the mother, in 30 April 1992. Over the intervening period of four and a half years, they had been subject in their home to what the

child consultant psychiatrist who examined them referred to as horrific experiences. . . .
The present case . . . leaves no doubt as to the failure of the system to protect these child
applicants from serious, long-term neglect and abuse' (para 75).

The Court found that no separate issue arose under Art 8.

As regards Art 6, the Court considered that it was applicable to the proceedings in
question, and it was contended by the applicants that the House of Lords' decision
finding that the local authority owed no duty of care deprived them of access to a court
as it was an exclusionary rule. The Court was not persuaded that this was the case and
held that the applicants' claims 'were properly and fairly examined in the light of the
domestic legal principles concerning the tort of negligence' (para 101). The Court
therefore found that there had been no violation of Art 6.

# (2)  REMEDIES

## X and Y v The Netherlands

## (1985) 8 EHRR 235

*Facts:*  X's daughter, Y, was mentally handicapped and lived in a privately run home
for mentally handicapped children. One day after her sixteenth birthday, Y was
sexually abused by B, a man living at the home. X filed a complaint with the police and
signed it himself as he considered his daughter unable to do so. The public prosecutor's
office decided not to open proceedings against B. X's appeals against this were
unsuccessful, the Court of Appeal deciding that the father's complaint could not be
regarded as a substitute for the complaint which the girl, being over the age of 16,
should have lodged herself. X applied to the Commission in 1980 alleging violations of
Arts 3, 8, 13 and 14.

*Commission:*  The Commission found a violation of Art 8 but not of Art 3. It was
decided that it was not necessary to examine the application under Arts 13 or 14.

*Court:*  With respect to Y's complaint, the Court found the facts to concern a matter
of private life, a 'concept which covers the physical and moral integrity of the person,
including his or her sexual life'. The Court referred to the positive obligations which
are inherent in Art 8 and noted that the nature of a State's obligation will depend upon
the particular aspect of private life that is at issue. It concluded that only criminal law
provisions could achieve effective deterrence in this area. As the criminal code did not
provide Y with effective protections, the Court concluded that she was the victim of a
violation of Art 8. Articles 3, 13 and 14 were not examined.

# (3)  PROTECTION

## A v United Kingdom (Human Rights: Punishment of Child)

## [1998] 2 FLR 959

*Facts:*  The applicant's stepfather was charged with assault occasioning bodily harm
contrary to s 47 of the Offences Against the Person Act 1861. It was not disputed that
the stepfather had caused severe bruising to the applicant, a 9-year-old boy, but it was
argued in his defence that the application of force amounted to reasonable chastisement

and was necessary since the child did not respond to parental discipline. The jury acquitted the stepfather of assault. A complained that, in failing to protect him from ill-treatment by his stepfather, the State was in violation of its obligations under Arts 3 and 8 of the Convention.

*Commission:* The Commission declared the complaint admissible and expressed the unanimous opinion that there had been a violation of Art 3, but that it was unnecessary to consider the complaint under Art 8.

*Court:* It was accepted that the injury caused to A was sufficiently serious to amount to ill-treatment proscribed by Art 3. The question to be determined in this case was whether the UK could be held responsible under Art 3 for the injury caused by the stepfather. The Court noted that States had an obligation to provide an effective deterrant against serious breaches of personal integrity. In the case of children and vulnerable individuals, the State had a greater duty to provide adequate protection. In this case, the failure to provide adequate protection against treatment or punishment contrary to Art 3 constituted a violation of the Convention.

## 12.8 ABDUCTION

### (1) RIGHT TO RETURN OF CHILDREN THE SUBJECT OF INTERNATIONAL ABDUCTION

### Ignaccolo-Zenide v Romania

### (2001) 31 EHRR 7

**Facts**: After a long custody battle during the course of which the applicant's ex-husband, DZ, had repeatedly defied court orders issued in both France and the United States granting the applicant custody of their two children, the ex-husband, a Romanian national, returned to Romania. The applicant, living in France, invoked the Hague Convention on the Civil Aspects of International Child Abduction 1980 and the French Central Authority asked the Romanian Central Authority to secure the return of the children. In 1994 the Court of First Instance of Bucharest granted an injunction obliging DZ to comply with the prior court orders. DZ took the children to an unknown destination, and appealed. DZ brought a number of actions by way of appeal, all of which were eventually unsuccessful. A number of attempts by the applicant to visit her children were unsuccessful, and DZ repeatedly breached obligations to attend meetings at the Justice Ministry with the children. In a letter in early 1997 the Romanian Ministry of Justice informed the French Ministry of Justice of its decision to order the non-return of the children, a decision based on the latter's persistent refusal to see their mother again. The applicant complained on the basis of a breach of Art 8.

*Court:* The Court held, by six votes to one, that Art 8 had been breached and ordered that damages be paid to the applicant. 'It is the Court's established case law that article 8 implies the right for a parent to such steps being taken as will reunite him with his child and the obligation for national authorities to take such steps' (para 94). The crucial point in this case was that of whether the national authorities took all the measures which they reasonably could to secure the enforcement of the injunction of December 1994. The Court noted that Art 11 of the Hague Convention demands that the requested authorities act expeditiously for the return of children, and while the first attempt by the authorities to act was timely, further efforts were not. There was also a total lack of action by the authorities for a subsequent period of over a year. No sanctions were imposed on DZ following a refusal to show the children to bailiffs appointed by the court, and there was no coercive mechanism to require attendance with the children at the Ministry of Justice. The Court found therefore that the authorities had not taken such measures to facilitate the return of the children as mentioned in Art 7 of the Hague Convention, and found, accordingly, that Art 8 had been violated.

## 12.9 LEGITIMATE REMOVAL OF CHILD FROM JURISDICTION

*UNITED KINGDOM CASES*

### Payne (Clive Anthony) v Payne (Andrea Catherine)

### Court of Appeal, [2001] EWCA Civ 166, [2001] UKHRR 484

*Facts:* M was a New Zealand citizen who married F, a British citizen, in 1996. A child was born. The marriage eventually broke down. M applied for permission to remove S, their child, from the UK permanently pursuant to s 13 of the Children Act 1989. The order was granted and F appealed, arguing that the authorities relied on at first instance were inconsistent with F's right to a family life under Art 8 of the Convention.

*Held:* The primary consideration was the welfare of S and the Convention did not affect this. The question was whether the proposals to remove the child from the jurisdiction were in the child's best interests, and whether there was a genuine motivation for the move. The court also had to consider the effect on the parent and the family of the child if the refusal to move was not granted, and the effect on the child of the loss of contact with the other parent, and any opportunity of continuing contact.

*Note:* Similar issues were addressed in the case of *Re GA (A Child)* [2000] UKHRR 572.

# Chapter 13

# EDUCATION

## 13.1 SCHOOLS

### (1) EDUCATION IN CONFORMITY WITH CONVICTIONS OF PARENTS

### Valsamis v Greece and Efstratiou v Greece

### (1996) 24 EHRR 294

*Facts:* In both cases, the first and second applicants were the parents of school children who were the third applicants. All applicants were Jehovah's Witnesses and maintained that pacifism was a fundamental tenet of their religion, which forbade any conduct or practice associated with war or violence. The children were asked by their schools to take part in a school parade to celebrate the National Day and they refused, stating that their religious beliefs prevented them from doing so. However, they were still expected to take part and were punished with suspensions when they did not do so. The applicants alleged violations of Art 2 of the First Protocol, and Arts 3, 9 and 13.

*Commission:* The Commission concluded that the relevant procession had no military complexion capable of offending pacifist convictions and that the penalty could not be considered as an attempt to indoctrinate the child with religious or philosophical convictions contrary to those of her parents. Accordingly, no violation of Art 2 of the First Protocol was found. With respect to Art 9, the Commission found that it does not guarantee the right to behave in the public sphere in a manner dictated by a religion or a conviction. Furthermore, making it compulsory for the child to take part could not be considered an attempt to indoctrinate her and Art 9 had not been breached. The suspension was found to be insufficiently serious to violate Art 3. However, as there was no effective remedy for the applicants under Greek law, violations of Art 13 were found.

*Court:* With respect to the alleged violation of Art 2 of the First Protocol, the Court found that the word 'convictions' denotes views that attain a certain level of 'cogency, seriousness, cohesion and importance' and that Jehovah's Witnesses do enjoy the status of a known religion. In the Court's view, the second sentence of Art 2 forbids States from pursuing an aim of indoctrination 'that might be regarded as not respecting parents' religious and philosophical convictions'. However, the Court could discern nothing 'either in the purpose of the parade or in the arrangements for it, which could offend the applicants' pacifist convictions'. Accordingly, by 7 votes to 2, no breach of Art 2 of the First Protocol was found. The Court also held that the impugned measure did not amount to an interference with the child's Art 9 right to freedom of religion, and that the suspension from school did not fall within the scope of Art 3. However, it was unanimously held that there was a violation of Art 13 in that the applicants were not able to put forward their arguable complaints and obtain redress before a national authority.

## (2) SEX EDUCATION

### Kjeldsen, Busk Madsen and Pedersen v Denmark

### (1976) 1 EHRR 711

*Facts:* The applicants were parents with children of school age. They lodged complaints with the Commission in 1971 and 1972 alleging that integrated compulsory sex education, as introduced in Danish State schools by statute in 1970, was contrary to the beliefs they held as Christian parents and constituted a violation of Art 2 of the First Protocol. The applicants also invoked Arts 8, 9 and 14.

*Commission:* The Commission found no violation of the Convention.

*Court:* The Court confirmed that the second sentence of Art 2 of the First Protocol is binding upon the Contracting States in the exercise of each and every function that they undertake in the sphere of education and teaching 'including that consisting of the organisation and funding of public education'. It also stated that the second sentence must be read together with the first: 'it is on to this fundamental right that is grafted the right of parents to respect for their religious and philosophical convictions'. Furthermore, the Court noted that there is no distinction between State and private teaching.

The Court explained that the purpose of the second sentence of Art 2 of the First Protocol is 'safeguarding the possibility of pluralism in education'. It is not limited to religious instruction and enjoins the State 'to respect parents' convictions, be they religious or philosophical, throughout the entire State education programme'. However, the Court confirmed that the second sentence does not prevent States from imparting through teaching or education information or knowledge of a directly or indirectly religious or philosophical kind. It does not permit parents to object to the integration of such teaching or education in the school curriculum 'for otherwise all institutionalised teaching would run the risk of proving impracticable'. The State must take care that information or knowledge included in the curriculum is conveyed in an objective, critical and pluralistic manner and, in the opinion of the Court, it is 'forbidden to pursue an aim of indoctrination that might be considered as not respecting parents' religious and philosophical convictions'. Examining the legislation in dispute, the Court found that it in no way amounts to an attempt at indoctrination aimed at advocating a specific kind of sexual behaviour. Further, 'it does not affect the right of parents to enlighten and advise their children'. No violation of the Convention was found.

## (3) CORPORAL PUNISHMENT

### Costello-Roberts v United Kingdom

### (1993) 19 EHRR 112

*Facts:* The applicant, at the time aged 7, attended an independent boarding school at which corporal punishment was administered. Eight days after receiving his fifth demerit mark, the headmaster punished the applicant by inflicting three 'whacks' on his bottom through his shorts with a rubber-soled gym shoe. On complaining to the police, the applicant's mother was told that no action could be taken unless there was visible bruising on the child's buttocks. An application was lodged with the Commission alleging violations of Arts 3, 8 and 13.

*Commission:* The Commission concluded that the punishment 'could not be said to have reached the level of severe ill-treatment proscribed by Art 3'. The Commission then examined whether that same punishment infringed the applicant's rights under Art 8. It found that on enrolling the applicant at the school, the parents did not waive his Art 8 right to respect for his physical integrity or consent to the interference. It concluded that Art 8 had been violated in that the corporal punishment constituted an unjustified interference with his right to respect for private life for which the State is responsible 'in so far as the English legal system authorised such interference and provided no effective redress'. The Commission also found a violation of Art 13 as, in its opinion, the applicant would have no prospect under English law of bringing a successful assault claim against his headmaster.

*Court:* The Court confirmed that although the treatment complained of was the act of a headmaster of an independent school, it was such as may engage the responsibility of the UK. In order for punishment to be degrading and in breach of Art 3, the Court found that 'the humiliation or debasement involved must attain a particular level of severity and must in any event be other than that usual element of humiliation inherent in any punishment'. It noted that the assessment of severity depends on all the circumstances of the case and, in the present case, the minimum level of severity had not been attained. The Court did not exclude the possibility that there might be circumstances in which Art 8 could be regarded as affording a protection which goes beyond that given by Art 3. However, the Court concluded that the treatment 'did not entail adverse effects for his physical or moral integrity sufficient to bring it within the scope of the prohibition contained within Art 8'. Furthermore, the Court found no violation of Art 13 as an effective remedy was available to the applicant: it was open to him to institute civil proceedings for assault.

## Campbell and Cosans v United Kingdom
## (1982) 4 EHRR 293

*Facts:* The first applicant's son, G, attended a school at which corporal punishment was used. Although the Council refused to guarantee that G would not be subjected to this measure, he was never punished. The second applicant's son, J, also attended a school at which corporal punishment was used. J was told to report to receive corporal punishment but, when he reported, he refused to accept the punishment. As a result, he was suspended from school and did not return. The applicants applied to the Commission in 1976 alleging violations of Art 3 and Art 2 of the First Protocol.

*Commission:* The Commission noted that discipline is a function assumed in relation to education and teaching, and that accordingly the State is obliged to respect the religious and philosophical convictions of parents. It defined the concept of 'philosophical convictions' as 'those ideas based on human knowledge and reasoning concerning the world, life, society etc, which a person adopts and professes according to the dictates of his or her conscience'. It concluded that the applicants' views on corporal punishment 'are indeed views of a clear moral order concerning human behaviour in respect of young children' within the meaning of the second sentence of Art 2 of the First Protocol. A violation of that Article was found. No separate violation was found in relation to the suspension of J and no violation of Art 3 was found.

*Court:*   As neither G nor J were in fact 'strapped with the tawse' the Court did not consider an actual application of corporal punishment but noted that provided it is sufficiently real and immediate, a mere threat of conduct may be in violation of Art 3. However, no violation of Art 3 was found as G or J had not undergone 'humiliation or debasement attaining a minimum level of severity'. With respect to the second sentence of Art 2 of the First Protocol, the Court found that discipline is an integral part of any educational system, and the functions assumed by the State extend to questions of discipline in general. The Court concluded that the applicants' views relate to a weighty and substantial part of human life and behaviour, 'the integrity of the person, the propriety or otherwise of the infliction of corporal punishment and the exclusion of distress which the risk of such punishment entails'. Therefore, these views were distinguished from opinions that might be held on 'other methods of discipline or on discipline in general'. A violation of the second sentence of Art 2 of the First Protocol was found. In relation to the suspension of J for nearly a whole year, a violation of the first sentence of Art 2 of the First Protocol was also found.

## 13.2   DISCRIMINATION

### Belgian Linguistic Case (No 2)

### (1968) 1 EHRR 252

*Facts:*   The applicants were parents of Belgian nationality who were French-speaking living in regions considered 'Dutch-speaking'. Their complaints to the Commission on their own behalf and on behalf of their children concerned Belgian legislation which provided that the language of education was to be that of the region in areas designated as unilingual. However, in bilingual areas, the maternal language of the child was the determinative factor and in six 'special status' communes, the language of education was optional provided the head of the family was a resident. If a school failed to comply with the legislation, it would be denied State support and official recognition. The applicants alleged violations of Arts 8, 14 and Art 2 of the First Protocol.

*Commission:*   The Commission concluded that the withdrawal of subsidies from schools providing complete or partial education in another language is in violation of the first sentence of Art 2 of the First Protocol read in conjunction with Art 14. It found a similar violation in respect of the prevention of children, solely on the basis of their parents' place of residence, from attending French language schools in one of the six communes. The refusal to homologate certificates relating to secondary schooling not in accordance with the language requirements was also found to be in violation of these Articles.

*Court:*   The Court stated that it cannot be concluded that the State has no positive obligation to ensure respect for the right to education. However, there is no question now of requiring a State to establish such a system 'but merely of guaranteeing to persons ... the right, in principle, to avail themselves of the means of instruction existing at a given time'. The Court confirmed that the right to education would be meaningless if it did not imply 'the right to be educated in the national language or one of the national languages'. The Court concluded that the first sentence of Art 2 of the First Protocol guarantees a right of access to educational institutions, and also that the individual has 'the right to obtain ... official recognition of the studies which he has completed'. However, the second sentence of Art 2 of the First Protocol does not secure for parents a right to have education conducted in a language other than that of the country in question. Similarly, Art 8 does not guarantee a personal right of parents relating to the education of their children.

Examining Art 14, the Court stated that the principle of equality of treatment is violated if the distinction has no objective and reasonable justification. The existence of such a justification 'must be assessed in relation to the aim and effects of the measure under consideration, regard being had to the principles which normally prevail in democratic societies'. The Court noted that a difference in treatment must pursue a legitimate aim, and there must be a 'reasonable relationship of proportionality between the means employed and the aim sought to be realised'. However, Art 14 read in conjunction with Art 2 of the First Protocol does not guarantee to a child or to his parent the right to obtain instruction in a language of his choice.

With respect to the State's refusal to establish or subsidise in the Dutch region primary school education in which French is employed as the language of instruction, the Court found no violation of Art 2 of the First Protocol, Art 8 or those Articles when read in conjunction with Art 14. In the opinion of the Court, it was a matter of legitimate public interest to ensure that all schools dependent on the State and existing in the unilingual region conducted their teaching in the language of that region. Similarly, no violation of the Convention was found with respect to the withdrawal of subsidies.

However, the legislation also prevented certain children, solely on the basis of their parents' place of residence, from attending French language schools at Louvain and in the six special status communes. The Court concluded that this measure was not justified in the light of the requirements of the Convention in that it involved 'elements of discriminatory treatment of certain individuals, founded even more on language than on residence'. For example, the Dutch-speaking children resident in the French unilingual region had access to Dutch language schools in the six communes. However, French-speaking children living in the Dutch unilingual region were refused access to French-language schools in those communes. A violation of the first sentence of Art 2 of the First Protocol, read in conjunction with Art 14, was found.

# X v United Kingdom
## (1982) 4 EHRR 252

*Facts:* The applicant, a prisoner in Dartmoor Prison, wished to follow a correspondence course in mechanical engineering as preparation for a degree. He paid for the course but was then refused time off work for study and had difficulty in obtaining access to textbooks. A prison tutor was of the opinion that the applicant could not cope with his studies. The applicant, a New Zealand citizen, believed that he would have been given better facilities and more encouragement if he had been British, in effect a claim of discrimination on the ground of nationality. The Home Secretary stated that prisoners were entitled to time off work for study only if they were receiving remedial education, following Open University courses, or engaged in full- or part-time study for a recognised qualification; the applicant did not fit into any of these definitions and so had not been allowed day-release from work. The applicant alleged breach of Art 2 of the First Protocol, in conjunction with Art 14, in that he had suffered discrimination in relation to the right to education.

*Commission:*   Referring to the decision in the *Belgian Linguistic Case (No. 1)* and *(No. 2)* ((1967) 1 EHRR 241 and (1968) 1 EHRR 252), the Commission stated that the right to education is not an absolute right to all forms of education, but a right of access to existing educational institutions. Thus 'where certain, limited, higher education facilities are provided by the State, in principle it is not incompatible with Art 2 of Protocol No 1 to restrict access thereto to those students who have attained the academic level required to most benefit from the courses offered'. Allowing the applicant to study in his spare time was therefore sufficient to comply with the right to education. Since the applicant had not offered any evidence that he would have been given time off work if he had been British, he had not shown that nationality was the basis of the difference of treatment. Although he was treated differently, in relation to time off work, from prisoners who were studying for Open University courses, remedial courses or other approved courses, this difference of treatment had not been shown to lack an objective and reasonable justification. Thus the application was declared inadmissible.

## 13.3   EXCLUSION AND SELECTION PROCEEDINGS AND ACCESS TO EDUCATION

### Chapman (Sally) and Others v United Kingdom

### (2001) 33 EHRR 18

*Facts:*   The applicants were members of five gypsy families who sought permission to live in caravans, but on land owned by them. The authorities did not grant them planning permission. As well as alleging that the authorities were in breach of Arts 8 and 14 and Art 1 of the First Protocol, three of the applicants alleged that their children and grandchildren were being denied the right to an education.

*Court:*   The applicants had failed to establish that there was in fact a denial of education as a consequence of a planning decision which was, in other respects, lawful.

*Note:*   The issue of planning permission and the rights of gypsies raised in these cases is considered in Chapter 18.

*UNITED KINGDOM CASES*

# R (on the application of B) v Head Teacher of Alperton Community School

## High Court, QBD [2001] EWHC Admin 229, [2001] ELR 359

*Facts:* Each of three claimants argued, in the context of disputes relating to non-admission (C) or exclusions from schools (B and T), inter alia, that certain provisions of the School Standards and Framework Act 1998 contravened Articles of the Convention, and that the court should make a declaration of non-compatibility with the Convention under the HRA 1998. In the case of C it was alleged that the provisions governing admissions appeals were in breach of Art 6 of the Convention as the panel members could be appointed, paid and trained by the LEA or governing body, and were therefore not independent. In the cases of B and T it was argued that as there had been an exclusion based on the ground of conduct amounting to a criminal offence either a civil right to a reputation and/or a criminal charge were involved and therefore Art 6 applied. The question arose, therefore, whether the Independent Appeal Panels (IAPs) were obliged to comply with Art 6 and, if so, whether the procedures set out in the HRA 1998, Sch 18 complied with the Article. The court also had to consider whether a right to education is a civil right in English law, whether the IAP determines a civil right to a reputation, and whether the proceedings involved proceedings in connection with a criminal charge.

*Held:* Following case-law from the Convention authorities it did not appear that the right to education could be characterised as a civil right such that Art 6 was applicable to disputes. In *Simpson v UK* (1989) 64 D&R 188, for example, the Commission had held that:

> 'Although the notion of a civil right under this provision is autonomous of any domestic law definitions, the Commission consider that for the purposes of the domestic law in question and the Convention, the right not to be denied elementary education falls, in the circumstances of the present case, squarely within the domain of public law, having no private law analogy and no repercussions on private rights or obligations' (para 45).

A finding of misconduct amounting to a serious breach of discipline leading to exclusion clearly affects the reputation of a child, but the issue in the present case was that of whether an IAP, dealing with an exclusion decision, determined the civil right to a reputation. The Court held that Art 6(1) was not applicable to IAP exclusion proceedings as:

> '... the civil law right to the enjoyment of reputation is not infringed in the course of proceedings (a) not directly decisive of reputation and (b) where the potentiality for damage has been recognised by proper procedural protection [and] An IAP is concerned to determine whether reinstatement should be ordered. The governing provisions are contained within a statutory disciplinary code applicable to schools, having the object of regulating, in the public interest, the proper and efficient provision of education' (para 57).

An IAP does not determine a criminal charge. 'Although expulsion is significant it does not lead to a denial of access to the educational system, nor does it constitute the determination of a criminal charge' (para 58).

*Note:* On grounds not connected to the application of the HRA 1998 the decisions taken by the IAPs in the cases of B and C were quashed.

# Chapter 14

# SEX AND GENDER ISSUES

## 14.1 SEX DISCRIMINATION

### (1) GENERAL PRINCIPLES

**Abdulaziz, Cabales and Balkandali v United Kingdom**

**(1985) 7 EHRR 471**

*Facts:* The applicants were women born outside the UK who had legally settled in the UK and had been given the right to remain indefinitely. They each married after coming to the UK and sought permission for their husbands to enter or to remain in the UK. Permission was refused in each case. The applicants claimed that UK immigration rules were discriminatory as to sex and race, and violated the right to respect for family life since the women were being deprived of their husbands. One of the applicants also alleged discrimination on grounds of birth. All three applicants alleged violations of Arts 3 and 8.

*Commission:* The Commission was of the opinion that there had been a breach of Art 14 in conjunction with Art 8, and that the absence of effective domestic remedies was a violation of Art 13.

*Court:* The rights of the applicants to a family life had to be balanced against the State's right to control the entry of non-nationals into its territory. There was no breach of Art 8, taken alone, since each applicant had the freedom to establish a family life in either her own or her husband's home country, and each applicant knew it was unlikely that her husband would qualify for UK residence. The Court went on to dismiss the allegations of discrimination on grounds of race or birth since there was no differential treatment on either of these grounds, but found that there was a violation of Art 14 taken together with Art 8 on grounds of sex. Under the Immigration Rules 1980, a husband settled in the UK had far more chance of obtaining permission for his wife to enter or to remain in the UK than did a wife in the same factual situation. The government had argued that this differential treatment was objectively and reasonably justified because it had the aim of limiting 'primary immigration' and there was a pressing social need to protect the domestic labour market in a time of mass unemployment. Since men were more likely to be seeking employment than women, male immigration was thought to be more dangerous to the labour market. The government further argued that preventing immigration was a method of securing good race relations. The Court rejected all these arguments, stating that 'the advancement of the equality of the sexes is today a major goal in the Member States. . . . This means that very weighty reasons would have to be advanced before a difference of treatment on the ground of sex could be regarded as compatible with the Convention'. The government had failed to show any convincing reason of sufficient weight to justify the differential treatment. The Court also found a violation of Art 13, but rejected the applicants' claim for compensation.

# Schmidt v Germany
## (1994) 18 EHRR 513

*Facts:* The applicant lived in a region of Germany where all male adults were in theory required to perform local fire brigade duties. In practice, service was replaced by a financial levy, which women did not have to pay. The Constitutional Court held that there was a risk involved in fire brigade duties which formed objective justification for the difference of treatment, and so only men should be subject to the levy. Women did in fact serve in the local fire brigade, so it was the levy which was the difference of treatment between the sexes. The applicant alleged that there had been a breach of Art 14 in conjunction with Art 4 in relation to forced labour, and with Art 1 of the First Protocol in relation to taxation.

*Commission:* The Commission stated that the difference of treatment was unjustified sex discrimination and violated Art 14 in conjunction with both of the above Convention rights. Although States do have a margin of appreciation in determining whether differences of treatment in similar situations are justified, the margin of appreciation in relation to sex discrimination is very narrow. Thus, the reasons behind a difference of treatment on grounds of sex must be extremely strong. The Convention is a living document which must be interpreted in line with modern ideas, and so historical and traditional reasons for differential treatment may become irrelevant. As equality advances, the roles of the sexes must be reinterpreted.

*Court:* The Court upheld the Commission's decision. However, the Court stopped short of discussing whether, in fact, there is any physical or mental difference about women which means that they are less well equipped to serve in the fire brigade. Since, in practice, the difference of treatment related not to service but to a financial levy, any such arguments could not form objective justification for the discrimination.

*Note:* A joint dissenting opinion was given by Judges Spielman and Gotchev, who argued that there had been no violation because: 'In our view this is not a difference of treatment founded exclusively on sex, but a difference based on fitness to carry out the difficult and dangerous tasks inherent in fire brigade duty. The legislature could legitimately consider that men are ordinarily better suited to such tasks than women . . . we believe that such a difference of treatment has an objective and reasonable justification'. Thus, even where sex discrimination is concerned, some Convention judges will consider direct discrimination to be justified, in contrast to the approach of UK law.

# Schuler-Zgraggen v Switzerland
## (1995) 21 EHRR 404

*Facts:* The applicant contracted a serious illness which required her to give up work, and she was granted an invalidity pension. Some 6 years later, she gave birth to a son. She was then given a medical examination in order to assess her ability to work. The subsequent report stated that she was completely unfit for clerical work, but 60–70% fit for housework. Her pension was cancelled on the ground that her family circumstances had radically changed due to the birth of her son, the improvement in her health and her ability to care for her son and her home. When she appealed she was denied access to her medical files. The domestic courts held that the applicant was not entitled to a pension since, even if she had been well enough to work, as a woman she was expected to give up her job once she became a mother and devote herself to housework.

The applicant complained that she had not received a fair trial due to the lack of access to her medical records, and that the court's assumption that she would have given up work to be a mother was sex discrimination.

*Commission:*   The Commission found that there had been no violation of Art 14.

*Court:*   The Court held that there had been a breach of Art 14. The domestic courts had assumed that the applicant would have given up work when she became a mother if she had not been unwell. This assumption 'cannot be regarded ... as an incidental remark, clumsily drafted but of negligible effect. On the contrary, it constitutes the sole basis for the reasoning, thus being decisive, and introduces a difference of treatment based on the ground of sex only'. Since there was sex discrimination, this difference of treatment could be justified only by extremely persuasive reasons, and no such reasons had been shown to exist in the present case.

## (2)   STATE BENEFITS

# Van Raalte v The Netherlands
# (1997) 24 EHRR 503

*Facts:*   Domestic law exempted unmarried childless women over the age of 45 from having to pay contributions towards child benefit. There was no similar exemption for men. The applicant was an unmarried, childless man over the age of 45 who argued that the exemption breached Art 1 of the First Protocol in conjunction with Art 14. The exemption was abolished by statute in 1989, and the applicant lost his domestic case for sex discrimination. The domestic courts held that the legislature had not intended to discriminate since the difference of treatment was based not on a difference in sex but on a difference in factual situation; women over 45 rarely procreate but men over 45 do. Thus, the women exempted would almost certainly never claim child benefit.

*Commission:*   The Commission found that there had been a violation by sex discrimination in relation to the liability to pay tax. It was 'doubtful whether the difference in treatment between men and women based solely on this biological difference could be regarded as proportionate to the aim pursued'. Women and men should be treated equally in social security law, and this difference in treatment was unjustified.

*Court:*   The Court held unanimously that there had been a violation of Art 14 in conjunction with Art 1 of the First Protocol. There was clearly a difference of treatment based on sex. Thus, it had to be determined whether there was an objective and reasonable justification for the difference. The Court pointed out that a central feature of the child benefit scheme was that all citizens were required to contribute, regardless of their potential entitlement. Thus the exemption contradicted the scheme's policy. Since, inter alia, unmarried childless women over 45 may adopt, foster or become stepmothers and thus claim child benefit, there was no logic to the exemption. None of the reasons put forward by the government could form an objective and reasonable justification, especially when set alongside the higher standard expected in cases of sex discrimination.

# Fielding v United Kingdom
## [2002] TLR 86

*Facts:*   The applicant complained that the British social security and tax legislation discriminated against him on grounds of sex and was contrary to Art 14 taken in conjunction with both Art 8 of the Convention and Art 1 of the First Protocol. Following the death of his wife in 1997, the applicant applied for social security benefits and bereavement tax allowance equivalent to those available to widows. His application was refused on the ground that the regulations governing the payment of widow's benefits and tax allowance were specific to women. Any appeal against this decision would fail because under UK law no equivalent benefit was payable to men.

*Court:*   Having received a declaration from the government in the context of a friendly settlement, the Court agreed to strike the case out of the list.

*Note:*   The Court also dealt with this issue in the case of *Cornwell v United Kingdom* (2001) 29 EHRR CD 62, judgment of 25 April 2000. The Welfare Reform and Pensions Act 1999, which came into force in April 2001, provides for bereavement benefits to be made available to men and women.

## PATERNITY RIGHTS AND BENEFITS

# Rasmussen v Denmark
## (1984) 7 EHRR 371

*Facts:*   The applicant was separated from his wife, who had custody of their two children. He began proceedings to prove that he was not the father of the younger child, but dropped the case once his wife agreed not to seek maintenance for that child. However, after their divorce, the ex-wife was granted a court order against him for maintenance of both children, and the applicant made the payments. The domestic court then refused him leave to instigate the paternity proceedings on the grounds that he had tacitly acknowledged the child as his. The welfare of a child required his or her parentage to be determined as soon after birth as possible, and the husband's interests were regarded as less important. Thus, time-limits applied to paternity suits by husbands, but not to those brought by mothers or guardians. The applicant alleged sex discrimination since his ex-wife had an unlimited right to challenge his paternity of the child, yet he did not.

*Commission:*   The Commission was of the opinion that there had been a breach of Art 14 in conjunction with Arts 6 and 8, in that the applicant had been subject to sex discrimination related to access to a court and respect for his family and private life.

*Court:* The Court held that the paternity proceedings were a determination of civil rights and obligations within Art 6, and that proving or disproving paternity was within the ambit of 'private life' under Art 8. There had been a difference of treatment between the applicant and his ex-wife. However, this discrimination had an objective and reasonable justification: the time-limits for paternity suits brought by husbands were introduced for reasons of legal certainty and to protect the child's interests. The legislature had assumed that the mother's interests were identical to the child's, which should prevail, but this was in line with the attitudes of the time. The legislation in question had since been modified to bring it in to line with modern thought. The difference of treatment was thus within the State's margin of appreciation, and so the Court held unanimously that there had been no violation of Art 14 in conjunction with either Art 6 or Art 8.

# Petrovic v Austria

## (2001) 33 EHRR 14

*Facts:* The applicant was a married university student who also worked part-time. His wife, a graduate, was a civil servant. After the birth of their child, the applicant took parental leave to care for the child while his wife returned to work. He claimed parental leave payments, but was refused on the ground that the benefit was payable only to mothers. Although the relevant legislation was later amended to allow payments to fathers who were primary carers, the change did not apply retrospectively to the applicant. He claimed sex discrimination in relation to his right to respect for private and family life, ie a breach of Art 14 in conjunction with Art 8.

*Commission:* The denial of the benefit in question was not in itself a breach of Art 8 since that Article does not oblige a State to give financial assistance to parents so that they can care for their children full time. However, the benefit exists in order to promote daily life and so its provision is a method by which the State performs its obligations under Art 8 to show respect for family life. Thus it was possible to argue a breach of Art 14 in conjunction with Art 8 here. The applicant was ineligible for the parental leave benefit simply because he was a man. There was, therefore, a difference of treatment on grounds of sex. Since sex equality is a major goal in modern society, such a difference of treatment will be justified only by very weighty reasons. There is no reason why fathers should be less able to care for a newborn child than mothers. If a State provides a scheme of parental leave payments, then they must be granted in a non-discriminatory manner. The lack of a common standard among Member States regarding social security schemes does not excuse any State's discrimination. No objective and reasonable justification had been demonstrated for the discrimination and hence there was a violation of Art 14 in conjunction with Art 8.

*Court:* The parental leave allowance fell within the scope of Art 8 since it was 'intended to promote family life and necessarily affects the way in which the latter is organised as, in conjunction with parental leave, it enables one of the parents to stay at home to look after the children'. Hence Art 14 could come into play. The Court agreed that there was a difference of treatment on grounds of sex, that equality is a major goal and, therefore, that very weighty reasons are needed to justify such a difference of treatment. However, such benefits originally applied only to mothers in all Contracting States, and have gradually been extended to fathers as societies' views of parenthood have changed. Hence the difference in treatment was within the margin of appreciation and there was no violation of Art 14 in conjunction with Art 8.

*Note:*   In a dissenting opinion at the Commission level, three commissioners argued that there were important differences of position between the mother and father of a young child, and so their positions were not analogous for the purpose of showing a difference of treatment:

> 'A consequence of the majority opinion would be to reproach a State for granting maternity leave to women without instantly providing men with equal benefits. This is not yet common ground in most Contracting States. On the contrary, the social development in this field has generally commenced through the establishment of a possibility for women to care for the new-born child. Only at a later stage have similar possibilities been granted to fathers ... even if the father and mother of a new-born child were in a relevantly similar position, the refusal of benefits to the father would nevertheless be compatible with the margin of appreciation afforded to the States.'

Judges Bernhardt and Spielmann gave a joint dissenting opinion to the judgment in which they argued that Art 14 had been breached:

> 'It is in reality the traditional distribution of family responsibilities between mothers and fathers that gave rise to the Austrian legislation under which only mothers were entitled to parental leave allowance. The discrimination against fathers perpetuates this traditional distribution of roles and can also have negative consequences for the mother; if she continues her professional activity and agrees that the father should stay at home, the family loses the parental leave allowance to which it would be entitled if she stayed at home. It is correct that States are under no obligation to pay any parental leave allowance, but if they do, traditional practices and roles in family life alone do not justify a difference in treatment of men and women.'

## 14.2   GAY AND LESBIAN CONDUCT

### (1)   ILLEGALITY OF GAY AND LESBIAN ACTS

### Modinos v Cyprus

### (1993) 16 EHRR 485

*Facts:*   The applicant was a practising homosexual and the president of the Liberation Movement of Homosexuals in Cyprus. He complained that a Cypriot statute, which rendered male homosexual conduct in private between adults a criminal offence, violated his right to respect for his private life within the meaning of Art 8, notwithstanding the policy of the Cypriot Attorney-General not to prosecute the offence.

*Commission:*   The Commission considered that, although some degree of regulation of male homosexual conduct by means of a criminal law can be justified 'as necessary in a democratic society', this would, however, require particularly serious reasons before it could be regarded as legitimate. On the present facts, no such reasons were established.

*Court:* The Court found that the Attorney-General had followed a consistent policy of not bringing criminal proceedings in respect of private homosexual conduct. However, this policy provided no guarantee that action would not be taken by a future Attorney-General to enforce the law, particularly when regard was had to certain statements made by government ministers which appeared to suggest that the relevant provisions of the criminal code were still in force. As a result, the Court considered that the existence of the prohibition 'continuously and directly affected the applicant's private life' and was thus a breach of Art 8.

## Dudgeon v United Kingdom
## (1981) 4 EHRR 149

*Facts:* The applicant complained that the law in Northern Ireland had the effect of making certain homosexual acts between consenting adult males criminal offences. He complained that, as a practising homosexual, he had experienced fear, suffering and psychological harm directly caused by the existence of the laws in question including fear of harassment and blackmail, which constituted an unjustified interference with his right to respect for his private life in violation of Art 8.

*Commission:* The Commission unanimously concluded that the legislation complained of interfered with the applicant's right to respect for his private life as guaranteed by Art 8.

*Court:* The Court, by a majority of 15 votes to 4, found that there had been a breach of Art 8 in regard to the existing law in relation to men aged over 21; but that it was for States to fix for themselves, in the first instance, any appropriate extension of the age of consent in relation to such conduct. The Court held that 'the very existence of the legislation continuously and directly affected the applicant's life: either he respects the law and refrains from engaging (even in private with consenting male partners) in prohibited sexual acts to which he is disposed of by reason of his homosexual tendencies, or he commits such acts and thereby becomes liable to criminal prosecution'. There was, however, a need in a democratic society for some degree of regulation of male homosexual conduct by means of the criminal law. Such regulation was justifiable where, for instance, there was a 'call to protect the public at large from offence and injury or to provide safeguards against the exploitation and corruption of those vulnerable by virtue of their youth'. Moreover, it was apparent that in recent years, the Northern Ireland authorities had reformed from enforcing the law in respect of private homosexual acts between consenting males and no evidence had been adduced to show that this had been injurious to moral standards or that there had been any public demand for stricter enforcement of the law. In the circumstances, it could not be argued that there was a 'pressing social need' to make such acts criminal offences. Accordingly, the applicant's right to respect for his private life had been violated.

# Norris v Ireland
## (1988) 13 EHRR 186

*Facts:* The applicant was an active homosexual and founder member and chairman of the Irish Gay Rights Movement. In November 1977, the applicant instituted proceedings in the High Court of Ireland claiming that certain laws prohibiting homosexual relations were invalid. Although empathetic with his plight, the High Court, and in turn the Supreme Court, dismissed his application. The applicant complained that the prohibition on male homosexual activity constituted a continuing interference with his right to respect for private life, contrary to Art 8 of the Convention.

*Commission:* The Commission declared the application admissible and by 6 votes to 5 expressed the opinion that there had been a violation of Art 8.

*Court:* The Court accepted, by 8 votes to 6, that there had been a violation of Art 8 and rejected the principal argument put forward by the government which was that, since the legislation complained of had never been enforced against the applicant, his claim was more in the nature of actio popularis by means of which he sought a review in abstracto of the contested legislation in the light of the Convention. The Court recalled that 'while Art 25 may not be used to fund an action in the nature of an actio popularis; nor may it form the basis of a claim made in abstracto that a law contravenes the Convention ... Art 25 entitled individuals to contend that the law violates their rights by itself, in the absence of an individual measure of implementation, if they run the risk of being directly affected by it'. Although the risk of prosecution in the applicant's case at that time was minimal, 'a law which remains on the statute book, even though it is not enforced in a particular class of cases for a considerable time may be applied again in such cases at any time, if for example there is a change of policy ... the applicant can therefore be said to run the risk of being directly affected by the legislation in question'. After examining the effect of the legislation complained of, the Court held that the applicant was substantially in the same position as the applicant in the case of *Dudgeon*, which concerned identical legislation in Northern Ireland. Thus, in a somewhat similar vein to the *Dudgeon* case, the Court repeated: 'in the personal circumstances of the applicant the very existence of the impugned legislation continuously and directly interfered with his right to respect to his private life under Art 8'. Since no evidence was adduced by the government which pointed to the existence of factors justifying the retention of the impugned laws, nor any evidence to show that there was a pressing social need to make such acts criminal offences, the Court found a violation of the applicant's rights.

# Laskey, Jaggard and Brown v United Kingdom
## (1997) 24 EHRR 39

*Facts:* This case concerned a group of homosexual men who were convicted of various offences against the person, including wounding and assault occasioning actual bodily harm. The charges related to incidents which spanned a 10-year period, and included 'maltreatment of the genitalia' with a variety of implements, beatings and branding. Some incidents left scarring but there were no permanent disabling injuries and no medical treatment was required. All of the injuries were inflicted with the consent of the 'victim' and conducted in private. The applicants had all pleaded guilty at trial since the trial judge had ruled that the consent of the victim could not provide them with any defence to the charges. Prison sentences were reduced on appeal and the House of Lords upheld the convictions. The applicants alleged breaches of, inter alia, Art 8, arguing that their convictions were an unjustifiable interference with their right to respect for their private lives.

*Commission:* The Commission accepted that respect for the health and rights of others may justify a State in prohibiting activities which cause or risk causing death or serious injury. Having regard to the type of activities in which the applicants engaged, the injuries could not be considered to be of 'a trifling or transient nature but rather of a significant nature and degree which on any view would be regarded as extreme'. Consequently, the interference with the applicants' right to respect for their private life was considered as 'necessary in a democratic society for the aim of protecting health'.

*Court:* The Court unanimously found that there had been no violation of Art 8. The activities involved a significant degree of injury or wounding that could not be characterised as trifling or transient, and this was in itself sufficient to distinguish the present case from those applications which had previously been examined by the Court concerning consensual homosexual behaviour in private between adults where no such feature was present. The Court rejected the allegation that the applicants were singled out because of the authorities' bias against homosexuals. Rather, the convictions were based on the 'extreme nature of the practices involved and not the sexual proclivities of the applicants'. Thus, the national authorities were entitled to consider that the prosecution and conviction of the applicants was necessary in a democratic society for the protection of health within the meaning of Art 8(2).

# ADT v United Kingdom
## (2001) 31 EHRR 33

*Facts:* The applicant had been charged and convicted of gross indecency with other men contrary to s 13 of the Sexual Offences Act 1956. Following a search of his premises, police officers seized photographs and videotapes containing footage of the applicant and other adult men engaging in oral sex and mutual masturbation. The sexual acts which formed the basis of the charge involved consenting adults, took place in the applicant's home, did not involve physical harm to the participants and there was no suggestion that the tapes were available for wider distribution. He complained that his conviction amounted to a violation of his right to respect for his private life, which is protected by Art 8 of the Convention. Furthermore, he alleged a violation of Art 14, which guarantees, inter alia, the right not to be discriminated against on the ground of gender, on the basis that domestic law did not regulate similar sexual acts between consenting adult heterosexuals or between lesbians.

*Court:* The Court was satisfied that a prosecution and conviction for gross indecency amounted to an unnecessary interference with the right to respect for private life, and held that the applicant had been the victim of an interference with his right to respect for private life both with regard to the existence of legislation prohibiting consensual sexual acts between more than two men in private and the conviction for gross indecency. The Court accepted that although sexual activities can be carried out in such a manner as to warrant interference by State authorities (see eg *Laskey, Jaggard and Brown v United Kingdom* (1997) 24 EHRR 39), the facts of this case were not sufficient to justify the legislation at issue. While satisfied that there was a violation of Art 8, the Court considered it unnecessary to examine the case under Art 14.

## (2)   THE AGE OF CONSENT

### X v United Kingdom (Wells v United Kingdom)
### (1978) 3 EHRR 63

*Facts:*   In 1974, the applicant, who was then aged 26, was charged with two offences of buggery in respect of acts committed with two males of 18 years of age. He pleaded guilty. The case was adjourned in order that a social enquiry and medical reports might be considered. The applicant was subsequently sentenced to 2½ years' imprisonment on the first count and 6 months' imprisonment on the second count, the two sentences to run concurrently. The applicant's appeal against this sentence was dismissed by the Court of Appeal in 1975. In the course of the Court of Appeal's decision, it was remarked that the applicant's connection with one of the 18 year olds 'was one which did not involve any force or particular unpleasantness at the beginning, but later in the history of the matter there was evidence that at some stage [the applicant] had virtually made a prisoner of [Y] and had beaten and forced him to take part in homosexual acts'. The court also considered that 'the fact that [the applicant] is oriented towards the late teenagers and the younger men of the next generation does make him a person who in our view is a danger to the public'. The applicant, having earned full remission of sentence, was released from prison on 31 January 1976. He complained to the Commission, inter alia, that his prosecution and imprisonment under the law as contained in the Sexual Offences Act 1956, as amended, which fixed the 'age of consent' for homosexual relations at the age of 21 (as it was then), constituted an unjustified interference with his right under Art 8. Similarly, he complained that the difference in 'the age of consent' for homosexual and heterosexual relations constituted discrimination against him under Art 14.

*Commission:*   The Commission concluded unanimously that the prosecution and imprisonment of the applicant under the impugned legislation was not a violation of Art 8. Similarly, the Commission also found that the difference in the 'age of consent' for homosexual and heterosexual relations did not constitute discrimination under Art 14. In view of the fact that there was an element of force used by the applicant, although he was not charged with mistreating or assaulting Y, the Commission felt that the prosecution and sentence of the applicant was justified according to the particular circumstances of the case, 'for the protection of the rights and freedoms of others particularly those who are specially vulnerable because of their age'. As regards the difference in age limit for homosexual and heterosexual relationships, the Commission was of the view that the age limit established in the UK 'must be examined on its own merits and in the context of the society for which it is considered appropriate'. Although it was suggested that the age limit of 21 may be regarded as high in the present era, especially when contrasted with other Member States of the Council of Europe, the Commission readily accepted the government's justification for the disparity: that, 'given the controversial and sensitive nature of the question involved, young men in the 18–21 age bracket who are involved in homosexual relationships would be subject to substantial social pressure which could be harmful to their psychological development'. Accordingly, the Commission found that the government had not gone beyond its obligation under the Convention and that the interference in the applicant's private life involved in fixing the age of consent at 21 was justified as being 'necessary in a democratic society for the protection of the rights of others'.

*Note:* The next case dealt with shows a change in the approach of the Commission and Court, indicating particularly that this is an area in which the requirements of the Convention may be adapted to keep pace with changing social patterns.

## Sutherland v United Kingdom

## (1998) 24 EHRR CD 22, Commission; [2001] TLR 279, Court

*Facts:* The applicant complained to the Commission that the fixing of a minimum age for lawful homosexual activities at 18 rather than 16 was in violation of his right to respect for his private life and was discriminatory, given that the age of consent was 16 for heterosexual activities.

*Commission:* The Commission found that there had been a violation of Art 8 taken in conjunction with Art 14. The Commission recalled that 'even though the applicant has not in the event been prosecuted or threatened with prosecution, the very existence of the legislation directly affected his private life: either he respected the law and refrained from engaging in any prohibited sexual acts prior to the age of 18 or he committed acts and thereby became liable to prosecution'. The Commission then rejected the government's argument that 'certain young men between the ages of 16 and 18 do not have a settled sexual orientation, and that the aim of the law is to protect such vulnerable young men from activities which will result in considerable social pressures and isolation which their lack of maturity might cause them later to repent; [thus] the possibility of criminal sanctions against persons aged 16 or 17 is likely to have a deterrent effect and give the individual time to make up his mind. Secondly society is entitled to indicate its disapproval of homosexual conduct and its preference that children follow a heterosexual way of life'. It was considered by the Commission that neither argument offered a reasonable and objective justification for maintaining a different age of consent for homosexual and heterosexual acts or that maintaining such a differential age is proportionate to any legitimate aim served thereby. Furthermore, 'current medical opinion is to the effect that sexual orientation is fixed in both sexes by the age of 16, and that men aged 16 to 21 are not in need of special protection because of the risk of their being "recruited" into homosexuality'. As noted by the British Medical Association, the risk posed by predatory older men would appear to be as serious whether the victim is a man or woman and does not justify a differential age of consent. As to the second ground relied on by the government, 'society's claimed entitlement to indicate disapproval of homosexual conduct and its preference for a heterosexual life style', the Commission recalled the court's words in the *Dudgeon* judgment: '"Decriminalisation" does not imply approval and a fear that some sectors of the population might draw misguided conclusions in this respect from reform of a legislation does not afford a good ground for maintaining it in force with all its unjustifiable features'. Thus, since no objective and reasonable justification for the maintenance of a higher minimum age of consent to male homosexual, than to heterosexual, acts was established, the application thereby disclosed discriminatory treatment in the exercise of the applicant's right to respect for his private life under Art 8.

*Court:* Following the conclusion reached by the Commission the law was eventually amended by way of the Sexual Offences Act 2000, which entered into force on 8 January 2001. The Court, at the request of the parties, struck the case from its list.

## (3) THE RIGHT TO FAMILY LIFE

### Application No 9369/81

(European Commission Procedure)
(1983) 5 EHRR 601

*Facts:* The applicants were in a stable homosexual relationship and complained about the refusal by the UK Immigration Authorities to allow the first applicant, a Malaysian citizen, to remain in the UK with the second applicant, a British citizen. They submitted that they had suffered discrimination on the basis of their sex in the protection of their right to respect for family and private life as guaranteed by the convention under Arts 14 and 8 respectively.

*Commission:* The Commission held that the complaints were manifestly ill-founded. Despite the modern evolution of attitudes towards homosexuality, such relationships did not fall within the scope of the right to respect for family life ensured by Art 8. In certain circumstances, restraints on such relationships could be considered to be contrary to Art 8, for example where a close member of a family is excluded from the country where his family resided. The Commission's approach in such cases is first to examine the facts of each case in order to find the extent of the claimed family link and also the ties with the country concerned, since the right to respect for family life does not necessarily include the right to choose the geographical location of that family life. In the circumstances of the present case, the Commission found that it had not been shown that the applicants could not live together elsewhere than in the UK or that the link with the UK was an essential element of the relationship. Thus, a refusal to allow the first applicant to remain in the UK did not constitute an interference with the applicants' right to respect for private life ensured by Art 8. The Commission found no indication that the proposed deportation of the first applicant was based on the fact of the applicants' homosexual relationship.

## (4) MILITARY SERVICE

### Application No 9237/81

(European Commission Procedure)
unreported

*Facts:* The applicant was serving as a non-commissioned officer in the army. On 26 August 1980, he appeared before a court martial charged with three offences under s 66 of the Army Act 1955 concerning homosexual conduct which the applicant had engaged in with a gunner in his regiment in Germany and with a civilian at home. The applicant admitted the charges and was sentenced to a reduction in rank and to 9 months' imprisonment with corrective military training followed by dishonourable discharge. The applicant successfully petitioned the confirming officer for cancellation of the custodial sentence. His sentence was otherwise confirmed and he was dishonourably discharged on 17 September 1980. The applicant complained to the Commission and alleged breaches of Arts 8 and 14, arguing that many other Member States did not have similar prohibitions on private consensual homosexual acts by serving soldiers. Further, the penalties of administrative discharge for suspicion of being homosexual and imprisonment and dishonourable discharge for homosexual acts were disproportionate.

*Commission:* The Commission confirmed that prohibition by criminal law of homosexual acts committed in private between consenting males amounts to an interference with the private life of those concerned. Nevertheless, some degree of regulation of male homosexual conduct can be justified 'notably where there is call to provide sufficient safeguards against exploitation and corruption of others particularly those who are specially vulnerable because they are . . . in a state of special physical, official or economic dependence'. In view of the circumstances of the case, although the proceedings against the present applicant involved a violation of Art 8, the argument of the government was accepted by the Commission: 'homosexual conduct by members of the armed forces may pose a particular risk to order within the forces which would not arise in civilian life and consequently it may possibly be considered as necessary for the prevention of disorder to maintain stricter rules over homosexual conduct in the military sphere than would be justifiable in the civilian sphere'. Accordingly, the measures taken against the applicant were deemed as being justifiable under Art 8(2) as being necessary for the 'prevention of disorder in the context of the military service'.

# Lustig-Prean and Beckett v United Kingdom
## (2001) 31 EHRR 23
# Smith and Grady v United Kingdom
## (2001) 31 EHRR 24

*Facts:* The applicants complained that an investigation into their sexual orientation and their subsequent discharge from the armed forces was a violation of their right to respect for private life. The current claim for non-pecuniary damage was based on a submission that the investigation was insulting, humiliating and degrading and had caused emotional and psychological damage.

*Court:* The Court held unanimously that all four applicants had been the victims of a violation of Art 8. The Court recalled that the interference with the applicants' rights in this case had been 'especially grave' and awarded each person £19,000, but rejected claims for aggravated damage and interest. In claiming pecuniary damage amounting to the difference between what would have been earned in the service and their civilian income, the applicants submitted that the discharge deprived them of their chosen careers and had had a profound effect on future career prospects. The Court took the view that a precise calculation of the exact sums necessary to make reparation was made difficult by the inherently uncertain character of the damage flowing from the violation. Whilst the Court rejected the government's suggestion that no award should be made in respect of future losses, it did acknowledge that the greater the interval since their discharge, the more uncertain the damage became. In this case, the Court considered it appropriate to award each applicant a sum in respect of loss of earnings, future loss of earnings and loss of the benefit of the non-contributory service pension scheme. The total amount awarded against the government, excluding costs and expenses, exceeded £325,000.

*Note:*    Changes were made to the discipline mechanism operating in the armed forces in order to reconcile the courts martial system with Convention obligations. These took effect in the Armed Forces Discipline Act 2000. The case of *Smith v Grady* is individually dealt with in Chapter 2.

## 14.3    TRANSSEXUALS AND GENDER REASSIGNMENT

### (1)   RECOGITION BY AUTHORITIES

### Rees v United Kingdom

### (1987) 9 EHRR 56

*Facts:*    The applicant was registered at birth as a female, was transsexual, and after medical treatment changed his name and began living as a male. An application to amend the birth certificate was refused. The applicant complained, alleging breaches of Arts 8 and 12.

*Commission:*    The Commission was unanimous in holding that, by not rectifying the applicant's birth certificate, there had been a breach of Art 8, but found no breach of Art 12.

*Court:*    The Court held by 12 votes to 3 that the respondent State had not violated Art 8. There was little common ground between the Contracting States in the area of transsexuality and laws were in a transitional stage. Accordingly, this was an area in which the contracting parties enjoyed a wide margin of appreciation in which a fair balance had to be struck between the general interests of the community and the interests of the individual. It was recognised that the UK authorities had 'endeavoured, albeit with delay and some misgivings, to meet the applicant's demands to the fullest extent that its system allowed'. Transsexuals were free to change their first names and surnames at will, and could have official documents issued in their chosen first names and surnames indicating their preferred sex by the relevant prefix (Mr, Mrs, Ms or Miss). This freedom gave transsexuals a 'considerable advantage in comparison with States where all official documents have to conform with the records held by the registry office'. The Court felt it significant that requiring the UK to adapt a system of registration of civil status to reflect the current status of the individual or a requirement to allow alteration of a birth certificate would not constitute an effective safeguard for the integrity of private life since it would reveal a change of sexual identity. The Court held that 'the right to marry guaranteed by Art 12 refers to the traditional marriage between persons of opposite biological sex'. The legal impediment on the marriage of persons who were not of the opposite biological sex could not be said to violate Art 12.

# B v France
## (1992) 16 EHRR 1

*Facts:* The applicant was a transsexual who underwent feminising hormonal treatment and then gender reassignment surgery and lived as a woman. She brought proceedings in a French court to rectify her birth certificate. The application was dismissed and she complained that the refusal of the French authorities to recognise her current sexual identity and, in particular, their refusal to allow her to change her civil status, constituted a breach of Art 8 of the Convention.

*Commission:* The Commission declared the application admissible and found that the refusal of the French authorities to recognise the applicant's true sexual identity, in particular the refusal to allow her the change of civil status, constituted a violation of Art 8. In reaching its decision, the Commission considered that the discrepancy between the applicant's appearance and the entries concerning both gender and forename on documents relating to her 'indisputably resulted in Miss B suffering particularly trying ordeals in her daily life; in particular the discrepancy forced her to reveal to third persons details of her private life, whether in performing everyday actions, travelling, finding work etc'.

*Court:* The Court found that the inconvenience complained of by the applicant reached a sufficient degree of seriousness to be taken into account for the purposes of Art 8, even having regard to the State's margin of appreciation in this field. The Court held that the fair balance which has to be struck between the general interest and the interests of the individual had not been attained and there had thus been a violation of Art 8. In distinguishing this case from the similar case of *Rees* (above), where no violation of Art 8 was found, the Court considered it to be significant that there were noticeable differences between France and England with reference to their law and practice on civil status, change of forenames and the use of identity documents.

# Sheffield and Horsham v United Kingdom
## (1998) 27 EHRR 163

*Facts:* The first applicant was registered at birth as being of the male sex. Prior to her gender reassignment treatment, she was married and had one daughter. Following a divorce, the applicant's former spouse applied to the court to have her contact with her daughter terminated. The applicant stated that the judge granted the application on the basis that contact with a transsexual would not be in the child's interest. The applicant further maintained that her decision to undergo gender reassignment surgery resulted in her being subjected to discrimination at work or in relation to obtaining work and attributed this in large part to the legal position of transsexuals in the UK.

The second applicant, a British citizen, had been living in The Netherlands since 1974 and acquired Dutch citizenship by naturalisation in 1993. She was also registered at birth as being of the male sex and in 1992 underwent gender reassignment surgery in Amsterdam. She applied to the British Consulate in Amsterdam, seeking a change of photograph and the inscription of her new name and sex in her passport, which was granted. She requested that her original birth certificate in the UK be amended to record her sex as a female. This request was rejected. She complained that she was forced to live in exile because of the legal situation in the UK. Both applicants complained that the lack of legal recognition of their gender reassignments constituted a lack of respect for their private life, a denial of the right to marry, and discrimination in contravention of Arts 8, 12 and 14.

*Commission:*    The Commission found that there had been a violation of Art 8 of the Convention. The applicants were 'subject to a real and continuous risk of intrusive and distressing enquiries and to an obligation to make embarrassing disclosure'. That these instances were not hypothetical was illustrated by the occasion when the first applicant, in court as surety, was required to disclose her original birth name which was in stark contradiction to her physical appearance. While it might be said that with care such situations could be avoided, the Commission argued that 'this in itself would threaten to impinge significantly on an individual's ability to develop and maintain relationships and to restrict the choices available in fulfilling personal and social potential'. The Commission rejected arguments put forward by the government that any alteration in the birth registration system in the UK would have detrimental consequences. Although the Commission agreed with the government that the area of transsexuality was still one of complexity and, in the midst of continuing research, what was significant was the fact that the 'medical profession had reached a consensus that transsexualism is an identifiable medical condition; gender dysphoria, in respect of which gender reassignment treatment is ethically permissible and can be recommended for the purpose of improving the quality of life notwithstanding that as yet there were no firm conclusions on the aetiology of transsexualism'. In light of this, the concerns put forward by the government, even having regard to its margin of appreciation, were not sufficient to outweigh the interests of the applicant.

*Court:*    In contrast to the Commission, the Court, by a narrow majority, found no violation of Art 8. In its view, the applicants had not shown that there had been any findings in the area of medical science which settled conclusively the doubts concerning the aetiology of the condition of transsexualism. 'It continues to be the case that transsexualism raises complex scientific, legal, moral and social issues in respect of which there is no generally shared approach among the Contracting States.' Although no violation was found 'this time', the Court issued the following warning to the respondent State: 'even if there have been no significant scientific developments since the date of the *Cossey* judgment which make it possible to reach a firm conclusion on the aetiology of transsexualism, it is nevertheless the case that there is an increased social acceptance of transsexualism, and an increased recognition of the problem which post-operative transsexuals encounter even if [the Court] finds no breach of Art 8 in this case the court reiterates that this area needs to be kept under review'. As regards the complaints under Art 12, the Court recalled what it had said in earlier decisions that the 'right to marry guaranteed by Art 12 refers to the traditional marriage between persons of the opposite biological sex and this is a matter encompassed within the power of the Contracting States to regulate by national law'. Thus the Court found no violation of Art 12. Similarly, the Court unanimously found no evidence to suggest that the government had overstepped its margin of appreciation in not according legal recognition to a transsexual's post-operative gender and that a fair balance had been struck. In the circumstances, there had been no violation of Art 14 either.

## (2)   THE RIGHT TO FAMILY LIFE

# X, Y and Z v United Kingdom

# (1997) 24 EHRR 143

*Facts:*   The first applicant, X, was a female to male transsexual. Since 1979, he lived with the second applicant, a woman. Their child, Z, was born as a result of artificial insemination by donor (AID). X acted as Z's 'father' in every respect since birth. X and Y attempted to register the child in their joint names as mother and father. However, X was not permitted to be registered as the child's father and that part of the register was left blank. Z was therefore given X's surname in the register. The applicants complained that contrary to Art 8, they were denied respect for their family and private life as a result of the lack of recognition of the first applicant's role as father to the third applicant and that the resulting situation in which they were placed was discriminatory in violation of Arts 8 and 14 taken together.

*Commission:*   The absence of an appropriate legal regime reflecting the applicants' family ties disclosed a failure to respect their family life. Accordingly, the Commission found, by 15 votes to 3, that there had been a violation of Art 8. The Commission held that, in the case of a transsexual who has undergone irreversible gender reassignment in a Contracting State, and lives with a partner of his former sex and child in a family relationship, there must be a presumption in favour of legal recognition of that relationship, the denial of which requires specific justification. Since no legitimate justification was forthcoming, a violation of Art 8 was found.

*Court:*   The Court held, by 14 votes to 6, that there had been no violation of Art 8. It had not been sufficiently established before the Court that there existed any generally shared approach amongst the High Contracting Parties with regard to the manner in which the social relationship between a child conceived by AID and the person who performs the role of father should be reflected in law. The issues in the case addressed areas where there was little common ground amongst the Member States and thus 'the respondent State must be afforded a wide margin of appreciation'. In the circumstances, the State was justifiably cautious in changing national law, since it was possible that the amendment sought might have undesirable and unforeseen ramifications. Accordingly, the fact that the law of the UK did not allow special legal recognition of the relationship between X and Z did not amount to a failure to respect the family within the meaning of that provision.

# Part 5
# RIGHTS OF EXPRESSION AND ASSOCIATED ISSUES

# Chapter 15

# CONSCIENTIOUS AND RELIGIOUS FREEDOMS

## 15.1 POSITIVE DUTY ON STATE TO ENSURE RELIGIOUS FREEDOMS ENJOYED

### Otto-Preminger Institute v Austria

### (1994) 19 EHRR 34

*Facts:* The applicant, a non-profit-making organisation aiming to promote creativity through the audio-visual media, operated a cinema in Innsbruck. At the request of the Roman Catholic Church, the public prosecutor instituted criminal proceedings under the charge of 'disparaging religious doctrines' to prevent the screening of a controversial film, *Council of Heaven*. Following a chain of proceedings, the Regional Court ordered the forfeiture of the film, inter alia, on the grounds that the film was 'primarily intended to be provocative and aimed at the church'. An appeal was declared inadmissible.

*Commission:* The applicant association alleged violations of Art 10 of the Convention on the part of the Austrian authorities, and the Commission found that there had been a violation.

*Court:* The government defended the restriction on the right to exhibit the film as being necessary for the protection of the rights of others and, in particular, 'the right to respect for one's religious feelings'. The Court noted that freedom of conscience and religion is 'one of the most vital elements that go to make up the identity of believers and their conception of life'. There were, however, tensions between beliefs and 'those who choose to exercise the freedom to manifest their religion ... cannot reasonably expect to be exempt from all criticism. They must tolerate and accept the denial by others of their religious beliefs, and even the propagation by others of doctrines hostile to their faith'. On the other hand, Contracting States may be expected equally to have an interest in controlling the way in which religious doctrines are opposed or denied, as 'in extreme cases the effect of particular methods of opposing or denying religious beliefs can be such as to inhibit those who hold such beliefs from exercising their freedom to hold and express them'. In this case, therefore, the Court held that the measures complained of pursued a legitimate aim under Art 10, as they were designed to fulfil the respondent State's positive duty to ensure compliance with Art 9.

*Note:* Although the Court in its judgment referred expressly to 'members of a religious majority or minority', it appears in this case to have placed some reliance on the fact that 'the Roman Catholic religion is the religion of the overwhelming majority of Tyroleans', and that 'the proportion of Roman Catholic believers among the Austrian population as a whole was already considerable – 78% – but among Tyroleans it was as high as 87%'. It appears therefore that the extent to which a State is required to protect religious sensibilities may depend in part on the extent to which the attacked beliefs are held.

## Buscarini v San Marino

## (2000) 30 EHRR 208

*Facts:* In May 1993 the applicants were elected to the General Grand Council of San Marino. Shortly after they requested permission to take the required oath without making any reference to any religious text. In support of their request the applicants relied on Art 4 of the Declaration of Rights of 1974 and Art 9 of the Convention. After some discussion the applicants took the oath as set out in the appropriate legislation, and, before the applicants applied to the Commission, the law was amended to allow an alternative oath to be taken.

*Court:* The Court held unanimously that the freedom enshrined in Art 9 entails, inter alia, the freedom to hold or not hold religious beliefs and to practise or not to practise a religion (para 34). Requiring the applicants to take an oath on the Gospels did constitute a limitation within the meaning of Art 9(2). The restriction concerned was clearly prescribed by law. Even if the aims of the government were legitimate the limitation would in any event be incompatible with Art 9. Requiring the applicants to take the oath on the Gospels was tantamount to requiring elected representatives to swear allegiance to a particular religion, which is not compatible with Art 9.

## 15.2 DISTINCTION BETWEEN HOLDING AND EXPRESSION OF BELIEF

## Handyside v United Kingdom

## (1976) 1 EHRR 737

*Facts:* The applicant was the proprietor of a publishing firm which published, amongst other titles, *The Little Red Schoolbook*. Subsequently, a warrant was issued under s 3 of the Obscene Publications Acts 1959 and 1964 and copies of the book were seized. The applicant was found guilty before a magistrates' court of two offences relating to the publication of the book. In an application lodged with the Commission, the applicant claimed that the action taken by the UK authorities was in breach, inter alia, of his right to freedom of thought, conscience, and belief. The applicant further relied on Art 10 of the Convention.

*Commission:* The Commission declared the application admissible insofar as it related to Art 10, but found that there had been no breach of Art 9, holding in part that there was a distinction to be drawn between the freedom of the applicant to hold the beliefs set out in the publication, but that the dissemination of these beliefs could, in this context, be curbed within the margin of appreciation left to the State. Particular emphasis was placed by both the Commission, and the Court subsequently, on passages in the book advising children to 'be yourself', which 'could have been interpreted as an encouragement to [children to] indulge in precocious activities harmful to them, or even to commit certain criminal offences'.

## (1)   FREEDOM TO WORSHIP

### Manoussakis v Greece

### (1996) 23 EHRR 387

*Facts:*   The applicants were Jehovah's Witnesses living in Crete. In 1983, they rented a room which was to be used 'for all kinds of meetings, weddings, etc of Jehovah's Witnesses'. In 1986, the local public prosecutor's office instituted criminal proceedings against the applicants, and, inter alia, accused them of having 'established and operated a place of worship for religious meetings and ceremonies of followers of another denomination . . . without authorisation from the recognised ecclesiastical authorities'. The applicants were eventually convicted and sentenced each to 3 months' imprisonment and a fine. An appeal was dismissed. The applicants complained, inter alia, of a breach of Art 9 of the Convention.

*Commission:*   The Commission was of the unanimous opinion that Art 9 had been breached.

*Court:*   The Court referred to the fact that Greek law lay down a general prohibition on the establishment of a church or place of worship of any religion that uses the term 'faith' other than the Orthodox religion, and that this prohibition could be lifted only by a formal decision or a specific discretionary measure. The government argued that the Court should take into account both the fact that virtually the entire population of Greece was of the Orthodox faith, and argued further that various sects sought to manifest their influence by 'unlawful and dishonest' means. Although the Court recognised that in this area Contracting States were consistently left a wide margin of appreciation, the relevant Greek legislation allowed far-reaching interference by the political, administrative and ecclesiastical authorities with the exercise of religious freedoms. The respondent State had tended to use these provisions to impose 'rigid, or indeed prohibitive conditions on practice of religious beliefs by certain non-Orthodox movements'. Accordingly, the Court held that in this case there had been a breach of Art 9.

## ISKCON (International Society for Krishna Consciousness) v United Kingdom

### (1994) 18 EHRR CD 133

*Facts:*   The applicant association, a registered religious charity, bought a nineteenth-century rural manor house in 1973 for use as a residential theological college for the promotion of Krishna Consciousness. The local authority stated that planning permission was not required, but later by agreement imposed the following conditions: no more than 1000 people could visit the manor on any day without the local authority's consent; but more than 1000 people could attend on 6 festival days each year. Several years after this agreement, following complaints from local residents about disturbances and the excessive number of worshippers, the local authority served an enforcement notice on ISKCON which alleged a breach of planning control by material change of use of the premises to include a 'religious community and public worship and public entertainment in connection with religious festivals'. ISKCON's appeal was rejected after an inquiry; the court regarded the planning conditions as maintaining a reasonable balance between the rights of worshippers and local residents. ISKCON and a group of representative worshippers alleged violations of Arts 9, 13, 6(1) and Art 1 of the First Protocol in conjunction with Art 14.

*Commission:* Planning control legislation is not usually in itself a violation of Convention rights since there is a wide discretion given to a State in this respect. However, the enforcement notices issued were an interference with ISKCON's freedom of religion, which included 'the freedom to manifest that religion in worship, teaching, practice and observance'. Thus, it was important to decide whether this interference was necessary in a democratic society. Planning legislation is generally accepted to be necessary in modern society in order to protect the rights of other residents and to prevent uncontrolled development. The enforcement notices were proportionate to these legitimate aims since adequate weight had been given to freedom of religion. The refusal of planning permission was based properly on planning grounds and not on any religious discrimination or prejudice. Thus, there was no breach of Art 9.

Further, in relation to Art 1 of the First Protocol, the enforcement notices aimed only to limit the use of the property to that which existed when ISKCON bought the manor; later contractual concessions could not be taken as creating a right regularly to have thousands of worshippers in attendance. The protection of property rights under that Article cannot be used to extend planning permission beyond that granted, since there is a difference between deprivation of possessions and control of the use of property. The planning controls were 'necessary and desirable in modern society in order to preserve and improve town and country landscapes'.

In relation to Art 14, there was no evidence of any racial or religious bias in the local authority's decision or the planning inquiry, and so that argument also failed.

Since ISKCON had never had an arguable claim of any Convention violation, a breach of Art 13 could not be shown. Thus the entire complaint was found to be inadmissible.

# Serif v Greece
## (2001) 31 EHRR 20

*Facts:* The applicant was convicted of offences under Arts 175 and 176 of the Greek Criminal Code for having usurped the functions of a minister of a 'known religion', and for having publicly worn the uniform of such a minister without the right to do so. The applicant had been elected to the position of Mufti of Rodopi in an unofficial election, and had not purported to fulfil any of the judicial functions which were entrusted to a mufti by Greek law. The applicant was given a commutable sentence of 8 months' imprisonment. The conviction was upheld on appeal, although the sentence was modified. The Court of Cassation rejected the final appeal by the applicant, based in part on Arts 9 and 10 of the Convention.

*Court:* The Court found unanimously that there had been a breach of Art 9 of the Convention. The fact that the applicant's conviction was based on the speeches and comments about religion, and appearing in the clothes of a religious leader, meant that there had been an interference with his right under Art 9. The interference in question pursued a legitimate aim, which was to protect public order. Any restriction on the freedom of religion must correspond to a pressing social need. There was no specific mention in relation to the conviction before the Greek court of any acts perpetrated by the applicant with a view to producing legal effects. The Court did 'not consider that, in democratic societies, the State needs to take measures to ensure that religious communities remain or are brought under a unified leadership' (para 52). The Court found that the interference with the applicant's right was not necessary, and was therefore in breach of Art 9.

## Grande Oriente D'Italia Di Palazzo Giustiniani v Italy
## (2002) 34 EHRR 22

*Facts:* The applicant was an association of Italian masonic obedience which had been in existence since 1805. Under Regional Law No 34 of 5 August 1996 the region of Le Marche provided, inter alia, that freemasons would not be eligible for nomination to 15 regional bodies. The applicant complained that these provisions were in breach of the freedom of association provided for within Arts 11, 13 and 14 of the Convention.

*Court:* The Court dealt with the issue only under Art 11. It found that there had been an interference with the right provided for in Art 11, which could be invoked by associations as well as by named individuals. The Court found that the restriction was not necessary in a democratic society, as 'freedom of association is of such importance that it may not be subjected to any form of restriction, even in the case of a person who is a candidate for public office, given that the person concerned does not himself commit a reprehensible act by belonging to the association' (para 26). Neither could the contested provision be justified by reference to the second sentence of Art 11(2). The Court found unanimously that the provisions of Art 11 had been breached.

## (2) STATE CHURCH PERMITTED
## Darby v Sweden
## (1991) 13 EHRR 774

*Facts:* The applicant was required to pay, as a portion of his tax liability, a sum to the Lutheran Church of Sweden ('the church tax'). The applicant submitted an appeal to the County Administrative Court on the ground, inter alia, that he was not a member of the Church of Sweden. Further appeals were rejected, although a reference to the Parliamentary Ombudsman eventually resulted in a change to the Dissenters Tax Act.

*Commission:* The applicant complained that the requirement to pay the church tax infringed his civil rights, and was in breach of Arts 9 and 14 of the Convention. The Commission held that there had been a breach of the Convention.

*Court:* The Court did not find it necessary to consider whether Art 9 had been breached, finding instead that the taxation provisions were discriminatory under Art 14, as they prohibited Swedish citizens to opt out of payment of the church tax if they were not members of the church. This option was not, however, open to the applicant, who was Finnish. Neither the Court nor the Commission found that there were any concerns caused by the strong links between church and State, and the taxation system as it related to members of the church.

## 15.3   RIGHT TO PROMOTE BELIEFS

### Kokkinakis v Greece

### (1993) 17 EHRR 397

*Facts:*   The applicant, a Jehovah's Witness, had been arrested over 60 times for proselytism, and was interned and imprisoned on several occasions. The applicant was arrested on a further occasion and, after a short trial, sentenced to imprisonment and a fine. The judgment made reference, inter alia, to the defendant's attempt 'to proselytise and, directly or indirectly, to intrude on the religious beliefs of Orthodox Christians, with the intention of undermining those beliefs, by taking advantage of their inexperience, their low intellect, and their naivety'. Appeals were dismissed.

*Commission:*   The applicant claimed that his conviction for proselytism was in breach of the rights set out, inter alia, in Art 9 of the Convention. The Commission was unanimous in holding that there had been a violation of this Article.

*Court:*   The applicant had focused on the logical and legal difficulty between drawing even a remotely clear dividing line between proselytism and freedom to change one's religion or belief. Freedom of religion included, the applicant claimed, the freedom to, either alone or with others, in private or in public, to manifest the belief, and to teach and publish. The government drew a distinction between 'bearing witness' and 'proselytism that is not acceptable'. The Court pointed to the fact that the freedom of thought enshrined in Art 9 was of vital importance to believers, but also 'a precious asset for atheists, agnostics, sceptics and the unconcerned'. The right, in principle, to try to convince one's neighbour, however, was necessary to ensure that the 'freedom to change one's belief' did not 'remain a dead letter'.

The Court accepted that the restriction on the right to proselytise in this case both was encompassed within a rule of law and pursued a legitimate aim. However, the Court did not accept in this case, in particular given that the national courts tended to apply the law in a cursory fashion, that the restriction was 'necessary in a democratic society', and, therefore, held that Art 9 had been breached. The measures adopted by the Greek authorities would have been acceptable only insofar as they were reconcilable with the combating of improper proselytism. Proselytism could be restricted if it took the form of exerting improper pressure on people in distress or in need, or the use of violence or brainwashing. In the light of the way in which the law was applied in this case by the domestic authorities, the Court did not consider it necessary to examine whether these factors were legitimate considerations in this case.

# Arrowsmith v United Kingdom

## (1978) 3 EHRR 218

*Facts:* The applicant, a pacifist campaigner, distributed a leaflet to soldiers at an Army centre, including troops who would soon be sent to Northern Ireland. The leaflet urged the soldiers to go absent without leave rather than serve in Ireland. The police asked the applicant to stop distributing the leaflets, but she refused and was arrested for conduct likely to cause a breach of the peace. She was convicted of statutory offences under the Incitement to Disaffection Act 1934 and sentenced to 18 months' imprisonment. The Court of Appeal dismissed her appeal finding that she had no lawful excuse or defence, even though the DPP had refused to prosecute in similar recent cases, but reduced her prison sentence. The applicant alleged breaches of Arts 5, 9, 10(2) and 14.

*Commission:* The Commission found that there had been a difference of treatment between the applicant and her companions, who had not been prosecuted. The arrest, prosecution and conviction had interfered with the applicant's freedom of expression, but 'they were motivated, not by her holding particular opinions, including pacifist views, but by the fact that her action in distributing the leaflets constituted the offence of incitement to disaffection'. Further, the difference of treatment was objectively justified by being based on differences of facts between the cases; the other protesters had heeded police warnings to cease distribution of leaflets. Hence there was no violation of Art 14 in conjunction with Art 10.

# 15.4  RELATIONSHIP WITH CHILDREN AND CHILD CUSTODY

## Hoffman v Austria

## (1993) 17 EHRR 293

*Facts:* After the applicant became a Jehovah's Witness, her ex-husband gained custody of their two children, who had been living with their mother. The domestic court held that, although removing the children from their mother might cause them distress, this had to be balanced against the dangers involved in their mother's religion. For example, the children's social life might suffer as part of a religious minority; there were medical risks involved in the faith due to its rejection of blood transfusions; and it was illegal under Austrian law for one parent to change a child's religion without the other's consent. The applicant alleged, inter alia, breaches of Arts 9 and 14.

*Commission:* The Commission argued that the domestic courts 'applied a criterion concerning the duties in the area of religious education which will normally exclude any Jehovah's Witness in a mixed marriage from being granted custody in the case of divorce ... Wherever a religious association is a lawful organisation it must be the consequence that a differentiation because of membership in this denomination needs very stringent justification'. Such justification could not be seen in the arguments made by the domestic court; a blood transfusion could be ordered by a court if necessary, and there is no great social stigma attached to minority religions. Thus, Art 14 had been breached, and the Commission did not feel it necessary to deal with the alleged breach of Art 9 since it had substantially the same issues as those above.

*Court:*   The Court agreed that there had been a violation. The domestic court had given too much weight to the illegality of changing the children's religion when it had not even been established that this would happen. The interests of the children should have been given the greatest weight, since Austria is a signatory to Art 5 of the Seventh Protocol, which also states that spouses are equal in parental rights. The lower courts had used expert psychological opinion as the basis of their judgments and had given custody to the mother; in contrast, the final domestic court had looked mainly at the mother's religious beliefs and behaviour. The discrimination was, therefore, unjustified since 'a distinction based essentially on a difference in religion alone is not acceptable'.

# 15.5   LIMITATIONS ON RIGHTS TO PRACTISE

## (1)   IN CONTEXT OF EMPLOYMENT

## Ahmad v United Kingdom

## (1982) 4 EHRR 126

*Facts:*   The applicant was a primary school teacher for special needs in London and a devout Muslim. He worked first at a school which was close to a mosque and asked to be allowed to be absent from school for about 45 minutes after the lunch break on Fridays in order to attend prayers. When he was transferred to another school, serious problems arose since he continued to be absent on Friday afternoons without permission. The applicant complained to the Inner London Education Authority (ILEA) that he had a right to attend the mosque for Friday prayer, and asked for the school timetable to be adjusted to allow this. The ILEA informed him that he could choose to work part-time, in effect for 4½ days a week, but if he continued to be absent for part of Friday afternoons, this change would be compulsory. The applicant resigned and his claim for unfair dismissal failed. He then alleged a breach of Art 9 in that 'a Muslim, who took his religious duty seriously, could never accept employment as a full-time teacher, but must be content with the lesser emoluments of part-time service, and would thus also be excluded from opportunities for promotion'.

*Commission:*   Freedom of religion under Art 9(1) includes the right to worship 'in community with others'. But 'even a person at liberty may, in the exercise of his freedom to manifest his religion, have to take into account his particular professional or contractual position'. The applicant had accepted a job which required him to work on Friday afternoons, and had not disclosed that he might need time off on Fridays until he had been employed for 6 years. Thus, there had been no interference with his freedom of religion under Art 9(1).

# Stedman (Louise) v United Kingdom
## (1997) 23 EHRR CD 169

*Facts:* The applicant was a practising Christian employed by a private company. She refused to sign a contract which would have required her to work Sundays on a rota basis, and was dismissed from her employment. She argued that her dismissal breached Arts 9, 8, 14 and 6.

*Commission:* The applicant alleged, first, that her dismissal was a violation of her freedom to manifest her religion in worship, practice and observance, and that the State had failed to secure that freedom. The Commission found that she had not been dismissed because of her religious beliefs but because she had refused to work certain hours. She had been free to resign and had not been pressured to change her religious views or to refrain from manifesting them. Thus, there was no breach of Art 9.

In addition, the applicant claimed an interference with her right to respect for her family life by requiring her to work on Sundays. The Commission found that 'given the almost inevitable compromise and balance between work and family commitments, particularly in families where both partners work', the requirement to work a 5-day week on a rota which included Sundays was not an interference with family life and so did not breach Art 8.

She also alleged religious discrimination in that Christians were not given the status of a minority religious group and received less protection than other religions in respect of religious holy days. The Commission found that her dismissal was not based upon her religious convictions and there was no evidence that she had been treated differently from employees of any other religious conviction. Thus, there was no evidence of discrimination and no breach of Art 14.

# Thlimmenos v Greece
## (2001) 31 EHRR 15

*Facts:* The applicant was a Jehovah's Witness who was convicted of insubordination before the Athens Permanent Army Tribunal for having refused to wear military uniform at a time of general mobilisation. The applicant served 2 years and one day of a prison sentence. In June 1988 the applicant finished second of 60 candidates in an examination to be admitted to the profession of chartered accountancy. However, the relevant professional board refused to appoint him on the grounds that he had been convicted of a felony. Appeals were unsuccessful.

*Court:* The Court was unanimous in finding that there had been a breach of Art 14 in conjunction with Art 9. Although Art 14 has no independent existence, for it to become applicable it suffices that the facts of a case fall within the ambit of another substantive provision of the Convention. While the Convention does not guarantee the right to freedom of profession, the applicant's complaint related to the fact that no distinction was made between persons convicted of offences committed exclusively because of their religious beliefs and persons convicted of other offences. The argument therefore was that the applicant was discriminated against on grounds of religion, contrary to

Art 9. While the State would have legitimate reasons to exclude those convicted of certain offences from professions 'a conviction for refusing on religious or philosophical grounds to wear the military uniform cannot imply any dishonesty or moral turpitude likely to undermine the offender's ability to exercise this profession' (para 47). The State in this case had violated the applicant's right by failing to introduce the appropriate exceptions to the rule barring persons convicted of a felony from the profession of chartered accountants (para 48).

## (2)   IN THE MILITARY

### Kalac v Turkey

### (1997) unreported

*Facts:*   The applicant, a judge advocate in the Turkish airforce, was compulsorily retired on the grounds that 'he had adopted unlawful fundamentalist attitudes'. An appeal was dismissed, and the applicant complained that his removal, on the ground that he was a practising Muslim, constituted a breach of Art 9 of the Convention.

*Commission:*   The Commission was unanimous in holding that the Convention had been breached.

*Court:*   The government argued that the applicant's compulsory retirement was not an interference with his freedom of belief or conscience, but was intended to remove from military service a person who had manifested his lack of loyalty to the Turkish nation which was founded on secularism. Facilities enabling members of the armed forces to practise their religion were in fact available, but the applicant's membership of the Suleyman sect, 'known to have unlawful fundamentalist tendencies', was held to constitute a breach of military discipline. The Court, referring to the *Kokkinakis* judgment (15.3), noted that a freedom to manifest one's beliefs was implicit in Art 9, but that not every act motivated or inspired by religion is protected. In choosing to enter the armed forces, the applicant had accepted a series of limitations on his freedoms which could not be imposed on civilians. The applicant would have been able to observe the normal obligations through which a Muslim practises his religion, and the Court concluded that, in this case, the authorities had not breached Art 9 in ordering the applicant's compulsory retirement.

## 15.6   OBLIGATIONS ON PUBLIC SERVICE EMPLOYEES

### Wille v Liechtenstein

### (2000) 30 EHRR 558

*Facts:*   The applicant was a former member of the Liechtenstein Government, and was then appointed to be President of the Administrative Court. In 1995, at a public lecture dealing with constitutional questions, which was reported in the press, the applicant suggested that the Constitutional Court was competent to decide on the 'interpretation of the Constitution in case of disagreement between the Prince (Government) and the Diet'. This followed a dispute between His Serene Highness Prince Hans-Adam II of Liechtenstein and the Government on political competencies in relation to the accession to the European Economic Area. This dispute was subsequently resolved on the basis of a common declaration. Following the reports of the lecture the Prince wrote a private letter to the applicant questioning his suitability for public office and his commitment to uphold the current constitution of Liechtenstein. The Prince indicated that he would not appoint the applicant again to any public office should he be proposed. Following the end of the applicant's first term of office the Diet proposed his reappointment, and the Prince refused his assent. The applicant complained, relying, inter alia, on Art 10.

*Court:* The right of recruitment to the civil service was deliberately omitted from the Convention, and the refusal to appoint a person as a civil servant cannot as such provide the basis for a complaint under the Convention (para 41). This does not mean, however, that once appointed a person cannot rely on the Convention when he has been dismissed if that dismissal violates one of the rights afforded under the Convention. The Court found that the letter of the Prince, and subsequent actions, constituted an interference by the State with the applicant's freedom of expression. The announcement by the Prince of his intention not to reappoint the applicant had a chilling effect on the applicant's freedom of expression, and was likely to discourage him from making such statements in the future. The lecture given by the applicant dealt with matters of constitutional law, and inevitably raised political questions. The views expressed were not untenable as they were shared by a number of persons in Liechtenstein. The Prince's subsequent action was disproportionate, and was not necessary in a democratic society. The Court found by 16 votes to 1 that there had been a breach of Art 10.

# Chapter 16

# PRESS FREEDOMS, PRIVACY, LIBEL AND SLANDER

## 16.1 JOURNALISTIC FREEDOM OF EXPRESSION AND PUBLIC INTEREST

### (1) CONFIDENTIALITY OF SOURCES

### Goodwin v United Kingdom

### (1996) 22 EHRR 123

*Facts:* The applicant was employed by Morgan-Grampian (Publishers) Ltd as a trainee journalist with *The Engineer*. Following the receipt of unsolicited information about Tetra Ltd, a computer software company, the applicant telephoned Tetra to check the accuracy of the information. The company suspected the information came from a missing draft of Tetra's confidential corporate plan, and obtained an ex parte interim injunction from the High Court restraining publication of any information derived from the corporate plan. All national newspapers and relevant journals were informed of the injunction. Notwithstanding this measure, Tetra wished to bring proceedings against the source for recovery of the missing document, an injunction to prevent further publication and damages for expenses.

The High Court ordered the applicant to disclose his notes and reveal his source on the basis that it was 'in the interests of justice' within the meaning of the Contempt of Court Act 1981, s 10. The order for disclosure was granted on the grounds of threat of severe financial damage to the business interests of the company, and consequently to the livelihood of their employees. In the Court of Appeal, Lord Donaldson described the threat as a 'time bomb' which could be effectively defused only by identifying the source. Leave was granted to appeal to the House of Lords. In construing the phrase 'in the interests of justice', Lord Bridge conducted a 'balancing exercise' involving a subjective assessment based on the evidence produced by the parties. The House of Lords held unanimously that disclosure of the journalist's notes did 'override the policy underlying the statutory protection of sources'.

*Commission:* The applicant complained that the order requiring him to reveal an anonymous source constituted an interference with his freedom of expression guaranteed by Art 10. The Commission was of the opinion that Art 10 required that any compulsion imposed upon a journalist to reveal his source should be limited to exceptional circumstances where vital public or individual interests were at stake. It was noted that the company had obtained an injunction restraining publication of any information derived from the source. There was no evidence that the source had conveyed the information to customers or competitors. Further, the Commission was not convinced that financial harm would have resulted from revealing the information and expressed concern that a disclosure order could have a 'potential chilling effect on the readiness of people to give information to journalists'. Finding no exceptional circumstances that would have justified a restriction on the applicant's right to freedom of expression, the Commission concluded there had been a violation of Art 10.

*Court:*   It was accepted that an order for disclosure of the documents did constitute an interference with the applicant's freedom of expression. Accordingly, the issue before the Court was limited to whether the interference was justified under Art 10(2). Relevant domestic law restricting freedom of expression was accepted as satisfying the requirement that any interference must be 'prescribed by law'. The applicant's argument that the Contempt of Court Act 1981, s 10 was too imprecise was rejected. Following consideration of national case-law, the Court rejected the argument that domestic courts had unlimited discretion to determine whether an order for disclosure should be made in the interests of justice. Moreover, it was not disputed that the protection of the company's financial interests amounted to a legitimate aim. Thus, the Court moved to consider whether there was a 'reasonable relationship of pro-portionality between the legitimate aim pursued by the disclosure order and the means deployed to achieve that aim'. This involved consideration of whether the necessity for the disclosure order had been 'convincingly established'. The Court considered that the justification for the disclosure order must be considered in the light of the case as a whole. The House of Lords had granted Tetra an order for disclosure on the basis that there was a threat of severe financial damage to their business. The purpose of the disclosure order was to bring about the same result as the ex parte injunction which prevented publication of information derived from the plan. In fact, the injunction was effective in stopping publication and the risk of the information being disseminated through the press was minimal.

The Court arrived at the conclusion that 'the disclosure order merely served to reinforce the injunction, the additional restriction on freedom of expression which it entailed was not supported by sufficient reasons for the purposes of Art 10(2) of the Convention'.

*Note:*   In a dissenting opinion, seven judges expressed concern that the Court could not undertake a detailed assessment of the company's interests, and that the domestic court was in a better position to evaluate the strength of conflicting interests on the basis of the evidence. In the opinion of the minority, the conclusion reached by the national court was within the margin of appreciation allowed to the national authorities.

## (2)   CONTEMPT OF COURT

### Sunday Times v United Kingdom
### (1979) 2 EHRR 245

*Facts:*   The applicants were a group of journalists, the publisher and the editor of the *Sunday Times*, which had published an article criticising the law in relation to claims for damages against drug companies, including Distillers, the manufacturers of thalido-mide, and urged Distillers to offer much higher settlements than it had previously done. There were almost 400 actions for negligence pending against Distillers at that time. Distillers approached the Attorney-General, arguing that the publication of the article was in contempt of court. However, the Attorney-General decided not to bring any charges. The *Sunday Times*' editor wished to publish a further article containing evidence which he believed would show that Distillers had not taken sufficient steps to ensure the safety of thalidomide for use in pregnancy before it was marketed to the public. The Attorney-General was granted an injunction by the House of Lords, which restrained publication of the second article since it would be contempt of court. The Commission found that there had been a breach of Art 10.

*Court:* The Court held that the injunction was an interference 'prescribed by law' within the meaning of Art 10, although it was granted to prevent the common law offence of contempt of court rather than a statutory offence. The words 'prescribed by law' are to be interpreted 'in a way that reconciles them as far as possible and is most appropriate in order to realise the aim and achieve the object of the treaty'. 'Law' includes common law, as long as the rule in question is clear, certain and consistent. The English law of contempt is unclear in its scope but its application to the proposed article's publication was foreseeable. The Court also considered that the injunction could be justified under Art 10(2) as maintaining the authority of the judiciary. The most difficult issue was whether the injunction was necessary in a democratic society and proportionate to the aim pursued. The Court held that the proposed article was written in moderate terms and was well balanced. Thus, the effect upon a reader would not have had adverse consequences for the judiciary. While courts are the 'forum for the settlement of disputes, this does not mean that there can be no prior discussion of disputes elsewhere, be it in specialised journals, in the general press or amongst the public at large'. The public, including thalidomide victims and their families, should be deprived of the information in the article only 'if it appeared absolutely certain that its diffusion would have posed a threat to the "authority of the judiciary"'. The thalidomide case was of such great public concern that the facts should be in the public domain. Thus, the injunction was not necessary and was disproportionate, and so formed a violation of Art 10.

*Note:* Nine dissenting judges gave a joint opinion which argued that the injunction was 'necessary' and that the words 'authority and impartiality of the judiciary' had been inserted into Art 10(2) specifically to allow an exception for the common law of contempt. Therefore, the UK should have been given greater scope with the law of contempt than was evident in the Court's judgment. It could be argued that the Court gave States an almost invisible margin of appreciation in this case.

## (3)   PUBLIC INTEREST

### Jersild v Denmark

### (1994) 19 EHRR 1

*Facts:* The applicant, a television journalist, interviewed a group of racist youths in Copenhagen as part of a documentary which was being made about the rise of violent racism among Danish youths. Several minutes of the interviews were broadcast, during which the youths made many racist, xenophobic and offensive statements. The youths were convicted of criminal offences related to the making of racist statements and the applicant was convicted of aiding and abetting their offences by causing the racist statements to be made public. The domestic courts considered that journalistic coverage of extreme views could be justified only if it was carried out with greater balance than the documentary in question had demonstrated. The applicant alleged a violation of Art 10 in respect of his criminal conviction and subsequent fine.

*Commission:*   The Commission found that there had been a violation of Art 10. The question was whether the interference with the applicant's rights was justified as necessary in a democratic society according to Art 10(2). In order to answer this question, it was necessary to look at the whole broadcast, not merely at the racist statements made during it. Although the Convention condemned racial discrimination and racism, the context within which the racist statements were made was such that it ridiculed those who held such beliefs and made it clear that the programme-makers themselves did not hold such racist views. The programme raised issues of great public concern, and the applicant's intentions were 'not to disseminate racist ideology but rather to counter it through exposure' by dissemination of an anti-racist message. Criminal sanctions must not be allowed to discourage such valuable functions of the media. Thus, there had been a breach of Art 10.

*Court:*   Whilst the Court emphasised the importance of combating racism and racial discrimination, it considered significant the fact that the applicant did not make racist statements himself but merely aided their dissemination in his role as a journalist. Although the media must not overstep the boundaries created in order to protect the rights and reputations of others, when information and ideas are of public interest then 'not only does the press have the task of imparting such information and ideas: the public also has a right to receive them'. The media act as a public watchdog and it is for them, not for courts, to decide which reporting techniques are appropriate to this task. The documentary, taken as a whole, had an anti-racist message and aimed to raise public awareness and concern. Criminal sanctions were therefore not justified in this case and Art 10 had been breached.

## Fressoz and Roire v France

## (2001) 31 EHRR 2

*Facts:*   The applicants were the former editor and a journalist working on the weekly satirical newspaper *Le Canard enchaîné*. In 1989 the paper published an article based in part on copies of tax returns submitted by a senior official within the Peugeot company. A criminal complaint was made relating to the returns, but the person responsible for removing them from the tax authority's files could not be identified. The applicants, however, were committed for trial on charges of obtaining and handling confidential information and stolen photocopies. On appeal the applicants were convicted, and this sentence was upheld by the Court of Cassation. The applicants relied on Art 10, and the Commission declared their application admissible.

*Court:*   The Court found unanimously that there had been a breach of Art 10. The government argued first that the applicants had not exhausted domestic remedies as they had not raised arguments relating to the application of Art 10 before the domestic courts. The Court found, however, that the issue of freedom of expression was at issue before the domestic courts, if only implicitly, and that the legal arguments had therefore included a complaint connected with Art 10.

There was no doubt that the applicants' rights to freedom of expression had been subject to interference, and that this was prescribed by law, and that this prescription served the legitimate aims of protecting the reputation or rights of others and preventing the disclosure of information received in confidence. The question then was that of whether the interference was 'necessary in a democratic society'. The Court was not convinced by the arguments of the government to the effect that the article was not in the public interest. It was published at a time of unrest in the car industry, with workers requesting pay rises that management was resisting, and the article showed that a senior manager had received a significant pay rise. However, journalists 'cannot, in principle, be released from their duty to obey the ordinary criminal law on the basis that Article 10 affords them protection' (para 52). The documents published had the effect of disclosing information which 'might have already been known to a large number of people' and 'accordingly there was no overriding requirement for the information to be protected as confidential' (para 53). The Court found therefore that there was not 'a reasonable relationship of proportionality between the legitimate aim pursued by the journalists' conviction and the means deployed to achieve that aim, given the interest a democratic society has in ensuring and preserving freedom of the press' (para 56).

# Ceylan v Turkey
## (2000) 30 EHRR 73

*Facts:* The applicant, who was president of the Petroleum Workers' Union, wrote an article in a weekly newspaper in Istanbul entitled 'The time has come for the workers to speak out – tomorrow it will be too late'. Following publication the Public Prosecutor at the Istanbul National Security Court indicted the applicant on charges of non-public incitement to hatred and hostility contrary to the Turkish Criminal Code. The applicant was found guilty, and sentenced to imprisonment plus a fine. The applicant's appeal to the Court of Cassation was rejected. The applicant served his full sentence, and lost his position as president of the union.

*Court:* The applicant's case was dealt with only in relation to Art 10. There was no doubt that there had been an interference with the exercise of the applicant's right to freedom of expression. Neither was there any doubt that this interference was prescribed by law for the purposes of Art 9(2). The applicant did not make any submission regarding whether the law served a legitimate aim. The Court accepted that, having regard to the sensitive nature of the security situation in south-east Turkey, the conviction could be said to have been in furtherance of the aims cited by the government (para 28). The Court reiterated the arguments it set out in eg *Fressoz and Roire v France* (2001) 31 EHRR 2 to the effect that restrictions on the freedom of expression must be construed strictly. Although the style of the article was 'virulent and the criticism of the Turkish authorities' actions in the relevant part of the country acerbic' (para 33), there 'is little scope under [Art 10] for restrictions on political speech or on debate of matters of public interest' (para 34). The background of the case was linked to the prevention of terrorism, but the applicant was writing in his capacity as a trade union leader, was a player on the political scene, and the article did not encourage the use of violence or armed resistance or insurrection. Taking this into account, and noting the severity of the sentence imposed, the Court concluded, by 16 votes to 1, that the conviction of the applicant was in violation of Art 10.

## Arslan v Turkey
## (2001) 31 EHRR 9

*Facts:* The applicant was the author of a prize-winning book called *History in Mourning, 33 Bullets*, which was first published in 1989, and dealt with the Kurdish question in Turkey. The Istanbul National Security Court conducted an investigation into the applicant, and had copies of the book seized as an interim measure. The public prosecutor charged the applicant with disseminating separatist propaganda. The applicant was subsequently convicted and sentenced to a term of imprisonment. Following the introduction of a new Prevention of Terrorism Act in 1991 the applicant's conviction was quashed and copies of the book returned. A new edition was published in 1991, and a new indictment was issued against the author and publisher. The applicant was again convicted, and sentenced to prison and a fine was imposed. An appeal was declared inadmissible. The applicant relied on Art 10.

*Court:* The Court held unanimously that there had been a violation of Art 10. The Court reiterated the arguments it made in *Fressoz v Roire* (see above). The book in the present case was in the form of a literary historical narrative. It was not intended to be a neutral description of historical events, and the author was highly critical of the actions of the Turkish authorities in the south-east of the country. However, there is little scope under the Convention for restrictions on political speech or on debate on questions of public interest. While several passages of the book 'paint an extremely negative picture of the population of Turkish origin and give the narrative a hostile tone, they do not constitute an incitement to violence, armed resistance or an uprising' (para 48). The Court was struck by the severity of the sentence, and the persistence of the prosecutor's efforts to secure a conviction. In conclusion the Court found that the applicant's conviction was disproportionate to the aims pursued and was not necessary in a democratic society.

## Erdogdu v Turkey
## (2002) 34 EHRR 50

*Facts:* The applicant was the editor of a periodical, the *Iscilerin Sesi*, based in Istanbul. In Issue 40 an article written by a reader was published under the heading 'The Kurdish Problem is a Turkish Problem'. The public prosecutor instituted criminal proceedings against the applicant, and in 1993 the National Security Court found the applicant guilty, sentencing him to 6 months' imprisonment and a fine of 50,000,000 Turkish liras. On appeal this sentence was modified. An appeal to the Court of Cassation was unsuccessful.

*Court:* The applicant relied on Art 10 before the Court, which held unanimously that there had been a violation of the Article. The key question before the Court was that of whether the restriction on freedom of expression was 'necessary in a democratic society'. In the Court's view it was clear that the article at the heart of the action was 'written in the form of a political speech, both in its content and the terms used' (para 61). The article was not 'neutral', and was intended to stigmatise the dominant ideology of the State, and the conduct of the authorities. However, the author did not call for violence, and did not in any way associate himself with the PKK. The national authorities had 'failed to have sufficient regard to the freedom of the press and to the public's right to be informed of a different perspective on the Kurdish problem, irrespective of how unpalatable that perspective may be for them (para 71). The measure could not be construed as being 'necessary in a democratic society'.

# News Verlags GmbH & Co KG v Austria
## (2001) 31 EHRR 8

*Facts:* The applicant company was the publisher of the magazine *News*. In 1993 it published a special issue of the magazine, which dealt with a letter-bomb campaign alleged to be initiated by members of a far right group, and for which B had been charged. Pictures of B with accompanying text identifying him as the bomber were published. B brought an action based on s 78 of the Austrian Copyright Act, which was upheld by the Court of Appeal in Vienna. The judgment had the effect of prohibiting the publication of B's picture in connection with reports on the criminal proceedings against him irrespective of the accompanying text. A further claim was upheld subsequently prohibiting the applicants from publishing B's picture in connection with statements in which B was referred to as the perpetrator of the letter-bomb attacks. These judgments were upheld by the Supreme Court. The applicant's complaint was based on the application of Art 10.

*Court:* The Court recalled that its well-established case-law established that the adjective 'necessary' within the meaning of Art 10(2) implies the existence of a pressing social need. In the present case the articles giving rise to the injunction were published against the background of intense public interest in what had been a spectacular series of letter-bomb attacks. B, being a right-wing extremist, had entered the public scene well before the attacks. The press has a duty in a democratic society to report and comment on court proceedings, which, 'provided that they do not overstep the bounds ... contribute to their publicity and are thus perfectly consonant with the requirement under article 6(1) of the Convention that hearings be public' (para 56). There may be good reasons for prohibiting the publication of a picture of an accused person, but no reasons to that effect were advanced in this case. Having regard in particular to the fact that it was not the use of the pictures by the applicants, but only their placement in relation to accompanying text, which interfered with B's rights the Court found that 'the absolute prohibition of the publication of B's picture went further than was necessary to protect B against defamation or against violations of the presumption of innocence' (para 59). The Court was unanimous in finding that Art 10 had been violated.

*UNITED KINGDOM CASES*

## Campbell (Naomi) v Mirror Group Newspapers Ltd
### QBD, [2002] EWHC 499, [2002] EMLR 617

*Facts:*   The defendant published a number of articles relating to the claimant. The articles focused on the fact that the claimant was, contrary to earlier assertions, a user of narcotics and had attended meetings of narcotics anonymous. A photograph was published of the claimant leaving a narcotics anonymous meeting. The claimant argued that the articles were in breach of her privacy, and that they should not be published unless there was an overriding public interest in doing so.

*Held:*   There was a private interest of the claimant worthy of protection, and her activities had the necessary quality of confidence about them. Information given to the publisher relating to her attendance at the narcotics anonymous meetings must have been given in circumstances which implied that they were confidential. It was recognised that awarding the claimant damages as sought would have a chilling effect on the media, but celebrities were entitled to a degree of privacy in accordance with Art 8. In particular confidential information and sensitive personal data should be kept private unless there was an overriding public interest in publishing it. In the present case the public did have an interest in knowing that the claimant had lied about her drug addiction, but a balance had to be struck between this interest and the claimant's right to privacy. Here the balance should be struck in favour of the claimant, and damages were awarded.

## Ashdown (Paddy) MP v Telegraph Group Ltd
### Court of Appeal, [2001] EWCA Civ 1142, [2001] UKHRR 1242

*Facts:*   The defendant newspaper had published a leaked secret minute written by the claimant detailing a meeting held with the Prime Minister. The claimant had argued, inter alia, that this was in breach of copyright. The defendant had argued that to restrict its right to publish such copyright material was to breach its rights to freedom of expression under Art 10 of the Convention. At first instance the judge had held that where an infringer of copyright could not rely on one of the statutory exceptions set out in the Copyright, Designs and Patents Act 1988 it could not seek to rely on the Convention in the alternative. The defendant appealed.

*Held:*   The freedom of expression guaranteed in the Convention did not normally confer the right to use another's work, and the form of literary work did not normally prevent the publication of information contained in that literary work. However, there might exceptionally be some cases in which the right of freedom of expression could come into conflict with the protection provided for by the Copyright, Designs and Patents Act 1988. In such a case the court was obliged to apply that Act in a manner which was consistent with the right of freedom of expression. In the present case the defendant had reproduced more of the document than it needed to do so in order to make its points, and the minute was deliberately edited in such a way as to provide the most colourful account. It was not the case that Art 10 allowed the defendant to profit from this use of copyright without payment to the author of the work. Appeal dismissed.

## Douglas (Michael) and Zeta Jones (Catherine) and Northern & Shell plc v Hello!

### Court of Appeal, [2001] UKHRR 223

*Facts:* The claimants were celebrities who celebrated their much-publicised wedding in New York. They sold the rights in photographs of the wedding to the proprietor of *OK!* magazine, the third claimant. Nine photographs of the wedding came into the possession of the rival *Hello!* magazine, and the claimants sought an injunction to prevent the publication of those photographs, relying on Art 8 of the Convention. At first instance an injunction was granted, and the defendants appealed.

*Held:* A general right to privacy was now recognised in English law in accordance with the obligations imposed by the HRA 1998 and Art 8 of the Convention. It was clear, however, that this right was not unfettered, and that there were different degrees of privacy. In the present case the wedding was not a private one, and the commercial sale of photographs had already restricted the privacy attached to it. An injunction preventing the publication of the photographs would not be appropriate, but the claimants would be able to seek damages following publication.

## Thompson and Venables v News Group Newspapers Ltd, Associated Newspapers Ltd and MGN Ltd

### QBD, Family Court, [2001] UKHRR 628

*Facts:* The claimants, who had been convicted of the murder of James Bulger while children, benefited from injunctions in place restricting the information which the media could publish. At the age of 18 these injunctions were to come to an end. The claimants, supported by the Attorney-General and the Official Solicitor, sought an extension of the injunctions such that they would continue to operate after the release of the claimants. The claimants relied in part on Arts 2, 3 and 8 of the Convention, and the court considered also the application of Art 10.

*Held:* There was sufficient evidence to convince the court that the claimants were, uniquely, at serious risk of attack and injury if their identities and whereabouts were disclosed following their release from custody. The right to life enshrined in Art 2 of the Convention required that steps be taken to protect the claimants from such attacks. It had already been recognised in cases such as *Douglas (Michael) and Zeta Jones (Catherine) and Northern & Shell plc v Hello!* (see above) that Art 8 could be invoked to protect the privacy of claimants in appropriate situations, although this had to be balanced against the right of the press to publish information of public interest, a right which could only exceptionally be curtailed. In this case it was necessary to grant indefinite injunctions restraining the media from publishing information which could lead to the whereabouts of the claimants being discovered.

## (4)  DEFAMATION

## Oberschlick v Austria (No 2)

## (1998) 25 EHRR 357

*Facts:*  A politician, the leader of the Austrian Freedom Party, had made a speech in which he praised all soldiers who had fought during the Second World War, even on the German side, and stated that only these men had the right to freedom of opinion since they had won it in battle and founded democratic society. The applicant, a journalist and the editor of a periodical, printed the speech with a commentary in which he stated that the politician was an idiot ('Trottel') rather than a Nazi. The applicant was convicted of defamation and insult offences, and an order was made for seizure of the relevant issue of the periodical. The applicant alleged a violation of Art 10.

*Commission:*  The Commission found that Art 10 had been breached by the unjustified interference with the applicant's freedom of expression. Although the protection of the reputation of others is a legitimate aim and the words in question could be considered insulting, 'in exceptional circumstances a statement which could be considered as insulting may be justified or at least excusable'. The applicant's statement was not an insult aimed at the politician but rather a reasoned critique of the latter's views, and as such was an expression of strong opinion in the same way as the politician's speech had been.

*Court:*  Freedom of expression extends to words which offend, shock or disturb, and politicians by definition are open to scrutiny and criticism by the media and public. The applicant's insult must be considered in the context of the whole article and of the speech which it criticised. The politician 'clearly intended to be provocative and consequently to arouse strong reactions'. Thus, the applicant's words were an opinion and not a gratuitous personal attack, and Art 10 was breached by his conviction. Two dissenting judges, however, argued that Art 10 should not be used in this way to 'protect primitive, fourth-rate journalism which, not having the qualities required to present serious arguments, has recourse to provocation and gratuitous insults to attract potential readers'.

## Thorgeir Thorgeirson v Iceland

## (1992) 14 EHRR 843

*Facts:*  The applicant, an Icelandic writer, published two newspaper articles on the subject of police brutality, alleging that unnamed officers were 'beasts in uniform' and that there were many unknown victims of police beatings and bullying. He also alleged that a particular paralysed man whom he had met in a hospital was one such victim; it appears that this was not true. He was convicted of criminal defamation against unspecified police officers and fined. He alleged breach of Art 10 by his conviction and of Art 6 by the fact that the public prosecutor had not attended all court sessions during the applicant's trial, leaving one judge in the role of court investigator and prosecutor, and hence the trial had not been impartial.

*Commission:*  The Commission was of the opinion that there had been no breach of Art 6, but that there had been a breach of Art 10.

*Court:* As regards Art 6, the Court rejected the applicant's argument of unfair trial since the judge in question had not taken on the prosecutorial role during the prosecutor's absence. In respect of Art 10, the Court stated that there was no reason to distinguish this case from cases such as *Oberschlick v Austria No 2* (1998) 25 EHRR 357, and others (see **16.1**(5)), which concern political comment; discussion of all matters of public concern should be dealt with similarly under the Convention. The applicant had fairly reported 'rumours' or 'stories' emanating from other sources in society and so it was unreasonable of the trial court to expect him to be able to establish the objective truth of these stories in order to avoid conviction for criminal defamation. Further, his criticisms were not of the whole police force, but of a few officers whose behaviour was a matter of serious public concern; thus, his conviction for damaging the reputation of the whole police force was not justified and might serve to discourage open discussion of matters of public concern. Thus, there was a breach of Art 10.

# Dalban v Romania
## (2001) 31 EHRR 39

*Facts:* The applicant, who died in 1998, was a journalist who ran a local weekly magazine called *Cronica Roma can*. In 1992 an article written by the applicant, headed 'Roman *IAS* defrauded of tens of millions' appeared in the magazine. The article related to a series of alleged frauds perpetrated by Mr GS, the chief executive of a State-owned agricultural company. The articles also named a senator, RT. An information was laid against the applicant on the basis that the article was defamatory, and he was convicted of criminal libel, resulting in a suspended prison sentence and an order that he pay damages in the sum of 300,000 lei. In addition, the applicant was banned from practising his profession for an indefinite period. The applicant appealed unsuccessfully save that the professional ban was set aside. Other organisations followed the story, and the Romanian Parliament's Committee for the Investigation of Abuses requested a public prosecutor to examine the allegations made. The Procurator-General applied to the Supreme Court to have the applicant's conviction overturned. The Court acquitted the applicant in relation to GS, finding that he had acted in good faith. In relation to RT the Court quashed the conviction, but held that the applicant, who had by now died, had been rightly convicted.

*Court:* The applicant's widow had standing to continue to pursue the case, brought on the basis of an infringement of Art 10. The judgment of the Romanian Supreme Court was not such as to deprive the applicant of his status as 'victim', and it lacked the 'adequate redress' as required by the Court's case-law (para 44). It was not disputed that the applicant's conviction constituted 'interference by public authority', and that this had been prescribed by law in accordance with Art 10(2). The question was whether, in the light of the case as a whole, the national courts had acted within their margin of appreciation. The articles related to a matter of strong public interest, and the duty of the press is to impart information and ideas on all matters of public interest. There was no evidence that the information given in the articles was totally untrue or designed to fuel a defamation campaign, and the conviction of the applicant was found, unanimously, to have been in violation of Art 10.

# Nilsen and Johnsen v Norway
## (2000) 30 EHRR 878

*Facts:* Both applicants were police officers, the former being President of the Norwegian Police Association, and the latter being Chairman of the Bergen Police Association. A book was published which suggested that the Bergen police were responsible each year for some 360 incidents of excessive and illegal use of force. A heated debate followed, with further publications making a series of allegations, and the Prosecutor-General's investigation concluded generally that the charges made were unfounded. The Norwegian Police Association and its Bergen branch brought defamation proceedings against one of the book's authors seeking to have various comments made by him declared null and void. This, following the judgment in *Thorgeir Thorgeirson v Iceland* (1992) 14 EHRR 843, was withdrawn. The author in turn instituted defamation proceedings against the applicants in which he was successful. The applicants appealed to the Supreme Court, which rejected both appeals. Later, the Supreme Court reopened a number of cases relating to police brutality in Bergen, and concluded that it was highly probable that some police officers had given false evidence during the original investigations.

*Court:* The Court held, by 12 votes to 5, that there had been a violation of Art 10 of the Convention. A significant feature of the present case was that the applicants had been sanctioned in respect of statements they had made as representatives of police associations in response to certain reports publicising allegations of police misconduct. There could be no doubt that any restrictions on the right to impart information on arguable allegations of police misconduct call for strict scrutiny by the Court. Equally, the same must apply to speech aimed at countering such allegations since they form part of the same debate. The question here was whether the applicants had exceeded the bounds of permissible criticism. Certain of the statements made by the applicants, such as one accusing one of the authors of telling deliberate lies, did exceed these bounds, and there would be no breach of Art 10 in declaring such an allegation null and void. In other respects, however, statements made by the applicants were not matters of fact, but were rather intended to convey the applicants' own opinions and were thus akin to value judgments. The Court held that:

> 'At the heart of the long and heated public discussion was the question of the truth of allegations of police violence and there was factual support for the assumption that false allegations had been made by informers. The statements in question essentially addressed this issue and the admittedly harsh language in which they were expressed was not incommensurate with that used by the injured party ...' (para 53).

The Court found accordingly that the limitation on the right of expression of the applicants was disproportionate in relation to the legitimate aim of protecting the reputation of the author, and that there had therefore been a breach of Art 10.

# McVicar v United Kingdom
## (2002) 35 EHRR 22

*Facts:* The applicant is a journalist who had written an article suggesting that the athlete Linford Christie regularly used banned performance-enhancing drugs. Following its publication in the magazine *Spiked*, Linford Christie commenced an action for defamation against the journalist, the editor, and the publishing company. Due to his inability to obtain legal aid or to pay legal fees, the journalist, John McVicar, was required to represent himself for the greater part of the proceedings. He complained that the unavailability of legal aid in defamation proceedings operated to deprive him of a fair trial. Furthermore, the exclusion of evidence at trial, the requirement that he bear the burden of proving that allegations made in the article were substantially true, the order for costs against him and an injunction restricting future publication of the allegations breached his right to freedom of expression, which is guaranteed by Art 10.

*Court:* The Court recalled that in order to comply with fair trial guarantees set out in Art 6(1), which include the right of effective access to a court and the right to present an effective defence, Contracting States must on occasion provide legal assistance. However, whether compliance with this provision requires access to free legal representation will depend upon the specific circumstances of the case. While acknowledging the physical and emotional strain resulting from defending a High Court action of this type, which attracted intense media attention, the Court observed that the applicant was a well-educated journalist capable of formulating a cogent argument. The Court was satisfied that the rules relating to the exclusion of evidence were clear and unambiguous and should have been understood by the applicant. Further, the outcome of a libel action 'turned on the simple question of whether or not the applicant was able to show on the balance of probabilities that the allegations at issue were substantially true' (para 55). Thus, the Court did not accept that the law of defamation was sufficiently complex to require a person in the applicant's position to need legal advice. Consequently, his inability to claim legal aid did not prevent him from effectively presenting his defence and did not render the proceedings unfair. Given the gravity of the allegations, the Court considered that the requirement that the applicant prove that they were substantially true on the balance of probabilities, and the granting of an injunction, amounted to a justified restriction on his freedom of expression under Art 10(2). Accordingly, the applicant's rights guaranteed by the Convention were not infringed.

# (5) POLITICAL CRITICISM AND THE RIGHT TO AN OPINION
## Lingens v Austria
## (1986) 8 EHRR 103

*Facts:* The applicant had written two articles, the first of which accused the Chancellor of being a Nazi sympathiser and an opportunist; and the second of which called him 'immoral' and 'undignified'. He had also suggested that the leader of the

Austrian Liberal Party should resign his parliamentary seat because he had served in the SS infantry. The Chancellor brought an action for criminal defamation and the applicant was convicted. He alleged a breach of Art 10.

*Court:* Since there was no dispute that the conviction for defamation was an interference with the applicant's freedom of expression, was prescribed by law and had the legitimate aim of the protection of the reputation or rights of others, the live issue was whether the conviction was necessary in a democratic society and proportionate to the legitimate aim. The Court stated that political criticism is an important function of the press. 'Freedom of the press ... affords the public one of the best means of discovering and forming an opinion of the ideas and attitudes of political leaders ... The limits of acceptable criticism are accordingly wider as regards a politician as such than as regards a private individual. Unlike the latter, the former inevitably and knowingly lays himself open to close scrutiny of his every word and deed by both journalists and the public at large, and he must consequently display a greater degree of tolerance.'

The words used by the applicant were value-judgements made in the exercise of his freedom of expression, and he had a right to his opinions about the Chancellor. He based them on undisputed facts and wrote the otherwise balanced articles in good faith. The conviction was a disproportionate interference with freedom of expression and was not necessary; thus, the Court was unanimous in its opinion that there was a breach of Art 10.

*Note:* This case demonstrates the priority given to freedom of expression by the Court, and also that different types of person may be accorded different levels of protection for their reputation.

## McLaughlin v United Kingdom
## (1994) 18 EHRR CD 84

*Facts:* The applicant, an active member of Sinn Fein, was elected as a local Councillor and became Chairman of the Council's Finance Committee. In 1988, the Home Secretary issued a Directive to the BBC and ITV which prohibited the broadcast of the spoken words of any person who represented or appeared to support a proscribed organisation, Sinn Fein, Republican Sinn Fein or the Ulster Defence Association, except in the case of an election broadcast or coverage of parliamentary proceedings. The Home Secretary argued that the ban was justified to prevent the spread of terrorism, and did not prevent speech being reported indirectly or the use of voice-overs and reconstructions. The applicant argued that the ban discriminated against him on the ground of political opinion, contrary to the Northern Ireland Constitution. He alleged breaches of Arts 10, 14 and 13 in that his freedom of speech had been unjustifiably limited, and that he was the victim of political discrimination since the ban did not apply to supporters of certain other political parties.

*Commission:* The Commission found that the interference with the applicant's freedom of expression was prescribed by law although the government power to ban broadcasts was of a broad, ill-defined nature; and that the interference had the legitimate aim of combating terrorism. The Commission also found that the interference was necessary in a democratic society; although the ban would have little direct effect upon the amount of terrorism, it is legitimate to deny publicity to certain causes. Although an elected representative needs freedom of expression in order to carry out his role and the media are an important source of political opinion for the public, the ban was not disproportionate to its aim of protecting the State from terrorism. Thus, there was no breach of Art 10.

Further, the Commission rejected the claim based on Art 14. Although there was differential treatment on the basis of political opinion, this was justified since it pursued the legitimate aim of prevention of the advocacy of terrorist violence and the ban was a proportionate measure compared to that aim. The ban had a limited operation, and so was not unreasonable. Thus the applicant's claim was inadmissible.

## Ozturk v Turkey
## Application No 22479/93, judgment of 28 September 1999, unreported

*Facts:* Criminal proceedings were brought against the applicant after he published a book titled *A testimony to life – Diary of a death under torture*, which gave an account of the life of one of the founding members of the Communist Party of Turkey, an illegal Maoist organisation. Copies of the second edition of the book were seized following an order made by a single judge of the National Security Court. The National Security Court found the applicant guilty of a number of offences, and imposed fines on him. The Court of Cassation declared that one part of the conviction should be set aside, but confirmed another. Subsequently charges were brought against the author of the book, but he was acquitted on the basis of an expert report prepared by three professors of criminal law which argued that there was nothing in the book which might be held to constitute the offence defined in the relevant Criminal Code. The applicant asked that his case be reconsidered, but was not successful.

*Court:* The applicant relied on Art 10 before the Court. The applicant's rights had been restricted in a manner that was prescribed by law, and pursued two aims compatible with Art 10(2): the prevention of disorder or crime. In exercising its function the Court 'must look at the interference in the light of the case as a whole, including the content of the impugned work and the context in which it was published' (para 64). The National Security Court had adopted two different stances in relation to the book, and 'the Court takes the view that this striking contradiction between two interpretations of one and the same book separated in time by about two years and made by two different benches of the same court is one element to be taken into consideration' (para 67). The words used in the relevant edition of the book 'cannot be regarded as incitement to the use of violence or to hostility and hatred between citizens' (para 68). The Court accordingly concluded that there had been a violation of Art 10 of the Convention.

# Jerusalem v Austria

## [2001] 12 HRCD 93

*Facts:*   The applicant was a member of the Vienna Municipal Council which also acts as the Regional Parliament. In 1992, in the course of a session of the Vienna Municipal Council the applicant gave a speech in which she referred to the dangers of granting subsidies to what she described as 'psycho-sects'. The applicant was highly critical of such sects, referring, inter alia, to their 'totalitarian character' and 'fascist tendencies'. The applicant named one association that she considered to be a sect. The association then filed a civil suit against the applicant requesting the court to grant an injunction to prevent her from repeating the statement that it was a sect. The applicant argued that she could demonstrate, if certain evidence was considered by the court, that the association was a sect, and also argued that she was expressing an opinion, and not a matter of fact. The court found for the association, and the applicant lost successive appeals.

*Court:*   The applicant relied on Art 10 to the effect that her freedom of expression was being unlawfully restricted. She had made the statements in relation to a political issue in the course of a debate in a Council session. The dispute in the present case related to whether the interference in question was 'necessary in a democratic society'. The applicant had enjoyed limited parliamentary immunity, but not in the context of debates of the Municipal Council. 'While freedom of expression is important for everybody, it is especially so for an elected representative of the people' (para 36), and 'the limits of acceptable criticism are wider with regard to politicians acting in their public capacity than in relation to private individuals' (para 38). In a number of cases the Court has distinguished between statements of fact and value-judgements: the existence of the former can be demonstrated, but it is impossible to prove the truth of a value-judgement. The Court was unanimous in finding that the statements made by the applicant were value-judgements, and not matters of fact, and that the Austrian courts had overstepped their margin of appreciation.

## *DEFAMATION OF JUDGES*

# De Haes and Gijsels v Belgium

## (1998) 25 EHRR 1

*Facts:*   The applicants had published five articles in which they strongly criticised the Appeal Court judges who had granted custody of two children to their father. The father had been charged with offences involving incest and child abuse. Although he had been acquitted, the applicants maintained that medical and other evidence proved his guilt. The Court of Appeal judges then brought successful defamation proceedings against the applicants, amongst others, on the basis that the articles had wrongly accused the judges of bias and amounted to a malicious and unfounded attack on the judges. The applicants alleged breaches of Arts 10 and 6 in that their right to freedom of expression had been infringed by the giving of higher priority to judges' privacy than to the public debate about incest. They also alleged that the domestic courts had wrongly interpreted Art 8 as protecting judges' attitudes and opinions rather than their private lives.

*Commission:* The main issue was whether the interference with the applicants' freedom of expression was 'necessary in a democratic society'. The Commission found that the articles had been based on facts and were supported by evidence, and had not been written merely to denigrate the judges. Although some statements in the articles were 'virulent', 'journalistic freedom … covers possible recourse to a degree of exaggeration, or even provocation'; and 'the general interest in a public debate which has a serious purpose outweighs the legitimate aim of protecting the reputation of others, even if such debate involves the use of wounding or offensive language'. Thus, there had been a breach of Art 10.

*Court:* The Court stated that the functioning of the judiciary is a proper subject for media inquiry. Although public confidence in the courts must be maintained by protecting judges from destructive and unfounded attacks, the applicants had based their articles upon thorough research and detailed evidence, including expert testimony. The articles' allegations were serious and in the public interest; the applicants were found guilty of defamation on the basis of opinions contained in their articles, and the factual truth of those articles had been treated as irrelevant. Hence, Art 10 had been breached.

## (6)   PRIOR RESTRAINT BY INJUNCTION

### Tolstoy Miloslavsky v United Kingdom

### (1995) 20 EHRR 442

*Facts:* The applicant wrote a pamphlet titled *War Crimes and the Wardenship of Winchester College* in which he claimed that Lord Aldington 'arranged the perpetration of a major war crime in the full knowledge that the most barbarous and dishonourable aspects of his operations were throughout disapproved and unauthorised by the higher command' and that he was 'a man with the blood of 70,000 men, women and children on his hands', amongst many other such allegations. Lord Aldington issued proceedings for libel against the applicant and a distributor, who both pleaded justification and fair comment. Record damages were awarded by the jury, being about three times the previous highest award. An injunction was also granted to restrain the defendants from publishing any part of the pamphlet or any similar allegations about Lord Aldington. The applicant alleged that the injunction violated Art 10.

*Commission:* The Commission accepted unanimously that there had been a breach of Art 10. The Commission found that the amount awarded in damages was not proportionate to the legitimate aim of protection of reputation. The injunction was also phrased in broader terms than was necessary.

*Court:* The damages award was unforeseeably high and almost impossible to overturn by appeal. Thus, although the libel itself was exceptionally serious, there was a violation of Art 10. But, although the applicant argued that the injunction prevented any comment on Lord Aldington's activities during the Second World War and might hamper the applicant's work as an historian, the Court held that the injunction was a logical consequence of the libel and was not phrased too broadly for the legitimate purpose of preventing further dissemination of the libel. Hence, the injunction did not breach Art 10.

*Note:*   The Commission and Court did not base their findings on any examination of the case against the applicant, but merely upon the proportionality of the remedies awarded against him.

## (7)   PRIOR RESTRAINT BY SEIZURE
### Vereniging Weekblad *Bluf!* v The Netherlands
### (1995) 20 EHRR 189

*Facts:*   The applicant association was the publisher of a weekly left-wing journal which had printed a confidential security service internal report as a supplement. Before the journal issue in question was distributed, the entire print run was seized. However, the journal staff reprinted the issue and sold 2500 copies in Amsterdam the next day. Three staff members had been arrested during the seizure but the charges against them were later dropped. Courts refused to order the return of the seized journals and withdrew them from circulation on the basis that possession of the journal was a criminal offence against national security. The applicants claimed that the seizure and withdrawal from circulation of the journal issue was a breach of Art 10.

*Commission:*   The Commission declared that the live issue was whether the seizure and withdrawal were 'necessary in a democratic society'. Although the security report was marked 'confidential', it was 6 years old and contained no highly sensitive material. Further, since a reprint had been widely distributed, the withdrawal from circulation was not justified under Art 10(2). Accordingly, there was a violation of Art 10.

*Court:*   The Court held that prior restraint is acceptable since: 'National authorities must be able to take such measures solely in order to prevent punishable disclosure of a secret without taking criminal proceedings against the party concerned, provided that national law affords that party sufficient procedural safeguards'. A State must be able to protect itself by keeping some information and operations secret. However, the State had recognised that the confidentiality of the information in question was not paramount, since no proceedings had been brought in relation to the distribution of the reprint. There was also a public debate at the time about the security service's activities. Since the information had been made public by the reprint, the withdrawal of the journal was not justified and there was a breach of Art 10.

## (8)   RIGHT TO ADVERTISE
### VGT Verein Gegen Tierfabriken v Switzerland
### (2002) 34 EHRR 4

*Facts:*   The applicant was an association existing with the aim of protecting animals, with particular emphasis on animal experiments and industrial animal production. It prepared a 55-second television commercial in response to various commercials prepared by the meat industry. When the videotape of the commercial was submitted for broadcast to the Commercial Television Company responsible for television advertising in Switzerland the applicant was informed that the commercial would not be considered for broadcast in view of its clear political character. The applicant was informed that it would be possible to show an advertisement emphasising the benefits of adequate animal rearing, and urging consumers to inquire into the origin of meat they were buying. The applicant requested a decision against which it could appeal, but it was told that the Commercial Television Company was not an official authority, and that there was no avenue for appeal. A complaint to the Federal Department for Transport and Energy was dismissed, and an appeal was made to the Federal Court. This found that the applicant was not entitled to have its commercial broadcast, and that Art 10 of the Convention had not been breached.

*Court:*   The Commercial Television Company was a private party, not being part of the State. However, it was established in *Marckx v Belgium* (1979) 2 EHRR 330 that 'there may be positive obligations inherent' in the guarantees set out in the Convention. Both the Commercial Television Company and the Federal Court made their decisions on the basis of s 18 of the Swiss Federal Radio and Television Act, which prohibits 'political advertising'. In these circumstances the responsibility of the State for any breach of Art 10 may be engaged. The interference was prescribed by law, inasmuch as, although the term 'political advertising' was vague, it would have been possible with foresight to determine that the commercial in question would have fallen within the rubric. The measure pursued a legitimate aim, which was to prevent financially strong groups from obtaining a competitive advantage in politics. In determining whether the interference was 'necessary in a democratic society' it was important to recognise that the margin of appreciation accorded to the State was reduced since what was at stake was the participation of the individual in a debate affecting the general public interest. The prohibition on political advertising did not extend to adverts in the press. The applicant was not a powerful financial group, and 'all the applicant intended to do with its commercial was to participate in an ongoing general debate on animal protection and the rearing of animals' (para 75). There was no objection by the authorities to any particularly disturbing scene in the commercial, and there was no other means by which the applicant could reach the entire Swiss public. Accordingly, the Court held unanimously that there had been a violation of Art 10.

## UNITED KINGDOM CASES

## Prolife Alliance v British Broadcasting Corporation
Court of Appeal, 14 March 2002, unreported

*Facts:*   The claimant appealed from a decision by Scott Baker J in which he refused to allow the claimant to apply for judicial review of a decision by the BBC not to broadcast the claimant's party political broadcast during the 2001 General Election Campaign. While accepting that the advertisement was accurate and was not sensational, the BBC and all other terrestrial broadcasters refused to carry it on the grounds that it contravened well-established guidelines of taste, decency and the public interest. The claimant argued that the refusal to broadcast the advertisement was in contravention of Art 10 of the Convention.

*Held:*   Party political broadcasts should only exceptionally, if ever, be refused for broadcast if they were truthful and unsensational, and in the present case there was no valid ground for refusing to broadcast the advertisement. In particular, the court held that the judge at first instance had not placed sufficient evidence on the overriding responsibility to protect political speech.

## 16.2   OBSCENE MATERIAL

### (1)   PRIOR RESTRAINT BY SEIZURE AND FORFEITURE

## Handyside v United Kingdom

## (1976) 1 EHRR 737

*Facts:*   The applicant had published the English version of *The Little Red Schoolbook*, a manual for teenagers which included information on sex, contraception, sexually transmitted diseases, pornography, homosexuality and abortion. The book was widely available in other European countries but, after negative press coverage of the intended distribution of the book in the UK, warrants were issued for search of the applicant's premises and seizure of copies of the book. A criminal prosecution was also commenced against the applicant for possession of an obscene publication for gain; after his conviction, a forfeiture order was made in respect of surviving copies of the book. A revised edition, with some of the offending passages removed, was later published without legal sanctions. The applicant alleged breaches of Arts 1, 7, 9, 10, 13, 14 and of Art 1 of the First Protocol.

*Commission:*   The Commission ruled out most of the alleged breaches, considering only Art 10 and Art 1 of the First Protocol in detail. It held that there had been no violation of Art 10 and that neither the seizure nor forfeiture and destruction breached the First Protocol.

*Court:*   The Court examined the delicate balance which must be maintained between freedom of expression and the protection of public morals. In respect of Art 10, the Court considered that there was no international or uniform concept of morality, and hence obscenity law would be better left to domestic courts to determine rather than to international judges. English judges were entitled to regard the book as dangerous to adolescents who would be likely to read it, and so impose prior restraint via seizure and forfeiture. The lack of legal action against the revised edition was evidence that the State was doing only that which was necessary to safeguard legitimate interests. Therefore, the Court decided that there had been no breach of Art 10.

*Note:*   The dissenting judgment of Judge Mosler was based upon the argument that, since the seizure and forfeiture orders were ineffective and did not achieve the State's purpose of preventing publication, the interference with the applicant's freedom of information could not have been necessary. In fact, only about 10% of the stocks of the book were seized.

# Otto-Preminger Institute v Austria

## (1994) 19 EHRR 34

*Facts:* The applicant was a non-profit-making association which ran a cinema in Innsbruck and had advertised future showings of a satirical film which included representations of God as senile, Jesus as feeble-minded and Mary as a wanton woman. The film was a version of a play written in 1894 which was banned in Germany; its author had been imprisoned for a blasphemy offence. Criminal proceedings were commenced against the applicant association's manager for blasphemy, but later dropped. Court orders were issued for seizure and forfeiture of the film, preventing the advertised showings from taking place. Performances of the play upon which the film was based did however take place, without legal proceedings being taken by the authorities. The applicant alleged that there had been violations of Art 10 by the seizure and forfeiture orders.

*Commission:* The Commission concluded that there had been violations of Art 10 in respect of both the seizure and the forfeiture. Article 10(2) allows restrictions of artistic expression if there is a pressing social need behind them, such as the prevention of disorder or the protection of others, but no such need existed on the facts since efforts had been made by the applicant to restrict the viewing to an interested adult audience who would not be offended by the film's content. Religious satire and caricature should not normally be completely prohibited, since this would be a disproportionate interference with the rights of the applicant to show the film and of its intended audience to view it.

*Court:* The Court referred to the necessity to balance freedom of artistic expression under Art 10 against freedom of religion under Art 9. Although some information and ideas may be suppressed by the State in order to protect the religious beliefs of others, freedom of expression includes the freedom to disseminate unpopular, shocking and disturbing information or ideas. However, causing gratuitous offence may legitimately be restricted. The concept of blasphemy cannot be considered in isolation from the society against which it is being judged, and the population of the Tyrol, where the showings were to take place, was strongly Catholic. 'The Austrian authorities acted to ensure religious peace in that region and to prevent that some people should feel the object of attacks on their religious beliefs in an unwarranted and offensive manner' and a State is 'better placed than the international judge to assess the need for such a measure in the light of the situation obtaining locally at a given time'. Thus, neither the seizure nor the forfeiture of the film were disproportionate measures, and so there was no breach of Art 10.

# Scherer v Switzerland

## (1994) 18 EHRR 276

*Facts:* The applicant was the owner of a gay sex shop which sold magazines, books and videos. The shop was advertised in specialist publications and bars but its purpose was not obvious from outside. The shop included a small private cinema which was advertised only by word of mouth and showed videos of sexual acts to persons who obtained membership cards and paid an admission charge. The shop was searched, and a film being shown in the cinema to nine customers was seized, together with the video recorder and the film's takings. The applicant was fined for displaying obscene items in public but was acquitted on appeal since only a few consenting people had seen the film and so his actions were not 'in public'. A prosecution appeal was, however, successful and the applicant's conviction was reinstated.

The applicant alleged breaches of Arts 6, 8 and 10. He argued that the criminal proceedings against him had been excessively long and unfair, and that the ban on showing the film on his own premises and his conviction for obscenity offences were against his rights to respect for private life and freedom of expression.

*Commission:* The Commission stated that whether the interference with the applicant's right was necessary in a democratic society depended on whether it reflected a pressing social need to protect the public. Thus, it was vital to establish whether the obscene material had in fact been displayed to the general public. There was no danger of unwilling adults 'being confronted' with the film since only those who wished to see it would be able to find the cinema. Nor could children gain access. The government had not shown any compelling reason why a small group of willing adults should be protected from the film, and so there was no pressing social need behind the applicant's conviction. Hence, there was a breach of Art 10.

## 16.3   ARTISTIC FREEDOM VERSUS OBSCENITY AND PROTECTION OF PUBLIC MORALITY

(1)   FILM

### Otto-Preminger Institute v Austria

(1994) 19 EHRR 34

See **16.2(1)**.

(2)   PAINTINGS

### Muller and Others v Switzerland

(1988) 13 EHRR 212

*Facts:*   The first applicant produced three paintings which were displayed as part of a contemporary art exhibition by the nine other applicants. The paintings showed a variety of sexual acts, some involving animals. The exhibition was free and open to the public. The paintings were seized and legally confiscated, and the 10 applicants were convicted of publishing obscene material. The applicants claimed that the courts had failed to take account of the freedom of artistic expression, and that the confiscation was unjustified. The paintings were returned on appeal after 7 years. The applicants alleged violations of Art 10 in respect of their criminal convictions and of the confiscation order. The Commission found a violation in respect of the confiscation but not the convictions.

*Court:*   The Court stated first that the applicants had indisputably exercised their right to freedom of expression by creating and exhibiting the paintings, since Art 10 includes freedom of artistic expression. There had also clearly been an interference with the exercise of that right. The Court then looked separately at the convictions and the confiscation orders.

As regards the criminal convictions, the Court found that the Swiss obscenity law was sufficiently certain to satisfy the 'prescribed by law' test and that there was a legitimate aim of protection of public morals. Thus, the key question was whether the convictions were necessary in a democratic society. The applicants had argued that freedom of artistic expression was so vital that bans and convictions damaged democratic society. However, the Court considered that the Swiss courts' view of the paintings as crude, hastily painted and 'liable grossly to offend the sense of sexual propriety of persons of ordinary sensitivity' was not unreasonable. The Swiss courts were entitled to consider the convictions and the imposition of fines necessary, since there is no uniform morality. Hence, there was no Art 10 violation.

In relation to the confiscation order, the issue was again whether it was a necessary measure in a democratic society. The applicants had argued that the confiscation was disproportionate to the legitimate aim of protection of public morals, whereas the government argued that the Swiss courts had taken the minimum action necessary and could have ordered the paintings to be destroyed. While the artist had lost the opportunity of exhibiting his paintings in more 'liberal' venues for more than 7 years, the Court again found that the issue of morality is within a State's margin of appreciation and so there was no violation. It was considered relevant that there was some case-law under which the artist could have applied to have the paintings restored to him more quickly.

*Note:*   Judge Spielmann gave a dissenting opinion in which he argued that Art 10 had been violated. Flaubert and Baudelaire were prosecuted for obscenity offences, yet their works are now considered classics rather than obscene and depraved. Baudelaire's conviction was overturned only 80 years after his death. States should:

> 'Take greater account of the relativity of values in the field of the expression of ideas. If, of necessity, we may regard State authorities as being in principle in a better position than the international court to give an opinion on the exact content of the requirement of Article 10 ... it remains unacceptable in a Europe composed of States that the State in question should leave such an assessment to a Canton or a municipal authority. If this were to be the case, it would clearly be impossible for an international court to find any violation of Art 10 as the second paragraph of that article would always apply.'

## 16.4   RIGHT TO INFORMATION

### (1)   RIGHT TO LIFE

# Open Door Counselling Ltd and Dublin Well Woman Centre v Ireland
## (1992) 15 EHRR 244

*Facts:*   The applicants were non-profit-making companies who provided counselling to pregnant women in the Dublin area, counsellors who worked for the Dublin Well Woman clinic, and Irish women of childbearing age. The Irish courts, after a complaint by the Society for the Protection of Unborn Children, issued an injunction to prevent the staff at the clinics from giving any information to pregnant women about the availability of abortion outside Ireland. The clinics provided counselling services which included discussion of abortion as an option and made arrangements to refer some women to abortion clinics in the UK. The Irish courts regarded this as a criminal offence of assisting an abortion, and Irish law recognised the right to life of a foetus from conception onwards. The applicants alleged a breach of Art 10. The Irish government argued, inter alia, that the women were not 'victims' of a violation of the Convention and so could not complain.

*Commission:*　The Commission's opinion was that the injunction violated Art 10 in respect of all the applicants.

*Court:*　The Court held that all the applicants were 'victims of a violation' of the Convention. The two Irish women were within the class of women of childbearing age who might be affected adversely by the injunction and so their application was legitimate. The injunction was found to be an interference prescribed by law since, given the protection of the rights of the unborn in Irish law, it was reasonably foreseeable that legal action would be taken against the two clinics. Although each State is entitled to reflect its own moral views in its law, and the rights of the unborn are protected by Irish law, the right to information can be limited in a democratic society only where such limitations are justified and necessary. Uncomfortable, disturbing or shocking information and ideas are protected by the right to freedom of expression, and the perpetual injunction in question was drafted in such absolute terms that its effect was disproportionate to its legitimate aim. The Court asserted that Art 10 should not be interpreted in such a way as to limit or to derogate from the right to life, but found that the injunction was also ineffective since many pregnant women continued to travel abroad in order to obtain abortions.

## (2)　NATIONAL SECURITY

### *Observer* and *Guardian* v United Kingdom
### (1992) 14 EHRR 153

*Facts:*　The applicants, a group of journalists, editors, publishers and owners of the *Observer* and the *Guardian* newspapers, published articles in 1986 containing details of alleged illegal activities by the security services, as exposed in the book *Spycatcher*. The newspapers had also published an article about an Australian case in which the Attorney-General tried to stop the book being published in Australia. The Attorney-General, wishing to obtain a permanent injunction against the newspapers to ban further publication, obtained interlocutory injunctions to prevent any more newspaper revelations before the case came to trial. In July 1987, the House of Lords upheld the interlocutory injunctions although *Spycatcher* had been published in America in the meantime and copies were available in the UK.

The government argued that the injunctions were necessary for the protection of national security and of the authority of the judiciary. The Commission considered that there had only been a breach of Art 10, both before July 1987 when *Spycatcher* was published overseas, and after that date.

*Court:* The Court regarded the injunctions as pursuing a legitimate aim, the preservation of national security and of the authority of the judiciary. When assessing whether the interference was necessary in a democratic society, the Court dealt separately with two time periods. Between 11 July 1986, when the interlocutory injunctions were granted, and 30 July 1987, when the House of Lords upheld them, there were relevant and sufficient reasons why the injunctions were necessary. But after 30 July 1987, *Spycatcher* had been published overseas and so the disputed information was no longer confidential. At that point, although further publication of details by the newspapers might still have affected the Attorney-General's case by harming the reputation of the security services, the reasons for the interlocutory injunctions were no longer sufficient. There was no longer any pressing reason for the permanent injunction since it would have a greatly reduced impact, and hence there was little reason to protect the trial. Thus, after 30 July 1987, the interlocutory injunctions 'prevented newspapers from exercising their right and duty to purvey information, already available, on a matter of legitimate public concern'. Thus, there was no violation of Art 10 before 30 July 1987; but there was such a violation after 30 July 1987.

*Note:* Judges Pettiti and Pinheiro Farinha gave a dissenting opinion in favour of finding a breach of Art 10 before 30 July 1987. They argued that the injunctions were granted as 'less a question of the duty of confidentiality than the fear of disclosure of certain irregularities carried out by the security service in the pursuit of political rather than intelligence aims', and so violated the right to receive information. The State should have taken action against the author of *Spycatcher* rather than restraining the freedom of the press.

## 16.5 FREEDOM OF EXPRESSION IN A COMMERCIAL CONTEXT

### Markt Intern Verlag GmbH and Beermann v Federal Republic of Germany

### (1989) 12 EHRR 161

*Facts:* The first applicant was a publishing firm run by journalists and the second applicant was its editor-in-chief. The first applicant had a range of functions related to defending the interests of small- and medium-sized retail businesses against larger companies, including supermarkets and mail order suppliers. It also published a number of newsletters and bulletins for specific types of retailers. The second applicant wrote an article in one of the bulletins aimed at chemists and independent retailers of beauty products. The article described a customer complaint against an English mail order firm, and asked readers to send in any similar complaints. The applicants had previously published other articles about the same firm in which they advised retailers and manufacturers to 'be cautious' in their dealings with the firm. The latter obtained an interim injunction to prevent the applicants from repeating such statements. The domestic courts issued a permanent injunction and fined the applicants for anti-competitive business practices. The Federal Constitutional Court then stated that freedom of the press had not been violated since that freedom cannot prevail 'where an item published in the press is intended to promote, in the context of commercial competition, certain economic interests to the detriment of others'. The Commission found that there had been a violation of Art 10.

*Court:*  The government had argued that the bulletin fell outside Art 10 since its aim was not to influence public opinion but to promote the economic interests of a group of businesses. The applicants accepted that they defended the interests of such a group, but stated that their publications satisfied the requirements of their niche audience, a group otherwise neglected by the press, and that to restrict the freedom of expression to political or cultural news would deprive a large percentage of the press of any Convention protection at all.

The Court found that information of a commercial nature cannot be excluded from the ambit of Art 10. Thus the main question was whether the interference with the applicants' right was necessary in a democratic society for the protection of its legitimate aim, the rights and reputations of others. 'In a market economy an undertaking which seeks to set up a business inevitably exposes itself to close scrutiny of its practices by its competitors. Its commercial strategy and the manner in which it honours its commitments may give rise to criticism on the part of consumers and the specialised press. In order to carry out this task, the specialised press must be able to disclose facts which could be of interest to its readers and thereby contribute to the openness of business activities. However, even the publication of items which are true ... may under certain circumstances be prohibited', and there are a variety of factors, such as the context of the statements and the method in which they were made, which domestic courts may legitimately take into account when deciding which statements are permissible. Publishing an account of an isolated incident without waiting to see the final result of the consumer complaint was likely to adversely affect the business against which the complaint had been made. It was within the State's margin of appreciation to prohibit such statements, and so there was no violation of Art 10. However, the decision required the President to use his vote.

*Note:*  This very close decision demonstrates the difficulty of balancing these rights. Seven of the dissenting judges regarded freedom of expression as being as important in relation to commercial practices as it is in relation to political activities, and stated that:

> 'The fact that a person defends a given interest, whether it is an economic interest or any other interest, does not ... deprive him of the benefit of freedom of expression. In order to ensure the openness of business activities, it must be possible to disseminate freely information and ideas concerning the products and services proposed to consumers. Consumers, who are exposed to highly effective distribution techniques and to advertising which is frequently less than objective, deserve ... to be protected, as do retailers.'

# Jacobowski v Germany
## (1995) 19 EHRR 64

*Facts:*  The applicant was dismissed from his employment as editor at a news agency by a combination of four separate dismissal letters, each on different grounds. His former employer also issued a press release in which it was alleged that the applicant had misled the board of directors, mismanaged the agency and behaved inappropriately to clients. After legal action, the applicant was granted a right to reply to the press release's allegations, but in the meantime he had assembled a file of negative press cuttings about his former employer and had distributed it to various journalists, with an accompanying letter which hinted that he might be setting up his own agency in the near future. He was then ordered by injunction to cease the distribution of his mailshots since his intention was to gain an unfair advantage over a competitor (his former employer), and argued that this injunction breached his freedom of expression under Art 10.

*Commission:* The Commission unanimously concluded that there had been a breach of Art 10, using arguments based on the law of defamation rather than unfair competition. The applicant's mailshot and letter, whilst containing serious criticism of his former employer, had to be viewed in the light of the attacks which had been made upon his own reputation and professional ability by the employer's press release. At the time when the applicant sent out his mailshot, he had no way of knowing that he would later be given a chance to reply to the allegations against him, and so was acting to protect his own reputation. Thus, the injunction was a disproportionate response and an unjustified interference with freedom of expression.

*Court:* The Court held that there was no breach of Art 10 since it was within the State's margin of appreciation to decide that the applicant's actions were essentially competitive in nature rather than a response to defamation against him. It was considered to be an important factor that the injunction merely prohibited distribution of the mailshot; the domestic courts had left it open for the applicant publicly to criticise his former employer in other ways, and so he remained able to express his opinions.

*Note:* Three dissenting judges regarded freedom of expression as the 'guiding principle' of the case and stated that any exceptions to this fundamental freedom should be construed narrowly. By distributing articles which were already in the public domain, the applicant could not be said to have given an unfair picture.

## Tele 1 Privatfernsehgesellschaft mbH v Austria
## (2002) 34 EHRR 5

*Facts:* The applicant, a company based in Austria, applied in 1993 to the appropriate Telecommunications Office for a licence to set up and operate a television transmitter in the Vienna area. The application was dismissed as no legislation had been enacted that would allow the introduction of regional television broadcasting, although regional radio licences were available. According to the Constitutional Broadcasting Law of 1974, it was left to federal legislation to deal with this issue. A number of appeals failed, and the Austrian Constitutional Court held that only the European Court of Human Rights could determine whether or not the impossibility of terrestrial television broadcasting by stations other than the Austrian Broadcasting Corporation was in breach of the Convention. The applicant complained that the refusal of a licence was in breach of Art 10 of the Convention.

*Court:* The Court found that the restriction complained of amounted to an interference with the applicant's exercise of its freedom to impart information and ideas (para 24). Article 10 allows States to regulate by a licensing system the way in which broadcasting is authorised in their territories. The monopoly system adopted by

Austria was capable of contributing to the quality and balance of programmes and was therefore consistent with Art 10(1) (see eg *Informationsverein Lentia v Austria* (1994) 17 EHRR 93). The refusal to grant a licence had a basis in domestic law, and it is in the first place for the national authorities, notably the courts, to interpret and apply the domestic law (para 28). The key question for the Court was that of whether the interference was 'necessary in a democratic society'. In this respect the Court considered the position in relation to three different time periods. In the first period, in relation to which the Court had already found the State to be in breach of Art 10, there was a breach due to the lack of legal basis of any licensing system. However, following changes to the Austrian legislation, the Court found that there was no ongoing breach. While there is no longer a justification for a far-reaching restriction such as that of granting a single broadcasting monopoly, it is not disproportionate, given the reach of other delivery mechanisms for broadcasters, to limit the granting of terrestrial broadcasting licences.

## 16.6   GENERAL PRIVACY ISSUES

### (1)   TELEPHONE TAPPING OF THIRD PARTY LINE

### Lambert v France

### (2000) 30 EHRR 346

*Facts:*   The applicant had several telephone conversations with B, whose line was being secretly intercepted in accordance with French law. B was being investigated for various offences, including theft, burglary, and handling. As a result of the interception of the conversations, the applicant was charged with handling. Domestic courts held that the applicant had no standing to challenge the interception order since it was related to a third party line. The applicant argued that the interception of the conversations which were used against him infringed Art 8. The Commission found that there had been a breach of Art 8.

*Court:*   The Court stated that telephone conversations are within the concepts of 'private life' and 'correspondence' for Art 8 and there had been an interference with Art 8. It did not matter that it was a third party's telephone line which had been intercepted, and the question was whether the interference was justified by being 'necessary in a democratic society'. The government argued that the tapping was necessary as a prime investigation tool. The Court stated that the domestic remedies available to the applicant were too limited to be effective, and the domestic court's reasoning about standing 'could lead to decisions whereby a very large number of people are deprived of the protection of the law, namely all those who have conversations on a telephone line other than their own ... the applicant did not have available to him the "effective control" to which citizens are entitled under the rule of law and which would have been capable of restricting the interference in question to what was "necessary in a democratic society"'.

*Note:*   In a concurring opinion, Judge Pettiti stated that:

> 'Intercepting telephone conversations is one of the most serious temptations for State authorities and one of the most harmful for democracies ... Abuses, however, are becoming more and more unacceptable, taking the form of monitoring wholly private

conversations on the pretext of spying on political entourages. In several Member States the supervision systems set up to control the monitors have proved inadequate and defective. Will it be necessary in the future, in order to protect privacy, to require people to get into "bubbles", in imitation of the practices of some embassies, in order to preclude any indiscretions? That would be to give in to Big Brother.'

## (2) SEARCH ORDERS

## Chappell v United Kingdom

## (1989) 11 EHRR 543

*Facts:*  The applicant ran a video club supplying second generation video cassettes to its subscribers. Many of the videos had been recorded in breach of copyright. A group of film companies and organisations representing film producers and distributors obtained an *Anton Piller* order to find evidence for a future breach of copyright action. The High Court ordered the applicant to cease dealing in unlicensed copies and returned the erased cassettes to him. The Commission found that there had been no violation of Art 8.

*Court:*  The Court was required to consider whether the interference with the applicant's right to respect for his private life was in accordance with law and necessary in a democratic society.

Since 'law' includes unwritten or common law, *Anton Piller* orders in general do satisfy that requirement, but the circumstances related to the specific order made against the applicant must also be examined. *Anton Piller* orders have a substantial body of case-law precedent and stringent safeguards do exist. The Court considered the applicant's rights had been respected by the order:

> 'An Anton Piller order is granted without the defendant being notified or heard and is capable of producing damaging and irreversible consequences for him. For these reasons it is essential that this measure should be accompanied by adequate and effective safeguards against arbitrary interference and abuse [but] ... The order made against Mr Chappell and his company was coupled with a number of safeguards.'

As for the necessity of the order, the Court agreed that some aspects of the search of the premises were 'disturbing', 'unfortunate and regrettable' and made the execution of the order 'more oppressive than it should have been'. However, 'the shortcomings in the procedure followed – which, by its very nature, was bound to cause some difficulties for the applicant – were not so serious that the execution of the order can, in the circumstances of the case, be regarded as disproportionate to the legitimate aim pursued'. Hence, there was no violation of Art 8.

## (3) RIGHT OF ACCESS TO PERSONAL INFORMATION ON FILE

## Leander v Sweden

## (1987) 9 EHRR 433

*Facts:*  The applicant worked as a temporary museum technician at a Naval Museum adjacent to a naval base in a 'restricted military security zone'. After 2 weeks, he was told to leave work pending security clearance. He alleged that his employment was scheduled to be for 10 months, whereas the government alleged that it was to be for 11 days only. The applicant was denied security clearance and was refused access to the information held about him on the security file maintained by the police. Swedish law allowed citizens access to secret police files about them 'in exceptional circumstances'. The applicant alleged that his former communist political affiliation and radical opinions had been unfairly used against him. He argued breaches of Arts 6, 8, 10 and 13. His complaint was that he had been prevented from obtaining permanent employment and dismissed from temporary employment on account of certain secret information which allegedly made him a security risk; this was an attack on his reputation and he ought to have had an opportunity to defend himself before a tribunal.

*Commission:*   The Commission found that there had been no breach of Art 8, and that no separate issue arose under Art 10.

*Court:*   The storing and release of information about the applicant's private life, coupled with a refusal to allow him an opportunity to refute it, was an interference with his right to respect for his private life. The protection of national security was a legitimate aim, and thus the main issues disputed were: whether the interference was 'in accordance with the law'; and whether it was 'necessary in a democratic society'.

Compliance with domestic law would not be sufficient, since the law must be accessible to the individual concerned and its consequences for him must be foreseeable. 'However the requirement of foreseeability in their special context of secret controls of staff in sectors affecting national security cannot be the same as in many other fields. Thus, it cannot mean that an individual should be enabled to foresee precisely what checks will be made in his regard by the Swedish special police system in its efforts to protect national security'. The law concerned was accessible, and the conditions under which secret files could be stored and released by the National Police Board were given in explicit and detailed provisions. Thus, the interference was 'in accordance with law'.

As regards the necessity of the interference, the Court stated that the applicant's legitimate interests had been adversely affected by the limitation of his access to jobs in certain fields of employment, but that the State's margin of appreciation as to the best means of protection of national security is wide. 'Nevertheless, in view of the risk that a system of secret surveillance for the protection of national security poses of undermining or even destroying democracy on the ground of defending it, the Court must be satisfied that there exist adequate and effective guarantees against abuse.'

On the facts, the safeguards in existence were sufficient, particularly since a decision to release secret information was supervised by members of Parliament who had vetoes. Thus, there was no violation of Art 8.

As regards Art 10, the Court held that: 'The right to freedom to receive information basically prohibits a government from restricting a person from receiving information that others wish or may be willing to impart to him. Article 10 does not . . . confer on the individual a right of access to a register containing information on his personal position, nor does it embody an obligation on the government to impart such information to the individual'. Hence, there was no violation of Art 10.

## (4)  SEARCH OF LAWYER'S OFFICE – LEGAL PROFESSIONAL PRIVILEGE

### Niemietz v Germany

### (1992) 16 EHRR 97

*Facts:*  The applicant, a lawyer, was involved in local politics and his office received mail addressed to an activist group with which he was strongly linked, the Anti-Clerical Working Group. A letter signed by a (probably fictitious) member of that group resulted in a criminal investigation for the offence of insulting behaviour. A warrant was issued for the search of the applicant's law office and of several other addresses, with the aim of establishing the identity of the writer of the letter in question. No relevant documents were seized.

The applicant alleged, inter alia, that the search had violated his right to respect for his home and correspondence (Art 8) and had impaired the goodwill of his law office and his reputation as a lawyer (Art 1 of the First Protocol). The Commission was of the unanimous opinion that there had been a breach of Art 8.

*Court:*  The Commission argued that the confidential relationship between a lawyer and his client justifies a finding that there had been an interference with the applicant's 'private life' and 'home'. The Court doubted that this was a sensible approach, preferring to state that it is neither possible nor necessary to attempt an exhaustive definition of these terms, and that there is 'no reason of principle why this understanding of the notion of "private life" should be taken to exclude activities of a professional or business nature since it is . . . in the course of their working lives that the majority of people have a significant, if not the greatest, opportunity of developing relationships with the outside world'. A person's work may 'form part and parcel of his life to such a degree that it becomes impossible to know in what capacity he is acting at a given moment of time'. Hence, professional activities could fall within the scope of protection of Art 8, and 'home' may include business premises. Thus, there had been an interference with the applicant's right to respect for his private life. The main point of contention was whether the interference was 'necessary in a democratic society'. The Court held that the measures taken were disproportionate to their legitimate aims: the offence under investigation was minor; the warrant was drafted very widely to allow the seizure of any documents concerning the letter-writer, without limitation; the search greatly interfered with professional secrecy; and 'the attendant publicity must have been capable of affecting adversely the applicant's professional reputation, in the eyes both of his existing clients and of the public at large'. Accordingly, there had been a violation of Art 8.

## (5)  INTERCEPTION OF CORRESPONDENCE

### Foxley v United Kingdom

### (2001) 31 EHRR 25

*Facts:*  The applicant complained that the interception of correspondence by the post office on behalf of the trustee in bankruptcy was an interference with his right to respect for his correspondence. Following the applicant's conviction and imprisonment for corruption, a trustee was appointed to manage his property and an order granted for all postal packets to be redirected for a period of 3 months. During this period the trustee opened, read and made copies of all correspondence, including letters from his legal advisers, before forwarding them to the applicant. However, the trustee continued to intercept correspondence and kept copies of some letters after the expiry of the order.

*Court:*   While accepting that the interception of a bankrupt's correspondence may be necessary in order to identify and trace sources of income, the Court noted that adequate and effective safeguards to ensure minimum impairment of the right guaranteed by Art 8 must accompany the implementation of these measures. The Court could find no justification for the copying and filing of documents attracting legal professional privilege and considered that the interception of any mail after the order had expired was not in accordance with the law as required by Art 8. Accordingly, the Court was satisfied that in this case there was a violation.

# Chapter 17

# FREEDOM OF ASSOCIATION, ASSEMBLY AND DEMONSTRATION

## 17.1 THE RIGHT TO PEACEFUL ASSEMBLY AND DEMONSTRATION

### (1) STATE'S POSITIVE DUTY TO PROTECT LAWFUL DEMONSTRATORS FROM REPRISAL

### Plattform 'Ärzte für das Leben' v Austria

### (1988) 13 EHRR 204

*Facts:* The applicant association was a group of doctors campaigning against abortion and urging legal reform on that issue. It held a series of demonstrations taking the form of religious services, assemblies and marches. Two of its demonstrations were disrupted by banned counter-demonstrations, in spite of a large police presence. The applicant alleged that the police had failed to provide sufficient protection for the demonstrations, and hence that there had been violations of Arts 9, 10, 11 and 13. Only the Art 13 allegation was found to be admissible by the Commission, which found unanimously that there had been a violation.

*Court:* The Court held that there is a positive duty upon a State to ensure that the right to peaceful demonstration and assembly can be exercised:

> 'A demonstration may annoy or give offence to persons opposed to the ideas or claims that it is seeking to promote. The participants must, however, be able to hold the demonstration without having to fear that they will be subjected to physical violence by their opponents; such a fear would be liable to deter associations or other groups supporting common ideas or interests from openly expressing their opinions on highly controversial issues affecting the community. In a democracy the right to counter-demonstrate cannot extend to inhibiting the exercise of the right to demonstrate.'

On the facts, Austrian law already took such positive measures via a criminal offence of disrupting a lawful demonstration and a statutory power to ban, terminate or disperse assemblies. These measures had not been shown to be inadequate. Although police had not intervened greatly in the counter-demonstrations, there had not been any serious assaults or lasting damage to property. The counter-demonstrations had been disruptive but not violent, and so the Austrian authorities had not been shown to have failed in their duties. Thus, there was no violation of Art 13 because there was no arguable claim that Art 11 had been breached.

## (2)  PROPORTIONALITY OF RESTRICTIONS TO LEGITIMATE AIM

### Ezelin v France

### (1991) 14 EHRR 362

*Facts:*  The applicant was a French lawyer who lived in Guadeloupe. He took part in a public demonstration against the convictions of three militants, during which offensive graffiti was painted onto public buildings. He was charged with a criminal offence and refused to give evidence to the investigating judge. The charges were later dropped. The Bar Council also found that there was no reason to discipline him. However, on appeal to the Court of Appeal, that decision was reversed and a reprimand was imposed on the basis that he had failed to 'disassociate himself from the demonstrators' offensive and insulting acts or leave the procession'. He alleged breaches of Arts 10 and 11.

*Commission:*  The Commission found that there had been a breach of Art 11. The right of peaceful assembly is a fundamental right in a democratic society, and 'is guaranteed to anyone who has the intention of organising a peaceful demonstration'. Although the demonstration had got out of hand, 'an individual does not cease to enjoy the right to freedom of peaceful assembly simply because sporadic violence or other punishable acts take place in the course of the assembly, if he himself remains peaceful in his intentions and behaviour'. The Bar's professional rules and disciplinary sanctions were 'prescribed by law' since their impact was predictable and they were not excessively rigid. The legitimate aim was that of preventing public disorder. However, the sanction was not necessary in a democratic society; what was expected of the applicant by the domestic Court of Appeal was a positive act of disapproval as regards the demonstration and its results, and 'a sanction based on the impression that the applicant's behaviour might have given is incompatible with the strict requirement of a pressing social need'.

*Court:*  The applicant had joined a lawful assembly and there was no evidence that he had been a party to the graffiti or alleged verbal threats. The disciplinary action clearly interfered with the exercise of his freedom of peaceful assembly, since an interference includes measures taken after the assembly. The main issue was whether that interference was necessary in a democratic society.

The Court found that the sanction was disproportionate to its legitimate aim of preventing public disorder:

> 'The proportionality principle demands that a balance be struck between the requirements of the purposes listed in Art 11(2) and those of the free expression of opinions by word, gesture or even silence by persons assembled on the streets or in other public places . . . the freedom to take part in a peaceful assembly – in this instance a demonstration that had not been prohibited – is of such importance that it cannot be restricted in any way, even for an "avocat", so long as the person concerned does not himself commit any reprehensible act on such an occasion.'

Hence, there had been a breach of Art 11.

## (3) PRIOR BANS OF RALLIES

# Rai, Allmond and 'Negotiate Now' v United Kingdom
# (1995) 19 EHRR CD 93

*Facts:* The applicants wished to stage a rally in Trafalgar Square in order to promote their views, including the view that the government should support peace negotiations in Northern Ireland even without a prior cease-fire. The applicants followed the procedures for approval of a rally. However, the Commissioner of the Metropolitan Police considered that the rally posed a danger to public order and, as a consequence, the Department of National Heritage banned the rally in accordance with longstanding government policy that no demonstrations were to be permitted in Trafalgar Square if they focused on events in Northern Ireland. The applicants argued that the ban infringed their freedom to manifest their beliefs in public, their freedom of expression and their freedom of peaceful assembly; and that they had been discriminated against on grounds of political opinion. They alleged breaches of Arts 9, 10 and 11.

*Commission:* The right to freedom of peaceful assembly is a fundamental right in any democratic society and protects every person who intends to organise a peaceful demonstration. Thus, there was an interference with the applicants' rights under Art 11. The applicants had argued that the assembly was banned not for any legitimate reason such as public order or safety but because it was controversial and likely to provoke public debate. The Commission decided that there was a legitimate aim involved: 'in the circumstances of Northern Ireland where sensitive and complex issues arise as to the causes of the conflict and any possible solutions, the government can be considered in its general policy of banning demonstrations concerning the subject to be pursuing the aim of preventing disorder and protecting the rights and freedoms of others'. There was no arbitrariness or bias evident in the government's policy; although a few demonstrations had in recent years been permitted in Trafalgar Square which concerned Northern Ireland, it was within the government's margin of appreciation to assess each application's merits and likely implications. Further, the refusal of permission did not form a blanket prohibition upon the holding of the rally, but merely prevented it from taking place at that one particular venue. There were other possible venues in central London, and so the Commission considered the restrictions to be proportionate to their legitimate aim and hence necessary in a democratic society. Article 11 had not been violated.

As for the allegation of discrimination on grounds of political opinion, the Commission found that there was a general policy of banning all Northern Ireland-related events in Trafalgar Square; it was only in exceptional cases where the event was regarded as 'uncontroversial' that permission had been granted. The events which had been allowed were three peace demonstrations which had no political overtones and a rally which was intended to commemorate the two World Wars, although it had in fact degenerated into a political rally. There was accordingly no evidence that the applicants had been the victims of any difference of treatment on political grounds. The applicants' entire complaint was held to be inadmissible.

## 17.2 RESTRICTIONS ON POLITICAL ACTIVITY OF GOVERNMENT EMPLOYEES

### Ahmed and Others v United Kingdom

### (2000) 29 EHRR 1

*Facts:* The applicants complained that regulations made pursuant to s 1(5) of the Local Government and Housing Act 1989 constituted an unjustified interference with their rights to freedom of expression, freedom of association and prevented them from taking part in elections. These regulations restricted the political activities of certain categories of senior local government officers. The applicants all held politically restricted posts and were required under the terms of their employment to refrain from engaging in certain political activities. Following an unsuccessful application in the domestic courts for judicial review of the regulations, an application was lodged with the Commission in September 1993.

*Commission:* The Commission was of the opinion that there had been an infringement of Art 10; that it was unnecessary to consider the complaint under Art 11; and that there was no violation of Art 3 of the First Protocol.

*Court:* The Court considered that the application of the regulations to the applicants pursued the legitimate aim of maintaining the political neutrality of local government officers. The regulations did not restrict the applicants' right to join a political party. The adoption of the regulations was considered a 'valid response by the legislature to addressing that need and one which was within the respondent's State's margin of appreciation in this area'. Accordingly, any interference with the applicants' right under the Convention was justified and there was no violation of Arts 10 or 11 and there had been no violation of Art 3 of the First Protocol.

### Chorherr v Austria

### (1993) 17 EHRR 358

*Facts:* The applicant had carried out a peaceful demonstration against the purchase of fighter aircraft by the Austrian armed forces. During a public military ceremony in commemoration of the fortieth anniversary of the end of the Second World War and the thirtieth anniversary of Austrian neutrality, the applicant and a friend distributed leaflets and wore huge banner-like rucksacks with slogans on them. A loud disturbance broke out among spectators whose view was blocked by the rucksacks, and police officers asked the applicant and his friend to cease their demonstration since they were disturbing public order. They refused, giving the right to freedom of expression as their reason, and were arrested for breach of the peace. The applicant was released from police detention after 3 hours. The domestic courts rejected the applicant's appeals against his arrest and prohibition from leaflet-distribution, on the ground that the actions taken against him were aimed at putting an end to a breach of the peace and not at preventing him from exercising his right to freedom of opinion. The applicant alleged breaches of Art 5 in relation to his arrest and detention and Art 10 in relation to the order to stop distributing leaflets and to remove his rucksack.

*Commission:* The Commission found that the Austrian reservation to Art 5, which provides that deprivation of liberty may be allowed for certain administrative offences including a breach of the peace, were drafted sufficiently narrowly to comply with Art 64. The applicant was arrested while committing two administrative public order offences and so his detention fell within the Austrian reservation and was not a breach of Art 5.

However, the Commission did find a violation of Art 10. The applicant had been physically removed from the ceremony and had been detained for some hours after it had finished, thus being prevented from expressing himself via his posters and leaflets. This interference was disproportionate to its aim of prevention of breach of the peace, since merely removing the rucksack would have ceased the disturbance.

*Court:* The Court agreed with the Commission that there had been no violation of Art 5 since the Austrian reservation was valid. However, the Court found that there had been no violation of Art 10 since it is within a State's margin of appreciation to determine which measures may be taken by authorities in order to ensure that lawful demonstrations and public events take place peacefully. The applicant must have realised, when he chose a public event for the venue of his protest, that he might cause a disturbance. The measures taken against him were not excessive in the circumstances. Therefore, there was no violation of Art 10.

# Vogt v Germany
## (1996) 21 EHRR 205

*Facts:* The applicant was a school teacher working in Lower Saxony. Assessments of her capabilities and work were entirely satisfactory. She was also an active member of the Communist Party, and in 1982 disciplinary proceedings were initiated against her on the grounds that she had failed to comply with the duty of loyalty to the Constitution that she owed as a civil servant under s 61(2) of the Lower Saxony Civil Service Act. A further indictment was drawn up in December 1986 specifying a range of political activities incompatible with the Act. In August of that year she was temporarily suspended from her post. Following a series of court actions and appeals the Federal Constitutional Court rejected the applicant's case on the grounds that it had insufficient prospects of success. In February 1991 the applicant was reinstated as a teacher for the Lower Saxony education authority following the repeal by the Land government of the decree on the employment of extremists in the civil service. The applicant alleged a breach of Art 10 of the Convention.

*Court:* The Court found that the Government did not contest the applicability of Art 10. The Court noted that while recruitment to the civil service was deliberately omitted from the Convention, once a person has been appointed they may complain if their dismissal or treatment is contrary to the Convention. The interference with the applicant's Art 10 rights was prescribed by law, and did pursue a legitimate aim in that it derived from civil servants' duty of political loyalty which was aimed at protecting national security, preventing disorder and protecting the rights of others.

The Court examined the duties owed by civil servants in Germany, and found that:

'... the absolute nature of that duty as construed by the German Courts is striking. It is owed equally by every civil servant, regardless of his or her function and rank. It implies that every civil servant, whatever his or her own opinion on the matter, must unambiguously renounce all groups and movements which the competent authorities hold to be inimical to the Constitution. It does not allow for distinctions between service and private life; the duty is always owed, in every context' (para 59).

The dismissal of a school teacher is a very severe measure. It has a significant impact on the reputation of the person in question, and also removes their livelihood. The applicant was a teacher of German and French in a secondary school, which was not a position that involved any security risks. There was no evidence that the applicant made anti-constitutional statements at school or personally adopted an anti-constitutional stance, and the party of which she was a member had not been banned by the authorities. Accordingly, the Court found that the dismissal of the applicant was in contravention of Art 10. The Court further found that Art 11 had, on the basis of the same reasoning, been infringed.

## Rekvenyi v Hungary
## (2000) 30 EHRR 519

*Facts:* An amendment to the Hungarian Constitution had the effect that as from 1 January 1994 members of the armed forces, the police and the security services were prohibited from joining any political party and engaging in any political activity. The applicant was a police officer. A complaint made to the Constitutional Court by the Police Independent Trade Union to the effect that the amendment infringed the constitutional rights of career members of the police was rejected on the grounds that the Constitutional Court had no competence to annul a provision of the Constitution itself.

*Court:* Before the Court the applicant relied on Arts 10, 11 and 14. The Court found that there had been no breach of the provisions of the Convention. The interference with the rights set out in Art 10 was clear, and the Court found that this was prescribed by law. In the Court's view 'the desire to ensure that the crucial role of the police in society is not compromised through the corrosion of the political neutrality of its officers is one that is compatible with democratic principles' (para 41). In the context of a State emerging from a totalitarian past such a provision took on a special significance. The Court found that, 'especially against this historical background, the relevant measures taken in Hungary in order to protect the police force from the direct influence of party politics can be seen as answering a "pressing social need" in a democratic society' (para 48). Although Art 11 has an autonomous existence the Court found that in the present case it must be considered in the light of Art 10, and here the same arguments could be applied to the case in respect of the application of Art 11. As there had been no violations of either of these Articles, there was no violation of Art 14 taken in conjunction with these Articles.

# Ahmed and Others v United Kingdom
## (2000) 29 EHRR 1

*Facts:*  The applicants were local government employees in a range of different positions. Following the raising of concerns about the political affiliations of such employees, a committee was asked to investigate the matter. It recommended that legislation should be amended so as to preclude senior local government employees from engaging in political activity. In 1990 the Local Government Officers (Political Restrictions) Regulations were laid before Parliament, coming into force in May. The applicants were all adversely affected by the Regulations' application. The applicants and their trade union were granted leave to apply for judicial review of the Regulations, and their application was subsequently dismissed in December 1991. A further appeal to the Court of Appeal was dismissed, and in both cases the courts held that Art 10 of the Convention did not assist the applicants' case.

*Court:*  It was not disputed that there had been an interference on the applicants' rights as set out in Art 10, or that, following *Vogt v Germany* (above), the applicants were protected by the Article. The applicants submitted that the Regulations were sufficiently imprecise as to render the restriction not one 'prescribed by law'. The Court found that taken as a whole the Regulations and the relevant primary legislation, together with a system of review provided for by way of appeals to industrial tribunals, meant that the restriction was prescribed by law. The applicants further argued that the restrictions could not be regarded as legitimate as the applicants' involvement in normal political activities did not represent any threat to the constitutional or democratic order. The Court did not accept that 'the protection of effective democracy can only be invoked as a justification for limitations on the rights guaranteed under Art 10 in circumstances where there is a threat to the stability of the constitutional or political order'. Rather:

> 'the notion of effective political democracy is just as applicable to the local level as it is to the
> national level bearing in mind the extent of decision-making entrusted to local authorities
> and the proximity of the local electorate to the policies which their local politicians adopt'
> (para 52).

The aim pursued by the Regulations was to underpin a tradition of a bond of trust between elected members and a permanent corps of local government officers. The Court accordingly held that the Regulations pursued a legitimate aim.

The Court then considered the question of whether the restrictions corresponded to a pressing social need and were proportionate. The committee had identified a problem, and a pressing social need for action in the area. The measures adopted were directed at the need to preserve the impartiality of carefully defined categories of officers and there was a procedure whereby officers could seek to avoid the application of the restrictions. The Court held by six votes to three that the Regulations did not breach Art 10.

# Refah Partisi and Others v Turkey

## (2002) 35 EHRR 3

*Facts:*   The first applicant was a political party, and the remaining applicants were politicians. The first applicant was dissolved by order of the Constitutional Court, and the remaining applicants were prohibited from sitting in Parliament for a period of 5 years as a consequence of their involvement with the party. The party was dissolved as it was found to be illegal as it operated against the principle of secularism which was secured by the Turkish Constitution.

*Court:*   By a majority of four votes to three the Court held that Art 11 had not been violated as there were legitimate aims in the restriction, and the measure was proportionate, even though, in a case such as this, the margin of appreciation accorded to the State had to be narrowly interpreted.

# 17.3   NEGATIVE RIGHT OF ASSOCIATION

## (1)   TRADE UNIONS

# Gustaffson v Sweden

## (1996) 22 EHRR 409

*Facts:*   The applicant owned a restaurant and a youth hostel which used casual employees. He was not a member of either of the two existing associations of restaurant employers and so was not bound by collective labour agreements and did not have to pay subscriptions to collective insurance schemes. He was given an opportunity to join an insurance scheme, but refused on the ground that he was against the system of collective bargaining; in any case, his arrangements were superior to those guaranteed under any of the possible collective schemes, and his employees shared his objections of principle. The Hotel and Restaurant Workers' Union then arranged a boycott of the applicant's restaurant, and three other unions later joined. Deliveries to the restaurant were stopped as a result. The applicant asked the government to intervene, to stop the industrial action and to force the unions to pay compensation to him. The government refused on the ground that it had no jurisdiction over such disputes. Further union action was taken against the applicant's youth hostel, and he eventually had to sell the ailing restaurant to a person who signed a collective agreement with one of the main unions. The applicant alleged breaches of Art 11, Art 1 of the First Protocol, Art 6(1) and Art 13. The State refused to support his complaint.

*Commission:*   Article 11 does impose on a State a duty to take some positive steps to ensure that freedom of association can be enjoyed effectively. That Article also includes negative freedom of association, ie the right not to join an association. The question here was whether the Swedish State was under an obligation to protect the applicant against industrial action in the present circumstances. The industrial action did affect the applicant's negative freedom of association since it was aimed at inducing him to join a collective bargaining agreement to which he objected. Although Art 11 itself gives trade unions freedom to promote their interests and those of their members, the State must protect against abuse of this freedom. Since the unions which took action against the applicant were not acting on behalf of any of his employees, who were in any case happy with their employment conditions, the industrial action was a dispro-portionate measure which had very harsh consequences. Thus, the State should have provided legal redress for the applicant, and there was a breach of Art 11.

The applicant had also argued that the State's failure to protect him against the boycott had forced him to sell his restaurant at an undervalue and so deprived him of his possessions. The Commission did not consider it necessary to discuss Art 1 of the First Protocol since it had already found a breach of Art 11. The alleged breach of Art 6(1) was rejected on the basis that there was no existing 'civil right' in this dispute. Article 13 was found to have been violated since the applicant had an arguable case under Art 11 and there had been no effective domestic remedy available to him, via a court or otherwise.

*Court:* The Court disagreed with the Commission and found that there had been no violation of any Convention right. Although Art 11 could apply to the present situation, 'in view of the sensitive character of the social and political issues involved in achieving a proper balance between the competing interests', the issue of whether a State should intervene to restrict union action is subject to a wide margin of appreciation. The unions did place great pressure on the applicant to sign a collective agreement, but he had been given an alternative; he could have signed a substitute agreement. Although this would have amounted to the same result since it would have involved collective bargaining, he would have been able to tailor it to his needs to some extent. In any case, collective bargaining is legitimate and recognised by several international treaties. Thus on balance, there was no breach of Art 11, and hence of Art 13. The reasons given for the Court's rejection of the remainder of the claim were broadly similar to those of the Commission.

*Note:* Judges Martens, Matscher and Walsh, dissenting, found that there had been a breach of Art 11. They saw the situation as 'a conflict between two fundamental rights, that of the trade union relying on its positive freedom of association and that of the employer who invokes a negative freedom of association'. The trade unions' legitimate aim was not as important a consideration as its effect on the applicant, who was forced into a situation which affected his negative freedom of association. He was unable to negotiate his own labour agreements: 'the individual must be free to act according to his convictions and, accordingly, be protected against having to go against those convictions as a result of constraining collective action by one or more trade unions'. Thus, unless the trade unions could be shown to be acting to protect specific employees, Art 11 would be breached on the present facts.

# Young, James and Webster v United Kingdom
## (1981) 4 EHRR 38

*Facts:* In 1975, British Rail reached a closed shop agreement with three trade unions, and so membership of one of those unions became a condition of employment with British Rail. The three applicants had all joined British Rail prior to that date, and were dismissed for not becoming members of one of the three unions. They were unable to satisfy the conditions to claim unfair dismissal, and did not fit the then sole ground of exemption from union membership on religious belief. All the applicants objected to compulsory union membership on political or conscientious grounds. They alleged breaches of Arts 9, 10, 11 and 13, ie of the rights to freedom of thought, expression and association, and the lack of an effective domestic remedy.

*Commission:*  The Commission was of the opinion that there had been a violation of Art 11; that it was not necessary to deal separately with Arts 9 and 10; and that there was no breach of Art 13.

*Court:*  The primary issue was whether the State was responsible for any breaches which might be found. Since Art 1 requires each Contracting State to secure all Convention rights and freedoms to those within its jurisdiction, the fact that domestic law made the dismissal of the applicants lawful was enough to trigger the State's responsibility for failing to secure any relevant rights and freedoms.

The applicants had argued strongly that a 'negative right' of association was implied in Art 11, ie a right not to be compelled to join an association, including a trade union. 'To construe Article 11 as permitting every kind of compulsion in the field of trade union membership would strike at the very substance of the freedom which it is designed to guarantee.' Thus, although the Court did not go so far as to wholeheartedly endorse such a negative right, it went some way towards this. Threats of dismissal are a very serious form of compulsion and so interfered with the applicants' freedom of association in the present circumstances. Further, 'an individual does not enjoy the right to freedom of association if in reality the freedom of action or choice which remains available to him is either non-existent or so reduced as to be of no practical value'; the applicants' choice of which union, if any, to join had been severely restricted. Article 11 has as one of its purposes the protection of personal opinion, and pressurising someone into joining an association against his beliefs therefore 'strikes at the very substance' of Art 11. The detriment suffered by the applicants was greater than that which could be justified by the legitimate aims of closed shop agreements, and compelling the unwilling to join an association does not serve its members' interests. Thus, there was a violation of Art 11. The Court did not consider it necessary to assess the remaining alleged violations.

## (2)  COMPULSORY MEMBERSHIP OF UNIONS

### Sigurdur A Sigurjonsson v Iceland

### (1993) 16 EHRR 462

*Facts:*  The applicant was granted a licence to operate a taxi cab. The licence contained a condition that he would join and remain a member of a named automobile association which had amongst its functions the representation of taxi drivers' interests. The applicant joined the association but stopped paying his membership fees within a year. He wished to continue to be a taxi driver but did not want to be a member of the automobile association. His licence was revoked and the domestic courts stated that he did not have any legal right to refuse to be a member of the association. The applicant alleged breaches of Arts 9, 10, 11 and 13.

*Commission:*  The Commission found that there had been a violation of Art 11 and that it was not necessary to examine the remaining allegations. The applicant had argued that a right to associate with others for the promotion of one's beliefs, opinions or interests is of little use if a person may be compelled to join an association with contrary aims. Thus, freedom of association must include a right not to associate with groups against one's wishes or interests. The Commission did not consider it necessary to determine whether there is such a negative freedom of association, since the forced membership had such the serious threat behind it of loss of livelihood it 'struck at the very substance' of Art 11. There were advantages in ensuring membership of the association, but these were not sufficient to justify the serious interference, and so the compulsory membership was a violation of Art 11.

*Court:* Compulsory membership of a private association is rare among the laws of Contracting States, many of which do in fact guarantee the freedom not to join, or to withdraw from, an association. This negative freedom is also becoming a feature of international law. Thus, Art 11 'must be viewed as encompassing a negative right of association', whether or not this is to be protected as strongly as the positive right. Hence, there was interference with the applicant's freedom of association. It was also considered important that the applicant objected to being a member of the association partly because he disagreed with its policies. Article 11 can guarantee the protection of such personal opinions, and so pressure to be a member of the association was also an interference with the right to an opinion. Although the association served both its members' interests and the public interest, compulsory membership was not the only method of ensuring that it could perform its useful functions. There was little to be gained by forcing objectors to join an association with whose aims they disagreed. Thus, compulsory membership was not necessary in a democratic society and was a disproportionate interference. Article 11 had therefore been violated. The Court did not find it necessary to examine the other alleged violations.

## (3)   OTHER ASSOCIATIONS

### Chassagnou and Others v France
### (2000) 29 EHRR 615

*Facts:* The applicants were opposed to hunting on ethical grounds. They complained that they had been obliged to transfer hunting rights over their land to municipal hunting associations with the consequence that they acquired membership of those associations and could not prevent hunting on their property.

*Court:* 'To compel a person by law to join an association such that it is fundamentally contrary to his own convictions to be a member of it, and to oblige him, on account of his membership of that association, to transfer his rights over the land he owns so that the association in question can attain objectives of which he disapproves, goes beyond what is necessary to ensure that a fair balance is struck between conflicting interest and cannot be considered proportionate to the aim pursued' (para 117). Accordingly, there had been a violation of Art 11.

*UNITED KINGDOM CASES*

## Royal Society for the Prevention of Cruelty to Animals v HM Attorney-General and Others

High Court, Chancery Division, [2001] UKHRR 905

*Facts:*   The RSPCA, which had a long-standing policy of objecting to hunting with dogs, adopted a membership policy which would preclude from membership those joining the RSPCA with the intention of overturning that objection. The RSPCA sought the guidance of the Court on the legality of its proposals in order to comply with its obligations under s 33 of the Charities Act 1993.

*Held:*   The RSPCA had the power to make rules relating to membership and had acted in good faith in making the suggested amendments. The rules governing the charity did not need to be read as prohibiting the adoption of the membership scheme on human rights grounds, and the RSPCA was not a public body within the meaning of the HRA 1998. However, in certain respects the scheme required amendment as the RSPCA did not have the power to exclude people simply because they fell within a specific category, and full consideration had to be given to the merits of each case in respect of existing members. In respect of applicant members they should be given some opportunity to put their case. As it stood the scheme was arbitrary.

# Part 6
# PROPERTY, COMMERCIAL AND EC LAW

# Chapter 18

# OWNERSHIP AND USE OF PROPERTY

## 18.1 PROPERTY RIGHTS AND LAND OWNERSHIP

## (1) RIGHT TO PEACEFUL ENJOYMENT OF HOME

### Sporrong and Lönnroth v Sweden

### (1982) 5 EHRR 35

*Facts:* In the *Sporrong* case, the applicants owned a property which was subject to an expropriation permit as part of a planned building project in central Stockholm. The permit, which also prevented building on the land, was extended repeatedly from 1956 until 1979, although the original permit had been set to lapse after 5 years and no compensation hearing had ever been held. In 1979, the permit was cancelled since the planned development no longer affected the building in question.

In the *Lönnroth* case, an expropriation permit was issued in respect of the applicant's property in 1971, and was set to be valid for 10 years. The construction of a multi-storey car park was planned. The project was postponed and the applicant, believing her property to be in urgent need of repair, requested that the permit should be withdrawn. Her request was refused on the basis that no derogation from the permit was possible. She attempted to sell the property on seven occasions between 1970 and 1975, but each potential buyer withdrew after consulting the council plans. She also had difficulty in finding tenants for the property. The expropriation permit and ban on construction ran for 8 and 12 years respectively.

The applicants claimed, inter alia, violations of Art 1 of the First Protocol, Art 13 and Art 14.

*Commission:* The Commission found a violation of Art 13, but not of any other Convention provision.

*Court:* In relation to Art 1 of the First Protocol, the applicants had argued that, although the measures affecting their property were lawful in themselves, the duration of the expropriation permits and prohibitions on construction were such that it amounted to an unjustified interference with their right to peaceful enjoyment of their possessions. They had lost the possibility of selling the properties at normal market prices, had been unable to carry out improvements or to build on their own land, and would have had difficulty in obtaining mortgages if they had sought them. The Court agreed that there had been an interference with the applicants' property: 'Although the expropriation permits left intact in law the owners' right to use and dispose of their possessions, they nevertheless in practice significantly reduced the possibility of its exercise. They also affected the very substance of ownership in that they recognised before the event that any expropriation would be lawful and authorised the City of

Stockholm to expropriate whenever it found it expedient to do so. The applicants' right of property therefore became precarious and defeasible'. The prohibitions on construction had a similar effect. Thus, the key question was whether the interference was justified.

Article 1 of the First Protocol contains three rules: the first is the principle of peaceful enjoyment of property; the second allows deprivation of possession only where certain conditions are met; and the third allows States to control the use of property by law. Logically, the Court had to establish whether the second or third rules applied, rendering the State's actions lawful, before it could determine whether the first rule had been violated. The second rule could not apply since there had been no legal or factual expropriation. The prohibitions on construction were within the third rule since they controlled the use of the property concerned, but the same could not be said for the expropriation permits. Therefore, the latter had to be considered under the first rule. The first rule requires that a fair balance should be struck between the interests of the community in general and the protection of the individual's fundamental rights.

While there is a wide margin of appreciation in a field as complex as planning law, 'the Court cannot fail to exercise its power of review and must determine whether the requisite balance was maintained in a manner consonant with the applicants' right to "the peaceful enjoyment of their possessions", within the meaning of the first sentence of Article 1'. The relevant law was inflexible, providing no possibility of modification of the terms of an expropriation permit, and the permits had been in force for extremely long periods of time, causing great uncertainty to the owners of the property. There should have been some provision for review of the permits at reasonable intervals. The combined legal measures 'created a situation which upset the fair balance which should be struck between the protection of the right to property and the requirements of the general interest; the Sporrong Estate and Mrs Lönnroth bore an individual and excessive burden which could have been rendered legitimate only if they had had the possibility of seeking a reduction of the time-limits or of claiming compensation. Yet, at the relevant time, Swedish law excluded these possibilities and it still excludes the second of them'. Hence the interference was disproportionate and violated Art 1 of the First Protocol.

*Note:*   Eight judges gave a dissenting opinion which argued that there had not been any violation of Art 1 of the First Protocol and that the majority had interpreted that provision in a way which did not correspond to its underlying meaning:

> 'The first sentence of the Article contains a guarantee of private property. It is a provision
> in general terms protecting individuals and also private legal entities against interference
> with peaceful enjoyment of their possessions. However, modern States are obliged, in the
> interest of the community, to regulate the use of private property in many respects. There
> are always social needs and responsibilities relevant to its ownership and use. The ensuing
> provisions of Article 1 recognise these needs and responsibilities and the corresponding
> rights of the States. The very essence of city planning is to control the use of property,
> including private property, in the general interest.'

*NUISANCE*

# Powell and Rayner v United Kingdom
# (1990) 12 EHRR 355

*Facts:* The applicants were all affected, to differing extents, by the noise of aircraft since they lived near Heathrow airport. Mr Baggs, a third applicant whose case was subsequently settled, lived approximately one-quarter of a mile from the southern runway and ran a poultry and market gardening business from home. His property had lost value due to its location and so he had applied for planning permission to change its use from residential to commercial, hoping that this would make it easier to sell. The planning permission was refused on the ground that the area was primarily residential and the proposed change of use would affect this.

The first applicant lived further from the airport and suffered less noise nuisance. Although the area was over-flown by a particular flight route, that route was used only for about 4 months of the year and in certain weather conditions.

The second applicant lived just over one mile west of Heathrow, beyond the end of a runway, and so his land was constantly over-flown and was subject to a high level of noise nuisance.

Each applicant argued, inter alia, a violation of Art 8 by the noise nuisance affecting his property.

*Commission:* The *Baggs* case was found to be admissible as to violations of Art 8, Art 13 and of Art 1 of the First Protocol. However, this case was withdrawn after a settlement was reached. The other two applicants were treated differently, with the Commission finding them to be admissible as to Art 13, but not as to any other argued breach. As a general principle, noise nuisance can form a breach of Art 8, but on the facts of the second and third application, the interference with the applicants' rights was justified. 'Considerable noise nuisance can undoubtedly affect the physical well-being of a person and thus interfere with his private life. It may also deprive a person of the possibility of enjoying the amenities of his home.'

The justification lay in the fact that 'the running of an airport and the increasing use of jet aircraft is in the interest of the economic well-being of a country and is also necessary in a democratic society. It is essential for developing external and internal trade by providing speedy means of transportation and it is also an important factor for the development of tourism'. The government had also attempted to limit and control the noise nuisance from Heathrow.

There was a breach of Art 13, since there was no domestic remedy available to Mr Rayner, the second applicant, for his arguable claim to a violation of Art 8. Article 1 of the First Protocol did not form an arguable claim since 'there was no evidence that the value of the applicants' property has been substantially diminished or that their property has been rendered unsaleable by aircraft noise'. The first applicant, Mr Powell, had no arguable claim because the noise nuisance was not considered significant enough.

*Court:*   The Court had jurisdiction only to consider the Art 13 claims. Section 76 of the Civil Aviation Act 1982 excluded liability for nuisance and trespass in relation to aircraft flights which complied with regulations as to reasonable height and navigation. This exclusion was not absolute and whether s 76 applied to a particular dispute was a question for a domestic court to decide. Thus, although access to a legal remedy was limited, unreasonable aircraft use and noise could still form the basis of a domestic action for trespass or nuisance. Thus, there was no violation of Art 13.

## Hatton and Others v United Kingdom
## (2002) 34 EHRR 1

*Facts:*   The applicants complained that the level of noise caused by aircraft using Heathrow airport at night was excessive and amounted to an interference with their right to respect for private and family life. Following the introduction of a noise quota scheme in 1993, which allowed aircraft operators to choose whether to operate a greater number of quieter aircraft or a lesser number of noisier planes, the number of aircraft taking off and landing between 4 am and 7 am had increased significantly. While acknowledging that night flights had increased, the government submitted that the applicants in this case were exposed to lower noise levels than applicants in previous cases, which had been declared inadmissible. Referring to the commercial significance and economic importance of night flights at Heathrow, the government submitted, in the alternative, that in deciding to introduce the 1993 scheme they had managed to strike a fair and reasonable balance between the various interests involved, and any interference with the applicants' rights was justified.

*Court:*   Drawing a distinction between the situation of the present applicants and that of the applicants in previous cases, the Court concluded that the outcome of previous decisions was not relevant to the present case. Although noting that aircraft using Heathrow were not owned or controlled by the government and thus the UK could not be said to have directly interfered with a Convention right, the Court emphasised that Art 8 imposed a positive obligation on Contracting States. Accordingly, the government had a duty to take reasonable and appropriate measures to ensure compliance with the Convention. The Court observed that in determining the steps to be taken to achieve a fair balance between the competing interests of the individual and the community as a whole, the State enjoyed a margin of appreciation. However, the Court emphasised that in striking the required balance, States must have regard not only to the economic well-being of the UK but also to the particularly sensitive issue of environmental protection. While accepting that night flights contribute to some extent to the national economy, the Court found that the importance of this contribution had not been assessed critically. Furthermore, only limited research had been carried out into the nature of sleep disturbance when the 1993 scheme was implemented. Although further research was under way, the results would be too late to have any impact on the increase in night noise caused by this scheme. In determining the adequacy of the measures taken to protect the applicants' rights, the Court considered that, in the absence of any serious attempt to evaluate the impact on the applicants' sleep patterns, it could not be satisfied that the government had struck the right balance in setting up the 1993 scheme. Accordingly, despite the margin of appreciation, the Court held by five votes to two that there had been a violation of Art 8. The applicants were each awarded £4000 in respect of non-pecuniary damage and a global sum of £70,000 was awarded for costs and expenses.

## (2)   RIGHT TO LIVE ON OWN LAND

### Buckley v United Kingdom
### (1996) 23 EHRR 101

*Facts:*   The applicant, a gypsy, owned land and parked her caravans upon it without having obtained the necessary planning permission. The local council later refused the planning permission and an order was made for the removal of the caravans. The applicant was then fined for breach of the enforcement notice. She argued that there had been a breach of Art 8 in that she was being prevented from establishing home on her own land, her children were being denied a stable environment and continuous education, and the family were being denied the right to pursue their traditional gypsy lifestyle.

*Commission:*   The Commission found that there had been a violation of Art 8. Although that Article does not contain a right to have a home, but merely to have respect for an existing home, a minority may claim the right to respect for its lifestyle within Art 8 since 'the concept of "home" within the meaning of Art 8 is not limited to those which are lawfully occupied or which have been lawfully established. "Home" is an autonomous concept which does not depend on classification under domestic law'. Where a case concerns a right to live on land without the required planning permission, the Commission will weigh up 'the general interests of the community in effective planning controls against the applicant's right to respect for her private life, family life and home, rights which are an intrinsic part of her personal security and well-being'. Since the applicant was a gypsy, her traditional lifestyle further restricted the options open to her. She could not reasonably be expected to move onto an official site and so she was being placed in a position where all her options involved insecurity and disruption to her family. This was an excessive and disproportionate burden upon her and so her specific interests outweighed the general interest on the facts.

*Court:*   The Court agreed that the applicant's unauthorised settlement on her own land fell within the concept of 'home' for Art 8. However, the Court stressed that the margin of appreciation under Art 8 is a wide one where planning controls are concerned. An official site nearby was not considered unsuitable, but merely less satisfactory than the applicant's own land. Individual preferences could not outweigh the general interest, and it was not within the Court's role to look at the merits of specific planning decisions, as long as the competing claims had been considered appropriately and fairly by the planning inspectors. Hence there was no violation of Art 8.

### Chapman (Sally) and Others v United Kingdom
### (2001) 33 EHRR 18

*Facts:*   The applicant was a gypsy who had led a life of constant travelling, moving with her caravan from temporary site to temporary site, and being subject to frequent harassment. Eventually the applicant bought some land with the intention of living on it in a mobile home. There was no official gypsy site within the area of the Three Rivers District Council in Hertfordshire where the land in question lay. The applicant and her family moved onto the land and applied for planning permission, which was denied. An enforcement notice was served, and a number of appeals were lost on the grounds that the interests of maintaining the green belt in which the plot was situated outweighed the interests of the applicant. During the time of the various procedures the applicant and her family established themselves in the local community.

*Court:* The applicant claimed that the refusal of planning permission was in violation of Art 8, and the Commission had found by 18 votes to 9 that there was no violation of this provision. Both parties in the case made extensive reference to the case of *Buckley v United Kingdom* (above). It was accepted by the State that there had been an interference by a public authority with the applicant's right to respect for her home, and the Court found that the measures 'pursue the legitimate aim of protecting the "rights of others" through preservation of the environment' (para 82). In its consideration of whether the interference was 'necessary in a democratic society' the Court drew attention to an intervention by the European Roma Rights Centre, which submitted that there had been a growing consensus about the need to take specific measures to address the position of Roma. The Court, however, was 'not persuaded that the consensus is sufficiently concrete for it to derive any guidance as to the conduct or standards which Contracting States [to the Convention] consider desirable in any particular situation' (para 94). In balancing the interests of those claiming protection for their home, and the State, the 'Court will be slow to grant protection to those who, in conscious defiance of the prohibitions of the law, establish a home on an environmentally protected site' (para 102). In the present case it was not the role of the Court to examine the national position *vis-à-vis* the provision of homes for gypsies, but rather the facts of the particular case, and 'the humanitarian considerations which might have supported another outcome at national level cannot be used as the basis of a finding by the Court which would be tantamount to exempting the applicant from the implementation of the national planning laws' (para 115). The Court found that there had been no violation of Art 8.

*Note:* The Court also dealt with this issue in the cases of *Lee v United Kingdom* (2001) 33 EHRR 29, *Smith and Grady v United Kingdom* (2001) 31 EHRR 24, *Beard v United Kingdom* (2001) 33 EHRR 19, and *Coster v United Kingdom* (2001) 33 EHRR 20.

## (3)   PROTECTION FROM HARASSMENT

### Whiteside v United Kingdom

### 7 March 1994, unreported

*Facts:* The applicant was a divorced woman who lived with her five children, four of whom had serious medical conditions. She had left the father of the two youngest children, alleging that he had become violent and abusive towards her, but he obtained access visits. The older of his children alleged that he had indecently assaulted her and access was then revoked, but since that date he allegedly instituted a campaign of harassment against the applicant. The applicant applied for an interlocutory injunction to restrain the man from harassing, threatening, pestering or using violence against her, but the injunction was refused on the basis that, at that time, there was no tort of harassment and no tortious or criminal act had been shown to have been committed or threatened by the defendant. The applicant was unable to pursue her claim, and alleged that the acts of harassment continued and that there had therefore been violations of Arts 8, 13 and of Art 1 of the First Protocol.

*Commission:* The Commission found that the alleged harassment suffered by the applicant could constitute an interference with the applicant's right to respect for her private life and for the enjoyment of her home, noting 'the persistent and distressing nature of the alleged conduct of Mr B and the consequent effect which it had on the applicant and the way in which she leads her life ... the responsibility of the State is engaged and it is under a positive obligation to secure the applicant's rights by providing adequate protection against this type of deliberate persecution'. However, there were remedies available to the applicant under domestic law, either for damages or an injunction, which would have provided her with effective relief. Thus, the application was held to be inadmissible.

## (4) SEARCHES AND INVASION OF PRIVACY

## Chappell v United Kingdom

## (1989) 11 EHRR 543

*Facts:* The applicant ran a video club supplying second generation video cassettes to its subscribers. Many of the videos had been recorded in breach of copyright. A group of film companies and organisations representing film producers and distributors obtained an *Anton Piller* order to find evidence for a future breach of copyright action; 377 pirated cassettes were among the items seized. He alleged a breach, inter alia, of Art 8 and of Art 1 of the First Protocol.

*Commission:* The Commission found that there had been no violation.

*Court:* The Court agreed that some aspects of the search of the premises were 'disturbing', 'unfortunate and regrettable' and made the execution of the order 'more oppressive than it should have been'. However, 'the shortcomings in the procedure followed – which, by its very nature, was bound to cause some difficulties for the applicant – were not so serious that the execution of the order can, in the circumstances of the case, be regarded as disproportionate to the legitimate aim pursued'. Hence there was no violation of Art 8.

## Gillow v United Kingdom

## (1991) 13 EHRR 593

*Facts:* The applicants were a married couple and the owners of a house in Guernsey. They had built the property themselves during a period of the husband's employment there. They had, during that period, occupied the house for about 2 years, but had subsequently left the island. Although it remained theirs, they let the property for about 18 years between 1960 and 1978. Wishing to return to Guernsey on the husband's retirement, they applied to the local Housing Authority for permission to occupy the house. Permission to occupy the property was refused under the Guernsey Housing Law 1969 and 1975 on the basis that they did not fulfil criteria relating to employment prospects and residence qualifications in Guernsey. Under that law, they were required to obtain a licence to occupy from the Housing Authority before resuming occupation. They subsequently entered into occupation of the premises without a licence and the husband was prosecuted for unlawful occupation. He was convicted and a fine was imposed by the magistrates' court. The Royal Court of Guernsey upheld the conviction and fine. The applicants claimed that the operation of the legislation was in breach of, inter alia, Art 8.

*Commission:* The key question was whether a fair balance had been found between the applicants' rights and those of the community in general. Any rule controlling the use of land had to be narrowly construed, with regard to whether the control rule pursues a legitimate aim in the public interest, and whether its effect upon the applicants was proportionate to that legitimate aim.

Thus, any control on the use of property, even if it has a legitimate purpose, would be in breach of the First Protocol 'if it is clearly established that there is no reasonable relationship of proportionality between the interference with the individual's rights and the general interest which gives legitimacy to the aim pursued'. The applicants' property was a home; the interference had therefore deprived them of almost the whole of its benefit, although they still had ownership. Thus, in spite of the control's legitimate aim, it was disproportionate and failed to pay due respect to the applicants' rights to enjoy their possessions.

*Court:* When the case reached the Court, it was realised that the claim under the First Protocol could not be sustained since Guernsey is not bound by that Protocol by reason of a technicality. However, this did not affect the Art 8 claim. The applicants had no other home and had been obliged to seek a licence to occupy their own property, with a criminal conviction as the end result of their occupation after the licence was refused. While there was a legitimate aim to the legal control on occupation, that of restricting the residential population of a small island to which many people wished to move, in order to promote the economic health of the island, many factors operated in favour of the applicants. The island's population was no longer increasing; they had no other home; and there were no other prospective tenants of the property, which would not receive vital repairs until the applicants could occupy it. Thus, the refusal of a licence to occupy was disproportionate and there had been a breach of Art 8.

# (5) THE OPERATION OF PLANNING CONTROLS

## Jacobsson (Allan) v Sweden

## (1989) 12 EHRR 56

*Facts:* The applicant was the owner of the land on which his home was built. The land was subject to building prohibitions and a ban on subdivision of the land. The applicant wished to subdivide the land into smaller plots or to build a small family house on the land, but permission was refused repeatedly by the local authority. Many appeals over a period of some 22 years were unsuccessful. The applicant alleged violations of Arts 6(1), 13, 17, 18, and of Art 1 of the First Protocol.

*Court:* The applicant had argued that the length of the prohibitions on building on his own land was a violation of Art 1 of the First Protocol. That there had been an interference with his rights was not disputed by the government. The Court pointed out that this case differed from *Sporrong and Lonnroth* (**18.1(1)**) in that at no time had the present applicant ever been threatened with expropriation; it was merely the case that his use of the land was controlled. The question was whether this control was a disproportionate interference with the applicant's rights. The Court found that it was not, and hence there was no violation of Art 1 of the First Protocol.

# ISKCON (International Society for Krishna Consciousness) v United Kingdom

## (1994) 18 EHRR CD 133

*Facts:* The applicant association, a registered religious charity, bought a nineteenth-century rural manor house in 1973 for use as a residential theological college for the promotion of Krishna Consciousness. The local authority stated that planning permission was not required, but later, by agreement, imposed conditions. Subsequently, the local authority served an enforcement notice on ISKCON which alleged a breach of planning control by material change of use of the premises to include a 'religious community and public worship and public entertainment in connection with religious festivals'. ISKCON's appeal was rejected after an inquiry; the court regarded the planning conditions as maintaining a reasonable balance between the rights of worshippers and local residents. ISKCON and a group of representative worshippers alleged violations, inter alia, of Arts 9 and Art 1 of the First Protocol in conjunction with Art 14.

*Commission:* Planning control legislation would not usually in itself constitute a violation of Convention rights, since there is a wide discretion given to a State in this respect. But the enforcement notices issued were an interference with ISKCON's freedom of religion, which includes 'the freedom to manifest that religion in worship, teaching, practice and observance'. Thus, it was important to decide whether this interference was necessary in a democratic society. Planning legislation is generally accepted to be necessary in modern society in order to protect the rights of other residents and to prevent uncontrolled development. The enforcement notices were proportionate to these legitimate aims, since adequate weight had been given to freedom of religion. The refusal of planning permission was based properly on planning grounds and not on any religious discrimination or prejudice. Thus, there was no breach of Art 9 and the entire complaint was found to be inadmissible.

# Varey v United Kingdom

## [2001] TLR 72

*Facts:* The applicants alleged, inter alia, that planning and enforcement measures taken against them in respect of their occupation of their land violated their right to respect for home, family and private life contrary to Art 8 and that they had no effective access to a court to challenge the decisions taken by the planning authorities, contrary to Art 6. The applicants, a group of local gypsies living in and around Stafford, had bought land on which they intended to live in order to maintain their traditional gypsy lifestyle, but were refused planning permission by the local council. Finding that the need for gypsy accommodation did not disclose the very special circumstances necessary to override the strong policy presumption against prejudicial development in the green belt, the Secretary of State for the Environment dismissed the appeal. In his view, granting the appeal would result in demand for further sites and weaken the Council's stance in resisting future development. The first applicant was convicted for failing to comply with an enforcement notice and fined £1000. The government informed the Court that the parties had agreed to settle the case on the terms that the government pay the applicants £60,000 and pay the applicants' legal costs.

*Court:*   In these circumstances, the court found that the matter had been resolved and the case was struck out of the list.

## UNITED KINGDOM CASES

## R v Secretary of State for the Environment, Transport and the Regions, ex parte Holding and Barnes plc and Others
House of Lords, [2001] UKHL 23, [2001] 2 WLR 1389

*Facts:*   It was argued in the context of a number of planning inquiries and decisions that the exercise by the Secretary of State of his power under various statutes, including the Town and Country Planning Act 1990, was not compatible with Art 6(1) of the Convention. The European Court of Appeal issued a declaration of incompatibility, finding that the proceedings in question involved the determination of civil rights, and that the Secretary of State lacked the requisite degree of independence. The Secretary of State had argued that while he was not an independent and impartial tribunal, individual Crown servants involved in the making of decisions were, and that the procedure as a whole was fair given the possibility of the right to appeal and judicial review.

*Held:*   The House of Lords, overturning the decision of the Court of Appeal, held that the process was not incompatible with Art 6. It was clear from the jurisprudence of the European Court of Human Rights that even if the Secretary of State himself was not independent, the question was that of whether taken as a whole there was sufficient judicial control over the administrative process. This depended on all the circumstances of a case, and the common law had developed the grounds of judicial review of administrative acts that were reflected in statute. It was appropriate in a democratic society that the grounds of expediency allowed decisions to be taken at the administrative level, but that in relation to findings of fact, or the evaluation of facts, some judicial oversight was necessary in order to provide for the safeguards guaranteed by the Convention. Those safeguards existed in the present cases.

## (6)  PROPERTY TRANSACTION PROCEEDINGS

## Eisenstecken v Austria

## (2002) 34 EHRR 35

*Facts:*  The applicant entered into a contract relating to real property with E, who subsequently died. This contract was approved, as required under Austrian law, by the local Real Property Transactions Authority. An appeal against the approval was launched by the administrator of the deceased's estate, and by the Regional Government. The applicant requested an oral hearing relating to the appeal, but the appeal was heard in camera, and the applicant was not permitted to make a representation at it. The applicant complained that the failure to permit him to present his arguments was in breach of Art 6.

*Court:*  Following earlier cases (eg *Ringeisen v Austria (No 1)* (1979–80) 1 EHRR 455), Art 6 is applicable to real property transaction proceedings. A reservation relied on by Austria on the basis of Art 57 was found to be invalid as it did not satisfy the requirements of Art 57(2). None of the competent authorities held a public hearing, and the applicant was in principle entitled to such a hearing as none of the exemptions laid down in Art 6 applied in the present case. There were no exceptional circumstances which would prevent the holding of such a hearing. The Court therefore found that unanimously that there had been a breach of Art 6(1).

## (7)  LICENSING OF PREMISES

### *UNITED KINGDOM CASES*

## Catscratch Ltd and Lettuce Holdings Ltd v Glasgow City Licensing Board (No 2)

Court of Session, Outer House, [2001] UKHRR 1309

*Facts:*  The relevant licensing board refused an application for an extension of a night-club entertainment licence. The applicant sought judicial review based in part on the application of Art 6.

*Held:*  Article 6 applied to licensing proceedings, but in the present case no specific issues were raised under the Article that were not covered under Scottish common law.

## 18.2  LANDLORD AND TENANT

### (1)  RIGHT OF LANDLORD FREELY TO MANAGE AND DISPOSE OF PROPERTY

## James v United Kingdom

## (1986) 8 EHRR 123

*Facts:*  The trustees of the estate of the Duke of Westminster brought an action claiming that the Leasehold Reform Act 1967 was an unlawful interference with their right to enjoy property in breach of Art 1 of the First Protocol. The estate was the freehold owner of more than 2000 expensive residential properties in London, most of which were let out on long leases. The terms of the leases had originally been freely agreed to by the predecessors in title to the current lessees. The legislation broadly created a scheme whereby holders of long leases could compel their landlords either: (i) to sell the freeholds of the properties to the lessees; or (ii) to extend the leases beyond the date envisaged by the original parties. This clearly involved a diminution of the landlords' ability to control their own property interests, although the legislation had made provision for compensation to be payable to the landlords according to a formula, and subject to review by the Lands Tribunal or by the Leasehold Valuation Tribunal.

The applicants claimed further that there was discrimination inherent on the legislation contrary to Art 14 on the basis, inter alia, that it focused upon one type of property only, and hence one type of landlord, namely long leases.

*Court:* Whilst the operation of the Leasehold Reform Act 1967 constituted a deprivation of the applicants' property rights in the cases complained of, the enactment could be justified as being in the public interest. The question to be considered was whether the deprivation was justified in the interests of wider social policy. The Court found that the principle of 'leasehold enfranchisement', the rights of long leaseholders to purchase their landlords' interests, and compulsory lease extension was a legitimate aim. Leasehold reform was a legitimate aim for the State to pursue. In the pursuit of that aim both the scheme itself, and the provisions for compensation, were both subject to the 'wide margin of appreciation' principle. Thus, unless the judgement of the national Parliament was manifestly without reasonable foundation in the enactment of the statute, the Court would not interfere. This was the case even if in some cases 'undeserving' tenants thereby benefited. Consequently, the State had not breached Art 1 of the First Protocol by depriving the applicants of their property.

## Melleacher v Austria
## (1989) 12 EHRR 391

*Facts:* The applicants were property owners who derived income from renting residential properties. Under the Rent Act 1981, a system of rent controls was implemented specifying maximum basic rents for certain classes of dwelling. In the applicants' case, the rents had been freely negotiated for 10 years, but had exceeded the newly imposed statutory maximum. The statutory framework had reduced the rent payable on one particular property to 17.6% of the original amount contractually agreed. They claimed that the legislature had interfered with the freedom of contract and deprived them of a substantial proportion of their future income in breach of Art 1 of the First Protocol of the Convention.

*Court:* The Court held, following *James v United Kingdom* (above), that in the implementation of social and economic policies, the legislature would be afforded a wide margin of appreciation. Unless the judgement of the national Parliament was manifestly without reasonable foundation in the enactment of the statute, the Court would not interfere. In this case, the reasons behind the legislation pursued a legitimate aim in the general interest, namely the reduction in disparities between rents for equivalent flats, and the combating of property speculation. The Court found that the measures taken did not amount to an expropriation of property as there was no transfer of property rights, merely a control of the use of the property. The relevant section of Art 1 referred to the entitlement of every natural and legal person to '. . . the peaceful enjoyment of his possessions. No one shall be deprived of his possessions except in the public interest and subject to the conditions provided for by law'. It was also provided, however, that those provisions would not 'in any way impair the right of a State to enforce such laws as it deems necessary to control the use of property in accordance with the general interest or to secure the payment of taxes or other contributions or penalties'.

The second paragraph of Art 1 of the First Protocol reserved to the State the right to control the use of property in the general interest. Such a right was especially called for in the field of housing. Whatever interference the State employed with property rights, it had to achieve a balance between the general interest and the protection of individual rights. Proportionality had to exist between the means employed and the aim pursued. Art 1 of the First Protocol did not preclude the legislature from interfering with existing contracts. Indeed, in remedial social legislation, it had to be open to the legislature to take measures affecting the further execution of previously concluded contracts. Even where the rent reductions were striking in their amount, 80% and above in this case, it did not follow that the reductions constituted a disproportionate burden.

# GL v Italy

# (2002) 34 EHRR 41

*Facts:* The applicant was the owner of an apartment in Milan, and served a notice to quit on a tenant. A court order granting possession was made, but the tenant refused to quit the premises. A statutory provision operated so as to suspend the enforcement of 'non-urgent' possession orders, and it therefore proved impossible for a bailiff to evict the tenant as an instruction to suspend the eviction was made by the Milan Prefect. The applicant, relying on Art 1 of the First Protocol, and Art 6, argued that the impossibility of enforcing the eviction notice infringed his property rights.

*Court:* The Court unanimously held that there had been a violation of Art 1. The second paragraph of Art 1 encompasses interference with property rights. The impugned legislation pursued a legitimate aim, and the question was that of whether there was a fair balance between this aim and the impact of the measure on the applicant. The system of staggering the enforcement of court orders was not in itself open to criticism, but in the present case the applicant was eventually able to recover possession of the apartment after a period of 3 years and 5 months from the making of the original court order of possession, and then only because the tenant spontaneously left. The Court found that an excessive burden was imposed on the applicant.

*Note:* This case substantially follows that of *Immobiliare Saffi v Italy* (2000) 30 EHRR 756, which dealt with the same Italian law.

## (2)   PROTECTION FROM EVICTION

### Spadea and Scalabrino v Italy

### (1995) 21 EHRR 482

*Facts:*   In April 1982, the applicants bought two flats with the intention of residing in them as their home. The flats were already let on a publicly controlled rent to two elderly ladies, Mrs B and Mrs Z. The applicants commenced proceedings to regain possession of the flats in October 1982, the leases being due to expire on 31 December 1983. The magistrate made an order for eviction in December 1984. However, pursuant to domestic law passed subsequently, the magistrate suspended enforcement of the evictions until January 1986. Enforcement of the evictions was suspended on three further occasions. In February 1988, the applicants were forced to purchase another flat. In August 1988, Mrs Z died and the applicants regained possession of her flat. Mrs B vacated her flat in February 1989.

The application was made on the basis of breaches of Art 1 of the First Protocol and of Art 14 of the Convention in that the legislation protected tenants to the detriment of landlords and that it only concerned the owners of buildings used for housing and not the owners of other types of property.

*Court:*   The Court held that the legislation in question was in the general interest and was consistent with Art 1. Article 14 will be breached and discrimination can occur where, without objective and reasonable justification, persons in 'relevantly' similar situations are treated differently. The distinction drawn between owners of non-residential property and the applicants in enforcing evictions was objective and reasonable given the aim of the legislation, ie to protect tenants during a serious housing shortage. Consequently, there had been no breach of Art 14 read in conjunction with Art 1 of the First Protocol.

## (3)   REASONABLENESS OF TIME FOR DETERMINING DISPUTES

### Pammel v Germany

### (1998) 26 EHRR 100

*Facts:*   In 1971, the applicant inherited land leased to Hoxter Town Council, which in turn sub-let the land for use as allotment gardens. The initial lease ran until September 1958 and was subsequently extended until September 1978. The applicant applied in September 1978 to Minden Administrative Court contesting the fixed rents set by the Land Government, and requested that it refer the constitutionality of the 1919 Allotment Gardens Act to the Federal Constitutional Court. Judgment on the issues was not given until September 1992. The applicant complained of the length of time it had taken the Federal Constitutional Court to review the Acts and alleged that that period of time exceeded the reasonable time referred to in Art 6(1) of the Convention.

*Court:*   The Court held that Art 6(1) of the Convention applied to all proceedings, the result of which is decisive of private or civil rights and obligations, even if they are conducted before a constitutional court. The character of the legislation which governs how the matter is to be determined is of little consequence. Furthermore, the reasonableness of the length of proceedings must be assessed in the light of the particular circumstances of the case as well as in the context of the complexity of the case, the conduct of the parties and the conduct of the authorities dealing with the case.

Article 6(1) of the Convention required the Contracting States to organise their judicial systems so that their courts could meet each of the Convention's requirements. This included the obligation to hear cases within a reasonable time. However, that obligation could not be construed in the same way for a constitutional court as for an ordinary court. Ultimately, it was for the Court in the last instance to verify that the obligation had been complied with. The applicant was not responsible for any of the delay, therefore in the light of all the prevailing circumstances, and having regard to the complexity of the case, the Constitutional Court proceedings did not satisfy the reasonable time requirement laid down in Art 6(1).

## Scollo v Italy

## (1995) 22 EHRR 514

*Facts:* The applicant bought a residential flat in Rome in 1982 which was occupied by a tenant. The applicant sought eviction of the tenant in 1983 on the grounds that the applicant was unemployed, diabetic, 71% disabled and needed the flat for himself. Furthermore, the tenant had stopped paying his rent. An eviction order was granted in 1983, but was subsequently suspended in accordance with a government policy of postponing eviction orders against residential tenants. The public authorities in Italy frequently intervened in housing legislation. The order for possession was further suspended on three later occasions. The tenant eventually left the premises of his own accord in January 1995, 11 years after proceedings had first been brought. During this time, and during several different periods when the suspensions were not in force, bailiffs acting on behalf of the applicant made 35 unsuccessful attempts to evict the tenant. The applicant applied on two occasions to the prefectoral committee, who had the power to grant police assistance in enforcing orders, but did not receive a reply. The applicant complained of an interference with his right to the peaceful enjoyment of his possessions as secured by Art 1 of the First Protocol, and that his case had not been heard within a reasonable time in violation of Art 6(1).

*Commission:* The Commission declared that there had been a violation of Art 1 of the First Protocol, and that it was not necessary to examine the complaint under Art 6(1). In doing so, the Commission applied the Court's decision in *Melleacher v Austria* (above). Whilst in this case there had been no expropriation of property, the measures in question concerned control of the 'use of property' by the State, and was open to examination under Art 1 of the First Protocol. The Commission reiterated the principle that States have a wide margin of appreciation in housing cases. The State's right to control the use of property had to be construed in the light of the general right to peaceful enjoyment of property, and hence a 'fair balance' had to be achieved between the general interest and the individual's fundamental rights. Here, the government were alleging that the suspension of evictions was dictated by an acute housing shortage, threatening considerable social tension. It was noted by the Commission that there were exceptions to the suspension provisions for lessors who required their properties urgently for themselves. In the applicant's case, he had indeed urgently required his flat, and this need was not disputed. In spite of this, the eviction was repeatedly postponed and he was unable even to receive a reply from the prefectoral committee. It was not submitted by the government that the tenant needed special social protection.

*Court:*   The Court said that the three elements of Art 1 of the First Protocol were not 'distinct' in the sense of being unconnected; the second and third rules had to be read in the light of the general principle. The measures in question undoubtedly amounted to a control of the use of possessions. The legislation had had a legitimate aim, being prompted by an immediate housing shortage. Once that was decided, it was necessary to determine whether the State's interference had been proportional. It was noted that housing shortages are an almost universal problem of modern society. The authorities had not, however, responded adequately to the applicant's needs. The means chosen by the government were appropriate to the legitimate aim. The restriction on the applicant's use of his flat resulted from the authorities' failure to apply the exceptions to the provisions which protected the right of landlords who urgently needed their property back. This amounted to a breach of Art 1 of the First Protocol. As to the claim under Art 6(1), the Court said that, while there had, strictly speaking, not been 'proceedings' to enforce the evictions, the measures taken to secure the evictions amounted to a dispute falling within the scope of the Article. The period taken to settle the dispute between the applicant and his tenant was 11 years and 10 months. This was too long, and there had been a breach of Art 6(1).

## 18.3   EXPROPRIATION

### Former King of Greece v Greece

### (2001) 33 EHRR 21

*Facts:*   The first applicant acceded to the Greek throne in 1964. In April 1967 there was a military coup in Greece and the applicant was deposed, although he remained in the country until December, when he left for Italy. A new Constitution was promulgated which guaranteed the right to property, but which in a unique provision provided also for the confiscation of all the movable and immovable property of the former Royal Family. This was put into effect by way of a legislative decree which confiscated the property, including that forming the basis of the present application, and which allowed for compensation of some 120,000,000 drachmas. Following the establishment of a democratic government an agreement was reached between the former King and the government relating to various properties formerly held by the Crown, although this was never put into full effect. Following the enactment of further legislation various court actions were initiated by the former King. These culminated in a judgment of the Special Supreme Court in 1997 which held that property claimed by the former King was lawfully the property of the State.

*Court:*   The Court held, by 15 votes to 2, that there had been a violation of Art 1 of the First Protocol. The argument of the Greek State that the property in question was inextricably linked to the institution of the Head of State and did not therefore fall under the notion of 'property' in Art 1 was rejected. The concept of possessions has an autonomous meaning independent from the formal classification in domestic law. History suggested that some of the royal property had been treated by the Greek State as being the private property of the Royal Family. The position of the respondent was therefore inconsistent, and the question for the Court was that of which property exactly was to be regarded as being the applicants' possessions. The Court found that the property which formed the subject matter of the present dispute did belong to the applicants. The deprivation of the property was by way of a legal measure properly undertaken. The question was then that of whether the deprivation was in the public interest. In that context the margin of appreciation given to Contracting States recognised in part that 'because of their direct knowledge of their society and its needs, the national authorities are in principle better placed than the international judge to appreciate what "is in the public interest" ' (para 86). In the present case the measure was taken in the national interest. The applicants submitted that the taking of the estates in question without compensation was 'wholly disproportionate'. The Court found that the applicants 'had a legitimate expectation to be compensated by the Greek legislature' (para 98). Accordingly, the Court held that the 'lack of any compensation for the deprivation of the applicants' property upsets, to the detriment of the applicants, the fair balance between the protection of property and the requirements of public interest' (para 99).

## Akkus v Turkey

## (2000) 30 EHRR 365

*Facts:*   In September–October 1987 the National Water Board (NWB) expropriated land belonging to the applicant, and paid compensation of 800–850 Turkish lira per square metre. A scientific study later assessed the value of the land at a higher level, and a court awarded the applicant additional compensation of 393.039 Turkish lira, as well as legal costs, in 1987. This was not paid until February 1992, following an unsuccessful appeal to the Court of Cassation by the NWB and the applicant's lodging of her case with the Commission. The applicant relied on Art 1 of the First Protocol.

*Court:*   The Court found by seven votes to two that there had been a breach of the Convention. The adequacy of compensation is diminished when there are unduly lengthy delays in its payment. At a time of inflation of some 70% per annum a delay in the payment of compensation by the State 'rendered that compensation inadequate and, consequently, upset the balance between the protection of the right to property and the requirements of the general interest'.

## Beyeler v Italy

## (2001) 33 EHRR 52

*Facts:*   The applicant had purchased, through an agent, a Van Gogh painting in 1977. The applicant was Swiss, and the painting was purchased from an Italian. The painting fell within the ambit of Italian legislation dealing with the right of the State to pre-empt private purchases in order to keep certain works of historical or artistic interest within Italy. The sale was notified to the relevant Ministry, but the fact that the sale was to a non-Italian was not disclosed. In 1988, after the State became aware of the ownership of the painting, the relevant Ministry informed the applicant that it wished to purchase the picture. By then, however, the picture had been resold to a collection in Venice. Six months later the national authorities asserted a right of pre-emption in respect of the 1977 sale. Compensation was paid at the 1977 price, well below current market value. The Italian courts held that any loss suffered by the applicant was a result of the failure to declare the full details relating to the purchaser in 1977. The applicant claimed, relying, inter alia, on Art 1 of the First Protocol, that the authorities had violated his right to property.

*Court:*   The Court held by 16 votes to 1 that there had been a breach of Art 1 of the First Protocol, which comprises three distinct, but connected, rules. These provide first, a general right to the enjoyment of property; secondly, that deprivation of property is subject to restrictions; and thirdly, that States are entitled to control use of property in accordance with the general interest. The first question in the present case was that of whether the applicant had a property interest in the painting. The applicant had, over a number of years, been in possession of the painting and was considered de facto by the authorities to have been the owner. These factors indicated that the applicant had a proprietary interest recognised under Italian law, which constituted a 'possession' for the purposes of the First Protocol. The exercise of the right of pre-emption undoubtedly constituted an interference in the applicant's use of the property, and the question then was that of whether the interference struck a 'fair balance' between the protection of the individual's right and the interests asserted by the State. The Court found that 'the control by the State of the market in works of art is a legitimate aim' (para 112). The applicant had not acted openly in concealing his nationality from the authorities and the original vendor of the painting. However, the Italian authorities had waited 5 years from becoming aware of the nationality of the applicant and making the decision to exercise their right of pre-emption, and their approach had vacillated over this period. The Court stressed that 'where an issue in the general interest is at stake it is incumbent on the public authorities to act in good time, in an appropriate manner and with utmost consistency' (para 120). The Court concluded that the applicant had had to bear a disproportionate and excessive burden.

# Chapter 19

# COMMERCIAL LAW

## 19.1  COMMERCIAL RIGHTS ARE ENCOMPASSED WITHIN THE MEANING OF CIVIL RIGHTS

### Benthem v The Netherlands

### (1985) 8 EHRR 1

*Facts:*  The applicant, who owned and ran a garage, was granted a licence in 1976 to operate a liquid gas petroleum delivery system. The Regional Health Inspector lodged an appeal which was successful. The applicant was told that, pending his appeal, he could erect the installation, but that the authorities would not be responsible for any financial loss if he did so. Subsequently, a Decree was issued by the Crown quashing the municipal authorities' decision, and revoking the licence. The applicant appealed unsuccessfully and, in February 1984, the installation was closed down. The applicant was declared bankrupt at the end of that year. The applicant claimed that the dispute related to civil rights and obligations, and that Art 6 had been breached as the matter had not been heard by an independent tribunal.

*Commission:*  The Commission held that Art 6 was not applicable in the present case, and that it was not necessary to consider further whether its requirements had been breached.

*Court:*  The applicant had argued that both the initial grant of the licence and its subsequent refusal by the Crown had decisively and directly affected his professional activities and contractual relations, and hence civil rights and obligations. The Court, reviewing its previous case-law, held that a 'genuine and serious' dispute as to the 'actual existence' of the right to a licence claimed by the applicant had arisen, and that the result of the proceedings in question was directly decisive for the right at issue. The licence in question was closely associated to the right to use one's possessions in conformity with the law's requirements, and also had a proprietary character, as the licence could be transferred to third parties. Although the government had claimed that the applicant was free to apply for a licence for an alternative site, a change of that kind would, in any event, have had adverse effects on the value of the existing business, on goodwill and the contractual relationships with the applicant's customers and suppliers. These factors confirmed the existence of direct links between the grant of the licence and 'the entirety of the applicant's commercial activities'. Accordingly, a civil right within the meaning of Art 6 was found to be at stake. The Court went on to find that the proceedings lacked the required guarantees to be compatible with the Convention, and thus found for the applicant.

## 19.2   DEROGATIONS FROM GUARANTEES NOT JUSTIFIED BY 'SPECIAL FEATURES'

### Funke v France

### (1993) 16 EHRR 297

*Facts:*   French customs authorities attempted to compel the applicant to produce documents which might provide them with evidence to commence a prosecution. His refusal to disclose the documents resulted in a court order for the production of his bank statements and the imposition of a pecuniary sanction. The applicant claimed that his conviction for refusing to produce self-incriminating documents violated his right to a fair trial and was in breach of the principle of the presumption of innocence.

*Commission:*   Before the Commission, the applicant argued that his criminal conviction for refusing to produce the documents requested by the customs authority violated his right to a fair trial, and was in breach of Art 6. He argued also that the search of his home violated Art 8. The Commission found, by a narrow margin, that there had been no breach of the Convention.

*Court:*   The government argued in its submissions that house searches and seizures were the only means available to the authorities for investigating offences falling under the relevant financial legislation. The Court accepted that this might be the case but noted that, at the time of the events, the customs authorities had very wide powers, including the exclusive competence to assess the expediency, number, length and scale of inspections. The Court found that Art 8 had been violated. In relation to Art 6, the applicant alleged that he was being compelled to co-operate in a prosecution mounted against him. The government emphasised the declaratory nature of the French customs regime, which benefited taxpayers, but which carried with it certain duties, including the requirement to maintain records and to make these available to the taxation authorities. The Court, however, held that 'the special features of customs law cannot justify such an infringement of the right of anyone "charged with a criminal offence" . . . to remain silent and not to contribute to incriminating [him]self'.

### Société Stenuit v France

### (1992) 14 EHRR 509

*Facts:*   The applicant company was accused of breaches of French economic legislation relating to price fixing. A fine of FF50,000 was imposed by the Minister of Economic and Financial Affairs by way of Decision, following consultation with the Competition Commission. The applicant appealed to the Minister to reconsider the Decision, and the appeal was dismissed. A further appeal to the *Conseil d'Etat* was dismissed.

*Commission:*   In its application to the Commission, the company argued that the proceedings taken against it were in breach of Art 6. The Commission expressed the unanimous opinion that Art 6 had been breached, and that the applicant had been denied the right to a fair and impartial hearing. Following the reaching of a friendly settlement between the parties, the Court agreed that the case should be struck out of the list.

## Saunders v United Kingdom

## (1996) 23 EHRR 313

*Facts:*   The applicant complained that the use in criminal proceedings of answers compulsorily obtained from him in a non-judicial investigation violated his right not to incriminate himself. He had been the Chief Executive Officer of Guinness plc when the company bought Distillers plc in April 1986, following a takeover battle with the Argyll Group plc. During an investigation into the activities of the company, he had been legally obliged to answer questions put to him by the DTI inspectors acting under statutory powers provided by s 432 of the Companies Act 1985. Failure to answer these questions could lead to a financial penalty or a prison sentence. The applicant was subsequently convicted of offences involving false accounting, theft and conspiracy. At his trial, the prosecution had been allowed to adduce in evidence incriminating statements made during his interviews with the DTI inspectors.

*Commission:*   The applicant argued that special features of proceedings could not be used to justify the denial of the right against self-incrimination, and that such a right should apply equally to all regardless of the nature of the allegations, or the level of education or status of the defendants. The UK argued that many jurisdictions permitted the compulsory taking of statements during investigations into corporate or financial frauds and their subsequent use in criminal trials. The UK argued that there was a strong public interest in the honest conduct of companies and in the effective prosecution of those involved in complex corporate fraud, and that in this respect a distinction could be drawn between corporate fraud and other types of crime. The Commission held that the privilege against self-incrimination formed an important element in safeguarding individuals from oppression and coercion, and should apply equally to all types of accused, including those alleged to have committed complex corporate frauds. The Commission found a breach of Art 6, in that the use of the evidence gathered was oppressive.

*Court:*   The Court did not accept the argument of the government that the complexity of fraud, and the vital public interest in its investigation, justified a departure such as this from one of the basic principles of a fair procedure. The Court accordingly found that Art 6 had been breached.

*Note:*   The Court noted that the guarantees of Art 6 did not extend to that part of the proceedings involving the inspectors, as these were essentially investigative in nature and the inspectors did not adjudicate either in form or in substance.

## 19.3   ENTITLEMENT TO PROPERTY

### (1)   ASSESSMENT OF COMPENSATION IN THE APPROPRIATION OF COMMERCIAL ASSETS

### Lithgow v United Kingdom

### (1986) 8 EHRR 329

*Facts:*   The applicants, who included both natural and legal persons, had various assets nationalised under the Aircraft and Shipbuilding Industries Act 1977. They accepted that the nationalisation itself was lawful, but contested that compensation received was grossly inadequate and discriminatory, and that there had accordingly been breaches of, inter alia, Art 1 of the First Protocol. This Article provides in part that 'every natural or legal person is entitled to the peaceful enjoyment of his possessions'.

*Commission:*   The Commission declared the majority of the applications to be admissible, but did not find that there had been any breach of the Convention.

*Court:*   The Court applied the terms of the judgment of *Sporrong and Lönnroth v Sweden* ((1982) 5 EHRR 35, and see **18.1**(1)) and considered the 'three distinct rules' dealt with in that judgment. The Commission, with the agreement of both the applicants and the respondent State, read Art 1 of the First Protocol as impliedly requiring the payment of compensation as a necessary condition for the taking of property of anyone within the jurisdiction of a Contracting State save in exceptional circumstances. The necessary balance between the demands of the general community that provides the justification for the taking of property, and the protection of the individual, would not be found to exist if the applicant had to bear 'an individual and excessive burden'. Thus, compensation terms would be material to the assessment of the determination of whether a fair balance had been struck. The applicants argued that the criteria for assessing the amount of compensation should be the same whether the case concerned nationalisation, or the compulsory acquisition of land. The Court was not able to agree with this proposition, holding that the valuation of major industrial assets was a far more complex operation than, for example, the valuation of a single piece of land, and that the standard of compensation could therefore be different. Compensation in this case was assessed with reference to the share values of the nationalised companies, and the Court found that this was appropriate. After a detailed assessment of the various conditions relating to the sums paid, the Court found that, in the light of the complexity of the issues, the government had acted within its margin of appreciation in setting the compensation rates.

## 19.4   RESPECT FOR BUSINESS PREMISES INCLUDED IN CONCEPT OF HOME

### Niemietz v Germany

### (1992) 16 EHRR 97

*Facts:*   The applicant was a lawyer whose law offices were searched in the course of a criminal investigation against a third party. Various files were examined in the course of the search. The applicant appealed against the search, but the regional court rejected his arguments, and further appeals proved unsuccessful. The applicant then brought a complaint to the Commission, alleging that Art 8 had been breached in that the search had violated his right to respect for his home and correspondence. In particular, the applicant argued that 'home' also covered business premises, such as a lawyer's office.

*Commission:*　The respondent State argued that the protections of Art 8 did not extend to the applicant's law office and his professional activities. The view of the Commission was that the application was admissible, and merited further investigation.

*Court:*　The Court held that a wide approach should be taken to the meaning of 'home' and 'private life', particularly in the light of the fact that the applicant's activities were ones which could be carried on equally well at home as in an office. Thus, the Court noted that 'activities which are related to a profession or business may well be conducted from a person's private residence and activities which are not so related may well be carried on in an office or commercial premises'. The fact that it would be impossible, or very difficult, to draw precise definitions of 'home' and 'business premises' meant that, in these circumstances, the concept of 'home' could be extended to cover some business premises. In relation to the protection of 'private life', the Court held further that 'it would be too restrictive to limit the notion of [private life] to an "inner circle" in which the individual may live his own personal life as he chooses and to exclude therefore entirely the outside world not encompassed within that circle'. Accordingly, the Court recognised that some personal relations arising in a business context may nevertheless fall to be protected by way of Art 8.

*Note:*　The protection accorded by Art 8 cannot, it is argued, be extended wholly to business premises under the concept of protection of the 'home'. In such a case, it might still be possible, however, to argue from the basis of a lack of respect for 'private life' (see DJ Harris et al *Law of the European Convention on Human Rights* (Butterworths, 1995), at pp 318–319).

## 19.5　FREEDOM OF EXPRESSION

### Markt Intern Verlag GmbH and Beermann v Federal Republic of Germany

### (1989) 12 EHRR 161

*Facts:*　The applicants were a publishing firm and its editor-in-chief. Markt Intern specialised in publishing bulletins aimed at specialised commercial sectors. On several occasions, companies which had suffered from the applicants' criticisms, or from boycotts instigated by the applicants, instituted proceedings against them for infringement of German competition law. Cosmetic Club International, an English mail order firm, obtained an injunction restraining Markt Intern from repeating statements published about the firm. On appeal, the regional court concluded that the applicants' conduct was culpable and, under the terms of the judgment, the applicants would be liable for a fine for each contravention. After further appeals, the Federal Court of Justice confirmed the ban on republication of the statements, and the Federal

Constitutional Court refused to hear a further appeal. The applicants claimed that the ban breached, inter alia, Art 10.

*Commission:* The government had argued that this case would fall at the extreme limit of the application of Art 10, and that the publication in question was not intended to influence or mobilise public opinion, but was intended to promote the economic interests of certain companies. The Commission held that the application was admissible, and that there had been a violation of Art 10.

*Court:* The Court noted that the contested article affected a limited circle of tradespeople, and did not directly concern the public as a whole, conveying information of a commercial nature. However, such information could not be excluded from the scope of Art 10, which does not apply solely to certain types of information or ideas or forms of expression. The Court held that the applicants had suffered an interference by public authority in the exercise of a protected right. This had been done in accordance with the rule of law, and the Court accepted that frequently laws are framed in a manner which is not absolutely precise, particularly so 'in spheres such as that of competition, in which the situation is constantly changing in accordance with developments in the market and in the field of communication'. In deciding whether the interference was 'necessary', the Court found it necessary to weigh the requirements of the protection of reputation against the right to publish the information. In this case, the article was written in a commercial context, but it intended legitimately to protect the interests of chemists and beauty product retailers. The Court found that the Federal Court of Justice had not gone beyond the margin of appreciation left to the national authorities, and that Art 10 had not been breached.

*Note:* Notwithstanding the finding that Art 10 had not been breached, the case remains important in establishing that corporations have the right to exercise freedom of expression, and that the denial of such a right has to be justified as being 'necessary in a democratic society'. This position was further confirmed in the case of *Autronic AG v Switzerland* (below).

## Autronic AG v Switzerland
## (1990) 12 EHRR 485

*Facts:* The applicant company specialised in dish antennae for home reception of television broadcasts. The company applied for permission from the Board of Directors of the Swiss Post, Telegraph and Telephone Services (PTT) for permission to show at trade fairs public broadcast Soviet television programmes which could be picked up from a Soviet satellite. The Board asked the Soviet authorities for permission, and a reply was never received. The PTT then told the applicant that permission would have to be refused, as approval had not been granted by the Soviet authorities, and the Radio Regulations 1959, as amended, therefore prevented any such reception. The applicant then applied for the issue of a declaratory order and statement to the effect that reception for private use of uncoded transmissions should not be dependent upon the approval of the authorities in the broadcasting State. This request was dismissed. The applicant company appealed, and relied in part on Art 10 of the Convention. The appeal board held that Art 10 applied only to information from generally accessible sources, which did not include the satellite in question, and rejected the appeal. A further appeal was rejected. The applicant complained that its right to freedom of information under Art 10 was breached, and that the requirement of the State's approval was disproportionate and unjustified.

*Commission:* The Commission found that the freedom of imparting and receiving information may consist of a series of acts which as a whole constitute the process of communication. By staging demonstrations of this process, the company would be part of the process. The fact that the applicant wanted to receive the programmes for the commercial purposes of selling its equipment did not alter the position. In fact, the technical equipment provided by the applicant formed an essential part in ensuring that the broadcasts at issue could be received. The Commission therefore found that the application was admissible, and that there had been a breach of Art 10.

*Court:* The Court held that neither the applicant's status as a company nor the fact that its activities were commercial could deprive the applicant of the protection of Art 10. The Court had held already that Art 10 'applies to everyone, whether natural or legal persons', including profit-making bodies. Further, Art 10 expressly refers to 'broadcasting, television or cinema enterprises'. The Court took the view that 'the reception of television programmes ... comes within the right laid down [in Art 10] without it being necessary to ascertain the reason and purpose for which the right is to be exercised'. The Court held that the restrictive measures taken by the authorities were not justified, and that the uncoded broadcasts, intended for television viewers generally within the Soviet Union, precluded their being described as 'not intended for the general use of the public' within the meaning of the Radio Regulations 1959. The Court therefore found that Art 10 had been breached.

## (1)  COMMERCIAL ADVERTISING

### Casado Coca v Spain

### (1994) 18 EHRR 1

*Facts:* The applicant, a lawyer, regularly placed adverts in the 'miscellaneous advertisements' pages of journals, and wrote to various companies offering his services. Disciplinary proceedings were brought against him by the Barcelona Bar Council, leading to the imposition of penalties and warnings. After further adverts were placed, the applicant was again reprimanded, and appealed to the national Bar Council. This appeal was rejected, as were further appeals to the Spanish courts, which held in part that the adverts in question went beyond the limits laid down in the rules of the Bar, being more than mere announcements of information. The applicant claimed, inter alia, that the rules were in breach of Art 10 because the Barcelona Bar Council had given him a warning for publishing a notice in a local newsletter. The Commission found the application admissible in respect of Art 10, and held that there had been a breach.

*Court:* The government argued in its submission that the applicant's notices did not in any way constitute information of a commercial nature, but simply acted as advertising, which did not come within the freedom of expression guaranteed by Art 10. The Court, following its judgment in *Autronic AG v Switzerland* (above), noted that Art 10 guarantees freedom of speech to everyone and that no distinction is made whether the aim pursued is profit-making or not. Information of a commercial nature is covered by Art 10. The notices in question merely gave the applicant's name, profession and contact details and were clearly published with the aim of advertising. Nevertheless, they provided persons requiring legal assistance with information that was of definite use and likely to facilitate their access to justice. The Court therefore found that Art 10 was applicable in this case but that, given the fact members of the Bar have a 'special status [giving] them a central position in the administration of justice as intermediaries between the public and the courts', and that rules curbing advertising were common throughout the Contracting States, the relevant authorities' reaction could not be considered disproportionate to the aims pursued.

# Chapter 20

# THE CONVENTION AND FUNDAMENTAL RIGHTS IN THE EC

*Note:* Most of the cases in this chapter are those heard by the courts of the EC: the Court of First Instance (CFI), and the European Court of Justice (ECJ). The CFI accepts direct actions brought against the institutions of the European Community, and appeal is available on points of law to the ECJ. The ECJ deals with references from the courts of the Member States made under Art 234 EC. In both courts, a single collegiate judgment is given, which is supplemented by an opinion delivered by one of the Advocates-General. The role of the Advocate-General is to assist the Court, and the opinion is not binding on the Court and not determinative of the outcome of the case. However, such opinions can add clarification, in particular to the development of the arguments and the progress of Community law. There is no process similar to that of the Convention structure whereby the Commission acts as a first filter on cases. These summaries are therefore dealt with in a different fashion from those of the Convention. A general discussion of the judicial developments in this area, and the link between the legal orders of the Community and the Convention, is given at **1.9**.

## 20.1 THE RELATIONSHIP BETWEEN THE EC AND THE CONVENTION

### (1) ACCESSION TO THE CONVENTION

### Opinion 2/94

[1996] ECR I-1759

*Facts:* The ECJ was asked to give its opinion on the question of whether the Community could accede directly to the Convention.

*Judgment:* The view of the Court was that there was no legal basis in the Treaty of Rome which would permit such an accession, and that general provisions of Community law which allow actions not otherwise specified in the founding treaties to be undertaken when they are necessary to allow the attainment of the objectives of the Community did not apply in this situation. The judgment means, therefore, that should the Community wish to accede, it would first have to amend the Treaty of Rome in such a way as to permit this.

*Note:* In 1977, the European Parliament, Council and Commission adopted a Joint Declaration which affirmed their commitment, and that of the EC, to the principles of fundamental rights set out in the Convention ((1977) OJ C103/1). A stronger step was taken in the enactment of the Treaty on European Union, Art 6(2) of which provides that: 'The Union shall respect fundamental rights, as guaranteed by the European

Convention for the Protection of Human Rights and Fundamental Freedom signed in Rome on 4 November 1950 and as they result from the constitutional traditions common to the Member States, as general principles of Community law'.

However, this Article is non-justiciable, which is to say that it cannot by itself form the basis for an action before the ECJ, although it might influence the Court in its interpretation and development of the law.

## (2)  FUNDAMENTAL RIGHTS GENERALLY IN COMMUNITY LAW

### Stauder v City of Ulm
### Case 26/69 [1970] CMLR 112

*Facts:*  The EC Commission took a decision in 1969 empowering Member States to provide subsidised butter for certain consumers in the Community in receipt of social assistance (69/71/EEC). The implementation of this measure in Germany required those seeking the subsidised butter to give to the appropriate retailer a counterfoil and coupon on which the name and address of the recipient was to be inserted. The plaintiff in the action, brought in Germany, argued that the measure was discriminatory and infringed basic provisions of the German Constitution. The German court asked the question whether the Commission's decision was 'compatible with the general principles of Community law in force' ([1970] CMLR 112, at p 115).

*Judgment:*  The Advocate-General, in his submission, stressed the view that 'common conceptions of value in the national constitutional law, in particular, national basic rights, must be established by comparative evaluation of the law and these common conceptions must be observed as unwritten components of Community law'. The Court found, on the facts, that it was not necessary within the terms of the decision for any one recipient of the subsidised butter to identify themselves. At the same time, the Court recognised the existence of 'general principles of the law of the Community of which the Court must ensure the observance' (at p 119).

*Note:*  The gradual recognition of the role of fundamental rights in the Community legal order (which culminated in the case of *Nold*, below) marked a change from earlier cases where the ECJ had held that it was not the place of the Court to consider arguments lying outside the direct remit of the Treaties. In this respect, the leading case, until *Stauder*, was *Stork v High Authority* (Case 1/58) [1959] ECR 17.

### Internationale Handelsgesellschaft mbH v Einfuhr- und Vorratsstelle für Getreide und Futtermittel
### Case 11/70 [1972] CMLR 255

*Facts:*  IHG, an export firm, forfeited a deposit of approximately DM17,000 after it failed to export 20,000 tonnes of maize. In the event, only 11,486 tonnes were exported within the time-limit, and in accordance with Regulation 120/67, the entire deposit was forfeited. The company brought an action in a Frankfurt court for the return of the deposit. In making a reference to the ECJ, the German court asked whether the relevant Community measures were lawful. In a series of related cases brought at the same time, questions focused in particular on the proportionality of a measure which required the surrender of a deposit without reference to the gravity of the breach of the condition. The domestic court was reluctant to find the measure lawful, on the grounds that it appeared to conflict with the principles of the German Constitution.

*Judgment:* The Court held that provisions of Community law could be judged only in the light of Community law, and that to allow Community law to be judged in relation to national law would possibly harm the uniform application of Community law. The Court put the matter very clearly: 'the validity of a Community instrument or its effect within a Member State cannot be affected by allegations that it strikes at either the fundamental rights as formulated in that State's constitution or the principles of a national constitutional structure' ([1972] CMLR 255, at p 283). At the same time, the Court held that the Community itself required that fundamental rights be respected, and that these constitute an integral part of the Community legal order. These rights were to be found in the traditions common to the Member States, although their application was to be ensured within the context of Community law, and that question could best be determined by the ECJ, which uniquely has the power to rule on the validity of Community measures. In its examination of the issues of the cases the Court found no reasons to strike down any part of the legislation.

## Jégo-Quéré et Cie SA v Commission
## Case T-177/01, judgment of 3 May 2002

*Facts:* The applicant company is a shipowner practising fishing activities in the waters south of Ireland. Before the CFI, and in reliance on Art 230 EC, the applicant challenged a Commission regulation aimed at preserving fishing stocks.

*Judgment:* The Court dealt only with the admissibility of the application. The Commission had argued that as the challenged legislation was in the form of a regulation it could not be challenged by an individual as the Treaty did not give individuals locus standi save in very restrictive circumstances. The Court accepted that the regulation was a 'true' regulation, and was not a decision in the form of a regulation, and accepted further that under pre-existing case-law the applicant would not have the locus standi to challenge the regulation. However, the Court held that individuals had the right to effective remedies where they were affected adversely by an act of the Community, and that it would be appropriate therefore to reconsider the strict interpretation previously given to the notion of individual concern in Art 230(4). In conclusion, the Court held that to ensure that effective judicial protections were available a person must be considered to be individually concerned by a Community measure in circumstances in which the measure actually affects his legal situation by restricting his rights or imposing obligations.

*Note:* This is a fundamental reassessment of the limits of Art 230 EC, and if this judgment is not reversed by the ECJ it will significantly extend the scope of judicial review of Community acts.

## (3)   THE CONVENTION AS A SOURCE OF COMMUNITY LAW

### Firma J Nold v Commission

### Case 4/73 [1974] 2 CMLR 338

*Facts:*   A Commission Decision, revising the terms of trading in relation to coal wholesalers, was challenged by the plaintiff before the ECJ. In essence, the plaintiff was not sufficiently large to meet the requirements of new contracts, and was thus excluded from its position as a direct wholesaler. The plaintiff argued in part that his property rights had been contravened in breach of the German Federal Constitution and the Constitution of the Land of Hesse. The applicant further contended that the measures in question were discriminatory as between different Community dealers.

*Judgment:*   The Court recognised that property rights were protected not only by the constitutional provisions relied upon by the applicant, but also by 'various inter-national instruments, particularly the [Convention]' ([1974] 2 CMLR 338, at p 354). The Court referred to its earlier judgments, in which it had recognised that general principles of law formed part of Community law (see above). The Court went further in this case noting that 'international treaties on the protection of human rights in which the Member States have co-operated or to which they have adhered can also supply indications which may be taken into account within the framework of Community law' (ibid). In this case, the Court, however, noted that even in these contexts, such rights usually allowed for limitations in the public interest, and that in the Community, such rights must therefore be considered in the light of the aims and objectives of the Community. It was the very essence of economic activity that decisions, such as those made by the Commission, would be taken and the applicant could not be protected from these in the absence of fundamental errors or procedural flaws.

*Note:*   Although this case marks a decisive step towards the recognition of the Convention as a source for fundamental protections in the EC, the ECJ took the decision only following the accession of France to the Convention, at which point all Member States of the EC became signatories to the Convention also.

### Cinéthèque SA and Others v Fédération Nationale des Cinémas Français

### Cases 60–61/84 [1986] 1 CMLR 365

*Facts:*   The case arose before the French courts, and concerned the application of provisions restricting the free movement of goods in the EC Treaty. The goods in question were video films (specifically *Merry Christmas, Mr Lawrence*), and France maintained in place national rules which prevented the marketing of video films until one year after the first exploitation of the film in cinemas. It was argued in part that these rules, which also applied to imported films, restricted unlawfully the flow of goods, contrary to Art 36 EC. A reference to the ECJ was made by the Tribunal de Grande Instance, Paris. The EC Commission, intervening in the case, argued that films are part of contemporary culture, and that protections designed to foster cultural growth and development could be legitimate even if they were to conflict with the application of Art 36. The question of the application of Art 10 of the Convention also arose, with the argument being made that the particular method of film distribution prescribed by France would be in breach of that Article, and that the ECJ was obliged to take this into account in making its ruling in the present case.

*Judgment:* The Advocate-General, who was not persuaded that the Convention was breached by the actions in question, dismissed the arguments based on Art 10. The Court went further, and was not prepared to consider whether the Convention rules had been breached or not. It thus made the relationship between Community law, Convention, and domestic law clear holding, inter alia, that: 'although it is true that it is the duty of this Court to ensure observance of fundamental rights in the field of Community law, it has no power to examine the compatibility with the European Convention of national legislation which concerns, as in this case, an area which falls within the jurisdiction of the national legislator' ([1986] 1 CMLR 365, at p 386).

## (4) THE DUTIES OF MEMBER STATES TO COMPLY WITH FUNDAMENTAL PRINCIPLES IN THE APPLICATION OF COMMUNITY LAW

### Wachauf (Hubert) v Federal Republic of Germany

### Case 5/88 [1989] ECR 2609, at p 2639 in particular

*Facts:* The plaintiff had brought an action in the German courts seeking the payment of compensation following the discontinuance of milk production. The payments were regulated under the Community milk quotas and production system, and the interpretation of various elements of those regulations were called into question. The question arose whether the landowner plaintiff, or a lessee of the landowner, was the beneficiary of the quota, and the domestic court was concerned that the case raised issues relating to unconstitutional expropriation without compensation in the allocation of the quota.

*Judgment:* The Court held that any Community rule which would have the effect of depriving a party without compensation of the fruits of his labour would be incompatible with the requirements of the protection of fundamental rights in the Community. When applying Community rules, Member States are themselves bound by these fundamental rights in turn, and must respect them insofar as possible. The rules in question left the national authorities a sufficiently wide margin of discretion to allow them to apply the rules in a manner consistent with the requirements of the protection of fundamental rights, and were not therefore themselves in breach of these principles.

# AM&S Europe Ltd v Commission
## Case 155/79 [1982] ECR 1575

*Facts:*   In this case, a challenge was made by AM&S Europe Ltd, an undertaking investigated in the course of competition proceedings by the EC Commission by way of Art 230 EC. Regulation 17/62/EEC gives the Commission the power to conduct all necessary investigations into undertakings in the enforcement of Arts 81 EC and 82 EC. To this end, Art 14 of Reg 17/62 empowers officials of the Commission to enter premises, search them, and to take copies of, or extracts from, documents held by the undertaking. In this situation, the undertaking in question refused to submit various documents requested by the Commission on the grounds that these had privileged status. The documents requested were communications between the undertaking and its lawyer, and the company claimed that they were, therefore, protected on grounds of legal confidentiality. The Commission argued that no such protection applied, and that the words of Reg 17/62 were not capable of being interpreted in such a way as to permit the protection claimed for the documents by the undertaking. A central question for the Court, the Regulation being silent on the matter, was the extent to which such a protection might exist, and whether such a protection could be properly incorporated into the law of the Treaty of Rome. The undertaking was supported in its application by the UK, and the Consultative Committee of the Bars and Law Societies of the European Community.

*Judgment:*   The Advocate-General conducted a wide-ranging survey of the positions adopted in respect of the protection of such information in the Member States. He concluded that, while protection was consistently given to lawyer–client communications in respect of the rights of the defence in criminal trials, no such systematic approach was taken in relation to administrative proceedings and commercial advice given by lawyers who were not independent of their client. The Court, agreeing with the Advocate-General, held therefore that EC law should adopt the consensus stance of the Member States, and give protection to communications between lawyer and client provided that such communications are made for the purposes and in the interests of the client's defence, and that they emanated from an independent lawyer (which is to say a lawyer not bound to the client by an employment relationship).

*Note:*   In seeking protections common to those found in the Member States, the Court should, in theory, be reinforcing its acceptance of the rights derived from the Convention, the universal acceptance of which by the EC Member States ensures that its norms were also common to the Member States.

It is perhaps significant that in the Competition Act 1998, which in effect is an incorporation into domestic law of Community competition law, the appropriate powers are specifically drafted so as to protect confidential information. Section 30 of that Act defines a privileged communication as being a communication 'between a professional legal adviser and his client' or 'made in connection with, or in contemplation of, legal proceedings and for the purposes of those proceedings'. In the parliamentary debates, it was confirmed by the Minister that 'it is the government's intention that the [UK authorities] should *not* be able to require . . . the production of legal advice and other material enjoying legal professional privilege, whether the lawyer concerned is an external lawyer or an "in-house" lawyer' (*Hansard* (HL) 17 November 1997, col 416). This is consistent with the approach adopted by the House of Lords in *Compton (Alfred) Amusement Machines Ltd v Customs & Excise Comrs (No 2)* [1974] AC 405. However, it is probably the case that the EC Commission, if investigating in the UK under the powers of Reg 17, could still demand material that would be considered to be protected for the purposes of domestic proceedings by virtue of the operation of the Act.

## Elliniki Radiophonia Tileorassi AE v Dimotiki Etairia Pliforissis and Sotirios Kouvelas

## Case 260/89 [1991] ECR I-2925

*Facts:* The case arose by way of an Art 234 EC reference from the Thessaloniki Regional Court, Greece. Elliniki Radiophonia Tileorassi (ERT) comprised television and radio broadcasting arms, and a production and marketing company. It was set up by, and subject to, the control of the Greek State which maintained, at the time, a State monopoly in broadcasting. In 1988, Dimotiki Etairia Pliforissis and the mayor of Thessaloniki established a television station which began broadcasting; ERT brought an action claiming that the actions of the defendants were unlawful under Greek law, and that they had caused damage to the plaintiff. Various questions were raised about the relationship of Community competition law to the situation, as well as aspects of fundamental rights under the Convention, and the ECJ was asked 10 questions. These included two questions relating to the position under Art 10 of the Convention, and question (10) asked 'whether the freedom of expression secured by Article 10 of the [Convention] . . . impose[s] per se obligations on the Member States, independently of the written provisions of Community law in force, and if so what those obligations are'.

*Judgment:* The Court reiterated its stance that fundamental rights form an integral part of Community law, and that the Convention 'has special significance in that respect' (para 41). Measures adopted by the Community which would be incompatible with these provisions could not, therefore, be upheld by the ECJ. However, the ECJ has no power to examine the compatibility of the Convention in relation to national law which falls outside the scope of Community law. Nevertheless, where a reference is made to the ECJ, it is the function of the Court to 'provide all the criteria of interpretation needed by the national court to determine whether those rules are compatible with the fundamental rights the observance of which the Court ensures and which derive in particular from the [Convention]'. Where domestic laws are being relied upon in situations which permit exceptions to the principles of substantive law set out in the Treaty of Rome (for example, in relation to the free movement of services), these laws are subject to Community scrutiny. In these circumstances, they must also be compatible with the fundamental rights, the observance of which is guaranteed by the EC. The domestic court, in assessing the provisions of domestic law, 'is to appraise the application of those provisions having regard to all the rules of Community law, including freedom of expression, as embodied in [the Convention]' (para 44).

## Society for the Protection of Unborn Children Ireland Ltd (SPUC) v Grogan

### C-159/90 [1991] ECR I-4685

*Facts:*    The ECJ was called upon to consider the application of the principles of the freedom to provide services arising under Community law in the context of the advertising and promotion in Ireland of abortion services located in the UK. The SPUC was prosecuted in Ireland for offences relating to the promotion and procurement of abortion services, and sought to rely both on the relevant provisions of Community law, and on the relationship of Community law with Art 10 of the Convention.

*Judgment:*    The ECJ did not have to rule on whether the Irish laws on abortion were in breach of the Community provisions on freedom to supply services. In this case, there was no commercial link between the SPUC and the providers of the abortion services in the UK. In these circumstances, the ECJ noted that it had the power to consider national law only insofar as it fell within the field of application of Community law, and that was not the case here.

*Notes:*    This was a particularly sensitive case, and although there had been several such prosecutions in Ireland, with the defendants seeking to rely on Community law, this was the first time when such a reference had been made. While the ECJ did not in the event rule on the legality of the Irish laws on abortion, there was strong concern that it might do so, and there is a wealth of commentary about this case. See, for example, DR Phelan 'Right to Life of the Unborn v Promotion of Trade in Services: The European Court of Justice and the Normative Shaping of the European Union' (1992) 55 MLR 670, and S O'Leary case note (1992) 17 EL Rev 138.

The response to questions raised concerning Art 10 of the Convention is considered at **20.2(5)**.

## Kaur (Surjit) v Lord Advocate

### [1980] 3 CMLR 79

*Facts:*    An Indian mother of three British-born children was threatened with deportation from the UK. She argued that the deportation would be a violation of Art 8 of the Convention, and that even if the Convention could not be relied upon directly, the effect of Community law was such as to allow her to rely on it under the European Communities Act 1972.

*Court (Court of Session Scotland):*    The Court accepted that, given a lack of basis for the appeal under domestic law, the principal issue in the case was whether rights arose under the Convention which would be enforceable in the Scottish courts. Lord Ross dismissed this possibility, holding that 'the Convention cannot be regarded in any way as part of the municipal law of Scotland'. The Court also had to consider whether, as counsel argued, the Convention was enforceable as part of Community law. Section 2(1) of the European Communities Act 1972 deals, inter alia, with the enforceability of all rights 'created or arising by or under the Treaties', and it was the argument of the plaintiff that these rights included the body of Convention law which had been accepted by the ECJ as being of relevance in informing its decisions. The decisive factor, Lord Ross held, was that 'although fundamental rights enshrined in the Convention are relevant to a consideration of the rights and duties of the Community institutions, and may be a background against which the express provisions of the [Treaty] have to be interpreted, they do not form an implied, unexpressed part of the Treaty itself'. Further, in this case, there was no Community content at all, as the plaintiff was not seeking to rely upon a Community law right. It would be necessary, for a domestic court to consider the application of the Convention in relation to a Community right, for the plaintiff to specify the Treaty Articles on which they were seeking to rely.

## (5)   APPROACH OF THE STRASBOURG AUTHORITIES TO EC MATTERS

### M and Co v Federal Republic of Germany

### (1990) 64 D&R 138

*Facts:*   The applicant was fined by the EC Commission following the finding of a breach of EC competition law. On appeal to the ECJ, the fine was reduced. The applicant then brought an action for damages against the FRG, which it argued had wrongly issued a writ of execution, on the grounds that the ECJ had violated the applicant's constitutional rights. The applicant alleged that the proceedings were unlawful under both the German Constitution and Art 6 of the Convention as the fine was disproportionate and excessive, and the company was fined on the basis of the faults committed by employees, but not by its managing partners.

*Commission:*   The Commission held that the application was inadmissible on the ground that a State could not be held responsible under the Convention in respect of action required of it by the requirements of Community membership. The Commission held that 'the transfer of powers to an international organisation is not incompatible with the Convention provided that within that organisation fundamental rights will receive an *equivalent* protection' (emphasis added). The Commission found that this was the case where the EC was concerned, and drew attention in particular to the joint declaration of the European institutions of 5 April 1977 ((1977) OJ C103/1) to the effect that they attached prime importance to the protection of fundamental rights.

*Note:*   It has been suggested that this decision is limited on its facts, and that it would not apply where the Member State was implementing its own legislation, even where that legislation was introduced in response to an EC requirement (see DJ Harris, M O'Boyle and C Warbrick *Law of the European Convention on Human Rights* (Butterworths, 1995), at p 28).

### Matthews v United Kingdom

### (1999) 28 EHRR 361

*Facts:*   The applicant was a British citizen resident in Gibraltar. In 1994, she applied to be registered to vote in the elections to the European Parliament. This application was denied, the applicant being told that, under the terms of the European Community

Act on Direct Elections of 1976, Gibraltar was not included in the franchise for such elections. Article 3 of the First Protocol to the Convention provides that: 'The High Contracting Parties undertake to hold free elections at reasonable intervals by secret ballot, under conditions which will ensure the free expression of the opinion of the people in the choice of the legislature'. The Convention and its Protocols extend to Gibraltar.

*Commission:*   The Commission declared the application admissible, but held by 12 votes to 5 that there had been no violation of Art 3 of the First Protocol.

*Court:*   The Court recognised that actions of the EU could not be challenged before it, as the EU is not a State party to the Convention. However, Contracting States themselves remained responsible for ensuring that Convention rights, where relevant, were guaranteed, and this obligation could not be set aside by subsequent Treaties entered into by the States. Legislation emanating from the EC institutions had the potential to affect the citizens of Gibraltar to the same extent as legislation originating in Gibraltar's own legislature, and the UK would thus be obliged to secure for the citizens of Gibraltar the rights guaranteed by Art 3 of the First Protocol, irrespective of whether the elections were domestic or to the European Parliament. The Court noted again that the Convention is a living instrument (see **2.3**) and found that although the role and place of the European Parliament had not been envisaged by the founders of the Convention, that did not preclude its falling within the definition of 'legislature' at the present time. The Convention had to be interpreted to take into account the changing constitutional structures of the State in question. Further, Gibraltar was affected by the supremacy of Community law asserted by the ECJ, as much as any other territory within the EC and, as such, Gibraltarians should have the same rights as other Community citizens to participate in the democratic process.

*Notes:*   This case throws into sharp relief the difficulties created by the overlapping jurisdiction of the EC, Convention and the European States. For the vote to be granted to Gibraltarians in relation to elections to the European Parliament, a unanimous vote of the Council of the EC is required, and Spain has to date resisted such a move. How then is the UK to comply with the requirements of the Convention in this respect? The answer may lie in Community law rather than in the law of the Convention. The remainder of this chapter deals with the extent to which Community law is required to conform to the law of the Convention.

## 20.2   SPECIFIC CONVENTION-DERIVED RIGHTS CONSIDERED BY THE COURT

### (1)   THE RIGHT TO A FAIR TRIAL

### Musique Diffusion Française SA v Commission

Cases 100–103/80 [1983] ECR 1825

*Facts:*   The undertaking, Musique Diffusion Française, brought an action for annulment against a Commission decision imposing fines following a finding that the applicant had engaged in restrictive practices in breach of Art 81 EC. The applicant relied in part upon Art 6 of the Convention, claiming that, in the proceedings before the EC Commission, it had been denied the right to a fair trial required by the Convention. In particular, the undertaking maintained that the contested decision was unlawful by the very fact that it 'was adopted under a system in which the Commission combines the functions of prosecutor and judge, which is contrary to Art 6(1) of the [Convention]' (para 6).

*Judgment:*   The Court held firstly that 'the Commission cannot be described as a "tribunal" within the meaning of Art 6'. However, the Court did hold that the Commission was bound, during its administrative procedure, to follow the procedural safeguards recognised and provided under Community law. It is a fundamental principle of Community law, the Court said, that a fair hearing be observed in all proceedings, including those of an administrative nature. In this context, the undertaking concerned must be 'afforded the opportunity, during the administrative procedure, to make known its views on the truth and relevance of the facts and circumstances alleged and on the documents used by the Commission to support its claim that there has been an infringement of the Treaty' (para 10). The Court concluded this part of its argument by stating that, while in this specific context Art 6 of the Convention could not be relied upon, Community law itself provided all the necessary guarantees to a fair hearing.

## Stichting Certifiicatie Kraanverhuurbedrijf (SCK) and Federatie van Nederlandse Kraanverhuurbedrijven (FNK) v Commission

## Cases T–213/95 and T–18/96 [1998] 4 CMLR 259

*Facts:*   The two undertakings were both organisations operating in the Dutch market for mobile hire-cranes. A complaint about their alleged breach of Art 81(1) was made to the Commission. The undertakings then notified to the Commission their statutes and rules, with a request for either negative clearance or an exemption under Art 81(3). Following a complicated chain of events, in the course of which the undertakings pressed the Commission for urgent action, and waived at one point their rights, the Commission issued its final decision, finding a breach of Art 81(1), ordering termination, and imposing fines (Decision 95/551 (1995) OJ L312/79). This Decision was made on 29 November 1995. The applicants subsequently sought to have the Decision annulled, arguing in part that the contested Decision infringed Art 6 of the Convention, in that they were denied a hearing 'within a reasonable time'.

*Judgment:*   Although it recognised that 'it is settled case-law that fundamental rights form an integral part of the general principles of law whose observance the Community judicature ensures' and that 'the [Convention] has special significance in that respect' (para 53), the CFI held that 'it is a general principle *of Community law* that the Commission must act within a reasonable time in adopting decisions following administrative proceedings relating to competition policy'. Because the matter then fell directly within the strictures of Community law, the Court considered that there was no need for it to rule on the status of Art 6 of the Convention. At each stage of the lengthy proceedings, the Court found that the Commission had either acted reasonably or 'not unreasonably'. Further, *Automec v Commission of the European Communities* (Case T-24/90 [1992] ECR II-2223) already makes it clear, the Court said, that the Commission is allowed within reasonable constraints to prioritise matters as it sees fit. The Court, therefore, rejected the plea of the applicants insofar as it was based on Art 6(1).

*Note:*   The approach of the CFI in this case has been criticised on the grounds that, although the Court purported to be reaching the same result as it would have done had it applied Convention law, the application of the general principles of Community law, which must be assessed in the light of the objectives of the EC, will not necessarily achieve the same result (see M Furse 'The Wronging of Rights – Editorial' (1998) *In Competition* 1).

## Mannesmannrohren-Werke AG v Commission
## Case T-112/98, [2001] 5 CMLR 1

*Facts:*   In the context of an investigation into breaches of Art 81 of the Treaty Commission officials carried out a dawn raid at the premises of Mannesmannrohren-Werke AG (MW) in Germany. Later a number of requests for information were made to MW, some of which it refused to answer on the grounds that to do so concerned the motives for meetings which had potentially illegal aims. MW relied in part on *Orkem SA v Commission of the European Communities* (Case 374/87), [1991] 4 CMLR 502.

*Held:*   The CFI accepted that, following *Orkem*, there was a limited right to silence in the context of competition-law proceedings, but rejected the argument that this should extend to matters that were purely factual. In respect of questions which compelled an applicant to admit that it was involved in illegal meetings the right to silence would exist. It was not lawful for the Commission to ask the applicant to give a value-judgement as to the nature of decisions taken at meetings.

## (2)   THE RIGHT TO PRIVACY
## Stauder v City of Ulm
## Case 26/69 [1970] CMLR 112

*Facts:*   The relevant facts are set out at **20.1(2)**. As well as arguing that the national provisions in question were discriminatory, the plaintiff further contended that, in being required to disclose his identity, Art 8 of the Convention was being breached.

*Judgment:*   The Court held that, when the correct version of the Community decision in question was referred to, it did not proscribe a named identification of the individual recipient of the butter, although equally it would not prohibit such an identification. However, in the present case, each Member State was free to choose its own method of 'individualisation', and that as properly interpreted, nothing in the decision in question jeopardised the fundamental rights which the Court was bound to observe.

# National Panasonic (UK) Ltd v Commission

## Case 136/79 [1980] ECR 2033

*Facts:* Using its powers under Reg 17/62 EEC, the Commission launched an investigation of the undertaking at its premises in Slough. Article 14(3) of that Regulation gives the Commission power to search premises of undertakings and to take copies of, or extracts from, documents. The undertaking, which had been given no prior notice of the 'dawn raid', claimed, inter alia, that such searches were in breach of Art 8 of the Convention as they constituted an infringement of the undertaking's right to privacy.

*Judgment:* The Court based its rebuttal of the undertaking's arguments on the text of Art 8 of the Convention itself. While recognising that its previous judgments had committed the Court to pay particular attention to the Convention as a source of rights, the Court noted that Art 8(2) itself provides a limit to the powers set out in Art 8(1). Thus, the application of the right may be limited to the extent to which it is 'in accordance with the law and is necessary in a democratic society in the interests of national security, public safety or the economic well-being of the country'. The Court did not consider that, in the light of the legitimate objectives of Reg 17/62/EEC, the Commission had been given rights which infringed the rights invoked by the applicant in the present case.

# A v Commission

## T-10/93 [1994] ECR II-179

*Facts:* This case came before the CFI as a staff dispute. Under Art 33 of the Staff Regulations for Employment by the Community institutions, every person is required to undergo a medical examination prior to being recruited as a Community official. The applicant underwent medical examination and voluntarily underwent screening tests for the human immunodeficiency virus (HIV). Subsequently, the Commission's medical officer wrote to the applicant expressing the opinion that the applicant was physically unfit to take up the post. The applicant appealed, claiming in part that the requirement of the medical examination was a breach of Art 8 of the Convention.

*Judgment:* The Court dealt with the arguments relating to Art 8 at paras 45–51 of the judgment. The Court accepted that the purpose of the medical examination was 'to safeguard the budgetary equilibrium of the institution concerned by preventing it from having to bear major expenses in the short or long term'. The examination would also ensure that successful candidates were assigned work to which they were suited and able to undertake. These objectives, the Court recognised, were perfectly lawful and were mirrored in the Member States where it was common practice to require public officials to undergo such examinations. The Court held that in these circumstances the very fact of the existence of the requirement of a pre-recruitment medical examination could not by itself be regarded as being in breach of Art 8 of the Convention.

*Note:* This was the first case in which the CFI expressly considered the impact of Art 6(2) on the Treaty on European Union, although its application did not assist the individual complainant.

## (3)  THE RIGHT TO FAMILY LIFE

### Demirel v Stadt Schwäbisch Gmünd
### 12/86 [1987] ECR 3719

*Facts:*   The plaintiff, a Turkish national, entered Germany in March 1983 to join her husband, also a Turkish national, who was lawfully resident in Germany. She made an undertaking to leave Germany on 11 June 1984, but did not do so. An order was subsequently made requiring her departure and, following an appeal, this was confirmed on 9 July 1985. She brought an action seeking annulment of the order. The domestic court raised questions relating to the relationship of the German laws governing family reunification, with an association agreement concluded between Turkey and the EC.

*Judgment:*   The Court referred back to its judgment in the *Cinéthèque* case (above), noting that it has the duty of ensuring that Community law is compatible with the Convention, but that it has no power to examine the issue in relation to national legislation lying outside the ambit of Community law. As the Court had already found that, while the association agreement was relevant, the national legislation in question was concluded outside its remit, the Court found that it did not have jurisdiction to consider in this case the relevance of Art 8 of the Convention.

## (4)  NON-RETROACTIVITY OF LEGISLATION IMPOSING PENALTIES

### R v Kent Kirk
### 63/83 [1984] ECR 2689

*Facts:*   Captain Kirk, a Danish trawlerman, was prosecuted by the British authorities and his vessel seized. On 6 January 1983, he had fished within 12 miles of the UK coast, contrary to the Sea Fish etc Order 1982 and Council Regulation 170/83, which entered into force on 25 January 1983. The Act of Accession of the UK to the Community of 1972 had, in Art 100, authorised derogations from the general principle of the equal conditions of access to fish stocks up to 31 December 1982. The Council of Ministers was not able to agree on new measures until 23 January 1983 and, in the interim period, the UK had taken unilateral steps in its adoption of the Order (albeit on the basis of the right to do so in Community law), which, on 5 January 1983, the EC Commission purported to authorise on a provisional basis. The Council Regulation, in Art 6(1), provided that various of its provisions were applicable from 1 January 1983. When prosecuted, the defendant relied in part upon the fact that at the time when he committed the allegedly unlawful act the Council Regulation had not been in force, that the domestic legislation was invalid as being ultra vires, and that a retroactive enactment was a breach of a fundamental right to legal certainty. A referral was made to the ECJ under Art 234 EC.

*Judgment:* The ECJ held that 'the principle that penal provisions may not have retroactive effect is one which is common to all the legal orders of the Member States, and is enshrined in Article 7 of the [Convention] as a fundamental right' (para 22). Accordingly, this right would take its place among the general principles of law recognised by the ECJ and upheld in the application of Community law. The retroactive measure could not, in the light of the facts of this case therefore, have the effect of validating a national measure imposing a penalty for an act which was not punishable at the time that it was committed.

## Officier van Justitie v Kolphinghuis Nijmegen BV

## Case 80/86 [1987] ECR 3969

*Facts:* This case raised questions in the complicated area of Community law of direct effect. The Dutch authorities had sought to rely on Directive 80/777, which had not yet been implemented in The Netherlands. Directives require, in order to become fully effective, implementation by national authorities. However, provided they are sufficiently precise, clear, and unconditional, and the time-limit for implementation has passed, they may give rise to obligations on the State and emanations of the States, and to rights for third parties generally. In the present case, a Dutch trader was prosecuted for stocking tainted mineral water, in breach of both domestic legislation and the Directive.

*Judgment:* The Court held, as a matter of Community law, that the national authority could not rely upon a Directive against an individual prior to the necessary implementation of that Directive by the appropriate national measure. To do so would be contrary to the principle of legal certainty, would undermine the distinction drawn in Art 249 EC between Directives and Regulations, and, in certain circumstances, could be tantamount to retroactive legislation.

## (5) FREEDOM OF EXPRESSION

## Vereniging ter Bevordering van het Vlaamse Boekwezen, VBVB, and Vereniging ter Bevordering van de Belangen des Boekhandles, VBBB v Commission

## Cases 43 and 63/82 [1984] ECR 19

*Facts:* The parties, VBVB and VBBB, notified to the Commission an agreement which had, in Holland and Dutch-speaking Belgium, an effect similar to that of the Net Book Agreement in the UK. In particular, the agreement made provision for collective exclusive dealing and collective resale price maintenance. Undeniably, this agreement was caught by the prohibition of Art 81(1) EC, but the parties hoped to gain the benefit of an exemption under Art 81(3) EC. The Commission adopted a Decision (82/123, (1982) OJ L54/36) in which it condemned the agreement, and refused to grant an exemption. In an action for annulment under Art 230 EC, the undertakings appealed to the ECJ. One of the applicants asked the Court to declare that the Commission was bound to follow Art 10 of the Convention, and that in banning resale price maintenance, which increased the diversity of books published and their availability, the Commission had not done so. The Commission, in turn, argued that the rules on competition cannot be incompatible with the principle of freedom of expression since their aim is not to affect that fundamental right.

*Judgment:*   The Court held that the Commission, in setting out its reasons, was not obliged to consider in the same level of detail all arguments made to it by concerned parties. Although it did not state unequivocally that the Commission was obliged to act within the bounds of Art 10 of the Convention, the Court implied as much when it discussed the substantive issue (at paras 33 to 34). The Court held in this instance that the parties had not, in fact, established a link between the action taken by the Commission in the context of competition policy, and the breach of the Convention that they alleged this action gave rise to. The Court held that 'to submit the production of and trade in books to rules whose sole purpose is to ensure freedom of trade between Member States in normal conditions of competition cannot be regarded as restricting freedom of publication'.

### Elliniki Radiophonia Tileorassi AE v Dimotiki Etairia Pliforissis and Sotirios Kouvelas
### Case 260/89 [1991] ECR I-2925

*Facts:*   The relevant facts are set out at **20.1(4)**.

*Judgment:*   The Court accepted, in its answers to the Greek Regional Court, that Art 10 of the Convention was a source of fundamental rights that occupied a special position in the Community legal order, and that in assessing the validity of a national law, which was required to be compatible with Community law, the provisions of the Convention should also be complied with.

### Society for the Protection of Unborn Children Ireland Ltd (SPUC) v Grogan
### Case C-159/90 [1991] ECR I-4685

*Facts:*   The ECJ was called upon to consider the application of the principles of the freedom to provide services arising under EC law in the context of the advertising and promotion in Ireland of abortion services located in the UK. The SPUC were prosecuted in Ireland, and sought to rely both on the relevant provisions of Community law, and on the relationship of Community law with Art 10 of the Convention. The ECJ was also called upon to examine the extent to which the prohibition on the provision of information was compatible with the general principles of Community law with regard to fundamental rights and freedoms.

*Judgment:*   The ECJ did not have to rule on whether the Irish laws on abortion were in breach of the Community provisions on freedom to supply services. In this case, there was no commercial link between the SPUC and the providers of the abortion services in the UK. The Advocate-General noted, in the context of Community law, the difficulty inherent in the balancing of two rights: the right to life; and the right to freedom of expression. The latter right is one of the general principles of Community law, on the basis both of the constitutional traditions of the Member States, and of the Convention but, in the context of the latter, was subject to limitations. The Court did not consider it necessary to follow the Advocate-General's arguments however, on the basis that it had the power to consider only domestic law insofar as it fell within the field of application of Community law, and that was not the case here in the absence of the link between the SPUC and the UK providers. However, the Court confirmed again that the principles of the Convention would be applied to the interpretation of Community law and implementing domestic law.

*Notes:*   This was a particularly sensitive case, and although there had been several such prosecutions in Ireland, with the defendants seeking to rely on Community law, this was the first time when such a reference had been made. While the ECJ did not in the event rule on the legality of the Irish laws on abortion, there was strong concern that it might do so, and there is a wealth of commentary about this case.

## (6)   RIGHT TO INFORMATION

## Council v Heidi Hautala

## Case C-353/99P, judgment of 6 December 2001

*Facts:*   Heidi Hautala was a member of the European Parliament and put to the European Council a written question relating to human rights abuses being perpetrated by those benefiting from arms exports from Member States. The Council replied to the effect that one of the considerations in making arms sales was that of respect for human rights in the country of destination. The reply further added that a report prepared by the Working Group on Conventional Arms Exports had been approved with a view to enhancing those criteria. Ms Hautala asked to see a copy of the report and her request was denied on the grounds that the report contained highly sensitive information. A formal application on the basis of Decision 93/731/EC (1993) OJ L340/43 on public access to Council documents was rejected by the Council. An action was brought before the CFI, which was subsequently appealed to the ECJ.

*Judgment:*   The CFI annulled the Council's refusal to grant access on the grounds primarily that the Council should have considered whether partial access could be granted, and had failed to do so. On appeal to the ECJ the Advocate-General relied on a number of documents including the Charter of Fundamental Rights of the European Union ((2000) OJ C364/1). A right to inspect public documents was in existence in many forms, including in the constitutional traditions of the Member States. In particular, the Advocate-General noted that it was not necessary to establish the existence of a clear principle, and that 'it may suffice that member states have a common approach to the right in question, demonstrating the same desire to provide protection, even where the level of that protection and the procedure for affording it are provided for differently in the various member states' (para 69). The Court followed substantially this opinion in its judgment, holding that refusal to grant partial access amounted to a breach of the right to information and the principle of proportionality.

# Appendix

# RELEVANT ARTICLES OF THE EUROPEAN CONVENTION ON HUMAN RIGHTS

## SECTION I

## RIGHTS AND FREEDOMS

*Article 2*

*Right to life*

1.   Everyone's right to life shall be protected by law. No one shall be deprived of his life intentionally save in the execution of a sentence of a court following his conviction of a crime for which this penalty is provided by law.

2.   Deprivation of life shall not be regarded as inflicted in contravention of this Article when it results from the use of force which is no more than absolutely necessary:

(a)  in defence of any person from unlawful violence;
(b)  in order to effect a lawful arrest or to prevent the escape of a person lawfully detained;
(c)  in action lawfully taken for the purpose of quelling a riot or insurrection.

*Article 3*

*Prohibition of torture*

No one shall be subjected to torture or to inhuman or degrading treatment or punishment.

*Article 4*

*Prohibition of slavery and forced labour*

1.   No one shall be held in slavery or servitude.

2.   No one shall be required to perform forced or compulsory labour.

3.   For the purpose of this Article the term 'forced or compulsory labour' shall not include:

(a)  any work required to be done in the ordinary course of detention imposed according to the provisions of Article 5 of this Convention or during conditional release from such detention;

(b) any service of a military character or, in case of conscientious objectors in countries where they are recognised, service exacted instead of compulsory military service;

(c) any service exacted in case of an emergency or calamity threatening the life or well-being of the community;

(d) any work or service which forms part of normal civic obligations.

## *Article 5*

### *Right to liberty and security*

1.  Everyone has the right to liberty and security of person. No one shall be deprived of his liberty save in the following cases and in accordance with a procedure prescribed by law:

(a) the lawful detention of a person after conviction by a competent court;

(b) the lawful arrest or detention of a person for non-compliance with the lawful order of a court or in order to secure the fulfilment of any obligation prescribed by law;

(c) the lawful arrest or detention of a person effected for the purpose of bringing him before the competent legal authority on reasonable suspicion of having committed an offence or when it is reasonably considered necessary to prevent his committing an offence or fleeing after having done so;

(d) the detention of a minor by lawful order for the purpose of educational supervision or his lawful detention for the purpose of bringing him before the competent legal authority;

(e) the lawful detention of persons for the prevention of the spreading of infectious diseases, of persons of unsound mind, alcoholics or drug addicts or vagrants;

(f) the lawful arrest or detention of a person to prevent his effecting an unauthorised entry into the country or of a person against whom action is being taken with a view to deportation or extradition.

2.  Everyone who is arrested shall be informed promptly, in a language which he understands, of the reasons for his arrest and of any charge against him.

3.  Everyone arrested or detained in accordance with the provisions of paragraph 1(c) of this Article shall be brought promptly before a judge or other officer authorised by law to exercise judicial power and shall be entitled to trial within a reasonable time or to release pending trial. Release may be conditioned by guarantees to appear for trial.

4.  Everyone who is deprived of his liberty by arrest or detention shall be entitled to take proceedings by which the lawfulness of his detention shall be decided speedily by a court and his release ordered if the detention is not lawful.

5.  Everyone who has been the victim of arrest or detention in contravention of the provisions of this Article shall have an enforceable right to compensation.

## *Article 6*

### *Right to a fair trial*

1.  In the determination of his civil rights and obligations or of any criminal charge against him, everyone is entitled to a fair and public hearing within a reasonable time by an independent and impartial tribunal established by law. Judgment shall be pronounced publicly but the press and public may be excluded from all or part of the trial in the interest of morals, public order or national security in a democratic society, where the interests of juveniles or the protection of the private life of the parties so require, or to the extent strictly necessary in the opinion of the court in special circumstances where publicity would prejudice the interests of justice.

2.  Everyone charged with a criminal offence shall be presumed innocent until proved guilty according to law.

3.   Everyone charged with a criminal offence has the following minimum rights:

(a) to be informed promptly, in a language which he understands and in detail, of the nature and cause of the accusation against him;
(b) to have adequate time and facilities for the preparation of his defence;
(c) to defend himself in person or through legal assistance of his own choosing or, if he has not sufficient means to pay for legal assistance, to be given it free when the interests of justice so require;
(d) to examine or have examined witnesses against him and to obtain the attendance and examination of witnesses on his behalf under the same conditions as witnesses against him;
(e) to have the free assistance of an interpreter if he cannot understand or speak the language used in court.

## *Article 7*

### *No punishment without law*

1.   No one shall be held guilty of any criminal offence on account of any act or omission which did not constitute a criminal offence under national or international law at the time when it was committed. Nor shall a heavier penalty be imposed than the one that was applicable at the time the criminal offence was committed.

2.   This Article shall not prejudice the trial and punishment of any person for any act or omission which, at the time when it was committed, was criminal according to the general principles of law recognised by civilised nations.

## *Article 8*

### *Right to respect for private and family life*

1.   Everyone has the right to respect for his private and family life, his home and his correspondence.

2.   There shall be no interference by a public authority with the exercise of this right except such as is in accordance with the law and is necessary in a democratic society in the interests of national security, public safety or the economic well-being of the country, for the prevention of disorder or crime, for the protection of health or morals, or for the protection of the rights and freedoms of others.

## *Article 9*

### *Freedom of thought, conscience and religion*

1.   Everyone has the right to freedom of thought, conscience and religion; this right includes freedom to change his religion or belief and freedom, either alone or in community with others and in public or private, to manifest his religion or belief, in worship, teaching, practice and observance.

2.   Freedom to manifest one's religion or beliefs shall be subject only to such limitations as are prescribed by law and are necessary in a democratic society in the interests of public safety, for the protection of public order, health or morals, or for the protection of the rights and freedoms of others.

## Article 10

### Freedom of expression

1.   Everyone has the right to freedom of expression. This right shall include freedom to hold opinions and to receive and impart information and ideas without interference by public authority and regardless of frontiers. This Article shall not prevent States from requiring the licensing of broadcasting, television or cinema enterprises.

2.   The exercise of these freedoms, since it carries with it duties and responsibilities, may be subject to such formalities, conditions, restrictions or penalties as are prescribed by law and are necessary in a democratic society, in the interests of national security, territorial integrity or public safety, for the prevention of disorder or crime, for the protection of health or morals, for the protection of the reputation or rights of others, for preventing the disclosure of information received in confidence, or for maintaining the authority and impartiality of the judiciary.

## Article 11

### Freedom of assembly and association

1.   Everyone has the right to freedom of peaceful assembly and to freedom of association with others, including the right to form and to join trade unions for the protection of his interests.

2.   No restrictions shall be placed on the exercise of these rights other than such as are prescribed by law and are necessary in a democratic society in the interests of national security or public safety, for the prevention of disorder or crime, for the protection of health or morals or for the protection of the rights and freedoms of others. This Article shall not prevent the imposition of lawful restrictions on the exercise of these rights by members of the armed forces, of the police or of the administration of the State.

## Article 12

### Right to marry

Men and women of marriageable age have the right to marry and to found a family, according to the national laws governing the exercise of this right.

## Article 14

### Prohibition of discrimination

The enjoyment of the rights and freedoms set forth in this Convention shall be secured without discrimination on any ground such as sex, race, colour, language, religion, political or other opinion, national or social origin, association with a national minority, property, birth or other status.

## Article 16

### Restrictions on political activity of aliens

Nothing in Articles 10, 11 and 14 shall be regarded as preventing the High Contracting Parties from imposing restrictions on the political activity of aliens.

## Article 17

### Prohibition of abuse of rights

Nothing in this Convention may be interpreted as implying for any State, group or person any right to engage in any activity or perform any act aimed at the destruction of any of the rights and freedoms set forth herein or at their limitation to a greater extent than is provided for in the Convention.

## Article 18

### Limitation on use of restrictions on rights

The restrictions permitted under this Convention to the said rights and freedoms shall not be applied for any purpose other than those for which they have been prescribed.

# PART II

# THE FIRST PROTOCOL

## Article 1

### Protection of property

Every natural or legal person is entitled to the peaceful enjoyment of his possessions. No one shall be deprived of his possessions except in the public interest and subject to the conditions provided for by law and by the general principles of international law.

The preceding provisions shall not, however, in any way impair the right of a State to enforce such laws as it deems necessary to control the use of property in accordance with the general interest or to secure the payment of taxes or other contributions or penalties.

## Article 2

### Right to education

No person shall be denied the right to education. In the exercise of any functions which it assumes in relation to education and to teaching, the State shall respect the right of parents to ensure such education and teaching in conformity with their own religious and philosophical convictions.

## Article 3

### Right to free elections

The High Contracting Parties undertake to hold free elections at reasonable intervals by secret ballot, under conditions which will ensure the free expression of the opinion of the people in the choice of the legislature.

# Index

References are to *page* numbers.